and
American
Culture

Dick Tracy and American Culture

Morality and Mythology, Text and Context

by GARYN G. ROBERTS

foreworks by
MAX ALLAN COLLINS
JEAN O'CONNELL
DICK LOCHER

McFarland & Company, Inc., Publishers
Jefferson, North Carolina, and London

The present work is a reprint of the library bound edition of
Dick Tracy and American Culture: Morality and Mythology,
Text and Context, *first published in 1993.*

Frontispiece photograph courtesy William E. Brown,
Bowling Green State University

LIBRARY OF CONGRESS CATALOGUING-IN-PUBLICATION DATA

Roberts, Garyn G.
Dick Tracy and American culture : morality and
mythology, text and context / by Garyn G. Roberts.
p.   cm.
Includes bibliographical references and index.

ISBN 0-7864-1698-X (softcover : 50# alkaline paper)

1. Dick Tracy (Comic strip)
I. Title.
PN6728.D53R63   2003   741.5'0973—dc20   92-56687

British Library cataloguing data are available

Cover illustration by Chester Gould ©Tribune Media Services

Manufactured in the United States of America

McFarland & Company, Inc., Publishers
Box 611, Jefferson, North Carolina 28640
www.mcfarlandpub.com

For Dad and Mom—
who have always been there

and

In memory of Chester Gould
and for all the people who were and are
part of the house of Dick Tracy

Chester Gould (photograph by Richard Pietrzyk)

Chester was a brilliant man, highly motivated by a great power that helped him attain his goals.
— MRS. CHESTER (EDNA) GOULD

Acknowledgments

The author expresses his thanks and love to all those people who have been there through the years; many of the same have lent their efforts, support, and guidance for the successful completion of this book. Particular appreciation is expressed to the following:

Max Allan Collins, Beverly Fletcher, Chester and Edna Gould, Jean Gould O'Connell, Dick Locher and Sara Moores Campbell, who graciously and unselfishly provided important information and moral support.

The Gilbert Dobrinskis, Mark S. Dorn, Lois Jancieski, the John Joswiaks, the Arthur Leppis, the Andrew A. Maattas, Deborah Magrum, Arthur G. Neal, the Fred and Raymond Schiffmanns, William "Bill" Schurk, and Ralph Wolfe.

My best-selling friends who have always offered practical advice, insight and support — Clive Barker, Robert Bloch, Ray Bradbury. And:

Bruce Ayres of Capital City Comics (Madison, Wisconsin).

Bill Blackbeard of the San Francisco Academy of Comic Art: preeminent authority on the American comic strip and invaluable advisor.

Ray B. Browne: good friend, mentor, visionary, genius.

Jim Cavett of Tribune Media Services.

John and Karen Dobrinski: good friends and family always.

Andy Feighery, Trevor Kimball, and the Dick Tracy Fan Club.

Gary Hoppenstand: good friend, cohort, professional, and band leader for this book. (Gary, when you are a best-selling author, don't forget your old buddy.)

William "Bill" Kerkes: good friend, typing teacher at Lakeland High, and father of my good friend, Mike (1959–1981).

Karen Kral Becker: high school English teacher and inspiration.

Robert P. Niedbalski: physician and friend.

Douglas A. Noverr: friend, mentor, professional, and talented scholar and editor instrumental on the stretch run for this project.

Randy Scott and Anne Tracy of the Russel B. Nye Special Collections Division of Michigan State University Library.

Ray Walsh, Bob Mark, Jay, Chris "the Rube," and all the good folks associated with Curious Book Shop (East Lansing, Michigan).

My friends and colleagues from the University of Wisconsin — Whitewater (Whitewater, Wisconsin), Bowling Green State University (Bowling Green, Ohio), Mankato State University (Mankato, Minnesota), and Michigan State University (East Lansing, Michigan). From Michigan State University — Joseleyne Ashford Slade, chairperson of the Department of American Thought and Language.

The thousands of students who have attended my classes in popular culture, English, American culture, and American thought and language since 1981. I love you all, and I hope that each of you learned half as much from me as I learned from you. No longer my students, you will always be my friends. I note in particular: from BGSU, Suzanne Brown (POPC 160, '81) and Robert "Bob" Craig (ENG 200, '84); from Mankato, Frank Lorentz and Traci Rostad (ENG 235, '86), James "Jim" Krapf (ENG 215, '87), the ENG 101 Honors Class '87, and the ENG 592 Class '87; and from Michigan State, Carla Austin (ATL 121, '87), Greta Leigh (ATL 172–3, '88), Gregory "Greg" Hill (ATL 171–3, '88-'89), Ryan Heath (ATL 171–3, '89-'90), Robert "Rob" Lunde (ATL 171–3, '89-'90), Randi Rummel (ATL 171–3, '89-'90), James "Jim" Van Dam (ATL 171, 173, '89-'90), Nancy Brown (ATL 173, '90), Michael Cohen (ATL 121–3, '90-'91), David C. Powers (ATL 150, '92), and the S.U.P.E.R. Class (ATL 121, Summer '89).

My wonderful relatives and friends whose names, though not listed here, are etched in my heart. And especially, Virginia, Nigel, Cocoa, Mookie, and Zen—with my love.

The families of Esther and Richard Brockling, Nesta and Phillip Fairfield, Naida and Donald Frankie, James and Jean Gilbert, Lida and Joseph Hindley, Ruth and John Larsen, Eileen and Donald Parker, Hilda and Paul Porter, Mae and Richard Slavens, Frederick and Francis Tody, and Geri and David Wrege.

Walter and Clara Gilbert, and Glyn and Marie Roberts: the fine folks, who, though gone to a better place, live in me every day, and whom I was blessed to have as grandparents.

Glyn Alyn Roberts, Cleo Ann Gilbert Roberts, and Thomas Norman Roberts (Dad, Mom, Tom) for unending support of, inspiration to, and understanding of a son and brother who chases cultural treasures of yesterday and today.

David Glyn Roberts (Dave), the best son in the world.

Table of Contents

Some Context for a Serious Study

The volume you hold in your hands is a remarkable achievement that is woefully overdue.

The comic strip *Dick Tracy* is a popular culture phenomenon of incredible impact and import. In the sixty-plus years the strip has appeared—leaving in its wake radio, cinema, and television adaptations, as well as toys, books, and countless "tie-in" products—Chester Gould's amazing creation has left its square-jawed impression on America and the world.

It is Dick Tracy who made the trenchcoat and snapbrim fedora the official uniform of the tough plainclothes detective and whose two-fisted approach ("Next time I'll shoot first and investigate later!") paved the way for every other tough detective from Mike Hammer to Dirty Harry.

It is the *Dick Tracy* strip that brought hard-hitting life-and-death action-packed melodrama to the comics page, previously dominated by humor strips (hence the term "comic" strips), ushering in the wave of adventure continuities that dominated the 1930s and 1940s.

It is *Dick Tracy*'s creator Chester Gould who virtually invented the modern police procedural story, depicting ballistics tests, line-ups, and lie detectors (among much else) before the mystery novelists or Hollywood got around to it.

Thus Jack Webb's *Dragnet* is *Dick Tracy* minus the larger-than-life villains and science fiction–tinged gadgetry, while Ian Fleming's James Bond draws on Webb's very discards.

And women detectives of film and fiction, from Angie Dickinson's *Policewoman* to Sara Paretsky's V.I. Warshawski, could not have walked their mean streets had not Tracy's policewoman assistant Lizz paved a way from the mid–1950s on.

Listen to the humorous radio shows of the Thirties, Forties and Fifties—Bob Hope, the Great Gildersleeve, Fibber McGee and Molly and the rest—and see how often a *Tracy* reference turns up. Or notice what a constant presence *Tracy* is in Warner Bros. and MGM cartoons, or in the movies, where to this day *Tracy* references abound. The film world's tributes to *Tracy* include Jerry Lewis, in *The Ladies' Man* (where Jerry mimics the two-way wrist radio and invokes classic villain Pruneface), and Robert Redford in *Three Days of the Condor* (which picks up on Chet Gould's ice bullet, and credits the reference!). And of course Warren Beatty paid Tracy the highest Hollywood tribute to date in his popular 1990 film.

As an influence on other creative talents, Chester Gould has few peers in American pop culture; and as a pop culture artifact, *Dick Tracy* has few peers—his very name has become as much a synonym for "detective" as Sherlock Holmes. (And Holmes never had as distinct, as consistent, as visual an image—although, ironically, Gould designed Tracy as a modernized Sherlock).

Why it has taken 60 years for a serious, scholarly, and yet lively study of *Tracy* to be produced is a mystery even Dick himself couldn't solve. There have been several books on the *Tracy* phenomenon, and good ones, but these have been light, if loving, looks at the subject. The two collections of strips I've edited with current *Tracy* artist Dick Locher include some wonderful insights and memories of how the strip has been created over the years. But until Garyn Roberts dug in, *Tracy* has been denied the serious consideration it deserves.

The author of this volume understands, and chronicles, the ongoing novel-in-progress that is a story strip, noting how changing times, the problems and fads and concerns of the day, are reflected in the stories of *Dick Tracy* on the comics page of the daily newspaper. He also examines the lives of those of us who have been involved in the *Tracy* strip's sixty-year-plus history.

While I've been lucky enough to provide words and adventures for Chester Gould's famous detective for 15 years, I can't speak for Chet himself in how he might react to this formidable study. My hunch is that he would express public embarrassment at his strip being taken so

seriously, and privately feel a good deal of pride. It became clear to me, in the time I was fortunate enough to spend with Mr. Gould, that Chet *did* understand exactly what it was he created.

At the same time, the production of the strip itself was what consumed Chester Gould's energy, what seized his full creative being. He never had much interest in the radio, movie or television versions of *Tracy,* and he paid scant attention to the licensing, other than to enjoy the proceeds. The real *Tracy,* to Chet, was the strip; all else was less than secondary.

Fortunately for us, Garyn Roberts has a different attitude. In this book he does the one thing Chester Gould could not do for *Tracy:* provide a serious, objective overview of the subject. Dick Tracy and I are grateful to have so diligent a chronicler.

Max Allan Collins

September 15, 1992

Dick Tracy's Sister Remembers

I was just four years old when Dick Tracy came into our family. Growing up with him and all the characters seemed natural—in fact, they were often at our breakfast table. I will never forget one morning in 1945 when my father came down to breakfast and announced that he had a new character. I could tell that he was especially pleased. "How do you like the name B.O. Plenty?" Back in those days, such a phrase (i.e. "B.O.") was never used, though one knew that it existed. My immediate reaction was, "Daddy, you really wouldn't use it, would you?" He looked at Mother and me and replied, "Can I help it if his name is Bob Oscar?" So B.O., in all his bewhiskered unkempt backwoods glory, became a relief character in the strip. On occasion, the main story would switch to this fellow's humorous, strange way of life, living at Sunny Dell Acres at the corner of Ecstasy Street and Rainbow Drive. Any day that Dad was sitting at his drawing board working and laughing, Mother and I knew that he was doing a sequence involving B.O. Plenty, his most favorite character.

Relief characters brought another dimension to the strip, playing against suspense and mystery in progress. My dad was a master at this technique. He knew how to keep reader interest high. He knew how to sell papers.

A multi-millionaire industrialist, Diet Smith, was another relief character who in 1946 developed the two-way wrist radio. My dad was very proud of this idea, and

thereafter, Tracy was seen at the top of each Sunday page talking into this amazing instrument. It later became a two-way wrist TV. The character of Diet Smith allowed my father to bring some of his other creative ideas to the strip, such as the atomic light and the magnetic space coupe.

After their marriage in 1926, Mother and Dad resided in Wilmette, Illinois, a suburb of Chicago. Then, in 1935, when I was eight years old, we bought an abandoned sixty-acre farm near the small town of Woodstock, which was within driving distance of the Tribune Tower. After remodeling, we moved to this wonderful country home, complete with a working farm with cows, pigs, chickens, ducks, horses, and a bull. We loved it. My father could be seen pitching hay to the cattle, or working in the fields during harvest when time permitted.

In those early days, my father made that 65-mile trip into the Tribune Tower five days a week. He gradually found that going in on Mondays was sufficient. The rest of the week, he worked in his large studio at home.

In 1945, my father's brother, Ray Gould, joined his staff as the lettering man on the strip, freeing his other assistant, Coleman Anderson, to help more with the backgrounds. In time, the weekly schedule was down to four days, Monday through Thursday. This left more time for research, thinking, and personal life.

Meals were a time we adored, a time to relax over food and conversation that always ended in laughter. My father with his anecdotes made mealtime an experience. He was a kind of one-man show, and Mother and I loved it. I often wondered how one man could have so many talents.

I remember the books that lined his studio-library shelves: books on criminology, police procedure, karate, microscopes, lie detectors, psychological experiments, handwriting, and chemistry (a class my father said he almost flunked except for his nimble cartoon character answers). He also subscribed to numerous police publications and an FBI monthly magazine.

Each week, my mother and I would read the finished strips and Sunday page before they were sent to New York. My dad decided that if there was anything we didn't understand, he would change it. As the excitement would mount, I couldn't wait to ask, "What's going to happen?" And my dad would invariably say, "I don't know yet." But by Monday, he would have thought of a solution. He believed if he himself didn't know the outcome, the reader wouldn't either. Only once do I remember his having Tracy up against a wall with no solution. The date was January 11, 1942. Tracy had been put down a 20-foot-deep caisson and a boulder rolled over the edge, working its way down to crush Tracy. My dad purposely backed himself into a corner believing he would come up with the best solution. He always came up with a thrilling ending, but not this time. Instead he had Tracy saying something like, "Gould, you can't do this to me!" and a hand holding an artgum was erasing Tracy's dilemma. J.M. Patterson nixed the idea, claiming that *Tracy* would lose its credibility. So the way it ended was that the caisson was actually a ventilator shaft with a wooden floor. Tracy heard voices below, yelled for help, and was sawed out and rescued just seconds before the boulder dropped through.

Later in 1953, my dad added Al Valanis, a retired Chicago policeman, to his

Chester looking on while wife Edna and daughter Jean read his completed six strips—1946.

staff to check his work for accuracy in police procedure and police law, as well as to exchange ideas from his years of experience. Though he met with Al for only several hours on Mondays, he found his knowledge indispensable throughout the following years.

During his years in writing and drawing Dick Tracy, it was the accuracy in police investigation that brought my dad great respect from police departments all over the country, and awards that were very dear to him. It wasn't unusual to see a police car drive into our courtyard and several policemen get out to shake my dad's hand and congratulate him on his strip.

I marveled at my father's mastery in storytelling in this medium of comic strip art. He felt that if Dick Tracy's success had a secret ingredient in his 46-plus years at the helm, it was this: over and above any good story, serious writing must be seasoned with humor to be complete. That excruciating suspense of a mystery story is enhanced, in fact, by a nervous laugh and parting quip that says, "All's well!"

Jean Gould O'Connell

June 11, 1992

The Enduring Qualities of "Dick Tracy"

A recent focus group on newspaper awareness made up of 30-year-old volunteers was surveyed by a national communications chain to see just how comic strips served the newspapers these individuals read. As might be expected, some comic strips ranked extremely high while others did not.

One question of the survey asked how recognizable each comic strip was. When this question was asked of *Dick Tracy*, the response went off the charts.

The next question asked, "If this feature was available in your newspaper, would you read it?" Comic strips which scored a five or above on a scale of one to ten were considered successes and features worth keeping. Again, *Dick Tracy* came through as it has for more than sixty years, scoring a very satisfactory six. This strip has been a success since its birth in 1931, and its appeal shows no sign of decline.

There is no other strip like *Dick Tracy*. A large portion of today's newspaper comics are made up of gags — most of them reflecting the everyday happenings of a middle class family. *Dick Tracy* does this and more, and this is what makes the strip altogether unique. Where else can one experience the flintiness of Flattop, a smirk of the evil B-B Eyes, and the total decadence of the criminal mastermind Pruneface?

New readers of *Dick Tracy* will thrill to high-speed chases and to the danger of machine gun slugs issued by the likes of No Face (a.k.a. "The Blank"). They will react to Tracy being dumped in wax, thrown down abandoned wells, tossed out of helicopters, and sealed in an old coffin. And what delight to watch Breathless Mahoney put her moves on Tracy as he gets too close to her murderous intentions! Everyone enjoys the humor of B.O. Plenty as he mangles Tracy's last name and then launches an arc of tobacco juice past him.

These new inductees into Tracyisms will be intrigued by Diet Smith's cutting edge, miraculous inventions that extract Tracy from sure-death situations. All of us remember, or know of, Dick Tracy's wrist radio and later his wrist TV.

Tracy, once regarded as a mainstay of Golden Age comic strips (which included *Krazy Kat*, *Skippy*, *Little Orphan Annie*, *Terry and the Pirates*, and *Prince Valiant*), remains a mainstay of contemporary newspaper comics pages. Of all these Golden Age classics, *Dick Tracy* alone remains in the spotlight today, capturing as much attention, defying death as boldly, and stalking super-evil geniuses as adroitly as he did in the 1930s. The title character is a tough, shrewd, colorful individual who tracks and corners the worst of society's villains with flair and daring.

Ah, but does he have a future? The better question is, "Does crime have a future?" Tracy will continue to thwart modern crime and its perpetrators as long as it and they exist. He will confront violent crime, white collar crime, electronic crime, and the like all undertaken by innovative, modern-day pirates and gangsters.

Newspaper comic strip readers today will get their laugh from the ever-popular "gag-a-day" strip. They will observe family relations that are very similar to those of their own families. But it is my guess that they will be just as entertained by a dirty rat named "Putty-Puss" who is about to remold his face into that of the mayor so that he can escape the elaborate trap Tracy has set for him. They will smile at the intricate plan of Fish Face as he squirms out of a flooded Chicago tunnel just as Tracy is about to net his catch.

This is what focus groups are telling us today. This is the blueprint for sustaining the newspaper business. Newspapers need comics that continue to attract readers, comics that serve the industry and the public in ways that few other features can. Comic strips can and will flourish above the ever-present, staccato news events that thrive on television and dominate the front pages of newspapers.

Thirty-year-olds, as well as our perennial readers and new readers, as far as I can discern, will look for Dick Tracy on the comics pages for a long time—because he is a survivor. *Dick Tracy,* in more ways than one, is still golden.

Dick Locher

July 8, 1992

A Piece to the Puzzle

In a very broad sense, of course, this book is a product of a lifetime nurtured in a Sixties childhood and a Nineties maturity; it is the result of personal experience and cultural heritage; it is also the work of many people other than the author. Though somewhat clichéd, the idea that no book is written strictly by one person applies here. The author's first truly tangible writing regarding *Dick Tracy* as a vehicle to understanding American cultural and political history and intellectual thought appeared as a master's thesis in 1982; that work was expanded into a Ph.D. dissertation in 1986. Both were done under the auspices of Chester Gould and Tribune Media Services.

This said, the present book is not intended to be the final word on *Dick Tracy* and American culture. (There have been several fine collections and studies done on various aspects of this topic; more will emerge as Chester Gould's *Dick Tracy* becomes increasingly recognized as canonical.) Instead, it should be considered a piece to a rather complex and important puzzle — the puzzle of the human experience and the place of the individual in that matrix.

In academe today, there exist some very important debates and related schools of thought. Appropriately, our university systems are busily expanding traditional cultural histories, and pedagogies regarding the same, by investigating and celebrating, with great alacrity

and fervor, such issues as ethnicity and gender.

Aside from these crucial issues, there rages another intense controversy which has engendered fierce passions from a variety of perspectives. The debate here centers on what precisely should be deemed Cultural (with a capital "C") and consequently worthy of scholarly inquiry, and what should not. Many scholars still hold to Matthew Arnold's 1864 edict that culture "is the best that has been known and thought"; many scholars still hold the idea that that which is popular (with a small "p," indicating relative worthlessness) is excluded from intellectual thought. Hence, p.c. (i.e. popular culture) is not always p.c. (i.e. politically correct) in the university setting.

Here again, Chester Gould's *Dick Tracy* serves as an important piece to a puzzle — the puzzle as to what should be regarded as canonical and what should not. Culture — for the purposes of this book being defined as the products of the life experience of a society (local, regional, or global) — is a complex of heritages and new discoveries that relies on narratives or similar emblematic representations of various sorts of articulation and preservation. There exist folk cultures, mass cultures, and elite cultures of diverse natures, and the distinctions between these are often blurred and even more often unimportant. Genrefication of social types and levels is only useful in a most broad and general sense, as is genrefication of literary forms. Many authors past and present have invested considerable time and effort to avoid such classification or categorization.

There does exist in some of the works of authors like Herman Melville, Charles Dickens, Edith Wharton, and Jack London a degree of sophistication and level of thinking that is perhaps more complex than in, for example, the dime novels and penny dreadfuls that were contemporary to the works of these authors. Yet Melville's revered classic, *Moby Dick* (1851), was not celebrated until "rediscovered" in the 1920s—his popular travel narratives, *Typee* (1846) and *Oomo* (1847), had long before established him as worthy of attention in the public's eye. Charles Dickens' writing, though acknowledged as the product of keen insight into the mid-nineteenth century human condition, is best appreciated as social melodrama of a "soap opera" variety from the period. Edith Wharton, the grand dame of turn-of-the-century intellectual thought and counterpart to such writers as Henry James, penned several popularly accepted ghost stories, and Jack London, internationally acclaimed best-selling author and social critic, relied on his reputation gained through sales of his "kitty and doggy" stories to sell his erratic, often painfully protracted, uninspired, and intensely subjective novels of criticism. Further, it was no accident that London clothed his pseudo-leftist, pseudo-intellectual discourse—such as that found in *The Iron Heel* (1908), *The Star Rover* (1913), and *The Scarlet Plague* (1913)—in the guise of rather simplistic futuristic fiction or science fantasy.

Did Chester Gould's *Dick Tracy* ever feature "the best that has been known and thought"? The answer is both yes and no, but is more importantly dependent on the training and cultural baggage of the individual reader of the comic strip. Degrees of art, literature, and intellectual thought are relative to the context in which they emerge and relative to the experience of the individual consumer. *Tracy* has achieved high status, on occasion, when considered in the context of other contemporary comic strips, and when considered in the context of its own past successes— successes measured in terms of their ability to reflect primary, life-structuring mythology, in terms of the optimal use of drawing in inherently confining, small, two-dimension comic strip panels, and in terms of the ability of the story line to entertain and enthrall readers.

Everything in society—including art and morality—is relative. Cultural phenomena cannot be appropriately studied in vacuums, and one cannot always effectively utilize established methodologies for understanding apples to appreciate oranges. But one can effectively apply paradigms to study fruit in general to better understand both apples and oranges. So can Chester Gould's *Dick Tracy* be intelligently compared to Nathaniel Hawthorne's *The Scarlet Letter* (1850), Albert Bierstadt's nineteenth-century romantic landscapes, and B.B. King's blues ballads? Sometimes. On a very general yet profound level, every product of culture is a fiction, is autobiography, and is metaphor.

Fans or "fanatics" and academics or "academicians"—the former hate the latter for their overanalysis and often speculative, seemingly unfounded hypotheses; the latter hate the former for their zeal, subjectivity, and willingness to be uninformed. Both are justified in their positions regarding the other, yet both are also unjustified in these positions. The fan/academic dichotomy or puzzle is best solved by synthesis—fans and academics need each other, and function best together on some middle ground. In short, fans—oftentimes better, more conscientious and comprehensive collectors and archivists of cultural documents and material culture than any other single group—provide the fodder for intellectual inquiry. Academics can provide meaningful, insightful examination of such cultural documents.

This synthesis of fan and academic is not, however, as easily achieved as one might think. There exist some deep-seated conflicts between respective paradigms. The famous *Saturday Night Live* sketch in which William Shatner tells a group of over-zealous *Star Trek* fans (aka "trekkies") replete with simulated Vulcan ears and period sideburns to "get a life" is uproariously funny because the stereotype of some SF, specifically *Star Trek*, fans is deadly accurate. Fans can lose, and have lost on occasion, all sight of objectivity. Conversely, the image of the egghead philosopher in the sterile ivory tower is also partially based in fact. There are indeed academics who profess and implement theories and hypotheses that are as ridiculous as Dr. Wertham's analysis of 1950s comic art. (Fans love to cite Wertham as an example of what poor scholarship can do. Not ironically, Fredric Wertham spent the remaining few decades of his life back-peddling from theories advanced in his infamous 1954 book entitled *Seduction of the Innocent.*)

There do exist, in academic settings, fields of inquiry which rely on very abstract, intangible "facts" or evidences as the basis of legitimation. The fields of "psychohistory" and "postmodern" literary criticism come to mind as examples of such fields of study. The more obscure and obtuse one can become in one's analysis, the better chance one has that no one will question one's findings. Unfortunately, some professionals do subscribe to the axiom, "Don't let facts get in the way of a good theory." But most fans and academics alike are not such extremists. Such stereotypes are never literally true for a particular group of people, though they are also never literally false. The vast majority of academics and fans mean well, and the vast majority of these two not-so-disparate groups engage in some of the most humane of efforts—such as providing relevant meaning to, and appreciation of, the human condition. Most academics dedicate their lives to understanding and teaching at great personal cost. This book serves as a middle ground between traditions of the seemingly, but not actually, disparate traditions of fandom and academia. Chester Gould, Rick Fletcher, Max Allan Collins, and Dick Locher were and are, in their own ways, each fans and each academics.

Chester Gould, creator and writer/artist of *Dick Tracy* between 1931 and 1977; Rick Fletcher, assistant and artist for *Tracy* between 1961 and 1977; and Max Allan Collins and Dick Locher, the long-time writer and artist team for *Dick Tracy*, have always realized the intimate connection between their creative work and American culture, the importance of being both canonical and revolutionary in their work, and the important role of academic inquiry into, and criticism and celebration of, what they have done and do. It is no surprise that all four of these individuals have embraced and revered higher education and credible analysis as essential to the appreciation of their art and craft, nor that they each contributed substantially and directly to this book. (All four were university educated, and all four have served in varying capacities for higher education as professors, instructors, and lecturers.)

Several fine collections of *Dick Tracy* comic strips have been produced in both hardcover and paperback book form throughout the years. These appeal to fans and scholars of all sorts. There also exist literally hundreds of scholarly, semischolarly, and informative articles on *Tracy* and related topics that date back to the debut of Chester Gould's famous comic strip. Coinciding with the release of the 1990 *Dick Tracy* movie was the release or re-release of several Tracy collections, studies, and related materials. At this time, Jay Maeder published a book which, though somewhat subjective in tone, is a masterwork in its own right. Maeder's *Dick*

Tracy: The Official Biography chronicles the origins of, and development of storylines for, *Dick Tracy*.

Of course, Gould himself, and others who have been intimately involved with the comic strip—most notably Max Allan Collins—have commented and written extensively about their work. Collins is responsible for much of the existing historical and archival work regarding *Tracy*. There have been others, fans and academics alike, who have enlarged our knowledge of *Tracy* and who have preserved the same for posterity.

In short, with rare exception, the people who work to preserve and celebrate the Dick Tracy legacy are a very caring, insightful, unselfish, and cooperative lot. This book is intended to modestly augment the fine work of these people; it is intended as a piece to the ongoing puzzle of the Dick Tracy legacy.

A primary objective of this book is to assimilate and expand upon existing knowledge of *Dick Tracy* as an American culture phenomenon, and to renew and spark interest in scholarly inquiry regarding that phenomenon. In this book, the reader will find straight histories, biographies, myth/symbol analyses, Caweltian formula applications, selected media theories, art criticism, literary criticism, aesthetical analyses, and more. Analysis is not used here for the sake of analysis; rather it is employed to make meaningful connections between established information and relevance to the human condition.

Reading has given me some of the greatest pleasures of my life. My mom and dad read to me and encouraged me to read almost from the start. When I had become a proficient reader at about age seven, I began to subject my brother Tom, 22 months younger than me, to my reading. Tom has always been the greatest of brothers, and he let me read him all sorts

of books. In 1967, aged six and eight respectively, Tom and I began to plumb the world of literature. We began with the new series of Big Little Books that appeared in 1967. At nighttime, Tom would often get into bed with me, or I with him, and we would read such classics as *Tom and Jerry Meet Mr. Fingers, Bugs Bunny in Double Trouble on Diamond Island,* and *Donald Duck: The Fabulous Diamond Fountain.* (Big Little Books cost 39 cents apiece in those days, and they disposed of our disposable income, which was chiefly generated from allowances.) Dad and Mom, of course, supplied us with other books as well.

Then the reminiscences began—Dad telling us that he had had Big Little Books as a child in the Thirties; he could even remember specific titles like *Mickey Mouse and Bobo the Elephant* (1935). Dad's stories of these books served as happy memories and as Tom's and my introduction to the lifestyle and culture of the middle class during the Great Depression.

A year or two later, more precisely by 1969, the new series of Big Little Books concluded with number 36; Tom and I had at least one copy of each of the series. We even had written for catalogs from an East Coast dealer who sold antique Big Little Books through the mail at what were, even by late Sixties standards, rather exorbitant prices. (Some of you may know who is referenced here.) We never could afford any of the "golden age" classics listed, but Dad could recite titles from memories of his childhood, and we could verify these titles in our catalogs. It was all very amazing.

Mom seemed to remember that her older brother, Tom's and my Uncle Jim, had once owned a Big Little Book or two when they were kids. Big Little Books had become one of many vehicles which transported Tom and me to the past, and which helped us appreciate American cultural history.

About 1970 or 1971, Tom and I spent

our first evening home alone without a babysitter while Mom and Dad went out for the evening. Earlier that same day, Dad had taken Tom and me to The Mill, a famous antique store still thriving today in Woodruff, Wisconsin. (Dad had run a want ad in the local newspaper for Big Little Books. The owner of The Mill, now long-time friend Dennis Howard, had sent us in response a postcard which stated that he had some old Big Little Books which he would sell or trade.) At the antique shop, the three of us discovered treasure. Dad bought Tom a Big Little Book entitled *Big Chief Wahoo* (1938) and bought me a copy of *Dick Tracy and the Man with No Face* (1938). Each had cost ten cents apiece in the late Thirties; Dad bought our copies for five dollars apiece. (Mom and Dad were spending ten dollars on Tom and me that day, and this was big money in those times. As I reflect on that expenditure, I am sure that they were rewarding us for staying home alone that night, but more importantly knew how impassioned we were with Big Little Books and wanted to share the heritage of their childhoods with us. This was indeed quite a brilliant move by two of the most insightful and caring parents that ever lived.)

That night, home alone with Tom, the television, our golden retriever dog and protector Taffy, and our Big Little Books, I carefully opened the cover of my newly acquired treasure. The pulpwood pages had an old, unique smell about them; they also contained what seemed to me then the most amazing stories and art possible. (Of course, as years progressed, my aesthetic values changed, evolved, and devolved — but, even back then I had a sense of what was good in the arts, and I knew that this story by Chester Gould had to be a classic.)

The story and drawings were thrilling and terrifying — especially when one was home with a younger brother and one of the gentlest dogs in the world. The first pages depicted the grim vengeance of the Blank — "The Man with No Face" — as he rescued a little boy named Junior (who seemed remarkably like Tom and me) from a horrible death, and then summarily executed two of his former underworld colleagues.

The Blank had done something very good, and he had done something that made me uneasy — he had taken the law into his own hands and killed two (admittedly bad) guys. There was a disturbing, profound message here, and it made me think for a long time.

Shortly thereafter, Dad helped Tom and me order other kinds of books by mail — using our allowance and helping us supplement these funds — from Publishers Central Bureau. The first book I ordered was Herb Galewitz's edited collection entitled *The Celebrated Cases of Dick Tracy 1931–1951* (1970). I read most of the book one Sunday in our family car en route to see Grandma Gilbert. I read so hard and long that I almost got sick in the car.

In 1973, I wrote the first of several letters to Chester Gould (Mom and Dad probably helped me address the first such letter to him in care of the *Chicago Tribune*.) Through the years, Mr. Gould responded to my every letter and I still have each of his replies. (Tom and I still have those *Big Chief Wahoo* and *Dick Tracy* Big Little Books, too.)

Later, I discovered that Gould was generally very faithful in responding to letters from young fans. (He had written Max Allan Collins years earlier, I learned.) My correspondence with Gould continued for years. The Tracy Big Little Book served, for me, as a piece to the puzzle called the Great Depression; Chester Gould's storylines in his famous comic strip provided me with important self-definition in terms of a large social order, morality, and mindset.

In this book I seek to place *Dick Tracy* firmly into a context of expanded social

Rescued by the Blank! — Reprinted by permission: Tribune Media Services. (From Large Feature Comic #1, Series 1: *Dick Tracy Meets the Blank*, 1939.)

and cultural history, to bring some existing ideas together and expand upon these ideas and provide a new perspective, and to apprise the reader of existing scholarship done on *Tracy*. Like all books, this one is defined by the parameters of time and space — a fixed amount of time for research and writing and a fixed number of pages to optimally relate the results of that research and writing.

Almost all of the chapters that make up this book could be expanded into free-

The grim vengeance of the Blank—Reprinted by permission: Tribune Media Services. (From Large Feature Comic #1, Series 1: *Dick Tracy Meets the Blank*, 1939.)

standing book-length studies of their topics.

What you now hold in your hands is the culmination of more than ten years of work; in a broader sense, it is the product of a lifetime for an individual who is thirty-something. It is a celebration, a loving tribute to many friends and an extended family. It is, I believe, a piece to the puzzle.

Garyn G. Roberts
Okemos, Michigan
May 25, 1992

CHAPTER 1

The *Dick Tracy* Comic Strip: An American Culture Phenomenon

"The moral objective is that of saving a people, or saving a person or supporting an idea. The hero sacrifices himself for something—that's the morality of it."
Joseph Campbell, *The Power of Myth* (1986)

Numerous methods of communicating an idea or thought exist, or have existed, in American society, and now in the world community. Various messages can be conveyed, and the media employed to disseminate these messages are improved and expanded upon daily. Through the media, American culture is widely promulgated and popularized. The Great Depression provided the circumstances for the development of significant, enduring sociohistoric events and advances; among these was the emergence or further development of a variety of popular media. Motion pictures, pulp magazines, story radio, Big Little Books, and comic strips enjoyed their respective golden ages during this time. In the fact and fantasy of the 1930s, a vast array of heroes arose to protect the social paradigm.

In October of 1931, a comic strip was born which chronicled the popular culture of the day, and which focused its content on the then socially prescribed "War on Crime." Its storylines, protagonists, and antagonists were intentional exaggerations of actual historic events and people. Ever conscious of newly documented police procedures, the strip's producer selected and effectively exploited a unique mass medium where he could convey a message

of high morality. The man was Chester Gould; the strip was *Dick Tracy*.

Born out of the ashes of the Depression, just as the mythic phoenix was born out of death, *Dick Tracy* thrived, and for more than sixty years has continued to thrive, as a reflection of public sentiment because of Gould's ability (and that of his successors) to tap into the experience of the masses. But the story only begins here. In the late Thirties the nation's attention shifted from concerns of severe economic conditions to a second world war, and Dick Tracy—nemesis of the underworld— could easily have fallen by the way. Instead, Gould turned the war years into *Tracy's* finest hours by further developing characters (including an array of increasingly grotesque, insidious, and socially deviant criminals), by moving crimes perpetrated from the local urban setting to the international scene, by refining and tightening his pen and ink drawings, and by providing the protagonist with a more defined nuclear family—until the Fifties when the comic seemed to get even better (if that was possible) in these ways and more. The strip responded to changing social history and sentiment, and Chester Gould, himself a product and affector of American popular thought, remained a

Dick Tracy—September 25, 1933. Reprinted by permission: Tribune Media Services.

dedicated student of newspaper headlines and police procedures. Gould's cultural inheritances and personal experiences produced a mindset highly congruent with established social attitudes. He stated, "I work from stuff [crime stories] that has actually happened, to get realism into the strip. I couple this with something highly imaginative, or fantastic. When you combine realism and the fantastic, you've got a story every time."[1] From *Dick Tracy*'s beginnings in 1931 through Gould's retirement from the strip in 1977, the man who first detailed graphic violence in comic strips studied the details of police procedure by working closely with the Chicago area police forces. His own personal experiences came to closely parallel those of real-life law enforcement officers. Almost from the start, the debate has raged as to who Dick Tracy was in real life. On several occasions Gould denied that the comic strip flatfoot was modeled on his own life. However, Tracy's personal values and philosophy were, except for the highly fantastic death trap sequences, first those of his creator. Chester Gould's cultural inheritance and personal experiences were

popularly accepted—they hit a "responsive chord." Coulton Waugh writes:

> The detailed picture of crime given in this strip was tried out on the public at first tentatively, but it was soon found that people liked it. The protests were drowned out by a roar of approval. The deep, human preoccupation with the morbid, with death, with diseased minds and bodies; the strange instinct that gathers men in a circle to gaze with a fascination at the shattered suicide, had found an outlet.[2]

To this day, Gould's successors (the root word "success" certainly does apply to these individuals) have followed in his footsteps.

The Thirties was a time of two distinct genres of American comic strips: the action/adventure drama and the domestic/situation comedy. The first genre was illustrated by Roy Crane's *Wash Tubbs* (4/21/24 debut); Harold Gray's *Little Orphan Annie* (8/5/24 debut); adaptations of Edgar Rice Burroughs' archetypal jungle man, Tarzan, by Hal Foster and others (Burroughs' creation first appeared in the October 1912 issue of *All-Story Magazine*, with the comic strip debuting on 1/7/29); and Alex Raymond's *Flash Gordon* (1/7/34 debut). In 1931, newspaper artist Chester Gould continued to submit sample ideas for comic strips to Captain Joseph Patterson of the Chicago Tribune–New York News Syndicate. The young artist had seen some of his comic art reach print during the Twenties, but at this time had had no major successes in the field. Patterson showed interest in Gould's samples of a new strip featuring a police detective, and he bought the idea, changing the title for the strip from *Plainclothes Tracy* to *Dick Tracy*. In October of 1981, Dick Tracy, along with Chester Gould and associates, celebrated the fiftieth anniversary of their famous newspaper strip. Gould died in 1985. In recent years, Max Allan Collins has scripted the stories and Dick Locher has done the drawing for *Dick Tracy*—two jobs which were done almost exclusively by Gould between 1931 and 1977, though Gould had assistants working for him almost from the start.

Comic strips have been one of the most pervasive media of the twentieth century. David Manning White estimated that during the early 1930s about three times as many Americans read the comics as read the important daily news.[3] "A 1938 Gallup survey revealed that 63 percent of adults read the daily comics and 73 percent of adults read the Sunday funnies. As for the kids, they weren't tallied at all as it was assumed that they all read the comics."[4] In an article written for *Life* magazine in 1944, John Bainbridge cited a then recent analysis which stated, "Comic strips are read with regularity by well over half of the country's adults and two-thirds of the children over six, a public of approximately 65,000,000 people."[5] So the comic strip, a seemingly simplistic combination of line drawings and dialogue and descriptions, had profound social significance as a popular art form. *Dick Tracy*, one of the most read strips of its time, not only had a profound effect on its readership, but it was also affected to a large extent by that same populace. The effects of *Tracy* on the readers may not be concretely quantifiable in all cases, but scholarly inquiry into the phenomenon provides important insight into American social history. As John G. Cawelti suggests in *Adventure, Mystery and Romance*, the successful story (in terms of mass acceptance and financial profitability) is the one that possesses a formula finely balanced by convention and invention.[6] Further, that story evidences a carefully constructed harmony between actual cultural history and created fantasy. *Dick Tracy* was and is proficient at both levels because Chester Gould made it so.

Referring to Thirties America, Stephen Becker stated, "If life was real and earnest, we would have real and earnest comics. If Capone was a national figure, Dick Tracy would shortly be even better

known."[7] The appeal of *Tracy* to its Depression audience was many faceted, but the strip's realistic portrayal of American life and dramatization of established and innovative police procedures have always been of prominent importance. The adventure and crime comic strips were significant developments for the times, but for the decades that have followed, Americans have hoped, and somehow known, that somewhere in the country there are straight, fearless, uncompromising, square-jawed cops like Dick Tracy.

Based on firsthand experience, most readers of *Dick Tracy* cannot relate to the violence and gore often found in, and more often attributed to, the strip. Yet most people learn of heinous crimes, cruelty, and savage acts via the media. What readers have traditionally related to in *Tracy* is the daily trials, tribulations, and resulting triumphs experienced by the hero and his family. Dick Tracy's family comprises the police force as well as his nuclear family and close friends. Comic strips unashamedly provide their readers with entertainment, enjoyment, and a measure of escapism. Yet, as David Manning White points out, the reader's response goes far beyond mere entertainment. "Readers find comics 'true to life,' mirroring life as they understand it. . . ."[8] Further, the comic strip provides a way for readers to understand life. Hence, *Dick Tracy* not only reflects common beliefs and values but also helps to create and supplement them. In the early Thirties, when newspaper readers followed accounts of gangsters and a variety of other social woes, they were able to enhance their perceptions with caricatures created and drawn by Chester Gould in a comic strip that was not far from the headlines. Regarding the relationship between daily news items and comic strips, Gould stated in a 1980 interview with Max Allan Collins and Matt Masterson:

> Today news is furnished to you by TV as much as 18 hours before you might see

the same story in your paper. I think the role of the newspaper dispensing news is pretty hard put, so I think the newspaper has to furnish an entertainment product — such as comic strips. If I were presently owner or publisher or editor of a paper, I would make it a practice immediately to print two of my comics at the bottom of the front page every day . . . just as a matter of headlines at the top. Two comics at the bottom of the front page. I think that would do an awful lot to bring back the prestige that newspapers used to have. They used to fight to get certain strips, they would outbid each other.[9]

People of the Thirties were aware of criminal activities through the media, and the cognizance was heightened by the captivating depictions of Gould.

The popular press sensationalized actions, exploits, and personalities of gangsters by giving them front page headlines. What had happened was that an undesirable byproduct of the American Dream had emerged and taken root. As a society, Americans discovered that not only was it possible for "good," hard-working people to achieve material success and the happiness equated with such success, but it was possible for entrepreneurs of lesser character to achieve at least the same level of prosperity. The dark side of the American Dream was more evident than ever. If the Vanderbilts, Carnegies, and Rockefellers in real life, and the heroes and heroines of Horatio Alger's nineteenth century novels of fiction could achieve happiness through the formula prescribed by the American Dream (i.e. hard work, thrift, and moral goodness), then the Capones and the Dillingers of real life and the Big Boys and Boris Arsons of *Dick Tracy* could also achieve happiness through a perversion of that formula (i.e. wile, cunning, and any brand of morality or none at all). Newspapers sold copy by reflecting public sentiment. Society of the Great Depression needed to learn of people achieving material success and all the glamor and benefits that go with such prosperity because

such stories provided a legitimacy or realism to people's own aspirations. Never mind how the success was attained, just be comforted in the fact it still could be achieved, or so society wanted to believe. Hence, the actions, exploits, and personalities of gangsters became front page headlines and the basis for great sensationalism and fantasy.

As depicted by the daily tabloids, the gangster's life was filled with wonderful things. Beyond enormous wealth conspicuously displayed in fancy cars, elegant clothing, exotic jewelry, and more, the gangster's lifestyle legitimated that which previously was socially taboo — alcohol during Prohibition, other forms of drug running, prostitution, and other illicit sexual behaviors epitomized by the naughty but oh-so-nice molls at the gangster's side. The gangster had become a folk hero, and he was perceived to be on the winning team. Perhaps crime *did* pay!

And established law enforcement agencies and their officials were often hurting their own cause. Corrupt police and ineffective police procedures became headline news because these individuals and events proved perfect counterpoints to the stories of successful and uncatchable gangsters. They added credence to the case for the gangster — it was a self-fulfilling prophecy. Consequently, if in the Thirties you were at all enamored with the likes of individuals such as John Dillinger (said to be the most charismatic of Depression era gangsters), the bad guys seemed to be the police. If you supported law enforcement and continued to learn of corrupt cops, wrongdoings, and inefficiency, you would naturally become less and less enamored with society's agency for protection of itself. It was very possible to be alienated by or ambivalent about law and order during the 1930s.

As a product of popular beliefs and values, *Tracy* exemplifies many of the proposals put forth by Richard Slotkin in his award-winning book *Regeneration Through*

Violence.[10] Dick Tracy employs violence to purge the social soul of its impurities, and this purgation entails destroying these malignancies with their own apocalyptic weaponry—death and destruction. Violence, then, is a means to the desired end; it is not only a good thing, it is prescribed for the maintenance of social morality. The bullets Tracy shoots through the heads of rogues might be deemed an example of commonly accepted fascism. Yet this action is all in the course of a day's work for the hero because it is demanded.

Beyond realism, *Dick Tracy* provides adventure and the allure of the grotesque and criminal. Grotesqueness and crime are synonymous in Gould's creation, and it is this association that keeps what could possibly otherwise have been an overly conventional and boring comic strip in the public eye.[11] The equating of freakishness with evil was nothing new when Gould and *Tracy* came along, but such equation did conflict with the rising glamorization of the gangster. In his strip, Chester Gould fiercely attacked the positive imagery of the criminal—*Tracy*'s artist was always an emphatic supporter of the American Dream as it related to good, hard-working people. If real-life gangsters were given names which celebrated their physiognomies and actions, Gould would give his villains in *Dick Tracy* names that condemned their physiognomies and actions. In this sense, this comic strip artist was a brilliant man—he did not simply portray gangsters as evil; he depicted the twisted social celebration of these rogues as evil also. In real life, Al "Big Boy" Capone was named for his high standing in society and seemingly infinite wealth; in *Dick Tracy* Big Boy was named for his fat, slovenly, bullying ways. In Depression America, John Dillinger was celebrated for his good looks, charm, and resourcefulness; in *Dick Tracy* Boris Arson (Gould's fictional portrayal of Dillinger) was an unattractive, conniving murderer, and his last name indicated a specific crime. In Chester

Gould's comic strip, the rogues were grotesque in appearance and morality, the former helping to illustrate the latter as deformity in physical appearance and body type indicated a kind of fatalistic, predetermined morality. In the relatively short history of the United States, Americans have traditionally held that the beautiful and hard-working are good (and hence realize the American Dream), while the ugly lack substantive purpose and thus are miserable failures. Via *Dick Tracy,* readers for over sixty years have been able to witness heinous crimes and then step away from them more fully appreciative of their own conditions which they, unlike some unfortunate comic characters, have the chance to live out. Depiction and reflection of social history in the form of hard-core melodrama, combined with a measure of grotesqueness, account for the appeal of the strip. The interesting players in *Tracy* are the bad guys and gals, not old square-jaw himself.

Chester Gould once acknowledged that a major motivation for him was money-making.[12] He noted that it is important to have dreams and aspirations, but that these only can be realized in our experiences with the use of money. His vision in this regard may sound cold and one-dimensional, yet material wealth was not Gould's sole inspiration for a widely received syndicated comic strip. His goal was to provide the American public with a very basic, simple message (and wave the flag a little at the same time). The essence of this message delineated the essential differences between good and evil. "*Dick Tracy* is the daddy of all cops-and-robbers strips, and Chester Gould . . . has been announcing to the world since 1931 that crime does not pay."[13] In *The Funnies: An American Idiom,* Robert H. Abel and David Manning White describe Gould's strip as a modern morality play. The beliefs which *Dick Tracy* reflects and shapes are basic and universally accepted, and are consequently unifying for many people.

During the Thirties and in decades since, the strip has grown and changed with the times, and Gould has presented the moral viewpoint of many. At the time of *Tracy's* inception, the artist was incensed by several years of recurring gangsterism.

An alarming percentage of the cops of the day were conniving and scheming with racketeers. Public faith in law enforcement was faltering, and rightfully so. Yet the people still wanted and needed to believe in good, straight, honest policemen. There was also a great deal of public sympathy engendered for the criminal who was believed to be persecuted and denied the chance at a decent life. Gangsters invariably seemed to arise from the ranks of the lower class, and they often were first generation immigrants looking for a better life. The fact that these individuals approached and achieved the American Dream by unconventional means was of little consequence except to intrigue the public. The end justified the means, and in the words of Mae West, "Goodness had nothing to do with it." From the start, *Dick Tracy* contested these ideas—ideas which were being reinforced circa 1930 in popular motion pictures like *Little Caesar,* and ideas which predicted the content of motion pictures made after the establishment of the 1934 Motion Picture Production Code in which "G-Men" were revered rather than their evil antagonists. *Dick Tracy* was popularly embraced because Chester Gould was a more than competent artist telling interesting stories in comic strip form for one of the country's two biggest newspaper syndicates, and because Gould was firm in his resolve that crime does not pay. As an artist and storyteller, Gould had to be emphatic and a little radical in selling a morality that was not wholly popular at the time. The Great Depression shook the moral foundations of American society for a period of time and brought confusion and uncertainty as survival concerns dominated people's lives.

At its inception, *Dick Tracy* was both accepted by, and satisfactory to, the consuming public. The title character was a plainclothes policeman who brought the toughest and vilest criminals to justice and who never wavered in his cause. Americans needed to see this; they were refreshed by, and made secure in, a belief in solid law and order that they held individually and communally. "An honest cop was much needed in places like Chicago and New York, to name but two cities . . . Gould's new strip was soon a success in these markets, as well as in other urban areas."[14] Ron Goulart writes that by 1937 *Dick Tracy* was the New York News Syndicate's third most popular strip. It was topped only by the well established *The Gumps* and *Little Orphan Annie;* the comedy of Sidney Smith's *The Gumps* was the most humorous and outrageous of the three. *The Gumps,* like *Annie* and *Tracy,* also placed heavy emphasis on themes of family and working through tough times together. Smith's strip had begun in 1917, and Harold Gray's *Little Orphan Annie* dated back to 1924, so they even more than *Dick Tracy* had spent by 1937 considerable time in the public eye. Simplistic domestic and situation comedy and fine, articulate drawing combined to support old American mythologies in *The Gumps* and *Annie.* Both Smith (who was replaced on *The Gumps* by Gus Edson after an untimely death caused by a car accident in 1925) and Gray were products of the middle class and the Midwest—Smith from Illinois and Wisconsin; Gray from Illinois and Indiana—and could depict Middle American values from firsthand experience. It is interesting to note that Gould spent his life in Oklahoma and rural Illinois, had lower-middle class origins, and so too was part of Middle America. The popularity of a comic strip was measured by the number of newspapers that included the strip in their copy. By 1939, *Dick Tracy* was in 160 newspapers.[15] Other media like story radio, motion picture features and serials, comic books, and Big Little Books were also utilizing the law enforcement hero at this time.

Since *Dick Tracy* was disseminated through numerous newspapers, the huge size of the audience is unquestionable. (The Chicago Tribune–New York News Syndicate was one of the two largest newspaper syndicates of the era. The other was the Hearst Syndicate.) Further, since most newspapers are read by a wide spectrum of individuals with diverse demographic characteristics, the heterogeneity of the audience is self-evident. At first glance, the comic appears to be solely adult-oriented due to its violent detective themes. Yet at second glance, one notes the all–American boy named Dick Tracy, Jr. (or just Junior), the ladylike and later motherly qualities of Tess Trueheart (Tracy's girlfriend, fiancée, and eventually wife), the humor and fallibility of Pat Patton (before he becomes police chief), and the family-like atmosphere surrounding the whole group of good guys and gals. Children are drawn to Junior, Tess, and Pat. The storyline may be related from any one of these characters' point of view. Tracy is appealing to children not just because of his exciting and dangerous work and what he stands for, but also because he is a prototypical father. Young readers of the comic believe Tracy embodies some of the most salient qualities of dad.

In a *Tracy* sequence from November 1932 (between the episodes of Dan the Squealer and Larceny Lu, Queen of the Stolen Car Gang), Junior is falsely accused of shooting Tracy and sent to a detention home. When the police take Junior away from Tracy's hospital bedside, where the young ward is talking to his mentor and father figure, to escort him to the orphanage, the great detective strikes the chief of police! For the next several weeks, Tracy vehemently chastises his own department and its officers for their treatment of Junior. It seems that at times even Tracy finds something more important than the law—his family. With his de-

manding time-consuming job, Dick Tracy does not seem as available for Junior as a conventional father might be, but no one protects and defends his family better.

Unlike Marvel comic books of the Sixties where readers could write to Stan Lee and see a response printed in the next issue of their favorite magazine, there has always been a lack of direct, critical contact between Gould (or his successors) and the audience. This has been true for a majority of comic strips and comic books throughout the years. As Abel and White note, "It is just because the characters are so 'real' that the authors remain anonymous even to the most constant readers. Awareness of the author would destroy the identity of his characters." In the reader's mind, "the man who writes about Dick Tracy is Dick Tracy."[16] Chester Gould, like Carl Barks (major Walt Disney studios comic book artist for decades) and many other comic art writers and artists, was essentially unknown to his audience for most of his career.[17] It is interesting to note that some artists like Gould and Barks were not recognized as profound comic creators until after they had left their famous works. When people read *Dick Tracy*, they read the story of Dick Tracy. (Little did they know that Tracy *was* Chester Gould.)

Dick Tracy is popular since its creator and perpetuators have adopted and adopt a wholly commercial attitude toward success. Market share is everything. When a form such as *Tracy* begins to stray from public interest, the artists have to adjust their product and its content to accommodate shifts in public sentiment. In this sense, there is no better monitor and censor of popular art than the producers themselves. These individuals, by necessity, keep one finger on the pulse of social sentiment, and they attempt to hit a responsive chord with another. Hence creators of the arts alter their themes in an effort to parallel changes in public taste. Chester Gould made shifts in the themes presented in *Dick Tracy* for this reason, but sometimes he was more successful than other times. Many people believed that Gould's adoption of outer-space settings and the placement of Tracy on the moon in the Sixties was not a totally successful shift in themes. The force behind a popular form necessarily continues to adjust the form until it plays the tune to which the public is marching. Further, in the case of the comic strip, the product has to be made available to the masses at a price which is attractive. Since in 1939 *Dick Tracy* was printed in 160 newspapers, and even more as time went by, and since many newspapers were read second- and thirdhand after the initial buyers and consumers were done with them, it seems apparent that the form has been accessible to a large segment of the American populace. And the price of newspapers has always been minimal. In the Thirties, daily newspapers typically cost no more than five or ten cents and Sunday editions were only slightly more expensive; today, most daily newspapers can be purchased for fifty cents or less and Sunday editions are generally no more than two dollars. Yet, the price of the popular art form is not measured solely in monetary terms. Investments in comic strips also include the individual's time expended reading the strip. Comic strips, then, must provide some hook which brings the reader back on a daily basis, creating a habit or ritual of sorts. In the comedy strip, that hook is humor of a level satisfying to the reader; in the action/adventure comic strip, the hook is the serial format which provides a daily cliffhanger. As an action/adventure strip, *Dick Tracy* has always provided captivating storylines that anticipate the next day's episode, and it has always provided interesting character types that further enhance the attraction of the strip. The consumer has to decide whether this available product, offered at a reasonable price, is worthy of attention and expenditure of time.

Newspaper publishers select comic strips based on how well the individual strips help sales of their papers. Had *Dick Tracy* not been a marketable commodity, it would not have been published in so many papers and would not still be around today. *Tracy* has been, and is, saleable because it has embraced, and continues to embrace, facets of the social consciousness. Particularly in the 1930s and 1940s, people bought newspapers for the funnies. Today this is not the case. Fifty years ago, *Tracy* or *Little Orphan Annie* or *Popeye* or *The Gumps* was often allotted one-third or one-half of a page, and on Sundays *Tracy* filled the entire first page of many newspapers' comic pages. Even Charles Schulz's *Peanuts,* Berke Breathed's *Bloom County,* or Bill Watterson's *Calvin and Hobbes* of contemporary times cannot boast that accomplishment.

Relatively simple, conservative themes abound in *Dick Tracy*. The basic central theme of the strip is that "crime does not pay." In an interview published in *The Celebrated Cases of Dick Tracy 1931–1951,* Chester Gould stated that he did not outline the whole story when he started a new saga.[18] Precisely how Dick Tracy was to triumph in the end over crime was never certain until the story appeared on the printed page. Gould felt that by writing the story as he went, he could keep the scripts interesting. He said that if he didn't know how the episode would turn out, the reader wouldn't either. In a sense, though, the story was always the same—Dick Tracy and his idealistic and hard-nosed American style of law enforcement subdued crime. Gould kept the storylines varied and inventive as he went, but the underlying current was the simple, conservative proposal that "crime does not pay."

Representational human elements with which the reader can easily identify (or wants to identify) are apparent in this strip. Settings and motifs for the strip have been derived from real life settings and occurrences of the times. This has made the stories highly believable and relevant to the readers. If not all cops of the Thirties were on the level, the American people wanted them to be so. But again, perhaps most interesting of all were the grotesque villains. These characters provided the critical invention to the police procedural formula that is inherently conventional. The rogues were physically bizarre and deformed, as were their actions—particularly the ingenious death traps they provided for the hero. Later, we will see some of the specific evils the grotesques perpetrated on Dick Tracy, including one of the most famous, ingenious, yet horrible death traps of all time—courtesy of Mrs. Pruneface in August 1943. The death trap provided the epic moment for each *Dick Tracy* adventure. These adventures typically averaged about three months of newspaper strips in duration. Readers not only wanted to see social reality reflected in the comic strip, they wanted to see their own personal realities, ideologies, and fantasies reflected and reinforced. They wanted to see straight cops, whether or not all cops were actually straight.

Dick Tracy, like all effective comic strips, demands a low level of attention or participation from its audience. Comic strips, unlike many political cartoons, are never, and were never, meant as vehicles of elitist thinking. Originally, as their name suggests, comics were conceived as a means for eliciting a laugh or chuckle from a brief moment of comedy captured in one or two frames. Chester Gould incorporated humor into *Dick Tracy* chiefly via the protagonist's sidekicks, Pat Patton and (later) Sam Catchem—themselves exaggerated stereotypes of the Irish and Jewish respectively. Patton is slightly overweight and slightly hot-tempered, and while he means well, he gets into mischief on occasion. Catchem has a big nose and a Howdy Doody–like face, so he is physically overstated. The majority of American readers have never wanted to begin or end a workday (or in the case of children, a day of

school or play) by picking up a newspaper and being bombarded with intellectualism. For most Americans, the day provides more than enough physical and mental challenges, and quite often the news in the newspaper is sufficiently disheartening. This is why so many more Americans have in years past bought the newspaper for its comics and its sports pages rather than for its news features.

Chester Gould and associates have been effective in *Dick Tracy* because they have catered to the whole spectrum of the American populace, including the lowest common denominator. Children can follow Junior, and minimally educated adults can follow *Tracy* with little effort. The comic strip at its best has always been a sort of silent film with subtitles. On several occasions Gould and his associates have been most powerful when few or no words of dialogue or description are employed in a frame or series of frames. Chester Gould's July 24 and 25, 1941, daily strips which were part of the "Who Shot Pat Patton? Story" are discussed in more detail in Chapter 4. It is highly unlikely that *Tracy* would be as popular and effective if the main character sat in a laboratory explaining to the reader, day in and day out, the virtues of scientific experimentation in ballistics as a means of crime detection. Gould spent time with the Chicago Police Department and got firsthand information from police technicians, as well as from lawmen on patrol. In the 1930s, he worked for a while with J. Edgar Hoover. These insights were frequently and consciously incorporated into his work.

David Manning White proposes five reasons why comic strips are read. While these explanations in themselves are not all inclusive, they do provide an important perspective on a phenomenon that is so pervasive in, and embraced by, the larger society. These are:

1. The comic strips are read because they provide some sort of satisfaction (some

tension reduction) for the reader, either in a conscious, purposeful way or in a mechanical, unconscious way.

2. Tensions may be reduced simply by a relief in monotony, by a break in accustomed activity, by the pure mechanics of variety (all characteristic of play), or through dramatic catharsis (which is characteristic of art, and which is dependent on ideas and symbols).

3. Catharsis requires interest (mobilization and focusing on latent tension in the audience) and interest involves empathy or identification.

4. Identification may take place at the level of fantasy, or because of the direct similarity between the depicted situation and that of the audience.

5. Differences of taste reflect the capacity of different themes to reduce tensions for particular kinds of readers.[19]

The satisfaction provided by *Dick Tracy* is visualization of "good" (in the form of established law and order) battling with and triumphing over "evil" (organized crime). The process occurs on both a conscious and unconscious level. Beliefs, values, ideologies are reflected, prescribed, and reinforced in this process. Established police forces defeating crime in epic confrontations are prominent in the mindsets of the individual readers, as are the minor albeit fleeting triumphs of gangdom prior to the epic moment. The detection of clues leading to solutions of seemingly perfect crimes is a ritual which enthralls *Tracy* readers. If the criminal mastermind is the magician creating the illusions, the detective hero has to be a similar sort of prestidigitator — who better to unravel the magician's deceptions than another magician?

The framework of the detective story acts as a giant puzzle, and the ritual of systematic detection leading to the solution of the puzzle provides the comfort and satisfaction of good triumphing over evil. The process provides a social construction of reality. In the 1920s and 1930s, the popular press celebrated and sensationalized the exploits of the gangster. At this

time too, J. Edgar Hoover emerged and molded the Federal Bureau of Investigation in his own image, and provided his own rituals of crime detection. These rituals have been engrained into America's collective consciousness for years, and as rituals they provide the comfort of the familiar induced by formulaic repetition. No matter how many times Tracy subdues a villain, the reader likes the reassurance that he continues to do so.

The primary convention in *Dick Tracy* is the repeated ultimate success of law and order. At the same time, the strip is inventive enough to relieve monotony in the readers' lives. The convention inherently also provides a familiarity that relieves tension through the mechanics of organization and order. The title hero serves as the ultimate symbol, embodying idealized characteristics; Tracy is the main beam in the house. At the same time readers, like Gould himself, were not and are not really sure that what happens daily in the story will culminate in the success of the detective. (In recent times, however, Max Collins more consciously plotted the storylines in advance and hence himself knew the outcome of the tale.) One can still hear New York Mayor Fiorello LaGuardia reading the funnies on the radio. He would say something like, "Let's see what Dick Tracy is doing today." Nobody knew! Adventures and tension releases were (and are) available daily in the comic, and there was satisfaction in knowing that eventually things would turn out for the best. Dick Tracy lives in a troubled world much like our own, but he provides an order (to his world and ours alike) that calms collective social apprehensions.

As the creator and longtime steward of *Dick Tracy*, Gould was especially adept at identifying and focusing on concerns and fears of his audience. He addressed all kinds of aspects of gangsterism and proposed seemingly logical solutions for the problem. These aspects included violence in the forms of insidious crimes like kidnapping, torture, and murder, perpetrated by grotesques of nature, for which the evildoer consistently atoned. Tracy, Patton, and others were unwavering in their commitments to justice, and were hence dispelling the qualms about cops going bad. Gould wanted us to identify with and emulate the good guys and gals.

In *Tracy,* there is a commonality between depicted situation and the experiences of the reader. The producers of the strip have continually based their stories on real life occurrences like the Lindbergh baby kidnapping, the famous escape of John Dillinger from jail, and the atrocities of Nazi Germany. This has created an empathy in the audience with the fictional caricatures. When real life is so closely paralleled and reflected, fact and fantasy become intertwined and are essentially one to the reader. Individuals can identify with the factual, based on their own experiences and exposure, and they want to identify with the fantasy evolving from the strip.

Diverse tastes reflect the capacity of different themes to reduce tensions for particular kinds of readers. Gould and his associates have created a smorgasbord which has an array of appealing qualities for a variety of consumers. This is evidenced in the heterogeneity of the readership. In the strip there are many sources of appeal and interest. These include:

1. crime detection
2. an idealized father-like hero
3. a child protégé
4. a love relationship between the hero and the lady
5. unique, interesting criminals
6. dangerous and potentially fatal situations created by the villains
7. authentic urban settings
8. an idealized family atmosphere
9. a measure of humor when it is appropriate
10. accurate depiction of documented police procedure and scientific crime detection.
11. fictional reflections of real-life historical events
12. ingenious and insidious death traps

The audience of *Dick Tracy* is attracted to the comic strip for a number of reasons, such as those aforementioned. Yet, other explanations exist. *Tracy* is often sensational, and it provides a degree of sadism and aggression in the forms of villainous acts like burnings, stabbings, shootings, and more for those who desire the same. The strip provides legitimate scapegoats in the forms of criminals who are continually pursued and eventually subdued; it also provides an idealistic, larger-than-life hero whom the reader can emulate. This idealistic hero is just that — someone to be idolized and glamorized. The secondary characters provide realism in the forms of humor and human frailty. The reader has the comfort of knowing that Dick Tracy will persevere and succeed. However, the audience likes to see the hero go through the orderly process, the ritual, which enacts the myth.

Richard Gid Powers has written several insightful articles on myth, ritual, the G-men, comic strips and other popular media, J. Edgar Hoover, and the FBI. Powers' landmark book, *G-Men: Hoover's FBI in American Popular Culture* (1985), may be the most important single work on these interrelated subjects of fact and fantasy. What becomes obvious from Powers' scholarship is that J. Edgar Hoover, bigger-than-life head of the FBI from 1924 until his death in 1972, had an intense love/hate relationship with the fictional G-men of the popular media.[20] Hoover was a master showman. As Powers notes, "Few American politicians have ever held the popular imagination in as firm a grip as did Hoover, and none ever maintained their grasp so long. It was Hoover's role as a public hero, a celebrity of the headlines, 'Public Hero Number One' as one pulp called him in the thirties, that was the ultimate source of his power."[21] Yet, J. Edgar Hoover had to be an all-powerful, pervasive character of the social consciousness because in the gangster, he had a formidable adversary. "It is one of the most important functions of the central authority (the president or his spokesman) to reaffirm public conventions whenever they come under attack, particularly when the threat is symbolic. To neglect this duty is to risk the accusation of encouraging or approving symbolic evil."[22] "From the earliest of days, victims of the Bureau have been prosecuted not for what they have done, but for what they have meant."[23]

Events relative to J. Edgar Hoover and the comic strip G-man are chronicled later in this work. For now, it is sufficient to know that Hoover critically reviewed factual and fictional stories of crime and its detection presented in the popular media of the 1930s. He was both enchanted and disenchanted with what he perceived to be occurring in these story forms, and he ultimately hired the writers and artists necessary to create his own comic strip, *War on Crime*, which debuted and concluded in 1936. Hoover was a big fan of Chester Gould and his fictional detective Dick Tracy because, though Tracy was an individualist who ironically stressed teamwork within his own police force, Tracy was not threatening to Hoover, who was anything but a fictional police detective. J. Edgar Hoover wanted only team players in his own war on crime—except that he, like Tracy, was very much the individualist— but Dick Tracy did not represent the Federal Bureau of Investigation (he was a cop) and did not, strictly speaking, claim to be retelling factual history in his adventures. Thus, Hoover found *Tracy* unobtrusive to the image he was establishing for the real-life FBI. The Bureau chief liked the ideology Gould's comic strip hero embodied. "In the action story the hero is a pure projection of the audience's fantasies of power, and so he has to embody the culture's most desired traits."[24]

Dick Tracy has been popular for some

sixty years for more than its captivating storylines and reflection of real-life history. Chester Gould's creation embodies things much more profound and mythic. In *Dick Tracy*, we find, among other ideologies, the "Myth of the Hero" and the "Myth of the Old Gothic Wilderness." Each of these myths is vital to the establishment of the strip as an epic. Famed myth/symbol scholar Joseph Campbell claims that the mythic hero goes through a series of intense sacrifices in an effort to achieve the moral objective of saving a people. This hero type is as old as the ages. Arthur Asa Berger writes:

> The ordeal is part of the general myth of the hero, a myth which seems to be ubiquitous, and which deals with the attempts of people (at whatever level of cultural development, it seems) to explain the human condition and man's place in the universe. The hero has an elevated status, but the cost of this superior position is the need to undergo "tests" and to suffer. Suffering ordeals purifies the hero and, at the same time, purifies the society.[25]

In an article for *Popular Culture in America* (1987), Franklin Rosemont claims that *Dick Tracy* is an extension of very, very old mythic and literary traditions. He states that in *Tracy:*

> We are in the old Gothic wilderness; it has been industrialized and urbanized, of course, and the moldering castles have been replaced by skyscrapers, but the atmosphere remains essentially the same. A cold metallic solitude rings through the Tracy epic in its early years. The streets glisten with greed and fear as we follow crazed killers in their gloomy sedans, roaring through the shadows to an inexorable doom. We read *Dick Tracy* the way we read Cotton Mather's *Wonders of the Invisible World*. Both are works of apoplectic puritanism, bursting at the seams with an uncontrollable and "righteous" fury. But we are as little interested in Gould's respect for the law as we are in the fine points of the old witchhunter's theology.

What interests us is the insuperable violence of the dramatic collisions and the
dazzling profusion of obsessive detail.[26]

Hence, Dick Tracy is a champion of ancient values and tradition who exists in a
modernly contextualized old gothic wilderness. His story, at least on the levels of
myth and tradition, is not wholly different
from that of Nathaniel Hawthorne's Young
Goodman Brown who goes into the forest
and meets the devil.

Should there be a question of legitimacy when studying comic strips as American culture phenomena? The answer is no.
Do the black and white drawing and storytelling in *Dick Tracy* represent the highest
plateaus of American intellectual art and
thought? Again, the answer is no. Neither
the art nor the storylines of *Tracy* are overly
complex, but the mythology involved is as
old and profound and universal as found
anywhere else. Remember, Chester Gould
was a student of, and claimed his only
artistic inspirations came from, the classics. As John Bainbridge noted in his 1944
Life magazine profile of Gould:

> Heywood Broun once pointed out that
> comic strips, in reality, constitute the pro-
> letarian novels of America. By this defini-
> tion Chester Gould, creator of the strip
> called *Dick Tracy*, must rank as one of the
> great writers of our time. He is formidably
> prolific, his characters have already passed
> into our folklore, and he has a following
> far larger than any author whose books are
> featured on the best-seller lists. In recent
> months a consistent best-seller among
> fiction titles has been the novel, *A Tree
> Grows in Brooklyn*. It has sold over
> 900,000 copies and been read, at a gener-
> ous estimate, by 4,000,000 people. *Dick
> Tracy* is bought every day in the year by
> 13,500,000 people and is probably read by
> twice that number. Literary critics were
> ecstatic about the Brooklyn book, finding
> it, as one said, "profoundly moving." Al-
> though no literary critic, even in Brook-
> lyn, has ever admitted being much stirred
> by *Dick Tracy*, a few million other percep-
> tive people apparently have.[27]

Premiere comic strip historian Richard
Marschall writes, "The comics' vocabulary
transcends the written words of balloons
and captions; it extends—expands—to
unique and meaningful signs and symbols:
motion lines, sweat beads, stars of pain,
sound-effect indications, all hovering
physically within the comic-strip universe.
They are not crutches for the cartoonist
but splendid means to tell stories in a way
different from, say, the novelist."[28] M.
Thomas Inge claims:

> Of all the popular arts, the comic strip is
> considered the most inconsequential.
> Produced by a daily deadline, read
> quickly and thrown out with the trash, and
> considered primarily to be a childish
> amusement, little appreciation has been
> accorded this uniquely American derived
> art form, even though at certain points in
> the history of journalism, the comics have
> spelled the financial success or failure of a
> newspaper. Some fine works of the imagi-
> nation and visual artistry have appeared in
> the comics in the course of their develop-
> ment, but they have been lost to cultural
> history because of their impermanent for-
> mat. There is evidence that William
> Faulkner—himself once an aspiring car-
> toonist—had a fondness for the funny
> papers that is reflected in his fiction.[29]

Phenomena take on epic American
culture proportions when they permeate
many aspects of the society. *Dick Tracy* has
appeared in several media since 1931 other
than the newspaper comic strip. Since its
infancy, the saga of America's number one
cop has been told via Big Little Books,
Feature Books, comic books, motion picture serials, "B" movies, radio programs,
novels, a television program, an animated
series of cartoons for television, and a fea-
ture-length movie starring Warren Beatty
in the title role. At its inception, the strip
was inspired by the social setting of the
Great Depression, and it was created by a
man who was acutely in tune with that environment. In *The Celebrated Cases of
Dick Tracy 1931–1951*, Chester Gould
commented that he was catering to his

neighbors with the strip by reflecting their beliefs and experiences.[30] Enduring comic strips like *Dick Tracy* are the ones that remain socially relevant through changing times. From the Thirties through the Nineties, *Tracy* has matured with America. Chester Gould and his successors have been revered for their replication of actual American lifestyles, and it is this representation that is so vital to the success of the saga.

A thorough understanding of social history as context for any cultural product is invaluable when appreciating the form. While theory is indispensable in providing a multitude of viable angles to an area of scholarly analysis, this same theory needs to be legitimated by a factual basis. In a cultural inquiry, what has happened and is happening is the essential focus. The human condition is, after all, the most important focus of scholarship.

Chester Gould originally conceived *Dick Tracy* as a barometer of the American experience. His invention flourishes on this and on other levels to this day. Vivid grotesqueness, heinous crime, and hardcore melodrama are effectively combined to communicate a message of high morality to the American people in this granddaddy of detective stories and adventure comic strips. Herein, beliefs, values and attitudes regarding truth, justice, and the American way are reinforced, reflected, and shaped, and in a time where heroes are scarce and ephemeral at best, the legend lives on. "Calling Dick Tracy, Calling Dick Tracy!"

Notes

1. George A. Brandenburg, "Gould-Tracy, Partners in Crime for 25 Years," *Editor and Publisher*, October 6, 1956, p. 14.
2. Coulton Waugh, *The Comics* (New York: Macmillan, 1947), p. 217.
3. Robert H. Abel and David Manning White, eds., *The Funnies: An American Idiom* (London: Collier-Macmillan, 1963). It is important to note that this book appeared in 1963, and that the readership of newspaper comics today is, with rare exception, diminished.
4. Herb Galewitz, ed., *Great Comics Syndicated by the Daily News–Chicago Tribune* (New York: Crown, 1972), p. vii.
5. John Bainbridge, "Chester Gould: The Harrowing Adventures of His Cartoon Hero, Dick Tracy, Give Vicarious Thrills to Millions," *Life*, August 14, 1944, p. 43.
6. John G. Cawelti, *Adventure, Mystery and Romance* (Chicago: University of Chicago Press, 1976).
7. Stephen Becker, *Comic Art in America* (New York: Simon and Schuster, 1959), p. 176.
8. Abel and White, p. 24.
9. *Nemo: The Classic Comics Library* 17, February 1986.
10. Richard Slotkin. *Regeneration Through Violence: The Mythology of the American Frontier 1600–1800* (Middletown, Conn.: Wesleyan University Press, 1973).
11. The police procedural is inherently one of the most pedestrian of the popular formulas of the mystery genre. Quite often, stories about the workings of law enforcement in the United States get almost exclusively caught up in redundant method and are hence mundane.
12. Mark Starr, "Durable Cop: After Four Decades Dick Tracy Remains Top Comic-Strip Hero." *Wall Street Journal*, March 12, 1974, p. 1.
13. Becker, p. 192.
14. Ron Goulart, *The Adventurous Decade* (New Rochelle, New York: Arlington House, 1975), p. 73.
15. Over the next few years, *Dick Tracy* appeared in several hundred newspapers. Today that figure has diminished, but it still remains in the hundreds. Publishers have been known to drop and add the strip almost daily, quite often in response to the ever-changing content of the storyline.
16. Abel and White, p. 238.
17. It has been the policy of Disney studios for many years to have its artists work solely under the Walt Disney byline. Carl Barks, who went virtually uncredited for decades, has upon his recent

retirement been rediscovered for his contributions to the business. His primary role with Disney was that of scripting and drawing comic book stories. Readers of Disney comic art began to recognize his style and deemed him "the good artist." In recent years, his discovery (or rediscovery) has brought about intense demand for his work.

18. Herb Galewitz, ed., *The Celebrated Cases of Dick Tracy 1931–1951* (New York: Chelsea House, 1970), p. ix.

19. Abel and White, pp. 233–234.

20. According to Powers, the term "G-men" was given FBI agents by "Machine Gun" Kelly after his arrest for his part in the kidnapping of an Oklahoma City oilman on July 23, 1933. See Richard Gid Powers, "J. Edgar Hoover and the Detective Hero" in Jack Nachbar's and John L. Wright's *The Popular Culture Reader—First Edition* (Bowling Green, Ohio: Bowling Green State University Popular Press, 1977). The term is generally defined as "Government Man."

21. Powers, pp. 201–202.

22. Ibid., p. 205.

23. Ibid., p. 208.

24. Richard Gid Powers, *G-Men: Hoover's F.B.I. in American Popular Culture* (Carbondale, Illinois: Southern Illinois University Press, 1983), p. 77.

25. Arthur Asa Berger, *The Comic-Stripped American* (Baltimore, Maryland: Penguin, 1973), p. 125.

26. Franklin Rosemont, "Surrealism in the Comics II," in Paul Buhle's edited *Popular Culture in America* (Minneapolis: University of Minnesota Press, 1987), pp. 130–131.

27. Bainbridge.

28. Richard Marschall, *America's Great Comic Strip Artists* (New York: Abbeville Press, 1989), pp. 9–10.

29. M. Thomas Inge, *Comics as Culture* (Jackson, Miss.: University Press of Mississippi, 1990), p. 79.

30. Galewitz, p. xiii.

CHAPTER 2

Chronicling a Culture:
A History of the Development
of the American Comic Strip

"It was once pointed out to me that the *New York Times* carries no comic strips and still is a great newspaper. My answer to that was, 'Think how much greater it would have been had it carried comic strips. It might have attained a circulation almost as great as the *New York Daily News.*'" — Chester Gould, from his remarks to the Newspaper Comics Council, November 2, 1972.

The comic strip, as we know it, has been a part of American culture since the late nineteenth century; the two-dimensional caricature, of course, dates back to the beginnings of humanity and ancient cave paintings. In recent centuries, the single frame political cartoon has evolved internationally with the newspaper, yet in America, it was not until the 1890s that the comic strip first appeared as a regular feature of newspapers. The comic strip, for the purposes of this book, is defined as a logical sequencing of line drawings — often compartmentalized into panels — which tells a brief story or elicits a chuckle or a smile, hence the term "comic." Originally, comic strips were designed as vehicles for humor. It was not until the early twentieth century that this new media form was employed to tell extended stories of adventure, mystery, and intrigue. In 1977, Bill Blackbeard and Martin Williams wrote, "Only in the past decade has the American newspaper comic strip begun to be recognized in its own country as an innovative and creative cultural accomplishment."[1] Blackbeard and Williams continue:

Many of our own historians of the arts, having borrowed their principles, procedures, and attitudes largely from European cultural historians, have proceeded to apply those principles only to such traditional categories as we have borrowed directly from abroad — to literary history, to the theater, to concert music, and the like sometimes pausing to scorn or reject these artistic genres that are particularly American, like the movies, Jazz, and the comics. Europeans, meanwhile, have applied their principles of cultural history and criticism in modified form to those American creations and transmutations which we still think of as our "popular" or even our "light" artistic pursuits.[2]

Today, in the early- and mid–Nineties, the comic strip has been rediscovered with great fervor. Publishing houses have emerged which have specialized in reprinting these cultural products of decades past in hardcover and paperback forms, in color (as in the case of Sunday strips) and in black and white (as in the case of daily strips). In San Francisco, Bill Blackbeard has championed the San Francisco Academy of Comic Art and has been

Little Orphan Annie—March 1, 1928. Reprinted by permission: Tribune Media Services.

instrumental in many such publishing ventures. Kitchen Sink Press of Princeton, Wisconsin, has produced several such books and series of books which collect and reprint classic comic strips. Individuals like Richard Marschall have made herculean efforts, with great results, to preserve and analyze the American comic strip medium. There cannot be enough positive said about the contributions of Rick Marschall. In Port Chester, New York, the Museum of Cartoon Art stands as a monument to this popular American art form. Established academic and international publishers like McFarland, the University Press of Mississippi, Oxford University Press, and Ivy League school presses such as those from Harvard, Yale, and so on, are beginning to realize the importance of scholarship on the American comic strip. There are, of course, many others. Why has the comic strip of yesterday become so popular today? The answer to this question is many faceted. First, "good" art—that is, art which achieves some universal aesthetic like an optimal combination of idea and line drawing within the context of the two-dimensional comic strip panel—is timeless. Second, comic strips from the Twenties, Thirties, and Forties, for example, often provide contemporary audiences with legitimation for their romantic visions of yesteryear— the older times being supposedly simpler and therefore better than the modern era. Third, comic strip artists of several dec-

ades ago had much more freer reign and creative control over their products. Hence, these works are much more complex, beautiful, and poignant than their contemporary counterparts.

Perhaps the single best and most representative volume of comic strip reprints from the 1980s forward published to date is Bill Blackbeard and Martin Williams' edited collection entitled *The Smithsonian Collection of Newspaper Comics* (1977). M. Thomas Inge's *Comics as Culture* (1990) stands as one of the single finest book-length analyses of the form and its place in cultural history yet put forth. And, through a variety of edited books and scholarly, insightful articles on the subject of comic strips, Rick Marschall has proven himself to be one of the finest comic strip authorities working today. Blackbeard and Williams set the boundaries for, and render a first-rate definition of, this media form. They write that a comic strip is a "serially published, episodic, open-ended dramatic narrative or series of linked anecdotes about recurrent, identified characters, told in successive drawings regularly enclosing ballooned dialogue or its equivalent and minimized narrative text."[3]

Most authorities on the American comic strip identify international and artistic precedents for the contemporary phenomenon which still thrives in newspapers nationwide. Most authorities also vary in what they claim as the "first" American comic strip. Pierre Couperie and Maurice

Horn cite several possible claimants for the title from the 1880s and 1890s.[4] Jerry Robinson and Herb Galewitz suggest that the comic strip, strictly speaking, did not appear until the 1920s.[5] Blackbeard and Williams cite 1896's *Yellow Kid* by Richard Outcault for the Hearst Syndicate as the first comic strip.[6] Yet the comic strip that fulfills all the requirements delineated above in Blackbeard and Williams' definition was *The Katzenjammer Kids.*

Hans and Fritz, the Katzenjammer Kids, appeared for the first time on December 12, 1897, in "The American Humorist," the Sunday supplement of William Randolph Hearst's *The New York Journal.* Rudolph Dirks was the creator and first storyteller of the Katzenjammer Kids saga. The strip, originally adapted from the German cartoon *Max and Moritz,* revolved around Hans and Fritz and their rebellion against any form of authority. "For Hans and Fritz, 'society is nix.'"[7] This famous comic strip has gone through a variety of writers and illustrators, and continues today, though in restricted form and in limited areas, almost 100 years later. Although several elaborate one-panel cartoons appeared during the years immediately preceding the arrival of *The Katzenjammer Kids* (including *The Yellow Kid*), no newspaper feature organized panels of comic or cartoon art into a logical, lineal sequence to tell a story until the debut of Dirks' comic strip. The importance of *The Katzenjammer Kids* extends further. "Katzenjammer" translates from the German to mean the "yowling of cats," and is the slang for a hangover in that country. The rebellious Hans and Fritz, whether in conflict with "der Mama," "der Inspector," or "der Captain," have contested social institutions such as parents and guardians, education, and government from the start. As a form of entertainment, this strip has enjoyed a good deal of success. Yet, on a larger scale, it has allowed its writers, illustrators, and audiences to look at social institutions and their implications.

During the first two decades of the comic strip, that period between 1897 and the close of World War I, the new medium essentially appeared on large, color-printed paper supplements of big-city newspapers. Blackbeard and Williams write that during this time, "Three comic figures of popular fiction dominated virtually to the exclusion of all others: the demon child, the clownish innocent, and the humanized animal."[8] *The Yellow Kid* preceded *The Katzenjammer Kids* by a matter of months and epitomized the most popular of the three aforementioned comic character types—the demon child. Richard Outcault's *The Yellow Kid* was, however, confined to one large frame of illustration, and did not evidence any logical progression of line drawings to relate a narrative, and thus was not really a comic strip—just as Gary Larson's contemporary comic art smash hit, *The Far Side,* is not, strictly speaking, a comic strip. Shortly after the emergence of Dirks' Hans and Fritz, Outcault's *Buster Brown* (May 4, 1902) and Winsor McCay's *Little Nemo in Slumberland* (October 15, 1905) appeared, along with an array of lesser known strips. The ideas of the demon child and the clownish innocent were not born, however, on the comic page. Such characters had pervaded folk culture centuries earlier. But the comic strip did become a vehicle which immortalized tales of such stereotypic individuals.

The humanized animal arose almost simultaneously with the trickster and innocent. For example, Buster Brown was accompanied by his dog Tige. Fred Opper, the comic strip artist most often remembered for his *Happy Hooligan,* provided the public with Maud the Mule in *And Her Name Was Maud* which began in 1904. J.M. Conde's Uncle Remus characters were part of a larger humanized animal community in *Uncle Remus Stories.* Yet, like the demon child and the clownish innocent, the humanized animal had been a staple of folk tales since ancient times.

There is a specific explanation for this. The mythic Greek slave Aesop is credited with early utilization of such animal characters in his stories with subtexts of social criticism.[9] By employing these animals as representations of the humans that surrounded him, Aesop was afforded the opportunity to parody and criticize individuals who would normally be hostile to direct scrutiny and condemnation. Animal characters act as non-threatening liaisons for social commentary. Stories which directly parodied his owners and masters would have gotten Aesop the severest of punishments; today, such direct stories would drastically limit the audiences of fictioneers of various media and genres. Animals which embody the frailties of humanity are less threatening than realistic human characters; these animals are safer. The comic strip and its descendants have thrived on the humanized animal since their earliest beginnings.

While—as Blackbeard and Williams point out—the first comic strips were organized around the exploits of the demon child, the clownish innocent, and the humanized animal, other variations and strains of character types soon appeared. Couperie and Horn write, "Originally comic strips were essentially humorous (hence their early baptism as 'comics'), but a great variety of themes were soon developed: the fairy tale, suspense, mythological tales, and even science-fiction appeared one after the other."[10] At the turn of the century, many of the newspaper strips were adult-oriented. Largely because William Randolph Hearst was the primary publishing force behind these strips, newspaper comics at this time were designed so that they would be acceptable facets of Hearst's "aristocratic" productions. Blackbeard and Williams write:

> The order of the day in the daily strips between 1907 and 1927 was satire, cheerful cynicism, and subdued slapstick, centered on helpless husbands, burlesque detectives, and inept scoundrels. But, new kinds of strips and heroes did enter the scene in the 1920s and shape the character of all strips in the following decade.[11]

Between 1907 and 1927 also, comic strips increasingly were targeted at larger audiences—audiences which included children. One such strip was a favorite of young Chester Gould; it was *Mutt and Jeff.* (See Gould's biography in Chapter 5.)

On November 15, 1907, H.C. "Bud" Fisher introduced *A. Mutt*, which was soon changed to *Mutt and Jeff.* One of the most famous vaudevillian teams of the comic page, Mutt and Jeff provided their audience with a form of comedy and satire that had been around for decades in other forms, and that would continue to thrive and grow in a variety of media during the first half of the twentieth century. The narrative device for *Mutt and Jeff*—perhaps the single greatest ingredient of this comic strip's success—centered on the interactions of the carefully drawn protagonists.

In 1917, Sidney Smith, under the tutelage of William Randolph Hearst's biggest emerging competitor, newspaper mogul Captain Joseph Medill Patterson, produced a comic strip which parodied domestic, middle class American families— *The Gumps.* Andy Gump and later his son Chester became enduring staples of the *Chicago Tribune,* the New York News Syndicate and comic pages everywhere. Maurice Horn writes, "*The Gumps* was intended only to chronicle the doings of a typical lower middle class family in Chicago when *Tribune* publisher Joe Patterson assigned the strip art and story to Sidney Smith in 1917, at a time when the *Tribune* was publishing no regular daily comic strip."[12] According to Herb Galewitz, Smith became a landmark comic artist when five years later he became the first cartoonist to receive a million dollar contract for his work.[13] The contract was for ten years of work at $100,000 per annum. To this day, a bronze statue of Andy Gump stands in Lake Geneva, Wisconsin—Smith's hometown. In 1935, however,

THE GUMPS—A PRESSING ENGAGEMENT

The Gumps—March 1, 1928. Reprinted by permission: Tribune Media Services.

tragedy struck: *The Gumps* was appearing in hundreds of newspapers and was at its height when Smith died in an automobile accident and *The Gumps*, while continuing for another 24 years, never again was the same. Sidney Smith proved to be a significant role model for Chester Gould. (See Gould's biography in Chapter 5.)

At the close of 1918, Frank King provided the Chicago Tribune and New York News Syndicate with another saga of middle class America, though King's strip did not debut until February 14 (Valentine's Day), 1921, in the established format of the comic strip. Horn writes, "In *Gasoline Alley* King introduced a fundamental innovation: the characters in the strip grew old along with the readers."[14]

> Much of the popularity that *Gasoline Alley* earned derived from its commonplace presentation of life as it was for many middle class Americans of this century, and accordingly it is an invaluable pictorial record of America's general way of life in our times.... It is evident, therefore, that *Gasoline Alley* is a neglected and important American work of art calling for republication in full to be made generally accessible for social study in institutions of learning.[15]

Sensing that the comic lacked an appeal to a larger audience which included women, Captain Patterson ordered Frank King to supply a baby in the storyline. The result was the debut of Skeezix Wallet on that first day of the strip, February 14, 1921. Walt Wallet, who was the bachelor hero of this comic representation of Indianapolis ("Gasoline Alley"), found the baby Skeezix on his doorstep. Young Skeezix, like the other characters of the strip, grew, and when World War II came around, the now post-adolescent young man enlisted in the military. Today, the saga of the Wallets continues. New characters have been introduced over the years, and others have expired, but the work carries on because it has remained representative of American life. Chester Gould's first known assistant on *Dick Tracy,* Dick Moores, was largely responsible for *Gasoline Alley*'s continued success in decades that followed. (See Moores' biography in Chapter 5.)

And there were still other comic strips that emerged and flourished. Frank Willard provided Patterson and the Chicago Tribune and the New York News Syndicate with *Moon Mullins* in 1923, largely as a competitive response to Billy De Beck's *Barney Google,* which was a popular strip of the *Chicago Herald* and other Hearst newspapers. "Moon's natural habitat, it turned out, was the circus, the neighborhood pool parlor, and any ritzy mansion he could bluff his way into for a free meal or two."[16] The strip was noted in the Thirties for its tightly woven storylines and cliffhangers. After Willard's death, the comic became gag oriented. Herb Galewitz writes:

Moonshine was a poolroom guy, always looking for the easy buck and a beautiful dame. His kid brother Kayo was wise beyond his years. He was also a bit of a cynic, which might stem from the fact that he had to sleep in a drawer. Moon and Kayo resided in the household of the ugly Emma Schmaltz, a boardinghouse owner with airs. Emma pursued Lord Plushbottom for ten years before he married her . . . .[17]

Today, the tales of Moon Mullins can still be found in newspapers nationwide. Upon Willard's death in 1958, Ferd Johnson took over the role as storyteller.

Murat "Chic" Young created a fictitious heroine who at one time was the subject of the most widely read comic strip in the world. Her name is Blondie, and she appeared in the strip with the same name for the first time in 1930. *Blondie,* like its predecessors *The Gumps, Gasoline Alley,* and *Moon Mullins,* was and continues to be popular because it celebrates the human spirit and the traditional American family, and it details the trials and tribulations, as well as the rewards, of being part of both nuclear and extended families. Chic Young was a master at eliciting a laugh or a chuckle from his readers because he had a keen insight into middle class America. While Blondie is the central character of this work, her interactions with her husband Dagwood Bumstead, her children Alexander and Cookie, the dog Daisy and her pups, the Ditherses, and the Woodleys have carried the script.

By the mid–Twenties, the domestic comedy newspaper strip had established itself as the dominant genre of the new medium. This particular comic strip genre has traditionally centered on the seemingly everyday activities of a family or pseudo-family group, and its focus is the daily social interactions of members of the family. Realistic settings, coupled with exaggerated stereotypes and events, provide a balance of reality and fantasy satisfying for the newspaper comic strip reader. The convention is the family group and its elaborate rituals; the invention is the response of group members to new events of each day. The invention reflects changes in sociopolitical thought and history.

Andy Gump and Blondie, along with their family members, are extensions of everyday life. Their popularity is largely attributable to their creators' and perpetuators' abilities to tap into social sentiment. Sidney Smith and Chic Young, for example, projected their own experiences onto the comic page. And since Smith, Young, and most other comic strip artists were products of middle class America, their stories were credible to their readers. Each of these artists related events in history that molded their thinking and reflected the experience of most comic strip readers. Popular entertainment and media are a very cannibalizing lot. If these masters of the comic strip could not and cannot cite specific influences from earlier comic art, they could and can refer to vaudevillians, popular authors and works, and so forth that they enjoyed and embraced, and then subsequently used to varying degrees in their own creative efforts. We all do this. Selected values and ideas which we use to construct our mindsets are modified based on new information. In the case of comic strip creators, artists, and writers, the result of this process is immortalized on the printed page.

The three primary character types, and themes surrounding them, that Blackbeard and Williams attribute to the comic strips of the late nineteenth and early twentieth centuries still thrived in the 1920s. The demon child, clownish innocent, and the humanized animal were and are all directly tied to the domestic comedy comic strips, and they are best described as formulas of the larger domestic comedy genre. In the Twenties and Thirties, variations and extensions of the genre began to appear. *The Gumps* and *Moon Mullins* were first stories of social interaction within the confines of a family group, but each strip developed a strong spinoff story. In these two particular instances, the spinoff was a variation of the demon child and clownish innocent formulas. By the end of the Twenties, the exploits of Chester Gump, Andy's son, were as vital to *The Gumps* as were the interactions of the larger family, or perhaps more vital. Similarly, Kayo became a central focus of *Moon Mullins*. In other instances, such as *Blondie*, the humanized animal rose to compete with the larger family unit for the foreground in the domestic comedy story. Stories centered on Daisy and her pups, and others, revolving around the children, Alexander and Cookie, became significant formulas within the larger genre.

The hallmark of the domestic comedy strip of the Twenties and Thirties was the character development which occurred in the better strips despite the limitations of the medium. The comic strip is a two-dimensional product which depends upon the linear progression of ideas, embodied in symbolic caricatures and settings, to relate a message. The better comic strip characters grew during the Twenties and Thirties, and the morality they conveyed was more complex and detailed than it is today. Trials and tribulations, and resulting moral growth, sometimes lasted for months. Comic strips of contemporary times are, with rare exception, dependent on short gags or superficial ideas that are limited to one day's telling. Such are the cases of *Herman, The Born Loser, Shoe,* and even *Peanuts* and *Calvin and Hobbes*. Space allocated comic strips in newspapers has become quite limited as editors and publishers have taken an increasingly heavy hand.

This problem of limited space and storyline is not unique to the domestic comedy genre of the comic strip. The Thirties saw the introduction of the second major comic strip genre—the adventure story. Today, adventure strips, which have

had an even more difficult time adjusting to changing newspaper policies, are few in number. It has become nearly impossible for these comics to carry on more than a generalized, superficial storyline. Max Collins and Dick Locher's *Dick Tracy* is the one rare and most notable exception. Perhaps this is getting ahead of the story.

The greatest human concern solidified itself as part of the comic strip in the mid–Twenties. Encounters with, escape from, and visualization of death were the basis of the newly evolving adventure genre. This genre was the second, and is apparently the last, of the major comic strip genres. While the domestic comedy remained a staple of the comic page despite shifts in emphasis and format, the saga of social interactions within a group now was augmented with the advent of tales of adventure, violence, death, and heroes. Jerry Robinson writes:

> Americans needed new heroes and heroines to divert them—Charles Lindbergh, Babe Ruth, Commander Richard E. Byrd, J. Edgar Hoover, and Amelia Earhart. Motion pictures, the dream factories for 100,000,000 Americans a week, supplied the romantic heroes and heroines: Fredric March, Clark Gable and Richard Dix, Joan Crawford, Jean Harlow and Greta Garbo. In the comic strips of the thirties, the adventure strip, a new genre, provided the action hero.[18]

The action hero and the adventure story were not new; they had appeared for years in seemingly all of America's popular media—dime novels, pulp magazines, motion pictures, and radio drama included. But this was a new twist for a new medium. What finer place for a fantastic adventure than next to even more fantastic accounts of real-life history and atrocities in the newspapers of the day?

Probably the most legitimate claimant for the title of first established adventure strip is Roy Crane's *Wash Tubbs*, though in the strictest sense there was a great deal of adventure in some of the earliest comic strip comedies. "Crane created *Wash Tubbs* in 1924, about the humorous escapades of a pint-size, bespectacled opportunist. In February 1929 Crane added a new character, Captain Easy, and the strip chronicled the rollicking adventures of the two footloose soldiers of fortune."[19] As the years went by, Easy became the more recognized figure of the two, and the strip was renamed *Captain Easy*. Stories of Easy and his comrades became epic adventures which featured exotic settings on land and sea, pitting the heroes against monstrous rogues and placing them in recurrent confrontations with death. Melvillian whales, mythic sea creatures, and cannibalistic island natives populated the world traversed by Captain Easy and Wash Tubbs.

The most famous of all adventure comic strip heroines appeared for the first time on August 25, 1924, several months after *Wash Tubb*'s debut. She was Harold Gray's Little Orphan Annie, and her story has been told ever since by the Chicago Tribune and New York News Syndicate. *Little Orphan Annie* premiered at a time in American culture when the comic strip was still a relatively new medium, and when the role of central protagonist was left primarily to the male of the species. The little waif with the red mop of hair was a Horatio Alger–like figure, spouting moral philosophy and struggling her way upward. While her adopted father, Daddy Warbucks, was a product of hard work, strict dogmatic morality, and the material wealth that comes from such qualities, Annie found herself most often on the other side of the tracks. She worked hard at whatever endeavors she undertook, always using her efforts to better the human condition as she encountered it.

Harold Gray had been Sidney Smith's assistant on *The Gumps* from 1920 until the time that Captain Patterson accepted *Little Orphan Annie* for publication in 1924. Annie reflected the struggle upward that

was so much a part of Gray's own life, and the comic named for her embodied much of how America envisioned itself. Al Capp, world famous cartoonist most often remembered for *L'il Abner,* wrote of Harold Gray:

> Harold Gray was a sharper observer of American trends, a truer prophet of America's future than Walter Lippmann. He created characters that have endured longer than Upton Sinclair's. He drew better pictures, in his seventies, than Picasso did. If he was that good, you may ask, why wasn't HE a political pundit, a revered novelist, or a master of modern art, as they were—instead of cartoonist? The answer is he WAS all that, as a cartoonist. And more. Because more of the world was affected by his political prophecy, transfixed by his story-telling, and compelled by his art than all the Lippmanns, Sinclairs, and Picassos who were his contemporaries.[20]

Gray established a tradition that was and is continued in many comic strips that followed. Annie became the number one heroine of the funny pages.

Philip F. Nowlan and Dick Calkins' *Buck Rogers* provided another such adventure heroine, though the comic strip in which she appeared was not named for her. Wilma Deering was Buck Rogers' female counterpart in the comic, and oftentimes it was Wilma who was the true star of this space opera. The strip was based on Nowlan's pulp novel *Armageddon 2419 A.D.,* which originally appeared in *Amazing Stories* magazine in 1928, and was first done for the John F. Dille Company on January 7, 1929. The value and ultimate fun of *Buck Rogers* was that it provided free expression of ideas. Nowlan and Calkins theorized what space travel would be like in the twenty-fifth century based on social perceptions and scientific knowledge of the times, and their strip met with great success because it provided excitement and escapism for the Depression-era audience. Buck Rogers represented American society's best guess at what interstellar life and travel would be like in the far distant future. As Buck saved Wilma from many death traps, or worse, so too did Wilma rescue the title character from similar situations. This dependence of the hero on the heroine, and conversely the heroine's dependence on the hero, led to an intimate bonding of Buck and Wilma which became one of the earliest love stories of the adventure strip. The hero had a vital counterpart, and he loved her as she loved him. Another degree of complexity and level of aesthetics was achieved for the adventure newspaper strip.

Less than two weeks after the debut of Buck Rogers on the comic page, another hero emerged who, along with a colorful female foil, rose to epic proportions as a legend of the newspaper page. His name was Popeye, and he first appeared in Elzie Crisler Segar's *Thimble Theatre* on January 17, 1929. *Thimble Theatre* had appeared over nine years previously, and had centered on a large cast of improbable stereotypic characters and their daily routines. At that time, the hero of the comic strip was Harold "Ham" Gravy, and he was accompanied by his girlfriend, Olive Oyl, and her brother, Castor Oyl. William Randolph Hearst was behind the promotion of Segar and his comic, yet neither Hearst nor Segar anticipated the success the comic strip would enjoy in the Thirties after the introduction of Popeye the Sailor. "Popeye ... devastated readers everywhere: nothing like the fighting, wisecracking, omnipotent sailor had ever been seen in the comics before."[21] Popeye soon replaced Ham Gravy as Olive's beau, and a number of other colorful characters were introduced during the Thirties, while lesser cast members from the early days of *Thimble Theatre* departed. The ageless ideology that good will ultimately engage and defeat evil became the mainstay for the now retitled *Popeye*—Segar and his successors made that quite clear. "Pop-

eye's fundamental honesty and loyalty— his absolute belief in right and wrong, with no grays—were but reflections of Segar," notes Bud Sagendorf, the man who continued *Popeye* after Segar's untimely death.[22] Olive quickly became Popeye's companion, accomplice, and foil. Very often the strip focused on Popeye's efforts to defend Olive's honor and his attempts to win her heart. In this sense, the comic is strongly oriented toward old-fashioned male chivalry, yet in a greater sense Olive Oyl chooses and implements her own destiny. While Popeye is the one most often rescuing Olive, Olive is the one who has chosen Popeye for the privilege of doing the rescuing.

The Thirties, as in the case of several other American mass media, proved to be the golden age for the comic strip. Ron Goulart, noted scholar and fine author, deems this the "Adventurous Decade" for the comic strip. Tales of adventure, mystery, and crime detection abounded on the comic page at this time. Goulart writes:

> The 1930's was a good decade for mystery fans. You could find detectives in just about every popular medium, from movies to radio to books and pulp magazines. And you also encountered them, unlike today, in great quantities in the comic sections of newspapers. Six days a week, and often in color on Sunday as well, there were tough cops, government agents, Scotland Yard 'tecs, reporters who dabbled in detection and even Sherlock Holmes himself.[23]

Domestic comedy comic strips flourished likewise during this period, and some of these, like *Blondie*, enjoyed steadily increasing acclaim. But the Thirties was the decade of the adventure comic strip. Countless heroes and heroines appeared, some endured, most grew as characters, and many disappeared in following years. Nevertheless, it was a glorious time for comic page justice. The socioeconomic conditions of the Depression provided a great deal to comment on, and the comic strip became a language system and system of symbols which articulated pertinent myths and values of society.

No sooner had this era commenced than one of the most famous comic strips and fictional detectives of all time appeared. He was Chester Gould's Dick Tracy, and he debuted in the *Detroit Mirror* on October 4, 1931. Today, *Dick Tracy* remains the most sociohistorically representative comic strip of all time; the title character is second in fame and notoriety as a fictional sleuth only to Sir Arthur Conan Doyle's archetypal Sherlock Holmes. In 1931, Gould and Captain Patterson realized that the comics that were monetarily profitable at the time were those which employed topics, settings, situations, and characters to which the reader could relate. Chester Gould made every effort to depict police procedure in as realistic a fashion as possible. He did this primarily by working with Chicago area police forces; by studying ballistics, new technologies, and related sciences; by investigating criminal behavior; and by reading accounts of gangsters and their exploits in the newspapers. Gould succeeded in his efforts because he employed a finely balanced blend of fact and fantasy in *Tracy.*

The violence inherent in gangland during the Thirties was a horrendous thing to present in a newspaper comic strip. Only in America, where there is a free press and free speech, was this possible. One of the narrative and illustrative staples of *Tracy* was the violent act. Though these acts are remembered more than they actually appeared, they are still today both a strength and a liability of the comic. In the heyday of *Dick Tracy,* bullets went right through people; in Gould artwork fires burned, water drowned and froze, and knives slashed rogues and innocents alike. Violence, though not new to the comic strip (it had appeared in various

forms in the 1920s adventure continuities), had reached new levels of intensity and had now become a staple, a central focus of the burgeoning medium. The extremes to which Chester Gould's Dick Tracy employed violence were justified as being socially accepted and prescribed means of purging evil or regenerating cultural morality; these acts very quickly and permanently reinstated good over evil.

Gould's work on *Dick Tracy* was so effective as a means of reflecting social mores and history that J. Edgar Hoover became interested. Hoover realized that *Tracy* enacted a wonderful ritual which reinforced, in a "black and white" fashion, the common American belief that "good" would ultimately triumph over "evil." The strip provided the public with a police force that worked, and one that could be idealized — something that was seriously lacking in the real-life drama of the time. Hoover believed that as a model of justice and moral goodness, *Tracy* affected America's thoughts and behavior. As head of the FBI, Hoover praised Gould for his work toward the betterment of society through the comic strip, and paid him one of the highest compliments possible when he tried to imitate Gould's work. Hoover hired a team of artists and writers, and the result was a comic strip called *War on Crime.* The strip featured actual cases of the FBI. The work lasted only for a short time and met with moderate success at best, quite possibly because it was too exclusively factual and consequently did not attain the necessary balance of fact and fantasy. (See Chapter 3 for further discussion of Hoover's *War on Crime.*)

Chester Gould was regarded as conservative to the point of extremism by some, and public expressions of his viewpoint in *Dick Tracy* brought various criticisms. So controversial and yet acclaimed were Gould and *Tracy* that another very popular social critic and comic strip genius parodied *Dick Tracy* in his work. The man was Alfred Gerald

Caplin—better known as Al Capp—and his work was the world-famous comic strip *Li'l Abner* which premiered August 20, 1934. (Capp was to comic strips as Philip José Farmer is to science fiction and fantasy, and as Clive Barker is to dark fantasy and imaginative fiction. He was the first successful artist in his field to liberally use sex as a theme in his art, and this is what he is often remembered for.[24]) Al Capp's parody of *Dick Tracy* was *Fearless Fosdick*, a comic strip within a comic strip. Capp's title character, Li'l Abner, followed Fosdick's adventures in his own newspaper's comic strip. (See Chapter 9 for further discussion on Capp's Fearless Fosdick.)

In short, Chester Gould and *Dick Tracy* made some very specific, significant contributions to the comic strip medium. First, Gould and *Tracy* helped issue in and define a new era—the era of the adventure strip. Chester Gould had grown up with the medium—the comic strip was barely three years old when Gould was born, and by the time Captain Patterson accepted *Tracy* for publication in 1931, Gould had matured with the medium; he knew what worked and what did not. (See Chapter 5 for more information on Gould and his early days with cartoon art and comic strips.) Second, several authorities have claimed that Gould's famous comic strip introduced violence to comic strips in its storylines. This claim is neither wholly true nor false, and needs to be qualified. *Dick Tracy* did not debut violence in the comic strip, but it did introduce a level of graphic, stylized violence that had not been seen before. It made violence a "black and white" issue—literally and figuratively; it both condemned and justified violence depending on the context in which it was presented in the strip. *Tracy* championed the Old Testament axiom of "an eye for an eye." Third, *Tracy* was so successful that it inspired, influenced, engendered imitation in, and was parodied by other comic strips—like the Hearst

Syndicate's *Secret Agent X-9*, J. Edgar Hoover's *War on Crime*, Al Capp's and *Li'l Abner's Fearless Fosdick*, and so on. In the 1930s, there were several *Dick Tracy*–like strips including Dick Moores' *Jim Hardy*, Norman Marsh's *Dann Dunn*, and others. Bob Kane—creator, writer, and artist for *Batman* in the comic books and then the comic strips—"recalling how he drew the stories in the early 1940s, says, 'I never wanted to make *Batman* too illustrative. I wanted it more like *Dick Tracy*. . . . Along with Chester Gould's *Dick Tracy*, *Batman* has the most bizarre and unique villains in comics. Indeed, it was *Dick Tracy* which inspired us to create an equally weird set of villains for *Batman*.'"[25]

Adventure on the newspaper page of the 1930s was not limited to *Dick Tracy*, however. On October 22, 1934, Milton Caniff's *Terry and the Pirates* appeared for the first time. Terry and his friends departed from newspapers in 1973, though Caniff had not worked on the project since the mid–Forties. In 1973, the comic suffered the fate of so many other adventure strips. The market was no longer tolerant of a watered-down version of a classic work that had endeared itself to the American public for years. An incredible array of rogues populated *Terry* in the early years—dragon ladies, yellow perils, ruthless pirates, and more. When World War II began, *Terry* adjusted to the evolving culture. War villains and air aces became the nemeses of the hero. Dismayed at the way in which *Terry* had become the property of the syndicate, Caniff left the work to pursue endeavors over which he had much more creative control. The most important result was his creation of *Steve Canyon* (January 13, 1947, to June 5, 1988), a premiere adventure strip of the Forties and Fifties. Yet Caniff will perhaps be remembered more for *Terry and the Pirates* than for anything else. "It can be said that no other strip (not even Foster's *Tarzan*) was so widely imitated by so many people; its techniques of lighting, framing and editing were assiduously studied not only by cartoonists but by movie-makers as well."[26] The adventure comic strip was now in its golden age.

A whole spectrum of adventure heroes and heroines populated the comic strips of the Great Depression. There were Vincent Hamlin's caveman, Alley Oop; Harold Foster's star of the Middle Ages, Prince Valiant; Lee Falk and Phil Davis' master prestidigitator, Mandrake the Magician; Alex Raymond's spaceman, Flash Gordon, and professional adventurer, Jungle Jim; and Dashiell Hammett and Alex Raymond's crackerjack hard-boiled detective, Secret Agent X-9—to name but a few. The adventure strip had established itself as the second and final comic strip genre. The cultural setting and the popularity of the comic strip as a medium allowed this story form to flourish like never before, and never since. Today, the adventure strip is in its twilight years, though the comic strip medium itself will probably endure for quite some time yet. Of the modern day adventure strips, Max Collins and Dick Locher's *Dick Tracy* is the lynchpin. Collins' attention to detail, to Gouldian tradition, and to new ideas, coupled with Dick Locher's masterful illustration and sense of humor, has made *Tracy* one of today's all-round finest comic strips. Probably for no other reason, adventure comic strips survive today because Collins and Locher's *Tracy* proves the potential for this comic strip genre in the Nineties. *Dick Tracy* in the 1990s is a pathfinder for all other adventure strips, and legitimates newspaper editors' and publishers' continued support of this form.

World War II saw the emphasis of the adventure story shift to themes of war and world conflict. At the same time, the domestic comedy presented families and pseudo-family life updated to accommodate domestic wartime concerns. The humanized animal remained a strength of this genre and in the Fifties continued to provide a vehicle for commentary on the day's events. In fact, in the 1950s, animals reached new heights in popularity as political crusaders during the postwar years. Perhaps the biggest contribution of the period was Walt Kelly's fictitious group from the Okefenokee Swamp.

The title character of Kelly's *Pogo* lived in a fantasy world where he was the moderator of a kaleidoscope of sociopolitical ideologies espoused by other animals. Pogo's first appearance was not in the comic strip medium, however. His was one of the rare cases of a character debuting in a comic book and then moving to the comic strip instead of the reverse. Walt Kelly's creation hit the newspaper page in 1948 and concluded July 20, 1975. It was begun again in 1989 by Kelly's successors. (Kelly had died in 1973.) Since Kelly's *Pogo* was highly political in content, it is not surprising that some of the residents of the Okefenokee were radical liberals while others were radical conservatives. Pogo himself was the arbitrator of the dynamic characters and ideas, and like many of the readers of the comic, Pogo was often appalled to discover some of the things he did. Pogo often tried to straighten up a world he never made.

On October 2, 1950, a comic strip debuted which centered on a group of adults in children's bodies and on humanized animals. By their actions and interactions as group members, the characters of Charles Schulz's *Peanuts* provided, and to this day provide, a message of high morality by which to live. Like *Blondie, Peanuts* enjoyed a period when it was the most widely read comic strip in the world. Charlie Brown, the central character of the comic strip, is Charles Schulz, and he is you and me. Charlie speaks to us about us. His female counterpart, Lucy, is more an antagonist than an accomplice, and is very outspoken, contrasting with the often shy and naïve Charlie. Charlie and Lucy and their group, still popular today and immortalized now in a variety of media, are effective because they confront universal trials and tribulations of life. *Peanuts* is also a vehicle of philosophy made possible by Charles Schulz's ability to tap into social consciousness. The heyday for *Peanuts* was the 1960s.

In the 1970s and 1980s, two new comics became immensely popular. The first of these was Garry Trudeau's *Doonesbury*, which began on October 26, 1970, and continues to this day, and the second was Berke Breathed's *Bloom County*, which ran from December 8, 1980, to August 6, 1989. *Bloom County* arose as a replacement for *Doonesbury* when Garry Trudeau took a leave of absence from comics between January 1983 and September 1984. Trudeau and *Doonesbury* returned, and Breathed and *Bloom County*, still very popular, continued also. In 1989, Breathed terminated *Bloom County* and began a new comic strip entitled *Outland* which retains some of the characters featured in *Bloom County*. The forte of each artist and his respective strip(s) is social satire—they are, as Kelly was, political cartoonists who have produced variations on the political cartoon. The fantastic atmospheres that Trudeau and Breathed paint work because of the incorporation of an element of realism. Both artists have hit a responsive chord in their dealings with current social issues.

In the 1980s and in the 1990s, the runaway favorite comic strip has been Bill Watterson's *Calvin and Hobbes*—a sort of *Dennis the Menace* (Hank Ketcham) and *Barnaby* (Crockett Johnson) hybrid for contemporary times. Debuting on November 7, 1985, *Calvin and Hobbes* was first collected in book form in 1987. That first collection and subsequent collections have each reached the *New York Times* Best-Seller List. Watterson's comic is so highly regarded because, like Schulz's *Peanuts*, it is tailored to make use of, rather than be hindered by, the constraints placed on comic strips in the Nineties; it

works within a tradition of the grandest of humanized animals—like those found in Walt Kelly's *Pogo*, Jeff MacNelly's *Shoe*, and Berke Breathed's *Bloom County*—and it is written and drawn by an accomplished political cartoonist who, like Jeff MacNelly and Dick Locher, starts with a very specific, isolated, funny, profound idea and then works from that idea.

The comic strips which have been, and continue to be, popular in American culture are those that reflect the ideology of the people. This story form, which is based on sequentially ordered panels of line drawings in a logical fashion to relate narratives, dates back to 1897 and Rudolph Dirks' *The Katzenjammer Kids*. Comic strips are language systems which embody popular myths, beliefs, and symbols of a society. More than ever before, this medium has been acknowledged as a "true" American art form.

Ultra-conservative, narrow-minded gatekeepers of aesthetics are able to deny the medium's validity as Art with a capital "A" no longer. Individuals like Rick Marschall, Bill Blackbeard, Ron Goulart, Maurice Horn, Jerry Robinson, M. Thomas Inge, and others are to be commended for their preservation of, and scholarship regarding, this most important medium, as are institutions like the San Francisco Academy of Comic Art and the Museum of Cartoon Art. These individuals and institutions have paved the way for much more extensive and comprehensive inquiry. While each has done his part in accumulating facts and figures and original artifacts, much more needs to be done in terms of putting the comic strip into an appropriate sociohistoric context. Previous scholarship has been general and has provided important overviews. In a few instances, as in Ron Goulart's *The Adventurous Decade*, detailed historical accounts have served as references for further study. But these accounts are relatively few in number. Much remains to be done. The stage is set for detailed analyses of a truly American art form—the comic strip. A variety of fans and scholars are now rising to the occasion. This is indeed an exciting time for comic strip research and scholarship. And *Dick Tracy* may be the most important comic strip of all time.

Notes

1. Bill Blackbeard and Martin Williams, eds., *The Smithsonian Collection of Newspaper Comics* (Washington, D.C.: Smithsonian Institution Press, and New York: Harry N. Abrams, 1977), p. 11.
2. Ibid.
3. Blackbeard and Williams' definition in *The Smithsonian Collection of Newspaper Comics,* p. 13.
4. Pierre Couperie and Maurice Horn, *A History of the Comic Strip* (New York: Crown, 1967), pp. 7–9.
5. Jerry Robinson, *The Comics: An Illustrated History of Comic Strip Art* (New York: Putnam, 1974), and, Herb Galewitz, ed., *Great Comics* (New York: Crown, 1972).
6. Blackbeard and Williams, p. 19.
7. Joe Musial, *The Katzenjammer Kids* (New York: Pocket Books, 1970), p. 2.
8. Blackbeard and Williams, p. 19.
9. Aesop, the legendary Greek slave of centuries ago, who is credited with the composition of numerous moral fables, was perhaps the first to realize the value of using animal caricatures to parody humans. While Aesop's actual existence has never been confirmed, legend has it that he was able to criticize his masters through his fables. What distanced Aesop's tales from real-life experiences was his use of animals. It is easier to observe an unreal talking duck do something foolish than it is to watch a somewhat real human story figure do the same.
10. Couperie and Horn, p. 23.
11. Blackbeard and Williams, p. 53.
12. Maurice Horn, ed., *The World Encyclopedia of Comics* (New York: Chelsea House, 1976), p. 296.
13. Galewitz, p. viii.
14. Horn, p. 275.
15. Ibid., p. 276.
16. Ibid., p. 503.
17. Galewitz, p. xii.
18. Robinson, p. 110.
19. Ibid.
20. Found in Al Capp's introduction to *Arf! The Life and Hard Times of Little Orphan Annie, 1935–1945* (New Rochelle, New York: Arlington House Publishers, 1970), unnumbered page.
21. Horn, p. 657.
22. Bud Sagendorf, *Popeye: The First Fifty Years* (New York: Workman, 1979), p. 39.
23. Ron Goulart, "The Funny Paper Detectives of the Thirties," *Alfred Hitchcock's Mystery Magazine,* Vol. 29, No. 3 (New York: Davis Publications, March 1984), p. 58.
24. Al Capp's voluptuous Daisy Mae, the perennial sweetheart and eventual wife of Li'l Abner, was a primary alluring facet of Dogpatch, the fictitious community around which the storyline was based.
25. Bob Kane quotes taken from "Tracy's Influence," *Batman: The Sunday Classics 1943–46* (Princeton, Wisconsin: Kitchen Sink Press, 1991), p. 208. This article is quite informative and insightful, detailing specific parallels in character type between *Dick Tracy* and *Batman.*
26. Horn, p. 654.

CHAPTER 3

Of Blue Knights and Social Injustices: The Police Procedural Detective Story and *Dick Tracy*

"Probably the tops in fan mail was a letter I once received from an Iowa convict who accused me of stealing incidents from the life of his father, who was then in an Arizona prison. I quickly explained that my ideas come only from newspaper reading and observation."—Chester Gould, "Dick Tracy and Me" (*Colliers*, December 11, 1948).

Chester Gould's *Dick Tracy* has been culturally significant and popular as a comic strip because it is more than just a good comic strip. From the outset, *Tracy* provided adventure and human drama via a carefully balanced blend of real-life social history and fantasy. It showcased issues of morality, be it individual morality or a collective conscience. The strip presented both rural and urban settings, and a smorgasbord of character types. These components make *Dick Tracy* more than entertaining formula fiction to this day. *Tracy* provided mystery and suspense. And it featured established police procedure and scientific advances in that procedure. Two elements significantly set Gould's *Dick Tracy* apart from other comic strips of the 1930s and the decades that followed. The first was a gallery of grotesque rogues. The second was the artist/storyteller's conscious effort to incorporate established police procedure into his storylines.

Chapter 1 addresses some of the complexity and significance of *Tracy*. It, like Chapter 2, also argues that the comic strip can be, and has been on occasion, a legitimate "Art" form. After all, some of America's greatest authors, like Mark Twain and William Faulkner, embraced the comic strip form as something worthy of regard and critical attention. *Dick Tracy* is a significant component of the world of the comic strip. It is also a significant component of the world of mystery fiction — specifically the mystery formula deemed the "Police Procedural." Further, *Dick Tracy* should not be denied status as legitimate illustrative art, and it should not be excluded in discussions of the police procedural formula. In fact, it should be central to any study or essay that claims to be at all comprehensive in its analysis of the police procedural in whatever medium or media. *Dick Tracy* has done more for the police procedural story than any other single contribution to the canon. *Tracy* was the archetype for this story form; it was the first such story to take the inherently very conventional procedure of real-life law and order and combine the same with the inventional and fantastic elements evident in outrageous character types.

31

Dick Tracy—November 23, 1932. Reprinted by permission: Tribune Media Services.

An appreciation of any cultural phenomenon is greatly enhanced by an understanding of the context in which that phenomenon emerged. Historical settings, sociopolitical thinking, intended audience, and the artist/author's motivations are important issues of context. Hence, it is incumbent upon any cultural study of *Dick Tracy* to place the work of Chester Gould and his assistants and successors on the famous comic strip in several different contexts. Further, a discussion of *Tracy* in the context of the police procedural story is crucial, as is a discussion of the contributions of Gould and associates to that story form.

In fiction, the popular mystery story has manifested itself in a variety of forms and variations for over 150 years. Although tales of intrigue and suspense have long been part of literature—as in the case of Homer's *The Odyssey*—the mystery tale was not solidified or clearly defined generically in terms of conventions and techniques until the advent of Edgar Allan Poe's stories about detective hero C. Auguste Dupin, who first appeared in "The Murders in the Rue Morgue" in 1841. The first identifiable formula of the larger mystery genre was that story of the "Classical Detective," in the cases of Poe's Dupin and Sir Arthur Conan Doyle's master sleuth, Sherlock Holmes, who debuted in *A Study in Scarlet* in 1887. Dupin and Holmes set the mold for the great consulting detectives that followed, like Agatha Christie's Hercule Poirot, who

debuted in *The Mysterious Affair at Styles* (1920) and Miss Jane Marple, who debuted in *Murder at the Vicarage* (1930); Dorothy Sayers' Lord Peter Wimsey, who debuted in *Whose Body?* (1923); and John Dickson Carr's Dr. Gideon Fell, who debuted in *Hag's Nook* (1933). These classical detectives were towers of intelligence, and they served as protectors of an otherwise helpless cast of characters. They solved puzzles for the love of the intellectual stimulus these enigmas provided.

America's first mass entertainment medium, the dime novel, emerged with mystery fiction and would not have succeeded on a commercial basis had the mystery not been a staple source of material. The mystery and its cousin, the western, were the two genres of fiction that sustained the dime novel and allowed it to prosper from about 1860 until 1912. Around 1912, when several events heralded the demise of this medium—including an increase in postal rates for novels sent through the mails—the pulp magazine arrived to fill the void. The pulp magazine, named for the cheap pulpwood paper upon which it was printed, was not as heavily dependent on the postal service for its distribution as was the dime novel—it sold primarily on newsstands. Also, the pulps were hybrids of the dime novels, and because of differences in format (i.e. pulps featured short stories, novellas, and other fiction forms, and hence were not strictly novels dependent on the mails), pulp magazines were not subject to the same high postal rates applied to dime novels when they were sent through the mails.[1]

With the emergence of the pulps, the mystery story exploded into a kaleidoscope of formulas and sub-formulas. The "hard-boiled detective" first appeared in the pages of *Black Mask* magazine in the 1920s, and heroes like Carroll John Daly's Three-Gun Terry Mack and Race Williams, Dashiell Hammett's Continental Op(erative) and Sam Spade, as well as Raymond Chandler's Philip Marlowe, boasted individual moralities in societies where everyone was corrupt. In 1931, Walter B. Gibson, friend and biographer of the Great Houdini, produced *The Living Shadow* under the pseudonym of Maxwell Grant. Enter one of the most popular of mystery heroes—the "avenger detective." Street and Smith Publishers' Shadow lived in the pulps for more than 300 novels and spawned a variety of colorful imitations like Popular Publications' Spider (not to be confused with Stan Lee's Spiderman who would not appear in comic books—not pulp magazines—until 1962 when he first appeared in Marvel Comics' *Amazing Fantasy* #15) and A.A. Wyn Publishing's Secret Agent X. *Weird Tales* magazine, a landmark publication of fantasy and weird fiction, produced a fare which included several enduring "psychic detectives" or ghost chasers. William Hope Hodgson's Carnacki the Ghost Finder, Seabury Quinn's Jules de Grandin, and August Derleth's Solar Pons combated foes and puzzles more threatening than death itself because their antagonists could control the world beyond. G-men wrestled with the devils of the "gangster story," and "magician detectives" and "gentlemen burglars" each had stories of their own.

However, detective heroes were not unique to dime novels and pulps. As the popular media evolved, mystery stories permeated each new means of communication. Motion pictures utilized the mystery as subject matter as early as the turn of the century. Mystery stories thrived in the highly imagination-dependent medium of story radio in the 1930s and 1940s. As World War II approached, the pulp magazine began to be replaced by the paperback novel. The idea of conserving paper and space not only appealed to the domestic market, but also made it possible for popular stories to be more easily sent overseas to Allied soldiers. The inscriptions on many paperbacks of this period stated that individual copies could be sent overseas for three cents apiece.

By the 1950s, the then new medium of television featured mystery stories on a regular basis. Consider the following representative list of 1950s mystery, police procedural, and true crime programs.[2]

1950s Mystery Television Programs

Title	Beginning Date	Network
Alfred Hitchcock Presents	October 2, 1955	CBS
Big Town	October 5, 1950	CBS
Bourbon Street Beat	October 5, 1959	ABC
Crime Photographer	April 19, 1951	CBS
Crime with Father	August 31, 1951	ABC
Danger	September 26, 1950	CBS
Hawaiian Eye	October 7, 1959	ABC
The Hunter	July 3, 1952	CBS
The Lawless Years	April 16, 1959	NBC

Title	Beginning Date	Network
Man Against Crime	October 7, 1949	CBS
Mark Saber	October 5, 1951	ABC
Markham	May 2, 1959	CBS
Martin Kane, Private Eye	September 1, 1949	NBC
Meet McGraw	July 2, 1957	NBC
Perry Mason	September 21, 1957	CBS
Peter Gunn	September 22, 1958	NBC
Philip Marlowe	September 29, 1959	ABC
Public Defender	March 11, 1954	CBS
Public Prosecutor	1947	Syndicated
Pursuit	October 22, 1958	CBS
Richard Diamond, Private Detective	July 1, 1957	CBS
77 Sunset Strip	October 1, 1958	ABC
Suspense	March 1, 1949	CBS
Suspicion	September 30, 1957	NBC
The Thin Man	September 20, 1957	NBC
The Vise	October 1, 1954	ABC

1950s Police Procedural Television Programs

Title	Beginning Date	Network
The Detectives	October 16, 1959	ABC
*Dick Tracy**	September 13, 1950	ABC
Dragnet	December 16, 1951	NBC
Gangbusters	March 20, 1952	NBC
The Lineup	October 1, 1954	CBS
M Squad	September 20, 1957	NBC
Naked City	September 30, 1958	ABC
Photocrime	September 21, 1949	ABC
Treasury Men in Action	September 11, 1950	ABC

1950s True Crime Television Programs

Title	Beginning Date	Network
Crime Syndicated	September 18, 1951	CBS
On Trial	November 22, 1948	ABC
Wanted	October 20, 1955	CBS

*See Chapter 6.

Several media were now featuring a variety of mystery formulas as well as an array of detective personalities, each with their own methods or style of crime investigation.

The police procedural is one such mystery formula. John G. Cawelti writes, "The changing cultural mythology of crime has given rise to many different popular formulas. Some of these have been essentially adventure stories or melodramas, but one of the most striking embodies the cultural mythology of detectives, criminals, police, and suspects in an archetypal form that is almost pure mystery."[3] Crime and its detection, whether factual or fictional, provide a catharsis for individuals and cultures alike in that the systematic, scientific dissection and thwarting of crime reinforces, in a rational way, the puritanical morality that "good" will always subdue "evil." Gary Hoppenstand states, "In detective fiction there abides a personification of the rational mind, a master game player, a character who can invite a reader's empathy while at the same time marshalling a society's cultural perceptions of right, moral and good around his presence."[4] The policeman is one such "master game player."

The formula in which the police detective and his rigid methods are central is the police procedural. This particular variant of mystery fiction is second in age only to the classical detective, and a survey of this formula is an essential aspect to the study of *Dick Tracy* since Chester Gould's creation is more than a comic strip: it is the archetype for the police procedural formula. Police and quasi-police figures had served in the background of many a social melodrama prior to the arrival of *Tracy,* but few had emerged as central heroes to their respective stories. None had established the prototype for the character that would in Gould's stories establish a whole new genre of fiction. But remember, "archetype" does not necessarily mean "first."

François Eugéne Vidocq (1775–1857) was a French detective and author who founded the Police de Sûreté. In many ways, Vidocq could be deemed a scoundrel. He proceeded from an audacious stint in the military to a life of crime and then to an extended jail term. In 1809, he became the first chief of Napoléon's police department. Chris Steinbrunner and Otto Penzler's *The Encyclopedia of Mystery and Detection* (1976) states that Vidocq's "agents were also former convicts whose practices were highly suspect."[5] Vidocq was forced to resign, and in 1832 he opened a private detective agency. His major contribution to the literature of crime fiction was the four-volume *Memoires* (1828–1829), a melodramatic autobiography of his career. Though highly fantastic and fictional in its content, the work did serve as an early document of French police procedure. Further, it inspired later authors such as Victor Hugo, Honoré de Balzac, and Edgar Allan Poe.

Stefano Benvenuti and Gianni Rizzoni write in *The Whodunit: An Informal History of Detective Fiction* (1980) that Vidocq's police methods were uncomplicated.[6] Vidocq and his men — mostly former criminals like himself — would infiltrate the underworld of the day disguised as rogues and villains (probably not a difficult transformation for this group) and would play on the sympathies of its members. Having gained the confidence of these murderers and thieves and extracted information from them, Vidocq and his agents would turn the information against them.

Charles Dickens is probably the most legitimate claimant to the title of author of the first police procedural–like stories. Dickens' social melodramas invariably centered upon themes of poverty, wealth, crime, and law enforcement. The detection of crime, often by systematic means established by law enforcement agencies, was very much a part of the entire body of Dickens' work; consider instances in such works as *Sketches by Boz* (1836) and *Oliver Twist* (1838), for example. Two of the author's works are, however, more often associated with mystery fiction than are the others. These are *Bleak House* (1853) and *The Mystery of Edwin Drood* (1870). *Bleak House* introduces Mr. Inspector Bucket, a character described by Dickens himself as a "sagacious, indefatigable detective officer." *Drood* is Dickens' most obvious contribution to the mystery genre. In *The Mystery of Edwin Drood*, Dickens provides a story wherein the solving of a seemingly impossible puzzle via relatively established procedure benefits the characters involved. *The Mystery of Edwin Drood* is, of course, never solved. Somehow this seems like the logical end for Dickens' literary career, which specialized in themes of the bleakness of social conditions and the dialectic between "good" and "evil"—wealth and poverty—and the gray areas in between. Like the conflict between good and evil, the novel's storyline is never wholly resolved. The romance of Dickens and his last, though incomplete, novel remains.

The parallel between Chester Gould's work and that of Charles Dickens is noteworthy. Several themes and settings found in *Dick Tracy*—some related to police procedure, some not—hearken back to those found in Dickens' work. For example, the parallel between the relationship of Dick Tracy, Jr., to Steve the Tramp and the relationship of Oliver Twist to his various masters is noteworthy. Particularly during the Depression years, Gould supplied *Dick Tracy* with stories of urban decay, homeless orphans adrift in a sea of poverty, and the filth and corruption often associated with those street people down on their luck who turn to vice and crime of all sorts—from petty thievery to prostitution to murder.

While most fans and scholars acknowledge the 1940s as Gould's and *Tracy's* finest decade, it was indeed the 1930s where the comic strip and its storyline found birth. Each decade of *Dick Tracy* has its own distinct charm, and the 1930s strips are no exception. In fact, the 1930s strips are among the finest of the *Tracy* canon as they evidence Gould's shift in style from cold, abrupt surrealism to smooth, finely tuned romance. During these years Chester Gould established and thoroughly developed his characters— Tracy himself would never again be as complex, as vulnerable, as rebellious; Tess would never again be as beautiful and alluring, as crude, as passionate, as independent; Junior would never again be as helpless, as innocent, as independent, as entertaining, as significant to the story. People down on their luck were the most pathetic and tragic in *Tracy* in the 1930s. Hunger was more intense, pain was more profound, and tears were more bitter. The Depression years defined the emotional and social content of *Dick Tracy*. Also, Gould was establishing the mythos for *Tracy* at this time. Never would the incorporation of reality, of established police procedure, be more evident. Dick Tracy discovered and scientifically analyzed "clews" on almost a daily basis. Never would more dirt, hair, fibers, and fingerprints be scrutinized under a microscope or coded messages be deciphered. Atmosphere, characterization, and established police procedure were everything. In short, Chester Gould's *Dick Tracy* storylines of the 1930s owed a great deal to Dickensian tradition.

Even Charles Dickens' *The Mystery of Edwin Drood* did not, however, in itself firmly establish the police procedural as a distinct mystery formula. In this novel, as in some of his others, Dickens writes at least in part in response to the development of the first real-life police force, created by Robert Peel in 1829 in Dickens' home city of London. *The Mystery of Edwin Drood* is best appreciated as a statement about social conditions of the times, and it is a worthy tribute to, and imitation of, the early mystery story produced by Poe in America.

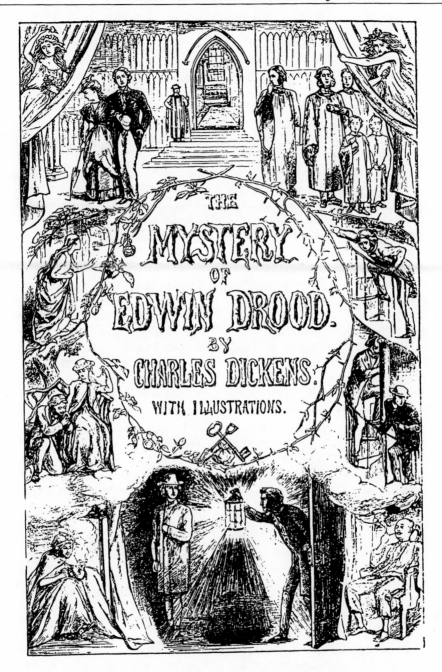

The Mystery of Edwin Drood **by Charles Dickens (April 1870).**

The police procedural has, until recent years, been given little attention by critics of mystery fiction, owing to the fact that stories of policemen and their rigid methods of detection have traditionally been some of the most conventional, and consequently most boring, mysteries written. The police officer is a two-dimensional, unimaginative character in an already solidly ritual-bound story form. Today the police procedural is one of the most popular formulas of all fiction. To

date, some of the best and most comprehensive scholarship on this formula has
appeared in the criticism of George N.
Dove and his Edgar Award–winning study
The Police Procedural (1982). Dove, however, focuses his discussion on the police
procedural as a story form confined to the
period from the close of World War II to
about 1980. George Dove's scholarship on
the police procedural during this time
frame is some of the finest such analysis
done to date. The author's book discusses
specific elements of this mystery formula, specific police detective types (like
women, black, Jewish, and Hispanic police
detectives), and specific authors of the formula (like John Creasey, Maurice Procter,
Hillary Waugh, Ed McBain, Bill Knox,
Nicholas Freeling, Maj Sjowall and Per
Wahloo, Collin Wilcox, and James Mc-
Clure). As we have seen, there were variants of the formula prior to 1940; there has
been a proliferation of followers since
1980. Any discussion of the police procedural and its development must refer to
Gould's famous comic strip. Without a
shadow of a doubt, the first stories where
police procedures were detailed and were
central to the storyline were those that appeared in Chester Gould's comic strip
Dick Tracy.

Chapter 5 includes a biography of
Chester Gould which explores Gould's
relationship to real-life law enforcement
agencies and their agents. What is important to note is that from its earliest days,
Dick Tracy consciously incorporated and
utilized up-to-the-minute police procedure. In fact, as years went by, Gould accurately documented and often predicted
the newest in such procedure and related
scientific technology. Consider the wrist
radio introduced in *Tracy* on January 13,
1946. No other single aspect of *Dick Tracy*
has received more press and coverage in
newspaper and magazine articles than the
wrist radio.

In *Dick Tracy*, the story of the development of the wrist radio ran for about

three months. The young inventor named
"Brilliant" invented the device for wealthy
researcher and business tycoon Diet
Smith—a physically obese man with recurrent ulcer problems who has remained
a staple character from 1946 to the present. (The *Tracy* strips from January to
March 1946 are reprinted in *The Original
Dick Tracy*, No. 2, Gladstone Publishing,
Ltd., 1990; Jay Maeder has also provided
an accurate and descriptive synopsis of
events in those days of the famous strip in
Dick Tracy: The Official Biography, Penguin Books, June 1990.)

Life magazine carried a photo essay in
its October 6, 1947, issue which announced
that the U.S. Bureau of Standards had
developed a "Dick Tracy wrist transmitter
which can broadcast messages for a mile."[7]
The essay explained how *Dick Tracy* introduced the idea for the invention, and
how Dr. Cledo Brunetti, chief of the ord-
nance engineering section of the National
Bureau of Standards in Washington, D.C.,
had made the idea practical and had built
a working model. The essay also provided
photos of Brunetti's real-life invention and
showed a policeman demonstrating its use.
There were numerous other articles regarding the wrist radio that appeared for
the next four-plus decades. Toy companies
produced replicas of Dick Tracy's new-
found aid in the war on crime, and the
Western Electric Company of Allentown,
Pennsylvania, presented Chester Gould
with a working model on June 13, 1952.[8]
Eventually the two-way wrist radio became a two-way wrist television in *Dick
Tracy.*

Though the wrist radio would remain
Gould's most famous *Tracy* invention, it
was not the last of the artist's inventions or
predictions in the strip that would one day
see real-life application. And Gould's successors on the comic strip made some
similar contributions. Gould forecast some
specific forms of space travel and rocketry;
though these predictions were not wholly
unique to him and were often less based on

scientific fact than his previous inventions, they provided the fodder for the storylines of the 1960s—perhaps the most controversial storylines of the canon. (See Chapter 4.) Nonetheless, magazines with large circulations like *National Geographic* and *Newsweek* acknowledged Gould's discussion of space travel as credible and insightful.[9]

All of Gould's assistants and successors on *Dick Tracy* made their own special contributions to the accurate portrayal of police procedure and related scientific technology in the comic strip. The recent collaborations of Max Allan Collins and Dick Locher make this obvious. Rick Fletcher, longtime Gould assistant and artist on *Tracy*, may have provided some of the most interesting contributions in this area. Fletcher was emphatic about accuracy and detail in the depiction of real-life history, specific weaponry like guns and their intricate components, new advances in the sciences and their related products, and police procedure. The story of "Art Deco" (a famous *Tracy* rogue created by the team of Fletcher and Collins) and the invention of "Nite-Site" are examples of such contributions of Fletcher. (See Chapter 5.)

In a 1955 article for *Guns Magazine* entitled "How Dick Tracy Gets His Man," William B. Edwards writes about Chester Gould's knowledge of guns: "Dick Tracy's guns are something of a problem to mild-tempered artist Chester Gould. He admittedly knows very little about firearms from a professional aspect. When he needs research for his cartoon strip, he visits the police department and gets assistance from officers who aid him in working actual criminal cases into Tracy's adventures."[10] In a 1974 article for *Argosy* entitled "Dick Tracy: The First Law and Order Man," John Culhane writes, "From the beginning, Gould has gotten inspiration for the strip from newspapers almost exclusively—the police news and all information about the operation of gangsters

and the war against them."[11] However, Gould also toured the FBI headquarters in Washington once, visited with J. Edgar Hoover, and once visited Scotland Yard where he was given demonstrations of its methods and techniques.[12]

Max Collins notes that *Dick Tracy* provided the visual picture of the policeman and his work.[13] The depiction of policemen as central to a mystery story began with *Tracy*'s debut in 1931 because creator Chester Gould based his stories on actual police history and scientific methods. Gould worked with the big city police of Chicago to provide realism in his fiction; he traveled with real cops in real squad cars and he observed scientific advancements made by these law enforcers. Gould was a participant-observer who realized that the marketable tale was the one which incorporated a high degree of recognizable reality as well as specialized work in its storyline. While the policeman had a role in the early works of Poe, came to Conan Doyle's Sherlock Holmes for advice, and hampered Sam Spade's private investigations, it was not until the advent of *Dick Tracy* that the law enforcement officer acquired a lead role in the mystery genre and became the protector of a cast of otherwise helpless innocents. The morality of Dick Tracy was, and is, the standard morality of American society. Collins states that Tracy, in his role as protector of society's morality, is a "by-the-book, company man."[14]

This idea of Dick Tracy is significant. As an organization man, Tracy could easily be a very flat, uninteresting character—and sometimes he is. These everyday qualities of being two dimensional and boring at times also make Dick Tracy a true-to-life representative of real-life police officers and organization men. But there is more to the comic strip detective hero than this. Gould gave his fictional hero a life outside of his career as a "law and order" man which, rather than contradicting the by-the-book credo and resulting lifestyle, actually augmented and supplemented it. Gould showed that it was possible to be a loyal, upright public servant, enjoy your work, and still revel in the rewards and pleasures of traditional (i.e., socially prescribed) family life. Starting in the 1930s installments of *Dick Tracy,* the title hero's life was split between the organization and his family, which extended to include his girlfriend and fiancée, a homeless orphan, and his friends on the police force. In short, the organization and the family were often not at odds and were also, not so ironically, one and the same.

Dick Tracy proved that an above average policeman doing his day-to-day job could be heroic and admirable. The procedure with which the comic strip police detective has always run his own life—a procedure which includes integrity, respect for the law, and self-discipline—is also the procedure which helps define the essence of the police procedural story. Chester Gould showed that the ideal police detective, whether in fact or fantasy, is the one who lives within a rigid personal credo and whose personal life affects, reflects, and defines the organization or company of which he is an integral part.

Claiming influence from several sources including Edgar Allan Poe and Sir Arthur Conan Doyle, as well as Winsor McCay's comic strip *Little Nemo* and Bud Fisher's comic strip *Mutt and Jeff,* Chester Gould denied any influence from the pulp mystery magazines.[15] But Gould certainly had to be aware of the traditions in the pervasive pulpwood magazines of the Twenties, Thirties, and Forties. In fact, two *Dick Tracy* panels from December 4, 1932, and September 6, 1936, contain references to "dime novels," each in a condescending fashion.[16] Conversely, it seems likely that many pulp authors took at least part of their leads from *Dick Tracy.* This is not only not surprising, but it is also to be expected since the media are a cannibalizing lot. Media theorist Marshall McLuhan termed this concept "rearview mirror-

ism."[17] Time-tested storylines that have turned profits for one medium are often revised and incorporated into new media. In the pulp magazines of the Thirties, G-men and police officers became central agents of justice. Magazines emerged which were solely dedicated to sagas of these keepers of the peace and their crime solving. Titles like *Crimebusters, Detective Fiction Weekly, G-Men,* and *G-Men Detective* had press runs in the hundreds of thousands and attracted large followings for their fictional policeman and special government operatives.

Dick Tracy—December 4, 1932, and September 6, 1936. Reprinted by permission: Tribune Media Services.

George Dove credits one pulp writer in particular with helping to solidify the police procedural. The author is Lawrence Treat. Dove writes, "Treat's *V as in Victim* . . . introduced a new way of dealing with the police story. The cops bore the burden of detection, but they were not 'heroes,' nor did they display any suggestion of awe-inspiring powers of ratiocination. For the most part they worked in teams, using the methodology normally employed by policemen in real life."[18] *V as in Victim* requires acknowledgment as an important contribution to the evolution of the police procedural, but it should not be considered the beginning or even archetypal story for this particular mystery formula. Too many events preceded Treat's novel in the realm of the police procedural—including some of Dickens' work and Chester Gould's *Dick Tracy*. Stefano Benvenuti and Gianni Rizzoni state:

> Some critics date the police procedural from Lawrence Treat's *V as in Victim* (1945), about the hardworking but human detectives Mitch Taylor, Jubb Freeman, and their associates. Treat, a New York native born in 1903, continued to write about Taylor and Freeman in a series of "alphabetized" novels and short stories, but he denies he had any intention of creating a new form of detective fiction.[19]

It is better, and more accurate, to claim that Lawrence Treat's *V as in Victim* helped consolidate and solidify the formula that had been around in various forms for about a century at the time Treat's novel first appeared.

Precisely what components combine to create the police procedural story in fiction? In Chester Gould's *Dick Tracy*, the formula is essentially defined as follows. An individual (or individuals) on the wrong side of the law is introduced and given a situation to exploit. These criminals are as grotesque and abnormal in physical appearance as they are grotesque and abnormal in personality and morality. The

rogues perpetrate what they believe to be the perfect crime—a crime which is supposed to generate some great personal benefit like monetary gain or revenge. The hero discovers the crime and begins pursuit of the offenders—a pursuit marked by a series of successes and failures for the detective hero. Innocent people often get hurt in the process due to their own personal ineptitudes and the increasingly maniacal actions of the criminals. The pursuit takes up most of the time used to tell the story, and it is characterized by the detective hero employing established procedure and scientific technology in a quest to detect and solve the trail of crimes and clues left by the villains. The tension builds as, much like the western story, civilization (represented by the hero) battles savagery (represented by the grotesque rogue) and the two factions ultimately meet in a confrontation that climaxes at an epic moment.[20] In short, the detective hero (Dick Tracy) is thrust into one of those famous Gould death traps (discussed in Chapter 4). The hero, through superhuman but not superhero feats, escapes and turns the tables on the criminal or criminals. The rogues atone for their crimes—more often than not, they die from the same apocalyptic weaponry that they had initially turned on society. Sometimes they are tried and imprisoned or even executed. Gould was, however, very cautious, thoughtful, and conservative in his allusions to capital punishment. In some cases, criminals are even rehabilitated as in the 1936 transformation of Lips Manlis into "Bob Honor."

Chester Gould proved that the dramatic presentation of fantasy based in reality found in sources like newspaper stories can make even the routine interesting, compelling, and entertaining. His successors, including Max Allan Collins and Dick Locher, have also verified this. Formula used to articulate a morality play can achieve the aesthetics of art. Variation in the formula in terms of procedure and scientific technology incorporated into storylines, coupled with fantastic, grotesque rogues, has kept *Dick Tracy* exciting for over sixty years. Hence, Gould's creation has always been more than a good comic strip, more than a good vehicle for action/adventure/mystery fiction—it is a synthesis of police procedure and mystery, reality and fantasy, form and function, formula fiction and art aesthetics.

The specific real-life police procedure reflected in Chester Gould's *Dick Tracy* has, of course, become an important yardstick by which all subsequent contributions to the canon of police procedurals have been measured in aesthetic as well as generic terms. The procedure in *Tracy* is essentially very rigid in nature; variance is only found in the order in which components of the procedure are followed. For example, sometimes the police detective hero has to trail and then entrap suspects before he can interrogate them; sometimes the police detective hero interrogates suspects, releases and then eventually entraps them. Significant components of real-life police procedure

reflected in *Dick Tracy* include crime scene examination, combing for and through clues and evidence, interrogation (both direct and indirect), specialized scientific methods and techniques, specialized methods of tailing suspects, and entrapment of suspects. In a period less than four weeks long (September 15 to October 9, 1933), each of these elements of police procedure is evident and crucial to the storyline which reveals "Boss" Jim Herrod—prominent politician and successor in crime and gang leadership to the now incarcerated Big Boy—as a big-time racketeer.

In the *Tracy* sequence from September and October 1933, the order of procedure begins with tailing a suspect. Dick Tracy, Jr., identifies two car thieves and uses a police call box to contact his namesake. Tracy and Pat Patton arrive on the scene in the daily comic strip from September 15 and capture one of the thieves. Tracy lets the second thief go. Tailing and surveillance ensue. The detective hero explains to Patton that he wants the suspect to think he is getting away. Dick Tracy plans to let the fugitive lead him to some larger evil—a car theft ring. Instead of

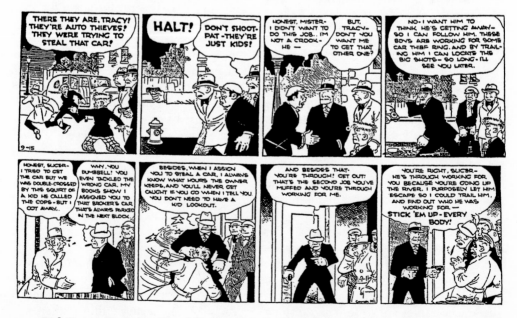

Dick Tracy—September 15 and 16, 1933. Reprinted by permission: Tribune Media Services.

Dick Tracy—September 18, 1933. Reprinted by permission: Tribune Media Services.

Dick Tracy—September 21, 1933. Reprinted by permission: Tribune Media Services.

Dick Tracy—September 27, 1933. Reprinted by permission: Tribune Media Services.

Dick Tracy—October 2, 1933. Reprinted by permission: Tribune Media Services.

Dick Tracy—October 9, 1933. Reprinted by permission: Tribune Media Services.

curing the symptom of the social evil (i.e., capturing the runaway suspect at the moment), Tracy wants to cure the cause of the problem (the larger car theft ring). This method of tailing a suspect is fairly straightforward, though not without its risks. Sometimes in *Dick Tracy,* and in other police procedurals that have followed, the suspect gets away. Established procedure of tailing narrows the margin of error and increases the probability of success, but it does not eliminate the possibility of error or necessarily guarantee success. In a relatively short period of time, the tailing leads to the arrest or death of the suspect and his cohorts. In the September 16 installment of *Tracy,* the police detective hero stands in the doorway of the car thieves' hideout, two handguns raised, and exclaims, "Stick 'em up—every body!"

The suspects do not get away in this case, and the final panel from September 16 visually depicts the criminals cowering in the face of the law. A fallen cigar, wide eyes, dropped jaws, and bodies in a state of recoil indicate that Slicer and his hoodlums are not so tough after all. (Also notice Dick Tracy's firmly set, square jaw and pursed mouth, and the straight, horizontal position of the guns in the detective hero's hands that parallel that jaw and mouth.) In this sequence is found the art of the procedural, the aesthetics by which all procedurals would be and have been eventually measured.

Combing for clues and evidence is another integral part of real-life police procedure and its incorporation into *Dick*

Tracy. Two days after Dick Tracy has arrested members of the car theft ring, he begins to comb through the evidence found at the thieves' hideout—in this case a record book kept by the rogues which specifically documents the public's car driving habits. On that day, September 18, 1933, Dick Tracy starts to realize and delineate the power and size of the even larger car theft ring still in operation. Mayor Freddy (Glad Hand) Turner asks, "But, Tracy, how does an illegitimate industry like this continue to exist?" The detective hero, now rewarded with the fruit of his combing of evidence—knowledge—responds, "I'll tell you why—*political fix and corruption.*" Tracy and his associates like Pat Patton have combed through record books, old files, carpet fibers, soil samples, garbage, fingerprints, and more ever since as part of virtually every investigation of criminal activity.

Interrogation of suspects is a most important weapon in the arsenal of police procedure. In the later days of September 1933, Dick Tracy conducts a rather controversial form of interrogation. The rogue "Slicer," a drug addict who has been placed in jail, is deceived into believing that the "shot" he is getting will remedy his withdrawal symptoms. What Slicer is really injected with is scopolamine, a form of "truth serum" used in the 1930s by police departments. Once the suspect is ready to be interrogated in the September 21 daily comic strip, Dick Tracy begins to systematically question the accused, building to the main point—specific information about the car thieves' ring. Patience and persistence elicit the responses Tracy is looking for. The craft of the interrogation, though somewhat advantaged by truth serum in this case, is found in the formation and articulation of questions that progressively build on each other, and whose answers lead to inescapable conclusions and even entrapment. But, like other facets of police procedure, interrogation of suspects and witnesses is not always an exact science guaranteed to produce desired results.

The interrogation of Slicer on September 21 is coupled with another often employed method in police procedure: the use of specialized scientific methods and techniques. The use of truth serum in this sequence is both interesting to the reader and somewhat controversial in general. Today, use of such drugs on a subject who is tricked into submitting to their use would be deemed an infringement on the personal and legal rights of the suspect. *Tracy* readers of the 1930s, however, probably were less sensitive to such invasion and were satisfied with the use of whatever techniques, scientific or otherwise, yielded results in the war on crime. Advances in science and technology were indeed reflected in Chester Gould's early *Dick Tracy* sequences and have been reflected by the collaborative team of Max Collins and Dick Locher. In fact, we know that particularly in the 1960s and early 1970s, Gould's use of science and technology in his strip sometimes drew criticism. (See Chapter 4's discussion of *Tracy* in the Sixties and Seventies.) Use of scientific techniques in real life and its reflection in *Tracy* could be interesting, but it could also be boring, as much police work requires rigorous routine and patience.

On September 27, Dick Tracy visited the scene of yet another gangland atrocity. The racketeers bomb Tony's store when he does not give in to their protection racket. Tony, however, is not as brave as he first appears. Tony is reluctant to reveal the names of the perpetrators to Tracy. Crime scene examination is central to the procedure of the police detective. In the September 27 installment of *Dick Tracy*, the ace detective uses crime scene investigation to generate ideas leading to what is usually the final element of the police procedural story—entrapment of the suspect(s).

Using a store as a front, Dick Tracy, Tess Trueheart, and Pat Patton entrap the bombers. Entrapment of suspects is oftentimes achieved by the police detective when he/she studies the routine of the guilty party and then uses the knowledge gained regarding routine and habit in order to trap the criminal. In the October 2 daily *Dick Tracy* comic strip, "Slip" Buckley is so captured. Slip is headed for jail, but entrapment of suspects does not always work as smoothly as in Buckley's case. Also, Dick Tracy has once again only thwarted a cog in the wheel of the car theft ring. He still needs to entrap the ringleader. With sufficient evidence gathered for conviction, Dick Tracy then moves on that ringleader—Boss Herrod. On October 9, Herrod is shot dead when he refuses to be taken alive. Entrapment, though sometimes part of the early stages of a police procedural, is almost always the conclusion to this story formula.

Dick Tracy and pulp magazines were not the only locus for the police procedural in the Thirties. Story radio was reaching ever-increasing audiences, and radio dramas featured many tales of mystery and intrigue and policemen in their "War on Crime." *Gangbusters* is perhaps the most celebrated police series ever to be broadcast on network radio, but there were other such programs. J. Fred MacDonald writes:

> For several years KEX (Portland, Oregon) produced *Homicide Squad,* basing its drama on the exploits of the local police department. *Calling All Cars,* directed on KFI (Los Angeles) by William N. Robson, as early as 1933 featured not only stories

from the Los Angeles Police Department, but utilized Chief of Police James Davis to introduce the weekly stories. *Tales of the Oklahoma Highway Patrol*, broadcast in 1937 on WKY (Oklahoma City), and *State Police Dramas* on WHAM (Rochester, New York) dealt with state agencies. And *G-Men in Action* on WNAC (Boston) in 1939 became one of the first series to focus upon activities of the Federal Bureau of Investigation.[21]

Gangbusters, was, however, the most slickly produced and most famous of such programs.

"And Now ... *Gangbusters!*" began each new episode of radio's number one police program. "*Gangbusters*, presented in cooperation with police and federal law enforcement departments throughout the United States. The only national program that brings you authentic police case histories."[22] Each week, a different law enforcement official hosted the program and provided a minimal commentary and contextualization, based on real-life police case history. Lewis J. Valentine, and later Colonel H. Norman Schwarzkopf, interviewed the guest hosts and helped to provide a dialogue which set up each program's storyline. Whistles, sirens, gunshots, and numerous other sound effects marked each presentation. While this police program sensationalized actual history and police procedure, it also augmented the audience's understanding of, and appreciation for, real-life crime and law enforcement. Jim Harmon states, "In 1935, Phillips H. Lord began what was to become *Gangbusters* by writing scripts based on the files of the Federal Bureau of Investigation."[23] Frequently FBI Director J. Edgar Hoover was displeased by Lord's heavy-handed use of gunplay instead of patient police work to bring down public enemies, and he ended the association after 26 weeks. Unperturbed, Lord gave his investigators city police badges in place of FBI IDs and continued his operation with even more lasting success. Lord

produced several follow-up radio dramas in the mold of *Gangbusters*, including *Counterspy*, which first appeared on NBC's Blue Network (later ABC) on May 18, 1942; *Mr. District Attorney*, which first appeared on NBC on April 3, 1939; *Policewoman*, which first appeared on ABC in 1946; and *Treasury Agent*. Each of these shows helped reinforce the credibility of established law enforcement systems. But, particularly in *Gangbusters*, Phillips H. Lord brought the police procedural to radio and made an important contribution to the formula. The real workings of crime, and the methods employed by social agencies to combat crime, were coupled with a dash of sensationalism and fantasy to advance the police procedural as a viable story formula in story radio, as well as in American popular culture.

While pulp magazines had provided stories of police and their methods, and radio dramas did their part, other advances were being made in the growth of the police procedural. Pulp magazines turned out an increasing number of such formulas, and police stories appeared not only in magazines of their own, but also as short stories in pulps which featured collections of mystery stories. Variations emerged. In *Ten Detective Aces* magazine, for example, cops and their counterparts abounded. Perhaps the most popular series to emerge from the pages of *Ten Detective Aces* was Frederick C. Davis' exploits of the Moon Man. A.A. Wyn Publishers of New York published 39 novellas about the Moon Man between May 1933 and January 1937. The first Moon Man story was entitled "The Sinister Sphere"; the last was entitled "Blackjack Jury." Stephen Thatcher (aka the Moon Man) was a cop and the son of a police chief, yet in his alter ego, Thatcher was an avenging Robin Hood! Stephen Thatcher served and upheld established law enforcement as a police officer, and ironically also worked against

From Headquarters Came That Death-Charged Message

"Calling Car 13!"

"Moon Man" Novelet

By FREDERICK C. DAVIS

Author of "Moon Doom," "The Murder Master," etc.

The Moon Man was at headquarters

Ripping the night air came that fatal message to a fatal car—"Calling Car 13!" And it plunged Great City into a mad whirl of murder. For that prowl car was riding to the hideout of Ned Dargan, the notorious Moon Man's assistant. Black powder scorched red blood. And Lieutenant McEwen cornered the Moon Man.

Frederick C. Davis' Moon Man in "Calling Car 13!" *Ten Detective Aces* (August 1934).

established law enforcement when he donned the outfit of the Moon Man—an Argus one-way glass fishbowl-like helmet and a black cape—and stole money from the wealthy, who in Davis' stories were almost always decadent and corrupt. By the end of the Depression, the police procedural had become so firmly engrained into popular consciousness that variations of the formula were now commonplace. In the character of the Moon Man, both the police officer and the avenger detective are found. Radio spawned a number of imitations of *Gangbusters*. Dick Tracy, strong as ever as a hero of the comic strips, moved also to the airwaves in 1935, and a decade later in 1949 the police procedural hit new heights with the debut of *Dragnet* on story radio. (See Chapter 6.)

Jack Webb had been writing for radio since 1947 when his brainchild, *Dragnet*, appeared two years later. Webb was the producer, director, and star of this drama about police and their activities, and a large degree of the success *Dragnet* won was due to his mastery. The fictional hero of the program was Sergeant Joe Friday.

> In the character of Sgt. Joe Friday are to be found many of the attributes of Johnny Madero, Pat Novak, and Jeff Regan [previous Webb detectives of story radio]. A cold and disciplined personality, Friday mechanically went about his duties for the Los Angeles Police Department. From the opening overview of the city as a reservoir of criminality, to the closing bittersweet announcement of the criminal sentences of the guilty, *Dragnet* projected an image of a corrupted civilization defended by dedicated but disspirited police, crushed by the enormity of perfection.[24]

Dragnet received public acclaim for two primary reasons. The first reason was that in an inherently conventional, highly realistic story formula dominated by rigid method, Jack Webb created and perpetuated a personality in Sergeant Friday that was colorful and inventional enough to balance the former. Joe Friday was so ultra-conservative, so routinized in behavior, and so two-dimensional in physical appearance and personality that he was actually interesting! The second reason was that, like its predecessors *Dick Tracy* and *Gangbusters*, *Dragnet* presented and reinforced a morality—a preferential bias for "good" over "evil"—that the consuming audience embraced. Jack Webb and *Dragnet* successfully promoted and marketed social thinking and social agencies. A

few years later, Webb and *Dragnet* made an effective transition to the then new medium of television; the visual picture of the police detective was further enhanced.

"The city in these pages is imaginary. The people, the places are all fictitious. Only the police routine is based on established investigatory technique."[25] So began a landmark event in the history of the police procedural—the Ed McBain 87th Precinct stories, which debuted in 1956 when *Cophater* first appeared in print. (Ed McBain is the pseudonym for Evan Hunter.) McBain's series was a hybrid of several established traditions in mystery fiction and the police procedural alike. This author did for the police procedural what Mickey Spillane did for the hard-boiled detective story. With his presentation of *I, the Jury* in 1947, Spillane continued the tradition of the private eye school of mystery fiction that had been pioneered by masters like Carroll John Daly, Dashiell Hammett, and Raymond Chandler in the 1920s and 1930s. Spillane brought this formula of mystery fiction into a post–World War II setting. Similarly, Ed McBain synthesized and expanded the police procedurals of Chester Gould, Phillips H. Lord, and Jack Webb into a 1950s context. Like Spillane, McBain's early novels tended to be highly action-oriented, and his stories were populated by beautiful girls and vicious killers—sex and violence being staple elements of these stories. As both authors advanced their respective series into several novels, the storylines became more polished, but some of the original action and excitement also diminished. Life was hard and fast for the very human, and consequently flawed, detective heroes of each of these authors. The evils of the underbelly of the city produced the antagonists for Spillane's and McBain's stories. The primary difference between Spillane's Mike Hammer and McBain's police heroes of the 87th Precinct was that the morality of the former was individual in nature while the morality of the latter was that of the larger society. If society and its counterpart rogues were corrupt, then Mike Hammer would be corrupt also, beating the evildoers at their own games. In contrast, Ed McBain's police force protected and enforced socially prescribed morality.

Sharp, brutal dialogue is a hallmark of the McBain's Precinct series. When *Cophater* first appeared in 1956, it was established as fact that both the techniques of crime and the methods used by police to combat the same were highly routinized and conventional in both fact and fantasy. While Chester Gould countered the problem of conventionality with a cast of lovable "good guys" and inventional, physically exaggerated, grotesque rogues, and Jack Webb developed the idiosyncracies of Sergeant Joe Friday, Ed McBain likewise developed a colorful array of detailed policemen and "bad guys." The array of characters that populates the world of Ed McBain's 87th Precinct is revealed to the reading audience, at least to a large extent, through ongoing dialogue. Perhaps no other mystery writer has so thoroughly mastered the use of dialogue to effectively relate a story. *Cophater* provides this example:

> "Where were you Sunday night?"
> "What time Sunday night?"
> "About 11:40 or so."
> "I think I was at a movie."
> "Which movie?"
> "The Strand. Yeah, I was at a movie."
> "Did you have the .45 with you?"
> "I don't remember."
> "Yes or no."
> "I don't remember. If you want a yes or no, it'll have to be no. I'm no dope."
> "What picture did you see?"
> "An old one."
> "Name it."
> *"The Creature from the Black Lagoon."*
> "What was it about?"
> "A monster that comes up from the water."
> "What was the co-feature?"

> "I don't remember."
> "Think."[26]

Such dialogue reveals the repetition, gamesmanship, and persistence required for police interrogation. It also reveals that many of the tools of law and order — like interrogation — do not guarantee success or results. Today, Evan Hunter continues the saga of the 87th Precinct under his pseudonym Ed McBain. These stories stand with *Dick Tracy* and *Dragnet* as landmark events in the development of the police procedural.

Just three years after the debut of Ed McBain's *Cophater,* another soon-to-be master of the mystery story produced the first of a new series of police procedurals. Enter Donald E. Westlake and his police detective Abraham Levine, who works for Brooklyn's 43rd Precinct. Westlake's detective first appeared in the December 1959 issue of *Alfred Hitchcock Mystery Magazine* in a story entitled "The Best-Friend Murder." In 1984, the Mysterious Press collected the Abe Levine stories of Donald E. Westlake in hardcover form. In the introduction for that book (entitled *Levine*), Westlake recounts the events leading up to his development of Levine and that first short story, "The Best-Friend Murder." Writes Westlake:

> It has become the convention that policemen, professional detectives, are "hardened" to death, "immune" to life untimely nipped. . . . But is the policeman not flesh? Doth he not bleed? Hasn't he in his own lifetime buried grandparents, parents? Isn't he aware of his "own" mortality? It was the idea of a cop, a police detective, who was so tensely aware of his own inevitable death that he wound up hating people who took the idea of death frivolously that led me to Abe Levine and "The Best-Friend Murder."[27]

Westlake has gone on to write several more short stories about his fictional cop, as well as many other short mystery stories and novels. To date, he has created several distinct series characters, and he has used several pseudonyms—like Richard Stark and Tucker Coe—as well as his own byline in his writing. In the 1990s, Donald E. Westlake enjoys a large following and is more popular than ever. Today, his stories are smoother and more polished than they were in the early years of his career, and those early police procedurals are old history. But Westlake—now equated with tight storylines, tremendous wit, fast-paced action, and hard-boiled P.I.s—has never been better than he was in those formative years.

Donald E. Westlake is a treasured discovery for the mystery fan, and several of his novels—including both grim and humorous storylines—have been made into successful motion pictures. One such novel and movie adaptation of the same effectively pokes fun at the police procedural formula. The novel *Cops and Robbers* (1972) features two of New York's finest—Tom and Joe—and the efforts of these two "nice guys" and "good family men" to rip off both Wall Street and the Mafia. The preface page to the first edition paperback reads: "and now Donald E. Westlake comes up with a realistic police thriller to top them all—*Cops and Robbers*. Remember *Dick Tracy* and *This Is Your F.B.I.* and other dramatic proofs that crime doesn't pay? Well, we've come a long way baby."[28] Westlake's stories bring the police procedural full circle. Max Allan Collins cites Westlake as one of his all-time favorite authors. (See Chapter 5.)

Joseph Wambaugh brought novels of policemen and established law enforcement to best-seller status with *The New Centurions* (1970), *The Blue Knight* (1972), and *The Onion Field* (1973). William J. Caunitz has also produced best-selling police procedurals. These include *One Police Plaza* (1984), *Suspects* (1986), and *Black Sand* (1989). Joseph McNamara, chief of police in San José, California, has written and continues to write popularly received police procedurals. The first such

McNamara thriller was *The First Directive* (1984), whose paperback edition states that McNamara is the only police chief in America with a Ph.D. from Harvard. During the Seventies and Eighties, there were other popular authors of the police procedural. These include those discussed in George Dove's study.

In 1971, a variant of the established police procedural was developed by Clint Eastwood in his fictional character Dirty Harry. Eastwood provided a new dimension to what was once a very conventional mystery formula. Harry Callahan (aka "Dirty Harry") is the police officer who stretches the acceptable methods of law enforcement to the limit and then, when necessary, breaks free of those methods and employs vigilantism. The conflict in the Eastwood films *Dirty Harry* and its sequels—*Magnum Force* (1973), *The Enforcer* (1976), *Sudden Impact* (1983), and *The Dead Pool* (1988)—is embodied in the character of Callahan. Harry works within the guidelines set forth by the police department when they suit his purposes— which is not very often. The Dirty Harry motion pictures illustrate a variety of weaknesses and shortcomings of this established social agency—Harry is caught between doing what is prescribed by law and what his individual morality dictates. This is the essence of a motion picture series which focuses on the realistic portrayal of crime and the police officers who combat the same. The Dirty Harry series is self-critical and examines the workings of real-life law enforcement.

In the 1980s, the police procedural exploded into a wide array of variations. *Miami Vice* (NBC, 1984–89) proved to be one of the most popular series ever to air on network television, and made Don Johnson and Phillip Michael Thomas celebrities for as long as the program remained in prime time. Robert Daley's *Year of the Dragon* and its movie adaptation both proved quite successful. In the 1985 movie adaptation of the 1981 book, Mickey

Rourke stars in a crime drama set in the exotic location of New York's Chinatown. Author Robert Daley had established himself as a best-selling author of police procedurals. Novels like Hal Stryker's *NYPD 2025* (1985) used futuristic settings to provide invention to the inherently conventional police procedural formula. But Stryker's conception in *NYPD 2025* was not so much original as it was imitative of a storyline found in the famous movie *Blade Runner* some three years earlier.

In 1982, Harrison Ford and Rutger Hauer costarred in one of the finest motion pictures of the decade, a filmic adaptation of Philip K. Dick's 1968 science fiction novel *Do Androids Dream of Electric Sheep?* called *Blade Runner*. The year is 2021, and ex-cop Rick Deckard is hired to "retire" several rogue androids who lurk among the hordes of humans. But the androids have very human qualities and do not want to be found. In one of the most apocalyptic tales of modern times, Deckard discovers the human qualities of his adversaries, unwittingly falls deeply in love with one female android and discovers that life in all forms is sacred. The story has profound subtext and is packaged in the guise of a police procedural set in the future.

During the 1980s and early 1990s, the police procedural has enjoyed some of its finest years. There has been a proliferation of such stories. Beyond popular novels and a variety of newly emerging writing talents in the field, television has exploited this formula. Though all four major networks and most cable channels provide their respective renditions of the procedural story, NBC seems to have dominated this area of television programming. NBC ran *Adam-12* from 1968 to 1975, and later introduced the critically acclaimed, award-winning *Hill Street Blues* in 1981. (*Hill Street Blues* ran on network television until 1987.) *In the Heat of the Night* (1988 to the present) and *Law and Order* (1990 to the present) have been recent successes on NBC. (*In the Heat of the Night* moved to CBS in 1992.) The story form is as popular now as it ever was. True crime programs—close cousins to the police procedural—have been highly popular on all television networks in the last few years.

The police procedural formula of the mystery genre is now a staple of the mystery writer's art. Often hindered by the necessity of close adherence to actual police methods, this story form has turned to even more inventional characters and settings to sustain itself. It has also merged with other story forms like that of the avenger in order to retain and broaden its market appeal. Through all of this evolution, several authors and their fictional police heroes and series have endured and even prospered. Most notably, these are Ed McBain's 87th Precinct novels and the *Dick Tracy* comic strip.

Chester Gould's essentially straightforward, conservative, and traditional police procedural has persisted despite the modernist and postmodernist influences on this story formula. Gould helped set the generic coordinates of the police procedural, and these have persisted because they are so basic and universal in nature, and because the creative talents on *Tracy* since Gould's retirement from the comic strip in 1977 (including Max Collins, Rick Fletcher, Dick and John Locher) have successfully perpetuated and expanded Gould's vision regarding such procedure. This procedure, coupled with real history, makes this comic strip culturally reflective and significant, and makes *Tracy* entertaining formula fiction.

Through the procedure of the police story, standard social morality is prescribed and reinforced, and our faith remains in, and is reinforced by, police departments—those gatekeepers of social morality that mete out justice. The ritual of solving crime through established means can be boring, can be interesting, and is almost always reassuring. The art inherent in successful formula fiction is found in the

Caweltian balance of convention and invention. (See Chapter 1.) Has the storyline of *Dick Tracy* ever become boring because of excessive convention? Sometimes. Is that same storyline often interesting? Yes, most often. We know that Dick Tracy will continue to utilize effective, established police procedure to thwart crime and its instigators, but we like the assurance that he continues to do so; we like to see the mechanizations of procedure grind slowly and faithfully to fruition. More than sixty years old, *Dick Tracy* remains the catalyst and archetype of this story formula.

Notes

1. Several sources recount the history of the rise and fall of the dime novel. See *Old Sleuth's Freaky Female Detectives from the Dime Novels,* edited by Garyn G. Roberts, Gary Hoppenstand, and Ray B. Browne (Bowling Green, Ohio: Bowling Green State University Popular Press, 1990). In short, the publishers of dime novels made money by selling their publications with low profit margins—margins typically measured by the cent and fraction of a cent—to a large number of buyers. "Dime" novels literally retailed for a nickel or dime apiece. Success came from quantity of sales, not profit per dime novel issue. When the rate for novels sent through the mails increased by only a penny or two per dime novel sent, the small profit margin per publication was lost.

2. Alex McNeil's *Total Television: A Comprehensive Guide to Programming from 1948 to the Present,* 3rd edition (New York: Penguin, 1991) is an excellent source of information on the history of network television.

3. John G. Cawelti, *Adventure, Mystery and Romance* (Chicago: University of Chicago Press, 1976), p. 80.

4. Gary Hoppenstand, "Murder and Other Hazardous Occupations: Taboo and Detective Fiction," in *Forbidden Fruits: Taboos and Tabooism in Culture,* edited by Ray B. Browne (Bowling Green, Ohio: Bowling Green State University Popular Press, 1984), p. 84.

5. Chris Steinbrunner and Otto Penzler, eds., *Encyclopedia of Mystery and Detection* (New York: McGraw-Hill, 1976), p. 403.

6. Stefano Benvenuti and Gianni Rizzoni, *The Whodunit: An Informal History of Detective Fiction* (New York: Macmillan, 1980), p. 5.

7. "Miniature Wrist Radio." *Life,* October 6, 1947, p. 63.

8. See Jay Maeder's *Dick Tracy: The Official Biography* (New York: Penguin, June 1990), p. 117.

9. Thomas Y. Canby, "Satellites That Serve Us." *National Geographic,* September 1983, pp. 281–291; "Dick Tracy in Orbit." *Newsweek,* January 14, 1963, p. 47.

10. William B. Edwards, "How Dick Tracy Gets His Man." *Guns Magazine,* August 1955, p. 16.

11. John Culhane, "Dick Tracy: The First Law and Order Man." *Argosy,* Vol. 379, No. 6 (June 1974), p. 44.

12. Ibid.

13. Collins interview—October 25, 1982.

14. Ibid.

15. Herb Galewitz, ed., *The Celebrated Cases of Dick Tracy 1931–1951* (New York: Chelsea House, 1978), p. x.

16. Gould's reference to "dime novels" in these cases should probably be taken in the broadest sense of the term to include everything from story papers of the nineteenth century to the pulp magazines of the first half of the twentieth century.

17. Marshall McLuhan, media expert and theorist, wrote several books on the subject, several of which deal with the idea of "rearview mirrorism." One such book is *Understanding Media: The Extensions of Man* (New York: McGraw-Hill, 1964).

18. George N. Dove, *The Police Procedural* (Bowling Green, Ohio: Bowling Green State University Popular Press, 1982, p. 10.

19. Benvenuti and Rizzoni, p. 165.

20. The notions of "savagery," "civilization," and "the western hero," as formulaic conventions of the western genre are discussed by John G. Cawelti in *The Six-Gun Mystique* (Bowling Green, Ohio: Bowling Green State University Popular Press, 1984).

21. J. Fred MacDonald, *Don't Touch That Dial!: Radio Programming in American Life, 1920–1960* (Chicago: Nelson-Hall, Inc., 1979), pp. 166–167.

22. *Gangbusters: "The Golf Course Murder,"* radio program.

23. Jim Harmon, *The Great Radio Heroes* (New York: Ace Books, Inc., 1967), p. 63.

24. MacDonald, p. 190.

25. Ed McBain, *Cophater* (New York: The New American Library, 1973), preface page.

26. Ibid., p. 92.

27. Donald E. Westlake, *Levine* (New York: The Mysterious Press, 1984), p. viii–ix.

28. Donald E. Westlake, *Cops and Robbers* (New York: The New American Library, 1973), preface page.

CHAPTER 4

From Historical Fact to Historical Fantasy: The *Dick Tracy* Comic Strip from 1931 to the Present

"The first colonists saw in America an opportunity to regenerate their fortunes, their spirits, and the power of their church and nation; but the means to that regeneration ultimately became the means of violence, and the myth of regeneration through violence became the structuring metaphor of the American experience." — Richard Slotkin, *Regeneration Through Violence* (1973)

John G. Cawelti writes in *Adventure, Mystery and Romance* (1976) that the commercially successful, popular art forms (in his discussion, story formulas) are those which evidence a fine balance of convention and invention, or the ritualistic and revolutionary. To become popular, then, stories must deal in both the familiar and the new, being careful not to lean too much in the direction of convention and thus become overly repetitive and boring while at the same time not favoring the invention and becoming so unreal and fantastic that the consumer cannot digest the story. The extension is that the popular story form is a finely crafted synthesis of fact and fantasy. Not only is this a logical and credible explanation for the commercial success of popular culture products as a whole and popular story formulas in particular, but it also provides profound insight into the mythmaking process and into the process of constructing social realities for the group and individual alike. This blend of fact and fantasy has been the foundation upon which the house of Dick Tracy was built, and upon which it con-

tinues to flourish. Richard Gid Powers writes:

Since popular culture consists in large part of fantasy projection and wish fulfillment, popular entertainment often predicts the kind of political action it will take to defuse the public's anxieties. Popular artists like Gould had detected a taste for the hot-lead and machine-gun style of law enforcement as early as 1931. The public had moved far beyond its leaders in tolerance for violence against lawbreakers. In their fantasies the public had already rejected Herbert Hoover's legalistic style of law enforcement.[1]

These fantasy projections and wish fulfillments provide ideal worlds and ideal solutions to perceived socially threatening problems.

The operative word here, however, is "perceived." While bigger-than-life villains haunt the "real" world and make excellent fodder for the fantasy world of *Dick Tracy*, they have also been the source of much sensationalism seemingly since the beginnings of journalism. "Crime had been a staple of American journalism since

1830 when Benjamin Day's New York *Sun* discovered what crime could do for circulations."[2] We generally associate crime lords like Al Capone, Pretty Boy Floyd, Baby Face Nelson, and John Dillinger with the Thirties, but there were others. Crimes of a bit less sensational nature, but every bit as heinous and even more pervasive, were perpetrated by a proliferation of less colorful and relatively obscure figures in rural and urban communities across America. Yet it was not only the media focusing attention on a few outlandish, saleable characters. During the Thirties, the new head of the Federal Bureau of Investigation, J. Edgar Hoover, seeking to present a positive image of the Bureau for public consumption, targeted the "Big Boys" as the focus of Bureau crime apprehension efforts. Charismatic villains were elevated to bigger-than-life statuses and became themselves extensions of fact into collective fantasy. Popular stories of this period had to present fantastic heroes who could compete with and subdue these seemingly superhuman monsters.[3] Chester Gould and Dick Tracy arose to meet the challenge. Richard Slotkin states that

> Myth-making is a primary attribute of the human mind and . . . the process of mythogenesis in a culture is one of continuous activity rather than dramatic starts and stops. True myths are generated on a subliterary level by the historical experience of a people and thus constitute part of the inner reality which the work of the artist draws on, illuminates, and explains.[4]

Slotkin continues, "The myth is articulated by individual artists and has its effects on the mind of each individual participant, but its function is to reconcile and unite these individualities to a collective identity."[5]

The *Dick Tracy* story, a sprawling, ongoing crime saga which has been told for six decades, has produced a rich array of characters—good and bad alike. The most enduring (and yet simplistic and two-dimensional) of *Tracy* characters are the "good guys" who not only seem to conform to social norms, but who also act as protectors of the larger social group. It is they who ultimately triumph in classic confrontation of good and evil, and they who are allowed to survive and continue because they conform to and represent desirable social values.

Continuity in *Dick Tracy* characters and storylines over the years passed has fostered growth and development of characters. The only exceptions are short-lived, minor characters and insidious villains who depart quickly from the story due to abrupt, usually violent demises. Grotesque criminals epitomizing the repulsiveness of evil and its minions abound in *Tracy*. If the title hero of the comic strip was intended to represent the goodness in humanity, Gould realized that that same hero would have to face an appropriate array of foils. Those whom Gould and his successors have provided Tracy have attained unique significances of their own, and these villains have become trademarks of the comic strip. The good guys in *Dick Tracy* and their socially established methods have served as the conventions and factual elements of the ongoing Dick Tracy story. The rogues' gallery that the producers of *Tracy* have amassed for over sixty years and the unique methods these rogues bring to traditional crimes provide the inventions and fantasy elements of the strip. Enduring story characters ("good," "bad," conventional, and inventional alike) and their presentations are those which reinforce beliefs and attitudes of the audience—in the case of comic strips, newspaper readers. *Dick Tracy* has consistently featured a repertoire of such characters. The title hero himself has become an archetypal figure of law and order in popular consciousness and popular fiction alike. Russel B. Nye states, "There are millions of adults who have known Li'l Abner, Dagwood, and Dick Tracy all their lives. Comics have provided for them a common experience through childhood, maturity, and old age, intertwined with memories of sorrow and happiness, courtship, marriage, parenthood, war and peace."[6]

Characterization in *Dick Tracy* has been the central strength and appeal of the strip since its inception. Like the larger Dick Tracy story, characterization is successfully achieved through a fine balance of fact and fantasy. The fantasy and invention that have balanced what is inherently a very repetitious, conventional thing—the method of the police procedural story—is the rogues' gallery begun by Chester Gould and continued by Collins, Fletcher, and Locher. Though criminals in *Dick Tracy* are often based on actual personalities of their times, they are improbable exploitations—both in action and physical appearance. Through gross exaggeration of their criminals' characteristics, Gould and his associates have consistently provided the consuming public with straightforward ideas. Gould has noted, "I wanted my villains to stand out definitely so there would be no mistakes who the villain was. I think the ugliest thing in the world is the face of a man who has killed seven nurses—or has kidnapped a child. His face to me is ugly. Or a man who has raped an old lady or young girl and robbed her of $3.40. I think this an ugly man."[7]

Perhaps even more than the good guys of *Tracy*, the bad guys change with the times. (Sure, Tracy smoked cigarettes in the early Thirties, and sure, he has had a variety of hair styles and configurations of facial hair through the years, but essentially the hero has remained unchanged.) Cawelti notes that changes in inventions reflect changes in social history and social thought.[8]

A good example of inventions reflecting social change is found in the evolution of science fiction literature. As advances in the "hard" sciences shed light on such things as man's exploration of the world and space travel, and new technologies emerge as reality, inventions in science fiction reflect this new knowledge. Today Jules Verne's *Twenty Thousand Leagues Under the Sea* seems on one level to be an entertaining, conventional adventure story; submarine travel (the primary invention of the story when it first appeared in France in 1870) is now seeming quite conventional. Yet, when placed in the context of 1870 France, the invention of the submarine tells us something of the public perception regarding this then revolutionary mode of transportation.

Similarly, story inventions in *Dick Tracy* have consistently reflected changes and advancements in social history and social thinking. "Popular legend and pulp novel transformed criminals like Billy the Kid and Jesse James into figures of romantic rebellion driven to a life of crime by oppressive land barons, grasping railroad tycoons, and crooked, greedy politicians. Later similar legends arose about the bank robbers, kidnappers, and murderers of the twenties and thirties, John Dillinger, Bonnie and Clyde, and Pretty Boy Floyd in particular."[9] Gould's representations of Al Capone and John Dillinger in the early and mid–Thirties in the characters of Big Boy (1931–32) and Boris Arson (1934–35) were replaced with war criminals in the late Thirties and early Forties. These figures included Karpse (1938), Pruneface (1942–43), Mrs. Pruneface (1943), Flattop (1943–44), and Brow (1944). In the paranoid Fifties the bad guys were individuals deemed radical, such as Crewy Lou (1951) and Joe Period (an Elvis Presley type from 1956), and so on.

Beyond characterization, the written word and the illustration depicting action are equally important elements of the comic strip storyline. Fixed, two-dimensional space allotted all producers of comic strips is the major constraint on both of these elements. The most artistic works in the field of story strips are those

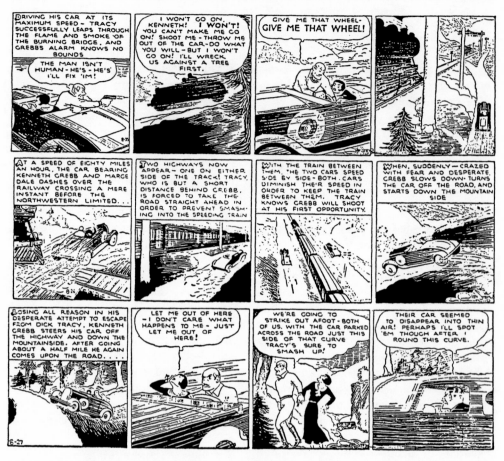

Use of angles, space, and dimension to give a car chase qualities of speed, recklessness, and danger—
Dick Tracy, August 25, 26, and 27, 1932. Reprinted by permission: Tribune Media Services.

which optimally and creatively work within this constraint. Word selection and illustration in *Dick Tracy* complement each other. Each, by necessity, is concise and to the point. Issues in the comic are straightforward and are presented in "black and white"—both figuratively and literally. Sharp, hard lines mark *Tracy* panels, as do intense, contrasting blacks and whites. Perspectives and angles at which scenes are presented enhance the line drawing and give dimensionality to the action. Spacing and positioning of caricatures and settings have also helped intensify the Dick Tracy story. These facets of the comic have provided the strip with its unique style and special imagery. Consider the mechanics of crime as de-

picted in the daily strips from August 25, 26, and 27, 1932, and June 8 and 9, 1933. The former set of dailies evidences Gould's use of angles, space, and dimension to give a car chase qualities of speed, recklessness, and danger. The latter strips literally and figuratively illustrate the blackness of a jailbreak and the techniques of crime.

The few comic strips that flourished in the Thirties and Forties which survive today have undergone some severe changes in format due primarily to editors and publishers of newspapers. Chester Gould was allowed over 170 words in one daily strip in the 1940s. Collins and Locher have been restricted to less than half that word count. Comic strips of contemporary times are substantially reduced in physical

Use of solid blacks to literally and figuratively illustrate the blackness of the techniques of crime—*Dick Tracy,* June 8 and 9, 1933. Reprinted by permission: Tribune Media Services.

size, and newspaper editors are much more critical or wary of controversial content in storylines. In the Thirties and Forties comic strips sold newspapers. People would sometimes buy newspapers for no other reason than to read the "funnies." Today, however, this is not the case. Of course, the hardest hit of the comics have been the story strips. The proliferation of new technologies and media is largely responsible for the decreased importance (in terms of generating profits) of the comic strip. Should the amount of space available to comic strip writers and artists continue to decrease, and it appears that this is a very real possibility, "story strips [may become] a dinosaur that might not be here in twenty years."[10] According to Max Collins, Charles Schulz was and is a genius in that he saw that comic strips were allotted increasingly smaller spaces in newspapers, and Schulz responded by creating a small-dimensioned strip in *Peanuts.* So there are several factors at work in all comic strips. Beyond a balance of fact and fantasy, there are characterization, issues of style and imagery, and, as time moves on, the possible decline of the medium in general as a commercially successful form.

The Thirties

Origins of a Hero

Like all archetypal heroes and famous comic strip adventurers of the Thirties, Dick Tracy has a significant origin. The origin story of the comic strip hero has two important functions. First, it provides the audience with a background in terms of the character's composite traits and lifestyle. Second, it sets forth a justification for the hero's cause and proceedings.

In the first daily episode of *Dick Tracy*

(*Tracy* debuted on October 4, 1931, in the Sunday edition of the *Detroit Mirror*, and the daily strip began on October 12 in the *New York News*), the newspaper audience learned very quickly of Dick Tracy's character and purpose. "His appearance in the *Chicago Tribune*, which became his headquarters, was delayed until Jan. 24, 1932."[11] In the first daily episode of *Dick Tracy*, the hero is the helpless witness to a holdup during which his girlfriend, Tess Trueheart, is kidnapped, and her father shot dead.[12] Emil Trueheart, Tess' father, was the owner of a delicatessen and was just beginning, after a lifetime of work, to enjoy a little financial comfort. Tracy has come to the Trueheart residence one evening to have dinner with the family of his sweetheart. Two gangsters enter the residence and shoot Emil. When Tracy attacks the gangsters, he is jumped and gun-whipped. He awakes to find Emil dead and Tess kidnapped. Tracy states, "Over the body of your father, Tess, I swear I'll find you and avenge this thing—I swear it."[13] The following day in *Dick Tracy*, Chief Brandon of the local police department asks, "Tracy—How'd you like to join the plainclothes squad? I think you'd be a big help in finding Tess Trueheart and catching her father's murderer."[14]

A hero was born whose cause was evident and justified, and who was destined to grow with the American public for more than sixty years. (Gould's origin story for Tracy was partially based on ideas from Captain Joseph Medill Patterson of the *Chicago Tribune* and *New York News*.) In *Comic Art in America*, Stephen Becker states, "*Dick Tracy* was the debut of violence in the newspaper comic strip. Previously, guns had been more or less taboo, and so had blood, and so had the techniques of crime."[15] This is essentially true, yet there were several popular adventure strips of the Twenties (like Roy Crane's *Wash Tubbs*) which did include some elements of violence. But until the advent of *Dick Tracy*, violence, gunplay, insidious

death, and torture had never been the focus of any comic strip. Gould and his mentor (Patterson) felt that the presentation of these controversial elements of life was appropriate if the means by which such evils were put down were established law and order and the police officers who upheld the same. Hence, by necessity Dick Tracy became a policeman, and unlike Walter Gibson's Shadow—another soon-to-be archetypal hero who debuted just a few months earlier in 1931 in the pages of a Street and Smith pulp magazine—Tracy did not often find himself outside the boundaries of law and order. From the beginning, Dick Tracy was designed to be a standard for honest Americans. He represented what Chester Gould wanted to be, and wanted each of his readers to be—an ideal citizen. Though Tracy was a fantastic extension of real cops, he did not lose his basis in fact. Tracy did not possess powers totally beyond human capabilities such as flight or X-ray vision like Jerry Siegel and Joe Shuster's Superman, who debuted in the comic book *Action Comics* #1 in June 1938. Rather, he was and is the guy who lives his life to the fullest because of and despite the constraints of law and order—something most of us would like to do but rarely manage.

Dick Tracy's heroic nature is the center of his appeal. Real-life people, as well as Tracy's police force associates created by Gould, have someone to emulate. Ron Goulart states that as a detective, "Dick Tracy fits right into the tough guy pattern of the 1930s. In his first newspaper appearance, October 4, 1931, Tracy talks in a tough, slangy style, takes a poke at a stick-up artist named Pinkie the Stabber, and solves a case for the chief of police."[16] We did not hear an extraterrestrial talk of planets in other galaxies; we heard a regular guy speak in terms that were as familiar as those of the next-door neighbor. But he is tougher and more determined than the average citizen who abhors crime and finds it hard, if not impossible, to do anything about.

However, Dick Tracy—particularly in the Thirties—was not without his tricks and gimmicks. Chester Gould acknowledged on several occasions that he was influenced by the classic works of Edgar Allan Poe and Sir Arthur Conan Doyle and their respective detectives, C. Auguste Dupin and Sherlock Holmes. In many ways Tracy was an American version of Sherlock Holmes, though he dealt more with common people and realistic crimes than did Holmes. Dick Tracy relied heavily on his deductive reasoning, as did his English counterpart, and particularly in the formative years of the comic strip, he used an old Holmesian motif—a plot convention nineteenth century dime novels like *Nick Carter* also exploited. Dick Tracy often wore disguises in his attempts to gain information that would assist in the bringing of criminals to justice. In an episode from 1936, the great detective dons the attire of a window washer. This was not the first time the great detective put on such calculated disguises; indeed he had done so almost from the start. These details illustrate his resourcefulness, intelligence, and determination once the course of his career was set.

Dick Tracy in Disguise à la Sherlock Holmes and Nick Carter—1936. Reprinted by permission: Tribune Media Services.

Tracy expressed an intolerant attitude toward criminal activities, which was representative of feelings of the times. "Heroes who were impatient with red tape, particularly nice-guy vigilantes like Tracy, were extremely popular in the Depression years."[17] It seemed that government could create policy, like the Volstead Act enforcing Prohibition, that affected only the honest citizen. While the rule making was hindering decent folks, gangsters and their lot were doing as they pleased. When it was time to crack down on criminals, the government seemed bogged down by its own policies. The term "vigilante" is not wholly accurate in describing Dick Tracy, however; the connotations of the term are too extreme. Otherwise the idea is clear. Tracy expressed prominent beliefs and sentiments during the Thirties, and was credible enough not to sound contrived. Chester Gould said it himself when he stated that the hero of his creation was "my own idea of a successful law enforcement officer."[18] His vision was obviously embraced by many faithful readers.

The Hero's Family

Chester Gould creations other than Dick Tracy have enjoyed a long life on the right side of the law. From the start, mainstays of the strip have been Chief Brandon, Pat Patton, and Tess Trueheart, though Brandon's role diminished as years went by. Chief Brandon is the fellow who encourages Tracy from the murder of Emil Trueheart on. Brandon's years of highest visibility in the strip were the early and mid–Thirties. During this time, with Tracy evolving as a character, Brandon was the authority figure to whom Tracy answered—with rare exception. As Tracy became better defined as a character, exercising a great deal of independence, Chief Brandon's role diminished. Throughout the Thirties and most of the Forties, Brandon remained in the background, appear-

The hero's family: Chief Brandon, Dick Tracy, Jr., Pat Patton, and Tess Trueheart—*Dick Tracy,* September 26, 1932. Reprinted by permission: Tribune Media Services.

ing rarely. Ironically, the episode which gave the character most time on center stage was the one in which he made his exit. On October 24, 1948, Brandon resigned from the police force, guilt-ridden by his error that had cost Diet Smith's young protégé inventor (Brilliant) his life.[19] Brandon had made a series of blunders through the years as chief of police, and this error was the culmination of these mistakes. Chester Gould had been working the Brandon subplot for years. The episode essentially closing this subplot was ample proof of Gould's ability to provide complexity and continuity to his storylines. This episode showed that Gould had a detailed memory of events and personae that had run through his famous comic from the start. Tracy's former chief did not, however, totally disappear from the comic strip. After a while, he reappeared in the strip as the proprietor of a greenhouse aptly named "Lawn Order."

Pat Patton, Tracy's friend, assistant, and comic relief, became the new chief of police when Brandon retired. Patton was never intended to be the equal of Tracy in terms of heroics (after all, the comic strip is not *Pat Patton*), but he has remained a staple of the comic. From the start, Patton's appeal has been his human frailty and humorous character. His broad smile and big eyes, as well as his tendency to overreact to many situations, make him the perfect counterpart for Tracy. Pat brings a

lightheartedness to *Dick Tracy* that tones down some of the bleakness inherent in stories of the very worst in humanity and realistic police procedure. The obvious question that arises is why Patton becomes the chief of police when Dick Tracy is the apparent choice for the position. The answer is that an action detective such as Dick Tracy could not survive in the fantasy world, or in the real-life commercial world, if he were chained to a desk. It is his nature to be out on the street confronting crime and its perpetrators in their natural habitat. Chester Gould wove a fictitious tale to answer the question for the readers

Chief Brandon—1936. Reprinted by permission: Tribune Media Services.

of the day. According to Gould, Tracy was offered the job and turned it down. (Tracy believed he could best serve the interests of law and order by remaining a street cop and detective.) Few other characters are as close to Tracy as is Patton. In the early *Tracy* strips of the Thirties, Pat is an overly eager, inexperienced cop. He grows with, and is shaped by, his hero friend. If Dick Tracy is the American Sherlock Holmes, then Pat Patton and Sam Catchem (who first appeared in *Dick Tracy* on December 24, 1948), are the American John Watsons.

Pat Patton was clearly designed to conform to and perpetuate the stereotype of the Irish cop. Chester Gould, ever conscious of the ethnic diversity and economic classes of the Chicago area and the home of his youth, Oklahoma, consciously incorporated a wide array of characters into his stories. Blacks, Asians, Native Americans, Europeans and various religious peoples and groups were represented from the early days in his strip. The rural and urban, poor and wealthy alike, all found their way into Dick Tracy's world. Like his Caucasian characters, Gould's representatives of varying ethnicities, religions, and economic strata found themselves on both sides of the law. Irish cops abounded in Gould's *Tracy,* particularly in the Thirties. Here, in the black and white line drawings of Chester Gould, as in real-life urban America, were found officers with names like Clancy, O'Brien, Flaherty, and so on. These individuals, as prescribed by the stereotype of the Irish cop, were slightly overweight, hot-tempered, and most often walked a beat with a nightstick. Patton was an extension of that tradition.

An important but often overlooked member of Dick Tracy's family is G-man Jim Trailer, who is significant as a character in *Tracy* for several reasons. Dick Tracy is a policeman, not a G-man (i.e. "government man"), and as noted earlier this very fact probably had a lot to do with J. Edgar Hoover's affection for the strip.

Pat Patton—1939. Reprinted by permission: Tribune Media Services.

(The comic did not directly have any impact on the images Hoover was trying desperately to equate with the FBI.) There have been times throughout the course of the past sixty years when Dick Tracy has been called upon to assist or do special duty for the government agency made famous by Hoover. Media other than the comic strip that have related Dick Tracy's adventures like movie serials have tended at times, correctly and incorrectly, to place Tracy in the G-man role. Gould himself, however, was very conscious of the distinction between policemen and G-men— so much so that he created a G-man counterpart for his police hero. Jim Trailer was that counterpart, and his name is indicative of his profession.

Another important member of Tracy's family is Tess Trueheart. Tess is with Tracy from the beginning, and she is the double victim in the origin story. In the early years of the strip, Tracy's girlfriend took an active role in thwarting criminals and their activities. Even more often, it seemed, Tess was the victim of crime. (She was kidnapped and held hostage on several occasions, for example.) Tess was sometimes brash, stubborn, independent, and foolish, and was sometimes a problem for Tracy. Likewise, she was also characterized at times as intelligent, charming,

Jim Trailer—1938. Reprinted by permission: Tribune Media Services.

reasonable, and impossibly patient, and on several occasions she even served as Tracy's rescuer. She was probably the most complex member of the Dick Tracy family—often moody and unpredictable, and often very alluring. The all-time master at depicting romance and sex in comic strips—and the pathos related to the same—was Milton Caniff. Of this there is no doubt when considering such relationships as those between the Dragon Lady and Pat Ryan in *Terry and the Pirates*. But Chester Gould was no bumpkin off the truck when it came to depicting love and romance in his strip. Tess could be a fiery blonde goddess, but only in her intimate relations with Tracy. *Dick Tracy* showcased this side of Tess most effectively in the Thirties.

But, we are getting ahead of the story. In the first months of 1932, Tess threw Dick's engagement ring into the river, and in 1939 she all but married a baseball player named Edward Nuremoh ("home-run" spelled backwards) who was using her to get an inheritance. Ultimately, however, after Tess rejected Dick, and Dick was demoted on the police force to a rural beat, Tess tipped off Tracy about the location and time of a gang meeting. After capturing the criminals, Tracy was reinstated at his old position on the force, and Tess made up with him. In 1939, Tess' relationship with Edward Nuremoh did not work out, and seeing the error in her ways, Tess made her way back to Tracy. Tess provided a vivaciousness in the Thirties that made her much more than a two-dimensional character. For a long time, the lovely golden-haired lady was the only female representative of the forces of law and order, though she was not officially a member of the police force. Years later, policewoman Lizz would appear on the scene.

One *Dick Tracy* episode from 1938 further proves that Chester Gould was able to deftly address and depict female sensuality and beauty. That which distinguishes art from the profane has often been arbitrary in nature. Nonetheless, the most ingenious of popular artists get around socially prescribed codes of morality, and in the process have managed to poke fun at the very institutions which

Breaking the engagement—*Dick Tracy*, January 13, 1932. Reprinted by permission: Tribune Media Services.

Romance and a proposal—*Dick Tracy*, January 2 and 3, 1933. Reprinted by permission: Tribune Media Services.

The hero and the lady—*Dick Tracy*, September 11, 1933. Reprinted by permission: Tribune Media Services.

Tess and Edward Nuremoh—1939. Reprinted by permission: Tribune Media Services.

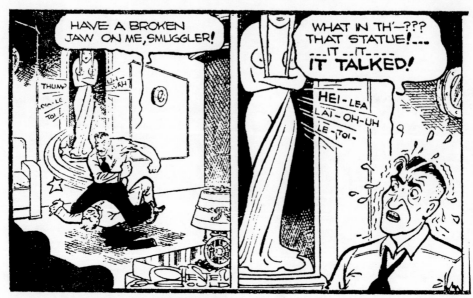

Feminine Sensuality—1938. Reprinted by permission: Tribune Media Services.

Feminine Sensuality—1938. Reprinted by permission: Tribune Media Services.

try to suppress their creative thought. Gould could not produce a scantily clad or naked person in *Dick Tracy*. Newspaper editors never would have tolerated such a thing. He could, however, produce a semi-nude statue that would, ironically, be acceptable or at least get past any media gatekeepers.

In 1932, a little nine-year-old waif stole a pocket watch from Pat Patton and met Dick Tracy for the first time. This street urchin, a boy with no name, eventually adopted the name of his hero who from the start had had undying faith in him, and Dick Tracy, Jr., emerged. Junior has a significant origin, though it is not as well documented as that of the title character. "A nine-year-old nameless street kid living under the thumb of thug Steve the Tramp meets Dick Tracy and begins a remarkable transformation and the start of a lifelong association."[20] The nameless kid moves from the Dickensian relationship of Oliver Twist to Fagin to the transformation from "rags to riches" epitomized by lead characters in Horatio Alger novels. Tracy cleans him up and gives him his first haircut and home. In the Thirties, Junior makes it big as a law-abiding citizen. As with so many fictional and real people, Junior finds an ideal role model in Dick Tracy. The character of Junior is an important dimension of *Dick Tracy*. Along with the title character, he has always been attractive to the youngest of comic strip readers. Junior was what many children would have liked to have been—a child protégé of the most likable detective ever. And Junior had plenty of care, love, and adventure. One can just imagine how exciting it would have been to be a youngster like Junior. True, he had his difficulties, like the time in 1937 when two of Supeena's mobsters tied him under a running car in a closed garage, leaving him to die of asphyxiation. But he always got out of those things either by his own ingenuity or the rescue of an adult (most often Tracy). In this particular incident, the killer, Frank Redrum (aka "The Blank"), was his unlikely rescuer.[21] Junior had a real sense of determination and purpose, like his mentor.

Dick Tracy, Jr.—1936. Reprinted by permission: Tribune Media Services.

Early Rogues and Real-Life Personalities

In the Thirties episodes of *Dick Tracy*, villains likewise—though the most inventional and outrageous of the *Tracy* characters—had their basis in fact. During this time, gangsters were taking on names based on their physiognomies as in the cases of "Baby Face" Nelson and "Pretty Boy" Floyd. Gould exploited this system of naming and incorporated it into his fictitious world of Dick Tracy. But big-time gangsters were not the only real-life source for Chester Gould's rogues' gallery. Rich-

ard Pietryzyk states, "The hardest of criminals have peopled the Tracy saga from the beginning, providing the detective with endless challenging situations. Early characters from the '30s were generally caricatures of various Hollywood personalities such as James Cagney, Greta Garbo, and Boris Karloff."[22] And, too, Gould often caricatured the well-known film roles associated with these personalities. Claudette Colbert appeared in the form of Jean Penfield, and Marlene Dietrich was parodied as Marro. Stooge Viller, who was one of the few *Tracy* rogues to become a continuing character, is reminiscent of Edward G. Robinson; Johnny Ramm physically resembled Clark Gable; and Stud Bronzen looks like Wallace or Noah Beery.[23]

Individuals like Cagney, Garbo, Karloff, Robinson, Gable, and others each possessed very distinctive physical appearances, and each played unique motion picture character types that were easily recognizable and easily satirized. Such coopting of very popular personalities of those times provided an immediacy and currency to *Dick Tracy* that made the comic strip both conventional and inventional. These caricatures provided a substantial and an intriguing subtext for Gould's work, and added to the appeal of *Tracy*.

Though many *Dick Tracy* characters of the 1930s were visual likenesses of various Hollywood stars and their film roles, it was the gangland personas that best represented crime. After all, real-life criminals epitomized crime better than actors who played criminals. Since 1931, several hundred characters have appeared in *Dick Tracy*, most of whom have been villains.[24] Rogues from the Thirties Gould strips were most often hard-core racketeers, blackmailers, kidnappers, and assorted gang leaders. Each believed he or she had the ability to pull off the perfect crime, and each, due to some flaw in character and soul, learned differently. There were Steve the Tramp, Dan the Squealer, Ribs Mocco, Stooge Viller, Larceny Lu, Boss Herrod, and Broadway Bates to name but a few from the early years.

Al Capone and Big Boy

Chester Gould's first larger-than-life rogue in *Dick Tracy* was a mobster named Big Boy. This character was "big" not only because of his position in the underworld, but also because of his physical size. As noted earlier, Big Boy was Gould's fantasy depiction of Al Capone. John G. Cawelti writes:

> The Capone legend provided occasion for the representation of crime as a social phenomenon. The way in which the social experiment of Prohibition gave rise to the Capone organization was invariably a part of the story as was an indictment of the extent to which the criminal gang had become allied with corrupt politicians and policemen. Journalistic and cinematic accounts of the Capone figure often portrayed the slum environment of the American city as the source of the criminal protagonist. But, above all, the Capone legend was the story of a great rise and fall, and in this way it coincided with the traditional moralistic pattern of the destruction of the criminal overreacher and with the archetype of melodrama.[25]

Chester Gould knew a good story when he saw one. He began exploitation of the Capone legend in *Dick Tracy* almost from the start.

The Lindbergh Baby and Buddy Waldorf

During the early and mid–Thirties, Al Capone's devious endeavors and the Lindbergh baby kidnapping were front page headlines. (Of course, in real life the two were unrelated events.) Gould tapped into these two national, highly emotion-evok-ing phenomena and incorporated Capone and the kidnapping into his *Dick Tracy*. Along with Dick Tracy, the evil mob lord Big Boy and the toeheaded little waif Buddy Waldorf were the instrumental players in this *Tracy* episode. Big Boy represented Capone in appearance and behavior (though somewhat fantastically), and Buddy Waldorf loosely represented the Lindbergh baby. There was little doubt that the storyline of 1932 featuring these characters was highly imaginative, but it was equally obvious where the basis in fact came from.

> H.L. Mencken called the Lindbergh case the greatest newspaper story since the crucifixion, and in terms of sheer volume of newsprint he was probably right. When the Lindbergh baby was taken from the family's house in New Jersey on March 1, 1932, the event touched off such a wild craze of public interest that it seemed as though the business of the entire country had come to a stop while the nation participated in the manhunt through the pages of their newspapers. Three months later the Congress passed the Lindbergh Kidnap Law, which, as usual, responded to a crime wave by throwing the F.B.I. at it. On September 14, 1934, after publicity which had turned everyone involved into a celebrity, the case was broken, and two years later the kidnapper was executed. The principal hero of the case, Colonel Schwartzkopf of the New Jersey State Police, went on to star as the announcer for Phillips H. Lord's "Gangbusters" (né "G-Men") radio show.[26]

In the comic, Big Boy abducts Buddy Waldorf. After weeks of chase scenes and further build-up of emotions, Tracy catches up with Big Boy. Tracy physically beats up the villain, incarcerates him, and rescues an unscathed Buddy Waldorf. The father side and protector role of Dick Tracy find illustration in this sequence.

Clearly, Al Capone was not accounting for his actions against society at this time. The Lindbergh baby was never rescued, and furthermore Capone never kid-

Big Boy—*Dick Tracy*, November 30, December 1 and 2, 1931. Reprinted by permission: Tribune Media Services.

napped the baby. Gould had produced a wholly fantastic depiction of real American historical events. There was nothing intellectual about it. People craved fantasy; they got more than enough reality in the front pages of the daily newspapers. The capture of Capone and the rescue of the Lindbergh baby were wish fulfillments for many American readers, fantastic and absurd as the storyline might seem. The headlines from the late edition of the *New York Times* of March 2, 1932, read, "LINDBERGH BABY KIDNAPPED FROM HOME OF PARENTS ON FARM NEAR PRINCETON: TAKEN FROM HIS CRIB: WIDE SEARCH." Almost immediately, Gould wrote the *Dick Tracy* episode featuring

Big Boy and Buddy Waldorf, and the fact and fantasy appeared together on newspaper pages from April 11 through May 28 in 1932.

John Dillinger and Boris Arson

Seemingly from the very beginnings of *Dick Tracy*, Gould made improvements daily in his storytelling and illustrations. Each new episode in 1932 and 1933 seemed more exciting, better plotted (though Gould never really outlined any of his stories in advance of their appearances in the newspaper pages), more solidly drawn, and better scripted than the one

Buddy Waldorf—*Dick Tracy*, May 20 and 21, 1932. Reprinted by permission: Tribune Media Services.

before. For the most part, criminals remained gang members and leaders, but their characters were slicker as well as more detailed and intense. Even more excitement was added as the episodes progressed. On the Sunday page of April 22, 1934, Tracy and Patton became trapped in a secret passageway where the ceiling, buzzing and crackling with live electrical wires, was descending upon them. (And you thought the exploits of Indiana Jones were new!) An early death trap for Tracy and associates, it would be followed by many more over the years.[27] In 1934, the

villains became even more insidious and intense. Rogues like Doc Hump, Larceny Lu, and Boris Arson appeared that year— three marvelously crafted characters. The premiere rogue for late 1934 and early 1935 was Boris Arson, Gould's rendition of John Dillinger.

In one episode with Arson and Chief Brandon, the escapades of John Dillinger provided the factual basis. This was a time in American history when Dillinger was a prominent leader in gangland, and newspapers sported his name on a regular basis. After numerous heinous offenses against

Jimmy White, an intense character—*Dick Tracy*, January 16, 1934. Reprinted by permission: Tribune Media Services.

An early death trap—*Dick Tracy*, April 22, 1934. Reprinted by permission: Tribune Media Services.

Boris Arson—1935. Reprinted by permission: Tribune Media Services.

society, Dillinger was eventually captured and jailed. But his time in stir was to be short-lived. In prison, Dillinger carved what resembled a crude gun out of a piece of wood and colored it with shoe blacking. The artificial weapon fooled prison guards and the gangster made his escape from Lake County Jail (Crown Point, Indiana) on the morning of March 4, 1934. In *Dick Tracy* not long after, Boris Arson carved a gun out of a potato and covered it with iodine to darken it. Arson escaped in a manner similar to that of the real gangster. This particular installment of *Tracy* also put Chief Brandon in a bad light once again—Brandon had supplied Arson with

Boris Arson—1935. Reprinted by permission: Tribune Media Services.

the potatoes from which came the artificial gun. In a newspaper photograph depicted in *Tracy*, Arson is pictured with his arm around the chief. Of course, the fictitious townspeople of *Dick Tracy* got the wrong idea. While crooked policemen and politicians were part of the fantasy and reality of the times, Brandon was not in collabora-tion with Arson. Several such embarrass-ing incidents would plague Brandon until his retirement in 1948.

Rogues of the Mid and Late Thirties

During the second half of the Thir-ties, villains continued to pour from the

Boris Arson—1935. Reprinted by permission: Tribune Media Services.

imagination and pen of Gould. Among others, there were Lips Manlis (one of the major grotesque villains of 1936) and the Purple Cross Gang (also from 1936). In 1937, the number one *Tracy* rogue was Frank Redrum (aka "the Blank"), who was bent on destroying his old gang members who had double-crossed him. The episode featuring the Blank introduced a rather complicated moral dilemma. And, Chester Gould communicated the complexity of the situation very effectively. The Blank systematically and efficiently killed his former partners—all of whom, in the larger sense of justice, got what they deserved. This revenge seemed at least in

Boris Arson—1935. Reprinted by permission: Tribune Media Services.

some ways, correctly motivated. However, the machinery of law enforcement not only protects socially prescribed morality, but it alone also possesses the authority to prosecute and punish violators of the code. The Blank was in the wrong, and Dick Tracy had to stop him.

In 1938, there were Stud Bronzen, Johnny Ramm (pictured in Sunday pages from April 24 and May 8 of that year), and Jojo Niddle (who meets his deserved demise at the hands of Tracy in the Sunday page of September 11, 1938). Scardol and Professor Emirc ("crime"

Boris Arson—1935. Reprinted by permission: Tribune Media Services.

spelled backwards) were among the *Tracy* rogues of 1939. And, an old favorite was back also.

In the Sunday page for Christmas Eve 1939, Dick Tracy let Stooge Viller escape in a taxi rather than shoot at him and risk hitting an unsuspecting member of the large holiday throng that surrounds them.

The Beery Brothers and Stud Bronzen

Stud Bronzen may have been the coldest and most heartless villain ever to pollute the world of Dick Tracy. Bronzen was Chester Gould's version of real-life Hollywood personalities Wallace and

The demise of Jojo Niddle—*Dick Tracy*, September 11, 1938. Reprinted by permission: Tribune Media Services.

Stooge Viller—*Dick Tracy*, **December 24, 1939. Reprinted by permission: Tribune Media Services.**

Noah Beery. Portrayal of the Beerys, however, went beyond imitation of physical appearance and exploited the mythology surrounding the personal and professional lives of the actors. In his autobiography, *Please Don't Shoot My Dog,* Jackie Cooper verifies the validity of Gould's depiction of Wallace Beery. Cooper claimed that in his relationships with Beery, "There was everything but warmth," and that though he made four movies with Beery, he "never had a comfortable moment with the man."[28] Certainly Wallace Beery was not a slave trader, mercenary, and murderer. But the rough, cold, mean persona that he exuded (on and off stage) as described by Jackie Cooper is translated into Gould's Stud Bronzen. Likewise, Wallace's brother, Noah, was particularly noted for his filmic portrayals of bad guys.

Bronzen debuted in *Dick Tracy* on December 11, 1937, and exited the strip on May 20, 1938. While Gould made a living at incorporating violence into the world of the comic strip and specifically into the world of *Dick Tracy*, it seemed that he took special pride in disposing of this character, one of his all-time nastiest rogues. Stud (whose name even suggests his cold, cruel tendencies) was wrapped up in a slave trade which used Chinese as the primary commodity. The story was set on the high seas and in Chinatown, but it was not the first such adventure to put Tracy on ships in pursuit of criminals. It was also not the first *Dick Tracy* story to incorporate diverse ethnic peoples and communities, nor the first to use Asians in its content.

Issues of Ethnicity

Chester Gould had been depicting all sorts of ethnic groups and peoples in his strip from the start. Asians, Native Americans, African Americans, and others were depicted in a variety of capacities in the comic. In *Dick Tracy,* there were a variety of ethnic stereotypes, and the characters so categorized found themselves on both sides of the law, and in situations of power and vulnerability alike. In short, Gould provided "good" Asians and "Yellow Perils" alike—both are found in the Stud Bronzen episode. Gould likewise filled his stories with blacks who found themselves on both sides of the law, and who often worked as valets, cooks, housekeepers, and other types of servants. Gould also provided images of Native Americans with whom he felt a sort of kinship since he had been raised in the Cherokee Strip region of Oklahoma.

As a popular artist of the 1930s, and as a progressive humanitarian (though definitely politically conservative at times), Chester Gould sought neither to create, perpetuate, deny, expand nor diminish popular stereotypes of the times. But he did exploit those stereotypes. Beliefs, values, and characteristics socially constructed and foisted off onto individuals and groups at this time simply made good conventions for stories. Chester Gould's message in *Dick Tracy* was that crime does not pay; it was not that one group was morally superior to another or that some ethnic groups are more prone to crime than others. Gould felt that human life in all forms was equally priceless. This is what makes the Stud Bronzen episode so appalling. When Bronzen disposes of his slave cargo by knocking his victims on the head with a club and then throwing them overboard to drown, we see Gould at his emotional best. This is shocking, hauntingly memorable material even for the highly fantastic world of the comic strip. Gould showed that crimefighting was a hard and often vicious business because these were the terms of survival dictated by criminals who had no conscience. The sentiment of fatalism was cold, hard, and dark—it was realistic.

The shocking violence of Stud Bronzen—1938. Reprinted by permission: Tribune Media Services.

The demise of Stud Bronzen—1938. Reprinted by permission: Tribune Media Services.

J. Edgar Hoover and the Comic Strip

The *Dick Tracy* criminals of the Thirties encountered by Tracy, his associates, and established police methods were to a large extent responsible for the balance of convention and invention, fact and fantasy,

achieved in the popular comic strip. J. Edgar Hoover was so impressed with this balance of fact and fantasy and its moral message that he praised Gould on several occasions for his work on *Dick Tracy*, and even commissioned his own imitation of *Tracy* called *War on Crime*. Prior to *War*

George the shoe shiner—*Dick Tracy*, January 18, 1932. Reprinted by permission: Tribune Media Services.

Della the colored cook—*Dick Tracy*, April 19, 1933. Reprinted by permission: Tribune Media Services. (Note also the Dickensian relationship between Steve the Tramp and the little waif who would later name himself Dick Tracy, Jr.)

Yellowpony—1935. Reprinted by permission: Tribune Media Services.

Memphis the valet—1936. Reprinted by permission: Tribune Media Services.

on Crime, Norman Marsh had produced *Dan Dunn,* which debuted September 25, 1933, and which was highly derivative of Gould's comic strip. Chester Gould's assistant on *Dick Tracy* during the early Thirties was Dick Moores. Moores produced his own comic strip, *Jim Hardy,* which debuted as a daily on May 9, 1936, just nine days before *War on Crime* first appeared. (Further information on Norman Marsh's *Dan Dunn* and Dick Moores' *Jim Hardy* is provided in Chapter 2; biographical

The remains of the Honorable Chiang, beloved mayor of Chinatown—1938. Reprinted by permission: Tribune Media Services.

Toyee and the "Yellow Peril" stereotype—1938. Reprinted by permission: Tribune Media Services.

Maybelle—1939. Reprinted by permission: Tribune Media Services.

Stereotyped qualities as story conventions—1939. Reprinted by permission: Tribune Media Services.

material related to Dick Moores is found in Chapter 5.) "On May 16, 1936, Hoover's comic strip, *War on Crime,* opened in forty-five papers across the country. Hoover had put together the whole package."[29] The group he assembled included artist Kemp Starrett, editor Doug Borgstedt, and writer Rex Collier of the *Washington Star,* who, according to Richard Gid Powers, was Hoover's "best friend in the Washington press corps." Hoover also arranged for the Ledger Syndicate of Philadelphia to carry the strip.[30]

But the strip lasted only a couple of years, concluding on January 22, 1938.

(Jimmy Thompson did the drawing for the last few months.) Powers suggests that the strip's demise was attributable to the lack of a solid fictional hero to pull the storyline together. Ron Goulart states that "once John Dillinger, Baby Face Nelson, Pretty Boy Floyd, and the other premium grade bandits had been used up, Collier increasingly had to resort to such distinctly lesser known figures as Two-Gun Brunette, and the feature gradually ran out of firepower."[31] Yet the explanation for the death of *War on Crime* is still larger than that. The comic was based on true FBI cases, and that was essentially all. It was simply too conventional. *War on Crime* was redundant, and it was far too similar to the front page headlines of the newspapers in which it appeared. A balance of fact and fantasy had not been achieved.

The Forties

World War II Storylines

When 1940 arrived, World War II was heating up. So too, was the action in Chester Gould's *Dick Tracy*. News of the global conflict dominated the media of the times (including newspapers, magazines, radio, and motion picture newsreels), and everything else seemed to pale in comparison. The war was on everybody's mind, and it was not easy to get anything else into the popular consciousness at that time—not even *Dick Tracy*. Chester Gould, always cognizant of the world around him, recognized the problem and reacted to changing circumstances. Perhaps more out of necessity than anything else, Gould "stepped on the gas" and he, along with *Dick Tracy*, roared into the new decade.[32]

Tracy villains were adapted to the changing world culture. Villains in the form of gangsters of the Thirties (epitomized by Gould's fictional interpretation of Al Capone, Big Boy) were updated in the Forties to include assassins and war criminals—the rogues of the new era. There were even Nazi sympathizers like Black Pearl (1940), B-B Eyes (1942), Pruneface (aka Boche, 1942), Mrs. Pruneface (1943), and Brow (1944). (Karpse, a poison gas dealer to hostile nations, had appeared as a war criminal as early as 1938.) *Tracy* storylines moved faster, dangers intensified, and the rogues became even more fantastic and outrageous. Further, Gould's style and imagery were even crisper and cleaner than they had been before. Lines were sharper; death seemed even colder. His colorful imagination augmented the colorful reality effectively, and because of this, *Dick Tracy* was able to keep the readers' interest even with the increasingly ominous front page news of a growing global conflict. Gould was often asked why Dick Tracy did not enlist in the armed forces when it appeared that everyone else had (including Skeezix of Frank King's *Gasoline Alley*). He replied that somebody had to stay home and fight the crime here.[33]

Perils of Water and Ice

The year 1940 brought the villainous Jerome Trohs ("short" spelled backwards; Trohs was a midget) and Mama, Yogee Yama, Black Pearl, and others. More than ever before, *Tracy* rogues were deriving their names from their invented physiognomies. Violence in Gould's strip intensified in the beginning of the 1940s, as it did for the duration of the decade. But the violence we associate with *Dick Tracy* during this period was actually less frequent than we remember it to be. The violent act in *Tracy* could be intense, but this act usually appeared only once or twice in a 12 or 16 week episode, and only appeared for a day or two when it did occur. In May of 1940, the devilry of Jerome Trohs produces one such violent act. The midget

decides he is going to permanently cripple Dick Tracy's shooting hand. After capturing and chloroforming our hero, Jerome puts Tracy's right hand into a vise. Fortunately for sensitive readers, while the actual vise is shown, the mangled hand is only presented "on camera" after it is bandaged. Indeed this was a shockingly graphic incident for the comic page, even for the strip that debuted violence as a central theme. As might be expected, the damage to Tracy's hand is relatively short-lived, lasting only a few weeks of strips. Trohs was later scalded to death by his fickle accomplice, the amazon woman named "Mama." (Jerome is trapped in a shower cabinet when Mama fills the cabinet with scalding water from a hose.)

In September of that same year, Yogee Yama provides a death trap for Dick Tracy and the "Professor" in which the pair of good guys are left to slowly drown in a watery grave. Due to a bit of luck and Tracy's resourcefulness, the pair survives. It is important to note that the resourcefulness of good guys and bad guys alike is often rewarded in *Dick Tracy*. However, resourcefulness is also supplemented by luck—luck which is more often afforded good guys than bad guys. The depiction of water by means of closely spaced, wavy lines, as evidenced in the *Tracy* adventure from Sunday, September 8, 1940, became a hallmark of Gould's strip in the Forties. This artistic motif would pervade the decade, and would later become legendary in the episode with Brow and the Summer Sisters.

In 1941, Krome, Little Facy Finny, the Mole, and other grotesques made their ways into the *Dick Tracy* rogues gallery. On the Sunday page from February 16, 1941, Krome, a professional killer, escapes from a runaway snowplow that crashes through an ice-covered river. The final *Tracy* panel for that day shows Krome in a position Jack Nicholson would find himself in some forty years later in the role of Jack Torrance in Stanley Kubrick's movie adap-

Jerome Trohs—*Dick Tracy*, May 2, 3, and 4, 1940. Reprinted by permission: Tribune Media Services.

tation of Stephen King's novel *The Shining*. Weak from the chase and soaked with ice water, Krome "settles down into the snow bank, a sardonic smile on his lips. His eyes stare glassily. His skin grows white—"

The Art of Gangland Execution

July 23, 24, and 25 of the same year present some rather violent moments when two gang members "rub out" a third so that he (Micky Stanley in the sequence) cannot confess to the police. The two murderers dress up in drag and pose as visitors of Mr. Stanley, who lies wounded

and helpless in a hospital bed (see p. 88). The last panel of July 24 sets the stage for the violence as one of the disguised rogues levels his tommy gun on Micky Stanley. The first frame for July 25 (a silent frame) requires no words to get its point across. We feel the tommy gun, angled down into the stomach of Micky Stanley, reverberate as it pumps hot lead into the victim's prostrate body. Closely spaced fine lines illustrate the recoil of the gun with each exploding round of fire. This is strongly violent material, even in the context of early Forties America.

On the Sunday page of August 31, 1941, the notorious racketeer Little Face

The demise of Krome—*Dick Tracy,* February 16, 1941. Reprinted by permission: Tribune Media Services.

Opposite: Dick Tracy and the Professor—*Dick Tracy,* September 8, 1940. Reprinted by permission: Tribune Media Services.

Exit Micky Stanley—*Dick Tracy*, July 23, 24, and 25, 1941. Reprinted by permission: Tribune Media Services.

Finny, is all but frozen to death in a meat locker, until the enterprising Charley Yemon ("money" spelled backwards) decides to make Finny pay "a couple of grand" for the aid of a doctor. Watch out Yemon! The fastest way in *Dick Tracy* to be terminated as a character is to cross both the good guys and the bad guys. Charley Yemon discovers this fact the hard way when Finny later turns the tables on him.

The year 1941 also brought the emergence of the infamous rogue named the Mole. Mole lives underground, or at least that is where he prefers to live, and like his rodent namesake likes to tunnel and dig. Particularly in the snout, Mole physically resembles the actual animal. The daily *Tracy* strips from November 28 and 29 show the Mole in his underground lair. Mole, like Stooge Viller of Thirties *Dick Tracy*, was one of the few rogues in Gould's comic strip not terminated at the end of his initial escapade.

Death as Allegory I: The Case of B-B Eyes

B-B Eyes, Tiger Lilly, and Pruneface were Gould's most noteworthy contributions to *Dick Tracy*'s rogues' gallery in 1942, but there were other characters—

Little Face Finny—*Dick Tracy*, **August 31, 1941. Reprinted by permission: Tribune Media Services.**

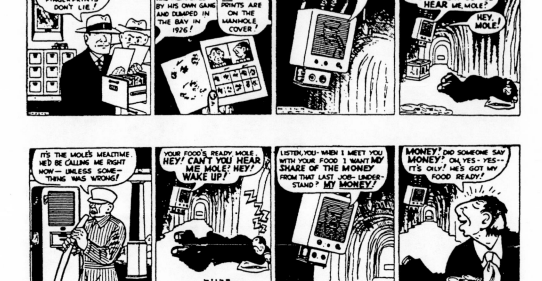

Mole—*Dick Tracy*, **November 28 and 29, 1941. Reprinted by permission: Tribune Media Services.**

good and bad alike—who debuted that year who had a substantial impact on the ongoing storyline. Most significant of these others was the troublesome Debby Thorndike, who, despite her good intentions, seemed to make Dick Tracy's days of early 1942 something of an ordeal. Debby's naïveté was a source of problems and caused her to fall into bad company. On the Sunday page of January 4, 1942, Dick Tracy and his audience learned of Miss Thorndike and her troubles. On the Sunday page of February 8, we see a bedridden Tracy suffering the consequences of his acquaintance with Debby—his broken leg at the hands of the "spit-fire debutante" confines him to a hospital bed. By Sunday, February 22, 1942, the troubles with Debby reach epic proportions as Tracy finds himself trapped with the girl in an old abandoned house that the vicious B-B Eyes has rigged to explode. The boiler is stoked up so it will explode, and Tracy is in danger of scalding to death or suffocating—a death trap similar to that employed in the 1990 Warren Beatty motion

picture. Once again, it looks like the end of the master sleuth—until Debby's Aunt Bea finds them in the house.

In the daily strip from April 18, the villainous B-B Eyes meets his demise in a most symbolic fashion. He is dumped into a watery grave with the rest of the refuse from a garbage scow. That day, April 18, society had disposed of two forms of refuse which were remarkably similar. Gould was indeed capable of profound subtext.

More Perils with Water and Ice

Boche, that Nazi criminal who was commonly known as "Pruneface" since his face was severely wrinkled like the surface of a dried plum, encountered his own death in early February 1943. Entrapped by Dick Tracy and associates in an old house with no heat—the thermostat is broken—and clothed only in pajamas, Pruneface does not last long in four degree weather. The manhunt was at last over, and the demise of Pruneface was most

Debby—*Dick Tracy*, **January 4, 1942. Reprinted by permission: Tribune Media Services.**

Debby—*Dick Tracy*, February 8, 1942. Reprinted by permission: Tribune Media Services.

B-B Eyes—*Dick Tracy*, **February 22, 1942. Reprinted by permission: Tribune Media Services.**

The demise of B-B Eyes—*Dick Tracy*, April 16, 17, and 18, 1942. Reprinted by permission: Tribune Media Services.

satisfying to readers. Boche had been calculating, vicious, and remorseless throughout the course of his tenure in Dick Tracy's world, at one time trying to kill the detective hero with lethal gas pellets. Remember that Axis villain Karpse had dealt in poison gas in *Dick Tracy* in 1938. Due to Hitler's use of such weaponry for mass execution of individuals in his interment camps, people of the period were hypersensitive to this particular technique of war. Yet once again, Gould and Tracy settled their score with the heinous rogue by employing the element of water and its

different manifestations as tools of retribution.

The following year, 1943, may have been *Dick Tracy*'s finest. Along with a colorful array of rogues which included 88 Keyes (a murderous, keyboard-tickling swindler who is much more ruthless than the 1990 Warren Beatty film portrays him) and Mrs. Pruneface (the hideous amazon wife of Nazi war criminal Pruneface, Tracy's victim of 1942), *Tracy*'s most famous rogue of all time, Flattop, emerged to terrorize the detective hero. Physical grotesqueness of villains and graphic depiction of violence were at all-time highs in 1943. More than ever before, people associated violence with *Dick Tracy.* Yet, while Gould used shockingly violent, graphic scenes in *Tracy* in 1943, these appeared far less frequently than people remember. Usually for each two- or three-month episode there were only a couple of really violent scenes, and these lasted only for a few days.

The heightened violence in *Dick Tracy* paralleled the escalated fighting in the European and Pacific theaters of World War II. Violence was large-scale in reality and in the comic strip world of Dick Tracy; it was an evil initially employed by villains — international and regional alike — that was often turned on its perpetrators to produce justice and thus sustain the status quo. Further, rogues that dramatically confronted the social order of Dick Tracy's domain during the years of America's involvement in World War II (about 1942 to 1945) were likewise dramatically stopped and punished. Characters like Mrs. Pruneface and Flattop took violence and sadism to new heights, or lows. And Dick Tracy responded with equal force.

Nazi Villainess: The Case of Mrs. Pruneface

One such graphic scene took place in August of 1943. *Life* magazine deemed it the "narrowest escape of Dick Tracy's career."[34] Seeking revenge on Tracy for the death of her husband, Mrs. Pruneface devises a devilishly clever and insidiously horrible end for Tracy. Having chained Tracy to the floor, Mrs. Pruneface and her henchman, Emil, place two melting blocks of ice on each side of the detective. (Tracy and the ice blocks are positioned in front of a hot oven which will accelerate the melting process.) On top of these they place a board with a spike driven through it. The spike is positioned directly over

Tracy's heart, and a heavy refrigerator rests on top of the spiked board. Once again, it looks like the end for our hero, and as the next few August days unfold in *Dick Tracy,* the ice gets smaller and smaller, and the spike inches closer and closer to Tracy's heart.

Since Dick Tracy is still combating crime today, we know that he somehow escaped this horrible peril. Tracy bounces on the floor enough to jar the ice over the necessary few inches to save his life. The spike does scratch his skin and rip his shirt. Mrs. Pruneface was one of Gould's most intense and menacing creations. She carried and liberally used a bullwhip, and her large-boned frame was topped by a skull-like face — she was hideously ugly. Mrs. Pruneface was bent on revenge, and she was bent on evil — she fulfilled the essential characteristics of the hated Nazi stereotype of the time.

On May 9, 1944, the *New York Daily News* carried an article by Al Binder and Kermit Jaediker which to this day illustrates the significance of the Mrs. Pruneface sequence to world society at that time. The article tells of a letter sent from the warfront by seven soldiers stationed in Italy. The letter, signed by Sergeant Aldo F. Tersillo and his colleagues, began:

> It is with the deepest regret that I am forced to submit a letter of this nature to you.
>
> We feel that it is not too much for you to ask of us to leave our families and dear friends in the U.S.A., to come over here to settle arguments of a handful of the moneyed men of the world; we think you have carried it entirely too far when you fail to keep us informed on the happiness and whereabouts of Dick Tracy and Smilin' Jack.
>
> The last we knew of poor old Tracy, he was staked to the floor under a huge ice-box supported by two cakes of ice. To top it off, he was in front of an oven which was heated to a high degree.
>
> What on earth happened to him?

88 Keyes—*Dick Tracy*, June 13, 1943. Reprinted by permission: Tribune Media Services.

Mrs. Pruneface—*Dick Tracy*, July 18, 1943. Reprinted by permission: Tribune Media Services.

In response, the *Daily News* sent back issues of the Sunday comic section from August 8, 1943, to what was then the present (May 1944).[35] Apparently news of Dick Tracy's exploits was in great demand, as were the latest baseball scores and standings of the day.

The Most Famous Rogue of All

Flattop was also a product of the war years, and he illustrated Gould's fertile imagination and ability to exploit these years in his fantastic world of Dick Tracy. "At a time when most villains expired from

The most insidious death trap of all — *Dick Tracy*, July 18, 1943. Reprinted by permission: Tribune Media Services.

the strip in 12 weeks, Flattop ran Tracy ragged for 5 months."[36] Max Collins notes that Flattop got his name from aircraft carriers of the period known as "flattops," and that Flattop was, as the fictitious Big Boy represented the real-life Al Capone and Boris Arson was reflective of John Dillinger, Gould's rendition of Pretty Boy Floyd.[37] Collins point out that Flattop, like Floyd and Gould himself, was from the Cookson Hills of Oklahoma. As with many previous *Tracy* rogues, Flattop's name reflected his physiognomy, as is evidenced in his debut in *Dick Tracy* on Christmas Day 1943. Just two weeks later in January 1944, we find Flattop at work attempting to eliminate Tracy. Flattop ushered in a new era for *Dick Tracy*'s rogues' gallery. In the 1930s, the rise in criminal activities was in several ways a direct result of hard economic times and restrictions imposed by the Volstead Act. For example, new markets emerged for illegally acquired goods such as liquor. During World War II, other commodities in short supply or

limited by rationing were provided by illegal business endeavors. These included food, rubber, metal, and gasoline. Criminals changed with the changing illegal market. The "big boy" mobster was replaced by the black marketeer and hit man embodied in Gould's Flattop.

Flattop was especially violent; bullets seemed to fly more frequently during his reign of terror than in any period before or since in *Dick Tracy*. He was also cold and calculating. But his demise was remarkably unnotable. Gould once again instituted the peril of water (or ice) motif by wedging Flattop between the braces beneath an old ship, where he is held fast under the water.

Death as Allegory II: The Case of Brow

As Flattop shoots his way into 1944, the action continues at a pace like that of a runaway train. On March 3, a man is

Meet Flattop—*Dick Tracy*, December 25 and 26, 1943. Reprinted by permission: Tribune Media Services.

Flattop and Tracy—*Dick Tracy*, January 15 and 17, 1944. Reprinted by permission: Tribune Media Services.

burned to death. Soon after, rogues such as (the) Brow, Shaky, and Snowflake appear, as do an array of innocents and victims including Vitamin Flintheart (a fantasy portrayal of John Barrymore), the Summer Sisters, and Gravel Gertie. Perhaps more than any other *Dick Tracy* rogue, the Brow emerged to rival Flattop for the title of most famous *Tracy* villain. Unfortunately, the 1990 smash *Dick Tracy* movie does not

More violence—*Dick Tracy*, March 3, 1944. Reprinted by permission: Tribune Media Services.

develop this character in any detail, and he is eliminated in the film's opening minutes.

The story of the Brow, the Summer Sisters, and Gravel Gertie may well have been the best single story of *Dick Tracy* and Chester Gould. This episode has been cited by several individuals, including Gould himself, as being one of their favorite *Tracy* stories. For this sequence, Gould developed a new and inventive graphic violence in the form of the Brow's spike machine. With this machine, depicted in the *Tracy* strips from June and July 1944, the Brow coerces the Summer Sisters into doing some of his dirty work. By July 10, the sisters get a moment of revenge on the Brow as he becomes entrapped in his own creation. The sharp spikes pierce his wrinkled brow and produce dark blood. But the Summer Sisters' revenge is short-lived.

The Brow escapes his own instrument of mutilation and death, and on July 31 he sends the two girls to a watery grave. Neither markedly good nor bad, the sisters become victims of the conflict between the two opposing forces. It takes three days for the sisters to drown in the sinking cab in which they are entrapped by the Brow. Gould's imagery here is shockingly realistic. One can feel the last gasps of air fleeting from the girls' lungs only to be replaced by algae-laden water. It is all very tragic, but it illustrates that in the world of *Dick Tracy* things are literally and figuratively black and white. There is no room for compromise.

The fact that Brow is a Nazi who, among other things, seeks to destroy the United States is seemingly downplayed throughout the course of the story. Events regarding the Summer Sisters and then Gravel Gertie take center stage throughout much of the Brow story. However, particularly at the beginning and end of the episode, Brow's Nazi sympathies become evident. With the demise of Brow, Gould waxed poetic more than he ever had before or after. Tracy flings a heavy glass inkwell at Brow and knocks him out a fifth or sixth floor window. The Brow, a foreign agent and espionage leader, is impaled by a flagpole which flies a U.S. flag.

The inkwell may very well be symbolic of Chester Gould's perceived control over his world of the comic strip. Gould in the guise of Dick Tracy and Gould himself may both have been reacting to the vile rogue, and the inkwell representing Gould himself may have been the artist/writer's contribution to the Brow's demise. Maybe not. However, the use of the inkwell as a weapon in this segment deserves careful consideration, scrutiny, and analysis for possibly profound subtext. Likewise, the conspicuous mention of the plaque with the honor roll of American men in service attached to the flagpole adds to the intensity of the literal and symbolic impaling of the war criminal. Once again, Gould's attention to detail is admirable and most effective.

The demise of Flattop—*Dick Tracy*, May 14, 1944. Reprinted by permission: Tribune Media Services.

The Summer Sisters and Vitamin Flintheart—*Dick Tracy*, June 4, 1944. Reprinted by permission: Tribune Media Services.

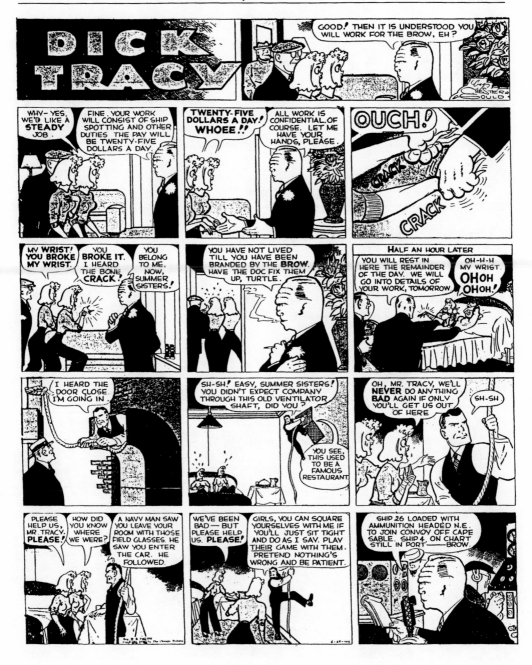

Brow and the Summer Sisters—*Dick Tracy*, **June 25, 1944. Reprinted by permission: Tribune Media Services.**

Brow—*Dick Tracy*, June 29 and 30; July 2 and 3, 1944. Reprinted by permission: Tribune Media Services.

Water and Ice Again; Increasingly Complex Continuities

Shaky was one of the all-time great rogues of *Dick Tracy* that appeared in the 1940s—specifically September 1944 to January 1945. Shaky suffered from an intense nervous condition which often gave him profound physical agitations. This Gould grotesque was also named

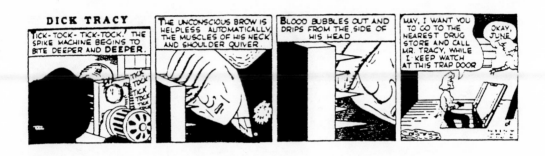

Brow—*Dick Tracy*, July 10, 11, and 12, 1944. Reprinted by permission: Tribune Media Services.

for the scams or shakedowns in which he was involved. Shaky died in a most insidious fashion in that, like Krome of 1941, he was frozen alive. Krome's demise was quite a bit more peaceful than Shaky's, however. In an attempt to escape Dick Tracy, Shaky hides in a hole in an old pier. Freezing ice breakers fatally trap him as he hides.

At about the time the Shaky sequence was playing in *Dick Tracy*, Chester Gould began to create increasingly complex continuities. The Shaky story would dovetail with the stories of Snowflake Falls, Vita-

min Flintheart, B.O. Plenty, Gravel Gertie, and Breathless Mahoney. Gould was beginning to integrate characters and episodes with a sophistication that would mark the 1950s *Tracy* continuities.

Beautiful and Deadly: Breathless Mahoney

Shortly after Shaky's death in January 1945, we learned that the deceased had a stepdaughter. The girl is an alluring young blonde who bears a striking resemblance

Death of the Summer Sisters—*Dick Tracy*, July 31; August 1 and 2, 1944. Reprinted by permission: Tribune Media Services.

to real-life movie goddess Veronica Lake. The continuity between stories is enhanced when Breathless discovers the skeletal remains of Shaky near the waterfront. We learn that Breathless is money-hungry, and that she will do everything necessary to get what she wants—even murder. Enter the neither markedly good nor evil B.O. (Bob Oscar) Plenty. Plenty is a rough-around-the-edges hillbilly type reminiscent of some of the folks Gould knew as a child in Oklahoma, and he is bent on getting the money which Breathless possesses. The conflict between the physically beautiful villainess and the unwashed country bumpkin makes for entertaining reading. Dick Tracy's role in this sequence is minimal, as the conflict between Breathless and B.O. dominates the comic strip's storyline. The episode is fast-moving, based heavily on coincidence, and full of minor leaps in logic—though minor incongruities in logic seemed to appear in Gould's *Dick Tracy* almost from the start. These inconsistencies were due primarily to the nature of the serial presentation of stories on a daily basis, and the fact that Gould did not plot the stories all the

Brow and Gravel Gertie—*Dick Tracy*, September 10, 1944. Reprinted by permission: Tribune Media Services.

way through since he liked the challenge of daily invention. Gould liked to rely on his instincts and on readers' daily anticipations of new developments in the comic strip. On her deathbed in the August 25, 1946, installment of *Tracy*, Breathless does partially redeem herself when she scrawls a final note from her hospital room. It reads, "Give him [B.O. Plenty] another chance. I forgive him."

The demise of Brow—*Dick Tracy*, September 24, 1944. Reprinted by permission: Tribune Media Services.

Comedy Relief: Enter B.O. Plenty

The most famous and enduring character to emerge in *Dick Tracy* in 1945 was not a rogue of the sort usually equated with the comic. Instead, B.O. Plenty was a misguided, somewhat lovable tramp who, thanks to his friends Dick Tracy, Diet Smith (who first appeared in 1946), and Gravel Gertie (from 1944), evolved into an upstanding citizen of Dick Tracy's world. He conversed in a hillbilly-like slang and

Shaky, Snowflake, and Vitamin Flintheart—*Dick Tracy*, **November 26, 1944. Reprinted by permission: Tribune Media Services.**

loved to chew tobacco. Gould said in later years that B.O. was one of his favorite creations, second only to Dick Tracy himself. On the March 31, 1946, Sunday page, B.O. moves into the new home that Diet Smith has given him, and hears the squeaky sing-ing of Gravel Gertie from a neighboring farmhouse. (Gertie, as we remember, had appeared as early as 1944 when she nursed Brow, who had been caught in his own spike machine.) Little does B.O. Plenty know that only months later, Gertie will

Breathless Mahoney—*Dick Tracy*, May 17, 1945. Reprinted by permission: Tribune Media Services.

Breathless Mahoney and B.O. Plenty—*Dick Tracy*, July 27 and 28, 1945. Reprinted by permission: Tribune Media Services.

become his bride. The escapades of B.O. Plenty and Gravel Gertie became a sort of ongoing comic relief for the larger *Dick Tracy* story. When B.O. and Gravel were married on August 18, 1946, they were not without presents and good wishes. *Newsweek* carried an article about the blessed event. According to the article, more than 200 presents arrived at the offices of the *Chicago Tribune*. These included a washrag, a gold wedding ring, soap, razors, and plugs of chewing tobacco. A similar generosity was experienced at the *New York Daily News*—a swanky hotel offered a bridal suite for the honeymooning couple. Gould said that he would put all the

presents into a special collection—the exception was the tobacco, which was to go to his tobacco-chewing assistant. "As to whether he'd spring the bridegroom (who spent the wedding night in the clink), again and for all time, Gould assured anxious fans aplenty: "Why shore," he said.[38] During the last few days of May 1948, Sparkle Plenty was born to B.O. and Gravel. "Her dazzling eyes and hip-length blonde hair immediately won the hearts of *Dick Tracy*'s 26 million readers."[39]

The *Tracy* rogues of the second half of the Forties were somewhat anticlimactic after the likes of Flattop, the Brow, and associates, but villains and villainesses such as Breathless Mahoney (1945), Itchy Oliver (1945), Shoulders (1946), Gargles (1946), Influence (1946), Coffyhead (1947), Mumbles (1947), Mrs. Volts (1948), Heels Beals (1948), Big Frost (1948), Pear Shape (1949), and Sketch Paree (1949) provided plenty of action for Dick Tracy in the postwar years. Mahoney, Influence, and Mumbles were among the most popular rogues of all time, with Influence and Mumbles involved in captivating storylines in which Tracy played a secondary role since the rogues themselves were so entertaining. Influence utilized special optical lenses which resemble modern-day contact lenses to hypnotize people into doing his bidding. (Influence worked his devilry on Vitamin Flintheart, as well as on others.) Mumbles was an inarticulate singer and speaker who utilized his front as leader of the Mumbles Quartette to perpetrate his evildoings.

More Comedy Relief:
Enter Sam Catchem

In 1948, Sam Catchem was introduced into the strip as a new partner for Tracy—Pat Patton had by this time been moved to the background of the storylines since he now replaced Brandon as chief. As Jay Maeder notes in his insightful and entertaining book, *Dick Tracy: The Official Biography,* Sam Catchem was based on Chester Gould's long-time friend, agent, and negotiator Al Lowenthal. Lowenthal "had a knobby nose and a face full of freckles and . . . was, in the late 1940s, nudging his client to incorporate 'a Jewish character' into the strip."[40] Maeder notes that this stereotype was never really played up in *Dick Tracy,* but that Catchem did often cry "Oi yi" and carry salami sandwiches in his coat pockets. Again, Maeder is authoritative on the origins and roles of Sam Catchem in *Tracy.* It should be further noted that Catchem was quite hu-

morous in appearance, and that his appearance was augmented by a sharp tongue which spewed forth a variety of witty wisecracks. He was much more humorous than the oft bumbling Patton— especially from 1948 on when Patton acquired the stern and stoic qualities often associated with the position of chief of police. Catchem did look a great deal like the up-and-coming children's television star, marionette Howdy Doody. (Howdy first appeared on television December 27, 1947.)

The Marriage of Dick Tracy and Tess Trueheart

In 1949, after 17 years of courtship and engagement, Dick Tracy finally married Tess Trueheart. The marriage was a long time coming. We remember the turmoils of the happy couple's early courtship and the indecisiveness of Tracy, in particular. The marriage occurred "off stage" and was announced in the Christmas Sunday page of December 25, 1949. Junior, Sam Catchem, and Pat Patton are the family members who are on hand for the announcement—Patton, who has known Tracy longer than anyone else in this episode, faints. Christmas strips have always been special events in *Dick Tracy.* This was one of the most memorable of all such strips. Against a backdrop of years of crimefighting and violence which made the strip famous, this quiet announcement of marriage may have been one of the most profound moments of the comic's history.

The marriage of Dick Tracy and Tess Trueheart at Christmastime was fitting. Chester Gould was rewarding the newspaper comics' most famous couple with one of life's most precious gifts—the gift of marriage, that socially prescribed recognition and consummation of a relationship based on true love, uncompromised trust, and unending respect. Gould also rewarded

Influence—*Dick Tracy*, February 8, 1947. Reprinted by permission: Tribune Media Services.

An announcement of marriage—*Dick Tracy,* **December 25, 1949. Reprinted by permission: Tribune Media Services.**

the pair with a house that Tracy bought Tess as a surprise wedding gift. The Christmas holidays of 1949 brought to fruition the American dream of the reward of hard work, patient waiting, saving, honesty, and moral goodness. Americans never tire of such rewards. Chester Gould had also provided a Christmas gift to his loyal readers in the marriage of the newspaper comics' most desirable and eligible flatfoot to the comics' loveliest lady.

The Sunday page from December 25, 1949, also includes the Crimestoppers Textbook, a feature of *Dick Tracy* that at this time was only a few months old. Junior and the Crime Stoppers (a club formed by Junior in April 1947) are not to be confused with the Crimestoppers Textbook which began as a regular feature of Chester Gould's *Dick Tracy* on Sunday, September 11, 1949.[41] Jay Maeder discusses the origin and early exploits of Junior and the Crime Stoppers in his book *Dick Tracy: The Official Biography*, one of the finest works of *Dick Tracy* scholarship.[42] The author discusses parallels between Junior and the Crime Stoppers and popular real-life boys' organizations like Sir Robert S.S. Baden-Powell's Boy Scouts, and parallels to other fictional children's groups of the comics like Little Orphan Annie's Junior Commando organization, and such groups as the Newsboy Legion and the Boy Commandos.

In regard to the significance of Junior and the Crime Stoppers as a club formed at the end of World War II, there is another important consideration. By 1947, *Dick Tracy* on radio was a dozen years old, had traversed more than one network, and was still a very popular series of the airwaves. (See Chapter 6.) Part of the popular appeal of *Tracy* on radio is attributable to Junior's role as narrator and officer of the Dick Tracy Secret Service Patrol Meetings. The radio programs which featured Junior and the meetings of the Dick Tracy Secret Service Patrol were extensions of Gould's comic strip. Very likely also, the introduction of Junior's Crime Stoppers

into the *Dick Tracy* newspaper comic strips of 1947 was Gould's tribute to and extension of the then highly popular *Dick Tracy* radio programs which featured Junior. Boys' clubs were immensely popular in both fact and fiction.

The Crimestoppers Textbook was a product of the Crime Stoppers, and this element of *Dick Tracy* has remained a crucial part of the comic strip long after Junior's boys organization faded into obscurity. (Originally, the Textbook was conceived as a scrapbook compiled by the Crime Stoppers; it is now the sole remaining legacy of the fictional club.) The Crimestoppers Textbook is still part of *Dick Tracy*; Max Collins and Dick Locher have kept Gould's invention intact, though they have sometimes replaced it with other features like Dick Tracy's Rogues' Gallery. In recent years, Barbara Collins (wife of Max Collins) has written the feature for the Sunday pages.

Synonymous with *Tracy* since 1949, the Textbook provides primarily practical and useful tips regarding personal safety, detection of crime, and protection of private property. The feature has also, on occasion, provided case history from true crimes. In a somewhat varied form, the Crimestoppers Textbook would later serve as a framing device for the *Dick Tracy* animated cartoons which aired on television between 1960 and 1962. (See Chapter 6.)

The Fifties

Paranoia, SF Movies, and Rock 'n' Roll

The Cold War was raging, invasion from Communists and outer-space aliens appeared inevitable, and a general state of paranoia permeated the social conscious-

ness as the Forties melted, though not nuclearly, into the Fifties. Science fiction and horror movies presented themes of invasion and showcased abominations of nature usually created by science gone wild. But these abominations of nature represented something much more culturally significant. *The Thing (From Another World)* (1951), *The Day the Earth Stood Still* (1951), and *Invasion of the Body Snatchers* (1956) were movies which reflected sentiments of the period and which were fraught with a subtext of fear. The study of psychology and the comic book were both misrepresented and misunderstood with the publication of Dr. Frederic Wertham's infamous book, *Seduction of the Innocent* (1954), and, coupled with various and sundry events, lead to the Comics Code controversy — a scandal which eventually reached Congress. A new breed of popular music called rock 'n' roll, derived from the heritages of Negro spirituals, the blues, folk music, and country music, was in its infancy. Pulp magazines were by now largely replaced with paperback books, and a new medium called television hit the market as an extension of story radio.

With the emergence of several new popular media and popular entertainment forms, social criticism of the same, and shifts in popular values and beliefs, Chester Gould was once again faced with the problem of adjusting the content in *Dick Tracy* so that it paralleled changes in American culture. The inventional elements of *Tracy,* the rogues and their crimes, evolved in character and complexity with the changing social sentiment, and thus kept Gould's comic strip relevant to his readership. In the Fifties, *Dick Tracy* stories remained captivating and interesting, though they were already beginning to show the effects of increasingly smaller comic strip sizes which were now part of all newspapers. "The syndicate decreed that the bottom portion of dailies should be expendable to allow certain newspaper clients to shave the strips and fit more on a page."[43] It was also becoming difficult, if not impossible, for Chester Gould to top some of the rogues and storylines he had generated in the preceding decade. In fact, the Forties episodes involving Pruneface, the Brow, and Flattop

would prove to be some of Gould's all-time finest. However, the crafty comic strip master extended the families of some of his earlier, very famous characters — good and bad alike — and adeptly expanded individual characters and synthesized them more significantly into the world of Dick Tracy. And *Tracy* in the Fifties provided continuities that were probably smoother and more logical than ever before. The pace of Gould's stories slowed a bit, which was not necessarily good or bad but simply different.

Chester Gould's strength as craftsman and artist was still firmly entrenched in his ability to tell an enthralling story and to relate a meaningful morality play; this strength was seen more than ever in complexities of storylines and character types, and it was increasingly evident in his drawing. For those enthralled with Gould's *Dick Tracy* in the Thirties, the Forties provided no disappointments. The writer/artist had matured and improved upon that which was already intrinsically and aesthetically art. In short, the crucial elements associated with *Dick Tracy* (i.e. good storytelling, meaningful allegory, complex and compelling characters, and mastery of pen and ink drawing) were all in place. For Chester Gould and *Dick Tracy,* the Fifties were likewise an era of stability and positive expansion upon success already established in the comic strip.

Regarding character types, talented *Tracy* fan and scholar Matt Masterson writes, "When I asked Chet Gould where he got the names for some of his characters, he told me he used to ride the train from his home in Woodstock, Illinois, to his studio in Chicago and sketch various people he observed on the train. He would exaggerate upon certain features or characteristics. The name would follow. . . ."[44] Like *Dick Tracy* of the Thirties and Forties, *Dick Tracy* of the Fifties adopted some very specific and unique themes, plots, and motifs. The innovations (let us deem them Caweltian inventions) tell us something about Chester Gould's convictions and beliefs, and something about social history of the era.

The Portrayal of Adolescents and Sex

As *Dick Tracy* entered its third decade, it did start to reveal some further, even more radical philosophies of its creator—again, this was neither good nor bad but simply a reflection of popular sentiment and of Gould's vision of the world. More than ever before or since, the villains in *Tracy* were adolescents and young adults, and more than ever before Gould questioned the preoccupations of the younger set—love and sex and the then current expressions of the same, including popular music. Perhaps the biggest single theme that evolved from the continuities of the Fifties was a distrust of the new and unconventional.

Extended Families and Media Villains

In 1950, Dick Tracy faced Wormy, Blowtop, and T.V. Wiggles. The complexion of Wormy's face was ridden with deep, wavey trenches; he physically resembled Pruneface. With the emergence of Blowtop (Flattop's brother), the Gouldian soap opera became even more intricate. Flattop had been acclaimed as *Dick Tracy's* most famous of all rogues, a figure who certainly could not be topped in popularity, yet this did not preclude creating a character who might approach Flattop's reprehensible charisma. In 1947, Gould had added Sparkle Plenty to the world of Dick Tracy in general, and to the family of B.O. and Gravel Plenty in specific, thus foreshadowing a trend toward extended families.

Blowtop, though somewhat renowed at the time as Flattop's brother, remains one of the great *Tracy* treasures as yet undiscovered by many. Chester Gould's visual depiction of the character was exceptional. As his name suggests, Blowtop possesses an extremely volatile temperment. He is every bit as mean, cold, calculating, and ruthless as was his kin. Debuting on March 29, 1950, Blowtop wastes no time in seeking revenge on our detective hero for the death of his brother, Flattop, and burns Dick Tracy's home to the ground. Perhaps it is his despicable nature that makes his stay in *Dick Tracy* seem very suspenseful and long. The story of Blowtop is one of Gould's all-time most captivating narratives. The reader really cannot wait until the blowhard gets his just deserts.

The story of T.V. Wiggles, that villain of Max Collins' 1992 novel *Dick Tracy Meets His Match*, is one of the first of the longer continuities that would characterize Gould's *Tracy* in the Fifties. Wiggles, like Blowtop, is absolutely despicable, featuring no apparent redeeming qualities of moral pulchritude. Several characters are exploited by the villain before he is terminated. His is an interesting, cruel, almost perverse story. Before he is stopped, Wiggles physically abuses Sparkle Plenty, Vitamin Flintheart, Dick Tracy, and B.O. Plenty. He cripples and uncripples Sparkle, physically beats Flintheart and Tracy on several occasions, and shoots B.O.

Wiggles is a big-time television mogul (television generally reaching mass audiences in 1948) who likes to manipulate everything and everyone and who feels that he is not accountable to anyone.

Besides providing a vicious killer and captivating storyline, the saga of T.V. Wiggles does provide a very poignant moment near its end. B.O. Plenty is hospitalized, and little hope is left for his recovery. All earthly options have been exhausted. In a moving scene from November 21, 1951, Dick Tracy calls on the ultimate redeemer as he prays over the prostrate, bedridden form of B.O. Tracy states, "His [B.O.'s] simple faith and homely, direct way stand out

Blowtop, Flattop's brother — *Dick Tracy*, April 4, 1950. Reprinted by permission: Tribune Media Services.

like a beacon in these confused days." The motif of praying over the hospital bed of the beloved would be utilized by Gould and his successors in years that followed.

At the end of 1950, December 20 to be exact, Dr. Plain debuted in *Dick Tracy*. The good doctor was not so morally good in terms of character. What he was good at was the use of pyrotechnics to perpetrate a variety of arsonous and murderous activities. Dr. Plain invented an artificial arm that mechanically started fires and that worked on the principle of a cigar lighter. But Dr. Plain's tenure in *Dick Tracy*, which ended by early February 1951, was conspicuously short considering the lengths of time his immediate predecessors, Blowtop and T.V. Wiggles, menaced Dick Tracy.

Empty Williams first appeared in *Dick Tracy* on February 6, 1951. Thinking he and his underlings are hijacking a truckload of valuable furs, Williams later discovers that his rather dense assistants grabbed the wrong truck and stole 120,000 diapers instead. Empty has acquired his name because he is missing the back part of his skull due to a bungled brain operation. The Empty Williams sequence sets up and reinforces two themes. First, with Sparkle Plenty's birth in the spring of 1947 and the subsequent theft of diapers, thoughts of babies were foremost on *Tracy* readers' minds. Second, with the physical deformity of Williams, Gould was reminding his audience that in *Dick Tracy* physical deformity often is symptomatic

of, prescriptive of, or representative of mental and social nonconformity. Gould postulated, perhaps partly from the heart and perhaps partly for the sole purpose of story convention, that there were reasons why people became or turned antisocial and thus evil. The Crewy Lou story, a classic from later in the *Tracy* canon, illustrates the credence Gould gave to theories of environmental determinism.

Enter Miss Bonnie Braids

On May 4, 1951, Tess presented Dick Tracy with a baby daughter. The Sunday page from May 20, 1951, related the story of Bonny (later Bonnie) Braids' name. Two days later, the teenaged Crewy Lou and Sphinx made their initial appearance in the comic strip. As the tale unwinds through the summer and autumn of 1951, Crewy Lou poses as a baby photographer in order to obtain access to private homes and then rob them. Sphinx is Lou's mute accomplice—he once fixed some poison for a pal and then accidentally drank it himself. Crewy Lou targets Tracy's house for robbery, and ultimately ends up stealing Tracy's car with Bonnie Braids in it. Suspense builds for weeks as Tracy and friends race against time to find and save the infant. Ultimately, Bonnie Braids is saved, and Crewy Lou blindly falls from a ranger's tower to her death some sixty-five feet below after being tear-gassed.

This particular sequence is one of the

all-time most famous from *Dick Tracy*, and like many of Gould's stories does contain some leaps in logic and contradictions due to the long, ongoing format of the comic strip. Some of the material and plotting, for example, seem added from thin air. Perhaps the most glaring incongruity in the Crewy Lou sequence is the moment when Tess and Bonnie are returning from a month-long vacation for which we never saw them leave. These kinds of errors had been part of *Tracy* since the start. However, given the nature of the story strip medium, Gould's techniques for plotting (see Chapter 5), and the overall genius of this continuity in retrospect, these kinds of errors in logic seem forgivable. Max Allan Collins writes about the Crewy Lou story:

> A few months before the beginning of this continuity, Gould began drawing his originals smaller, reflecting the smaller size the strip was printed in most newspapers [paper shortages during the war opened the door to editors shrinking the publication size of comics]. Now somewhat limited visually, Gould poured on the steam where the stories themselves were concerned. Certainly this story—the first complete continuity of the shrunken-art period—demonstrates Gould flexing his every muscle as a writer.[45]

Spinner Record, a dealer in collectable records whose specialty was murder, debuted November 26, 1951, in *Dick Tracy*. He was both an adolescent and inextricably tied to the evils of the new popular media and entertainment forms. All indications point to the young man's involvement with progressive music as the cause of his departure from social mores.

But rock 'n' roll records were not the only things that adversely affected vulnerable adolescent minds. In a comparatively short (by Fifties standards) continuity about Dick Tracy, Jr.'s, blossoming relationship with one Miss Model Jones

(January 23 to March 27, 1952), Gould showed us that there can be other evils of environment. The evil in the story of Model is alcohol and the alcoholism to which Model's parents and hence entire family have fallen victim. Model's father, mother, and brother Larry are pathetic, abusive creatures. Larry is nothing more than a juvenile delinquent of the worst sort.

While this rather bleak subtext of the evils of alcohol misuse pervades the story of Model Jones, there is another highly important element of this particular sequence that needs to be addressed. We remember that Chester Gould was a genius at portraying so many aspects and facets of the human experience. We also remember that he was quite adept at engendering empathy from his readers for his characters, and that he was very talented at relating extremely poignant, passionate love stories—the most famous of which began in 1931 when we met both Dick Tracy and Tess Trueheart and were made privy to their intimate relationship. In the story of Model Jones, Gould likewise tears at the reader's heart. The story generated about the pure, honest love relationship between Junior and Model is sensitive, insightful, and profoundly sad. It makes the reader thrill with delight and cling to hope, and it makes the reader crash emotionally and despair. Model and Junior are victims of the cruelest game of all—a love relationship abruptly cut short. Chester Gould was a master at capturing the human experience; at protecting, celebrating, and reinforcing social morality; and at working magic with the deceptively limiting medium of the two-dimensional comic strip panel to capture intangible universals. For this reason alone, any minor incongruities in logic and sequencing are quickly dismissed. Among other things, Chester Gould was an expert of the love story.

The year 1952 witnessed the appear-

Opposite: **Empty Williams—*Dick Tracy*, April 22, 1951. Reprinted by permission: Tribune Media Services.**

ance of the adolescent, Frank Sinatra–like singer named Tonsils and a master criminal named Mr. Crime. Mr. Crime was a crime lord remarkably similar to some of those that would later appear in the James Bond novels of Ian Fleming. His hands-off approach to the perpetration of crime at its basest levels would later be seen in such Bond villains as Ernst Stavro Blofeld, Doctor No, Auric Goldfinger, Mr. Big, Hugo Drax, and others. (Fleming's first Bond novel, *Casino Royale,* appeared in 1954.) Mr. Crime and his man-killing barracuda, which Crime kept in his swimming pool, were still conducting business in *Dick Tracy* in January 1953.

More Relatives and Adolescents

In 1953 Odds Zonn and Pony and 3-D Magee appeared in *Dick Tracy;* each were part of Gould continuities for several months that year. Uncle Canhead, B.O. Plenty's brother and Sparkle Plenty's uncle, also enjoyed a long though bittersweet tenure in the comic strip. Gould's sequences were now consistently long, involved, ongoing affairs, and some characters—good and bad alike—lasted longer than others. By 1954, Alex the Timer (bomb expert for the Mole), Open-Mind Monty, and Dewdrop appeared as new additions to the *Tracy* rogues' gallery. Rughead, named for his rather overstated toupee, debuted at year's end and continued well into 1955.

The infamous and nefarious Mumbles, one of those rare famous *Dick Tracy* grotesques (like Stooge Viller from the Thirties and Mole from the Forties) who reappeared in the comic strip after his initial escapades and capture, was joined by George Ozone in 1955. The 467-pound murderer and generally unpleasant person named Oodles dominated Dick Tracy's detective efforts for a good part of the year, too. Nothing Yonson, so named because his facial features were almost nonexistent,

and Joe Period also appeared. Yonson was a throwback to Little Face Finny of the Forties. Joe Period, an Elvis Presley type (and in this case the parallel is negative, not positive), was another of Gould's spoiled, rebellious juvenile delinquents of the Fifties. Joe later teamed up with Flattop, Jr., and was around well into 1956.

Also in 1955 came the debut of Lizz, a photographer turned policewoman. Lizz was rumored to be one of Gould's favorite creations, and assuredly was one of his readers' favorites also. Lizz represented the women cops common to police departments of the Fifties. She was progressive, hard-working, intelligent, compassionate, beautiful, and tough. As years have gone by, Lizz has had a number of extended sequences centering on her role in *Dick Tracy* as a policewoman.

More Police Procedure

Chester Gould and *Dick Tracy* never lost sight of the importance of accurate and up-to-the-minute depiction of real life police procedure to their story comic strip. The Sunday page from August 7, 1955, served to remind readers of the importance of such procedure, though regular readers of the Sunday pages were generally reminded of such techniques in the weekly Crimestoppers Textbook. After the Mumbles case and before the next case (regarding Oodles), Gould found some precious time to elaborate some real-life police procedure. As a comic strip artist, Gould was an expert at utilizing time—of maximizing the use of every panel and every written word; of maximizing the use of every daily installment of the comic strip, whether a part of a larger continuity or a transition between sequences. The August 7, 1955, Sunday page served as such a transition. On this day, Dick Tracy schools his junior officers about some specific procedures. Sam Catchem, talking

Opposite: **Bonny Braids**—*Dick Tracy,* **May 20, 1951. Reprinted by permission: Tribune Media Services.**

The return of Mumbles—*Dick Tracy*, May 8, 1955. Reprinted by permission: Tribune Media Services.

Joe Period, Nothing Yonson, and Lizz—*Dick Tracy*, November 23, 1955. Reprinted by permission: Tribune Media Services.

Flattop, Jr., and the ghost of Skinny—*Dick Tracy*, August 15, 1956. Reprinted by permission: Tribune Media Services.

to Chief Patton, says, "Chief, it isn't always the sensational gun battle that licks crime." Patton responds, "No, Sam, most of its done right in the classroom."

Joe Period and Flattop, Jr., are Dick Tracy's primary quarries during 1956. Max Allan Collins and Dick Locher's *Dick Tracy's Fiendish Foes: A 60th Anniversary Celebration* (1991) reprints the entire run of *Dick Tracy* in 1956, and thus the editors of the volume, Collins and Locher, show us the maturity and complexity of Chester

Opposite: Crewy Lou and Sphinx—*Dick Tracy*, June 17, 1951. Reprinted by permission: Tribune Media Services.

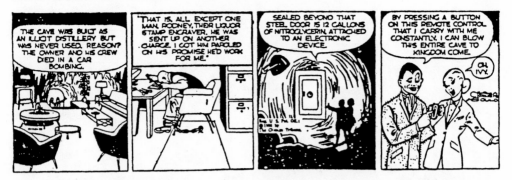

Ivy and Flossie—*Dick Tracy*, October 26, 1956. Reprinted by permission: Tribune Media Services.

The Kitten Sisters—*Dick Tracy*, February 25, 1957. Reprinted by permission: Tribune Media Services.

Gould's writing at this juncture of his career. Ivy and Flossie were rogues at the end of the year.

The Kitten Sisters, murderous female acrobats, tag-team their victims, including Dick Tracy, in the early months of 1957. This rather incestuous group of girls, with close-cropped hair and extreme hatred toward males, may have been intended to represent public sentiment against homosexuals, specifically lesbians in this case, and the evils of what was then perceived as deviant, countercultural behavior.

Elsa Crystal and Pantsy were other *Tracy* rogues of 1957, but the most interesting addition to the strip over all that year may have been Morin Plenty. Morin is the father of B.O., and with his much younger wife Blossom, he haunts Dick Tracy's community for several months in 1957. He is an extension of B.O. and even

characters like Sam Catchem who were designed to provide comic relief to the grim goings-on. Like his son, Morin is adept at falling into trouble and requiring Tracy's services for rescue. There was indeed an element of formula, of recurring plot structures, character types, motifs, and so on, in Chester Gould's art. It should also be noted that much of the evil perpetrated by Pantsy in 1957 has to do, once again, with record albums or "platters."

Pantsy continued as a villain in *Dick Tracy* in 1958; however, Miss Egghead, a wealthy woman who indulged in the questionable sport of gamecock fighting, was the primary rogue for the year. Miss Egghead was later joined by an accomplice named Chicory. Gould added a visiting "good guy" to the side of law and order in 1958, ironically in the person of a member of the Cuban Secret Police. (One would suspect

Opposite: A lesson of police procedure—*Dick Tracy*, August 7, 1955. Reprinted by permission: Tribune Media Services.

Morin Plenty and Blossom—*Dick Tracy*, June 3, 1957. Reprinted by permission: Tribune Media Services.

Elsa Crystal—*Dick Tracy*, October 23, 1957. Reprinted by permission: Tribune Media Services.

Chicory—*Dick Tracy*, July 26, 1958. Reprinted by permission: Tribune Media Services.

that Chester Gould would not have introduced a hero with such political and ethnic backgrounds five years later.) The character's name was Wunbrow.

In 1959 Gould highlighted two naïve and misguided victims and two grotesque rogues in *Dick Tracy*. The former were the eccentric and wealthy E. Kent Hardly and the foolish and villainous, though not murderous, Matty Munkie—a television star. The latter were Willie-the-Fifth and Flyface.

The continuities of *Dick Tracy* in the Fifties are best characterized as longer in

Opposite: Morin Plenty and Blossom—*Dick Tracy*, May 5, 1957. Reprinted by permission: Tribune Media Services.

Miss Egghead—*Dick Tracy*, October 14, 1958. Reprinted by permission: Tribune Media Services.

Tracy and Lizz subdued by Willie-the-Fifth and Flyface—*Dick Tracy*, November 7, 1959. Reprinted by permission: Tribune Media Services.

length than earlier ones, more complex and intricate in storyline and character type, and filled with the political thought of the period. Themes of adolescents gone bad, the negative effects of newly emerging popular media and entertainment forms, and suspicion of anything that was not conservative and traditional in nature dominated *Tracy* sequences. And, in a sense there was just cause for these dominant themes. In response to the Crewy Lou story of 1951, one young woman from Missouri actually celebrated the appearance of the kidnapper of Bonnie Braids by getting her hair cut in the same radical fashion as Crewy Lou's.[46] Near the end of the decade, it was apparent that Gould's famous strip would continue to evolve and reflect changing cultural history as the Sixties approached. The space age was just around the corner.

The Sixties

As the Fifties came to an end, Dick Tracy continued to fight social injustices on a grand scale, but once again a transformation was becoming evident in Chester Gould's famous comic strip. For the most part, the outrageous, vividly grotesque and colorful war criminals of the early Forties had been replaced by villains who were often adolescents and who were often associated with the burgeoning popular media and entertainment forms of the Fifties. In the Fifties, story sequences slowed in pace and became more complex and intricate in nature. But, with the advent of such rogues such as Rhodent, Willie-the-Fifth, and Flyface in 1959, Gould had once again, at least momentarily, relied on criminals' extremes of physiognomy to carry story lines. This was the beginning of a new era which focused on extremes of invention and fantasy, and an era which brought Gould and *Dick Tracy* their greatest criticism. At the beginning of the Sixties, the continuation of Willie-the-Fifth and Flyface and the introduction of a rogue named Spots seemed to validate the return to extremes of invention. Many, however—including newspaper publishers, editors, and readers, as well as *Dick Tracy* scholars past and present—believe that the comic strip's storylines took a turn for the worse shortly thereafter. A minority opinion has held that on the contrary *Tracy* of the 1960s revealed Chester Gould as a great visionary as well as a great cartoonist and chronicler of social history.

Two of the best authorities on Sixties *Dick Tracy*, Max Collins and Jay Maeder, provide several perspectives on the famous comic strip during this time. In his *The Dick Tracy Casebook: Favorite Adventures, 1931–1990*, co-edited with Dick Locher, Max Allan Collins provides some of the most insightful, concisely stated commentary yet to appear on this particular subject. Collins writes:

> The 1960s were by no one's yardstick the glory years for Chester Gould's *Dick Tracy*. Gould's diatribes against hippies and his "Law and Order First" campaign made the once cutting-edge strip seem to some readers crankily, creakily Establishment-oriented. (Ironically, many counterculture "underground" cartoonists—including Art Spiegelman, Kim Deitch, Gilbert Shelton, and Robert Crumb, who visited Gould's Tribune Tower office in the late sixties—continued to extol the virtues of *Tracy*'s creator, both for his storytelling and his graphic mastery.)[47]

Obviously, there was mixed sentiment regarding Chester Gould's new direction for *Dick Tracy* in the 1960s. Yet the period did produce some noteworthy accomplishments.

In 1960, Willie-the-Fifth and Flyface, those two grotesques of 1959, continued in *Dick Tracy* until May. They remained as repulsive as ever. During the last days of January 1960, Gould's work offered fine storytelling, sharp drawing, and the humor—some of Gould's best yet—of B.O. Plenty juxtaposed against the grotesqueness of Willie-the-Fifth and Flyface. The *Tracy* strips from the 25th, 26th, and 27th of that month remind us that all comic strips, including those like *Dick Tracy* which feature very melodramatic, depressing, and violent themes are by definition somewhat "comic" in nature. Even the ultra-conservative Harold Gray and his *Little Orphan Annie* provided instances of levity.

By May 1960 a noticeable shift in storyline and character type began to become evident. Rogues named Spots and Odgen arrived on the scene to kidnap a young Hawaiian girl (Little Pineapple) and wreak general mayhem for months to come. Though Collins writes that "Spots is a terrific villain who somewhat resembles the earlier thirties fiend the Blank," the story of Spots, Ogden (poetry-spouting buffoon and all-around bonehead), and Little Pineapple, is really quite uninteresting, serving as little more than melodramatic fluff. Nonetheless, as evidenced in the August 20, 1960, installment of *Tracy*, Gould's mastery of black and white, of light and dark, and of overall artistic composition is still in place.

Pseudo-melodrama carried over from 1960 into 1961, as characters like Aunt Soso and Little Boy Beard, and their stories begun at the end of 1960, moved into the new year. The story of Little Boy Beard, which is not really a crime sequence, produces characters that are very banal (they are unimaginative and one does not really

Spots and Ogden—*Dick Tracy*, August 2, 1960. Reprinted by permission: Tribune Media Services.

Spots—*Dick Tracy*, August 20, 1960. Reprinted by permission: Tribune Media Services.

like or dislike them) and is generally drawn out and uninteresting. *Dick Tracy* stories of the early Sixties were perhaps even worse than those that would be attacked just a few years later as being less than optimal! Gould was grasping at straws. This lapse does not diminish fans' love and respect for Chester Gould and his strip; the early Sixties was simply a period when the artist/writer had to rethink his strategies regarding the accurate portrayal of real life. This rethinking process took a couple of years to work itself out and culminated in the moon sequence, which, though criticized by many, was actually better than continuities like those featuring Little Boy Beard. It is amazing that as a true comic strip genius—a one-man band of epic proportions—Chester Gould had not reached such a lull in his previous thirty years on the comic strip.

In 1961, ex-mayor Happy Voten, Trusty Hubbub, and Mona the Mouthpiece appeared in *Tracy*, the latter two being villains of sorts. These characters and their stories were quite uninteresting. The highlight of 1961 was the brief return of Mary Steele—former wife of Hank Steele, Junior's biological mother, and all-round rather tragic character. (Mary had been part of *Dick Tracy* almost from the start.) On November 4, 1961, Mary Steele dies when a golf ball from a nearby golf course crashes through her window and hits her in the temple. At the time, she is sitting in a rocking chair, reading a story to two children. Tracy never tells Junior that the elderly lady who has died is in fact the boy's mother whom he knew during his early childhood. Shortly thereafter, however, flowers are mysteriously placed on Mary's grave by an unknown benefactor

Opposite: Flyface, Willie-the-Fifth, and the humor of B.O. Plenty—*Dick Tracy*, January 25, 26 and 27, 1960. Reprinted by permission: Tribune Media Services.

Brush—*Dick Tracy*, March 7, 1962. Reprinted by permission: Tribune Media Services.

whom we are led to believe might be Junior, thus indicating that Junior knew of his mother's passing. The sequence draws on the grand tradition of the classic *Dick Tracy*, and was one of Gould's last looks backward as he began to move into a new era with his famous comic strip.

The year 1962 featured Tommy Mc-Conny (aka "Ivy Gallows"), the man who accidentally hit the golf ball that killed Mary Steele and who not so accidentally escaped prison back in 1921 when he was sentenced to be hanged for murder. Because of the golfing incident, McConny is rediscovered by chance. The ex-con unintentionally hangs himself in the ivy growing up a wall of the building from which he is trying to escape. Jockie Lyceum, an actor who designs a facial wig for himself and who is also known as the Brush, becomes part of the ongoing *Dick Tracy* saga on January 24, 1962. By the end of 1962, the 52 Gang troubled Dick Tracy's world, and early indications of a move toward outer space settings started to become apparent.

The following year, 1963, brought with it Mrs. Peek, Thistle Dew, Uncle Punky, the Pallette Twins, and Smallmouth Bass. Thistle Dew and Uncle Punky were the primary rogues that year, and their crimes, motivated by revenge for the death of Thistle's father and Punky's brother, targeted Junior—the artist whose

sketch sent the deceased to the electric chair. The Thistle Dew story is a sort of bastardized version of, and tribute to, the Model story of 1952 in that it chronicles a love relationship involving Junior which goes wrong. The difference, of course, is that Model genuinely cared for Junior and was, along with Junior, the victim of a horrible fate that ended their relationship. Thistle Dew's intentions with Junior, though somewhat softened as the story unfolds, are not honorable. She is bent on trapping Junior and turning him over to Uncle Punky, who plans on exacting his revenge. The saga completed, Gould returned to outer space themes for good.

Jay Maeder writes, "On December 31, 1963, the Dick Tracy Strip as anyone had known it effectively ceased to exist."[48] Harsh words indeed. Max Collins somewhat more objectively writes:

> Gould's decision to take Tracy to the moon pleased few of his fans, though Chet himself loved these sequences. Marrying Junior Tracy off to the exotic Moon Maid seemed, to some of the faithful, a mistake of major proportions: In the late forties and the fifties, Gould had clearly set events in motion so that Junior would one day marry Sparkle Plenty (whom Moon Maid resembled in some regards). And outfitting Tracy and crew in flying magnetic moon buckets violated Gould's stated

Opposite: Dick Tracy in outer space—*Dick Tracy*, December 6, 7 and 8, 1962. Reprinted by permission: Tribune Media Services.

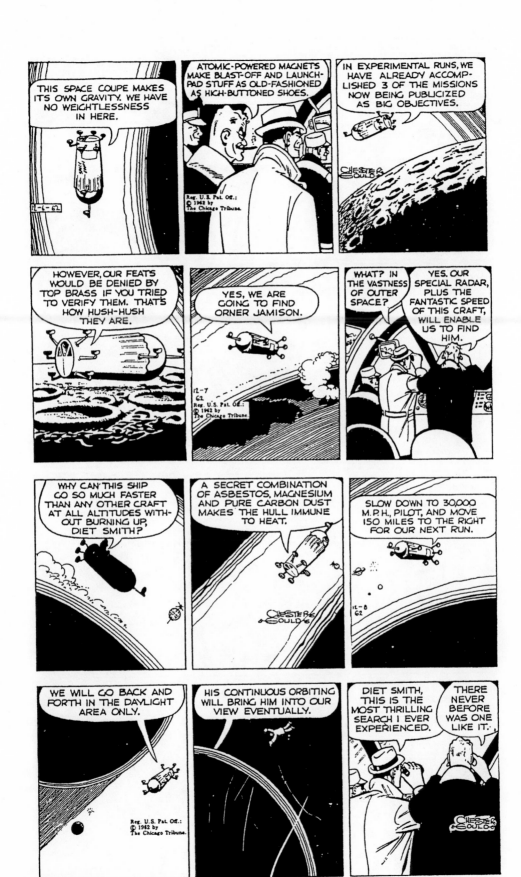

intention to keep Tracy only one simple remove away from reality. Taking Tracy into outer space, and giving him science fiction gadgetry, went well beyond the Two-Way Wrist Radio, satellite television hookups, and openheart surgery, to name a few of Gould's one-step-ahead-of-the-times visions.... Editors and readers were as uncomfortable with Tracy in a Space Coupe as they'd have been with Buck Rogers or Flash Gordon in a squad car.[49]

In 1964, the most controversial of all *Dick Tracy* characters appeared, and she was on the side of law and order! She was the Moon Maid. Dick Tracy in outer space meeting extraterrestrials was a little too much for some people. Yet for others, including Gould himself, this seemed to be the logical progression for the storyline. (Accompanied by his inventor and philanthropist friend Diet Smith, Tracy made his way into space for the first time in 1962 in pursuit of the 52 Gang.)

The controversy stemmed from the fact that Chester Gould had from the outset reflected real-life history, peoples, social thought, police procedure, and scientific advancement in *Dick Tracy*. He had implemented invention and fantasy as extensions of real life. When Dick Tracy began excursions into outer space in 1962, many readers and fans felt that the previous fantasy based on reality was now fantasy based on fantasy, and consequently these readers and fans felt that *Dick Tracy* had become too unbelievable — the fine balance of Caweltian convention and invention was no longer intact. Though this became a common criticism of Gould's strip in the 1960s, there were those — including Gould himself — who felt that the move of America's number one detective hero from the squad car to outer space was logical. The January 14, 1963, issue of *Newsweek* carried an article which elab-

orated still other concerns about the Moon sequence. It stated, in part:

Since Chester Gould created the comics' top-cop Dick Tracy in 1931, life has been a consistent imitator of his art. The two-way wrist radio, for example, was developed by Western Electric six years after Tracy first used it; "Telegard," pioneered by Tracy, is now familiar as closed-circuit TV for keeping watch on prisoners and shoplifters. So, it was understandable that not even Diet Smith's "Space Coupe" looked far-fetched to most readers when Gould introduced it in the Tracy strip last October. But science-minded Tracy fans were outraged. Gould "hasn't the slightest respect for the fundamental laws of nature," one wrote to his favorite paper. The way Diet Smith explained it to Tracy, the Space Coupe was powered by sixteen "atomic energizers that amplify magnetic ears." It could hurtle through space or the earth's atmosphere at more than five times "orbiting speed" [or 85,000 mph] — thus defying Newton's second law, for at this speed, the spacecraft would wholly overcome earth's gravity and veer wildly far out in space. Most baffling of all was how two Gould characters could be shot into orbit from the Coupe, without exploding instantaneously in the vacuum of space. Winding up his Space Coupe episode last week, Gould remained as lock-jawed as Tracy on how it works. "I'm no spaceman. I'm a cartoonist," he said. "But I do a lot of research in crime labs and science books." Could the world expect Space Coupes soon? Gould wouldn't say, but Diet Smith let drop that the "fire and brimstone stuff [of rocketry] is diversionary . . . while this vehicle gets into production."[50]

Max Collins suggests that the moon stories which evolved from this period of Gould creativity and lasted for a number of years to follow were indeed too fantastic. Collins may have been one of the first to observe that the moon sequence was fantasy based on fantasy, and not fantasy based on reality. He notes, "Dick Tracy did not belong

Opposite: **Thistle Dew and Uncle Punky — *Dick Tracy*, January 21, 22 and 23, 1963. Reprinted by permission: Tribune Media Services.**

in space. He belonged in a squad car."[51] (Later, we will see what Collins did with the moon storylines after he assumed the writing responsibilities for *Dick Tracy*.) And, there was and is a substantial faction of *Tracy* fans and scholars alike who are firmly entrenched in this camp of thought. Likewise, however, a healthy percentage of the strip's followers have supported and embraced this period. "When you combine realism with the fantastic, you've got a story every time," Gould stated in 1981.[52] And Gould defended his storylines of the Sixties as based on realism. At the time of Gould's death in May of 1985, *Chicago Tribune* writers Wes Smith and Kenan Heise noted:

> It was in the panels of *Dick Tracy*, not in scholarly journals, that the world first learned of two-way wrist radios (1946), closed-circuit television, space shuttles, and a lunar golf course, which appeared in Mr. Gould's comic strip two years before Alan Shepard hit a golf ball on the Moon. Olga, a Tracy villain, performed the first human heart transplant in 1963. Dr. Christian Barnard didn't do the first actual human heart transplant until four years later.[53]

There is indeed a certain charm to this often underrated period of *Dick Tracy*. Collins provides the following qualification: The strengths of the 1960s are not in the area of story but in the artwork. "These years might be described as Gould's pop-art period; his dramatic use of striking black-and-white composition hit its peak around 1968. . . . This is the period that influenced Warhol, Lichtenstein, and other purveyors of pop art."[54] And this period in *Tracy* does serve as an important counterpoint to early *Dick Tracy* episodes in that the moon sequence does get us to think about the respective roles of fact and fantasy in this comic strip. The stories from this period were still often entertaining, the artwork was still exceptional—this was still Gould, just not classic Gould.

The moon people in general, and the Moon Maid specifically, were very interesting (if not wholly believable) creatures. They possessed intellectual and reasoning abilities that appeared in many ways superior to those of humans. Moon Maid herself was an alluring, fascinating, talented, and sensual creature. She was beautiful in many different ways, and one cannot help but believe that she did have quite an appeal to readers of the day. In her, we see once again that though a master of the police story, Chester Gould was also a master of depicting genuine, intense, and unperverted sensuality and love. Junior Tracy was indeed lucky to know her as he did, just as he was fortunate to know Model Jones of 1952.

Dick Tracy, Jr., and the Moon Maid were married on October 4, 1964 (33 years to the day after the debut of *Tracy*) at Diet Smith's Earth Complex. Honey Moon Tracy was born on September 12, 1965, aboard the Space Coupe, which at the time was located between the earth and the moon. Gould's moon sequence, like it or not, was destined to last for about fifteen years.

In 1965, Matty Square, Mr. Bribery, and Ugly Christine were primary nemeses of Dick Tracy. Haf and Haf (reminiscent of Bob Kane's Two-Face from *Batman*) was Gould's major contribution to his *Tracy* rogues' gallery in 1966. The Chin Chillars and Piggy were the main foes of Dick Tracy in 1967—Piggy a classic caricature in his own right. Purdy Fallar and Posey appeared for the first time as *Dick Tracy* villains in 1968.

In 1968, *Time* magazine printed an article in its June 28 issue which essentially accused *Dick Tracy* of inspiring Sirhan Sirhan to assassinate Robert Kennedy. The day after Kennedy's death, a particularly violent *Tracy* daily strip appeared by coincidence and was the focus of the trumped-up controversy. In one sense, the particular episode of violence referenced in *Time* was really nothing that had not

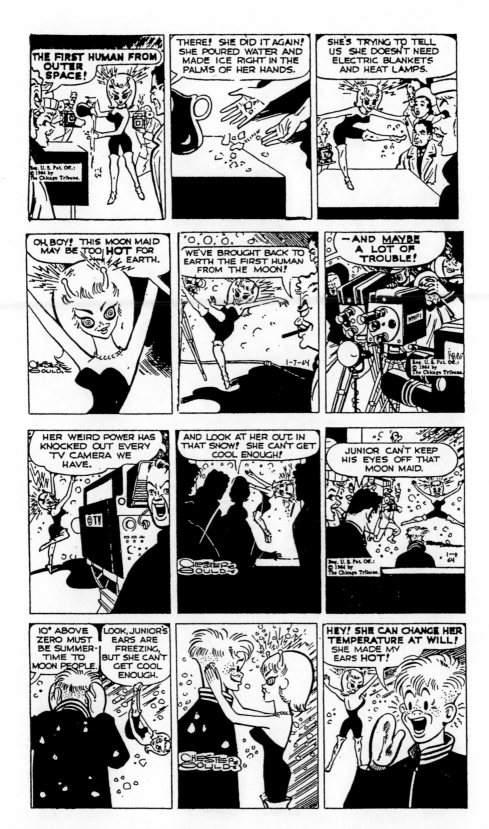

Moon Maid and Junior—*Dick Tracy*, January 6, 7, and 8, 1964. Reprinted by permission: Tribune Media Services.

Moon Mail and Junior—*Dick Tracy*, **January 16, 17, and 18, 1964. Reprinted by permission: Tribune Media Services.**

Moon Maid and Junior—*Dick Tracy*, April 2, 3 and 4, 1964. Reprinted by permission: Tribune Media Services.

Moon Maid and Junior — *Dick Tracy*, April 13, 14 and 15, 1964. Reprinted by permission: Tribune Media Services.

Piggy and Moon Maid—*Dick Tracy*, November 20, 1967. Reprinted by permission: Tribune Media Services.

Purdy Fallar—*Dick Tracy*, May 3, 1968. Reprinted by permission: Tribune Media Services.

Selected panels, out of context, presented by *Time* magazine in its June 28, 1968, issue. Reprinted by permission: Tribune Media Services.

appeared in the comic during its 37 previous years. In another sense, particularly when taken out of the context of events leading up to this particular fictitious violent act in the comic strip, this segment does seem a bit extreme in that Dick Tracy *appears* to resort to violence (in this case the vaporization of master villain Intro) without exploring other options and without giving the rogue a chance to surrender. Further, the detective seems to relish this particular violent

end more than usual. Perhaps Gould had gone too far, but upon further investigation, perhaps not. The violent act is indeed justified when one considers Tracy's previous encounters with Intro. Further, the author of the *Time* article took outrageous liberties with the cutting and pasting of panels which did not appear side by side in the original presentation. Even the casual observer can see that the three panels reprinted in that *Time* magazine article are disjointed. Besides the obvious lack of

Golfing on the moon with Dick Tracy and Diet Smith—*Dick Tracy*, March 25, 1969. Reprinted by permission: Tribune Media Services.

Sparkle Plenty and Vera Alldid—*Dick Tracy*, May 21, 1969. Reprinted by permission: Tribune Media Services.

continuity between panels, there is also the conclusive evidence of both the second and third reprinted panels containing copyright information that was reprinted only once per day. The *Dick Tracy* panels presented in this magazine are clearly taken out of context, and would have made Dr. Wertham proud. (See Chapter 6, the section on comic books.)

The year 1969 saw the emergence of several new catalysts of evil in Chester Gould's comic strip including Mr. Litter, Scorpio, and 2 Finger. Vera Alldid, an aspiring cartoonist, emerged as Sparkle Plenty's beau. Readers had to be somewhat saddened by the betrothal of Sparkle to someone other than Junior. But then, Junior was already married. Perhaps Gould was simply trying to portray the reality that sometimes even things as wondrous as love do not always work out as planned. As Chester Gould and *Dick Tracy* approached their fortieth anniversary together, the moon sequences continued.

The Seventies

Since the moon phase of *Dick Tracy* continued into the Seventies, the characters of the early and mid–Seventies were primarily extensions of those created in the Sixties. Some of these characters—good and bad alike—were more colorful and interesting than others. Two of the new good guys of the early Seventies included Groovy Groove (who debuted in 1970) and Peanutbutter (who debuted in 1972). Groovy, a middle-aged but nonetheless "hip" police officer, became Lizz's romantic interest. He died in action several years later. Peanutbutter was a

Peanutbutter and Groovy—*Dick Tracy*, December 10, 1972. Reprinted by permission: Tribune Media Services.

young boy who was a sort of throwback to the old Crime Stoppers Club. Rogues from the first half of the Seventies, who interestingly enough were somewhat reminiscent of the old Gouldian grotesques, included Diamonds (1970), Pouch (1970), Johnny Scorn (1971), Mr. Pike (1973),

Smelt (1973), and Brain (1974). Z.Z. Welz, Chilly Hill, Hairy, LeMaude, and Bulky were characters added in 1975.

To his credit, right up to the point of his retirement from *Dick Tracy* Chester Gould was always very conscious about reflecting changing cultural attitudes and current socio-political thought. In fact, sometimes the comic strip genius tried too hard at capturing cutting-edge trends and commonly held ideologies. The moon sequence, some would argue, is an example of Gould trying too hard. *Dick Tracy* in the Seventies, an extension of Sixties *Tracy*, may have been another period when he tried too hard, when he may have reduced the message of his world famous comic strip to ultra-conservative, puritanical themes.

This said, the ways in which story themes developed and story characters evolved in the Seventies are best explained by considering the proposal that Chester Gould at this time may have been too conscientious, too focused in his work. The appearance of Groovy Groove, a likeable enough and entertaining character, and the changes very evident in the personae and depictions of Dick Tracy himself and Lizz, support this hypothesis. Groovy Groove is a "hip," "mod," "with-it," "New Age" sort of cop. And Tracy and Lizz follow his lead. Dick Tracy's hair becomes a little longer, as do his sideburns; he grows a pencil-line mustache and dons wildly informal sportswear. Somewhere since her first appearance in *Tracy* in 1955, Lizz has changed from an alluring, very feminine blonde to a rather scraggly haired, brunette tomboy. (She has always maintained her tremendous intelligence, street smarts, and humanitarian qualities.)

One final note in this regard. Lizz's love for Groovy Groove, which is indeed reciprocated, is significant. From all indications, it is apparent that Groovy is considerably older than Lizz, and this reflects Gould's attempt to capture the more liberal ideologies of what would have been for him the younger set of the Seventies. We had seen May-September romances in *Dick Tracy* before, most notably in the 1957 appearance of Morin Plenty and his young bride Blossom. (In fact, Morin and Blossom's romance seemed more like a March-November relationship.) But in the case of B.O.'s father and his bride, readers are to take this rather unconventional marriage as a logical extension of the tradition of hill folk from which individuals like Morin, Blossom, B.O., and others come. The relationship between Lizz and Groovy is best appreciated not as a parallel to that of Morin and Blossom, but as Gould attempting to reflect the lifestyles of the younger set of the Seventies. One has to give the artist/writer credit here. Chester Gould, himself a rather conservative traditionalist, was probably not enamored with this particular lifestyle, but he was open-minded enough to reflect what he perceived as a popular reality in his comic strip. Lizz agreed to accept Groovy's marriage proposal on the condition that he leave the police force. They never married.

The romance between another couple at this same time was rocky at best. Cartoonist Vera Alldid was not the ideal mate for Sparkle Plenty, as the readers already knew. In fact, Alldid was a bit of a cad, often taking Sparkle for granted and often being undependable. In the Sunday page of December 21, 1975, (see p. 146) Gould reminded us of the power of the comic strip form, of the potential for art in that form, of the effectiveness of the judiciously employed silent panel, and of his own unique and wonderful talents as a comic strip artist/writer, which never left him. This Sunday page, perhaps Gould's best of the Seventies and one of his best of all time, speaks for itself. No words or explanation can do it justice.

Lispy, Puckerpuss, the Gallstones, Bolo, Big Charley, and Perfume appeared in 1976. The sequences involving these characters were entertaining and effective, but not overly profound. Judging by the artwork and storylines, it is apparent that Gould's assistant, Rick Fletcher, had a great deal to do with the ongoing success of the famous comic strip at this time. Fletcher was one of Gould's and *Tracy's* great, generally unrecognized treasures.

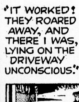

Lizz—*Dick Tracy*, June 8, 1975. Reprinted by permission: Tribune Media Services.

More than people will probably ever know, Fletcher helped keep *Dick Tracy* going so that he, Gould, and Max Collins could take the famous comic strip into the Eighties.

By 1977, having completed over 46 successful years as the mastermind behind *Dick Tracy*, Chester Gould announced his retirement. His last direct contributions to the drawing of the strip appeared on Christmas Day that year, though he would continue in a sort of advisory capacity to Rick Fletcher and Max Allan Collins for a few more years. Young, critically acclaimed author of detective fiction Max Allan Collins was hired by the *Chicago*

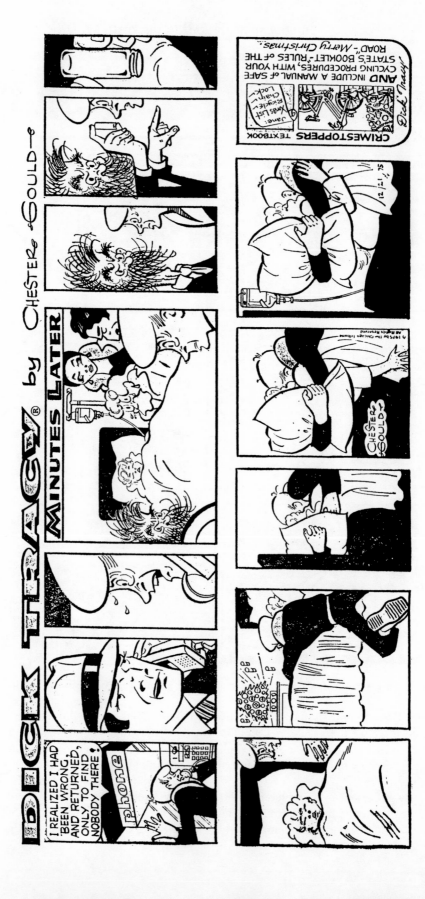

The Iceman, Sparkle, and Tracy—*Dick Tracy*, **December 9 and 10, 1978. Reprinted by permission: Tribune Media Services.**

Opposite: **Sparkle Plenty and Vera Alldid**—*Dick Tracy*, **December 21, 1975. Reprinted by permission: Tribune Media Services.**

Tribune to script the comic strip. Veteran cartoonist and longtime Gould assistant Rick Fletcher assumed full illustrative duties of the strip.

Max Collins wasted no time killing off the Moon Maid and the Moon Valley storyline which had been part of *Dick Tracy* ever since Diet Smith had taken Tracy into space via Space Coupe in the early Sixties. In 1978, Moon Maid (who was married to Junior at the time) died when the car she was about to drive exploded. The Moon people closed diplomatic relations with earthlings for good. It was the end of an era. Collins felt that there were too many characters in the strip at that time, and remained firm in his resolve that stories of outer space were too fantastic for the tough guy cop who emerged as gangland's nemesis in the Depression-era America. Vera Alldid, the cartoonist who debuted in

Tracy in 1969 and was now Sparkle Plenty's husband, was also eliminated from the storyline, setting the stage for the inevitable marriage of Sparkle and Junior. Max Collins believed that "people saw Dick Tracy as a detective that belonged on earth"[55] By 1978, Collins and Fletcher were firmly in the driver seat of Gould's vehicle for fantastic representation of reality. Things looked good: characters engendered genuine pathos; drawing was crisp, clean, and effective; storylines and action were fast-paced and well plotted. The Fletcher/Collins story of the Iceman proved this. In 1979, Dick Tracy and Tess Trueheart had a second child, a son named Joseph Flintheart Tracy. For better or worse, a new period of *Dick Tracy* was ushered in in the late Seventies. Gould's ship would move forward or sink. Collins and Fletcher were the pilots at the helm.

The Eighties

Rick Fletcher and Max Collins brought *Tracy* into the Eighties with a special flair. So often in the history of comic strips, when a landmark comic strip artist/writer retires, the strip retires too. Very few of the classic comic strips begun in the first half of the twentieth century have survived the retirement of their original creative forces. These exceptions include Frank Willard's *Moon Mullins* (continued by Ferd Johnson), Frank King's *Gasoline Alley* (continued by Dick Moores and then Jim Scancarelli), Harold Gray's *Little Orphan Annie* (continued by Leonard Starr), and Chester Gould's *Dick Tracy* (continued by Max Collins and Rick Fletcher, and then by Max Collins and Dick Locher).

Two of the major contributions of Fletcher and Collins to the *Dick Tracy* rogues' gallery are Angeltop (Flattop's little girl, done in collaboration with Chester

Gould in 1977) and Torcher (1980). Like Gould had done in years previous—particularly in the Thirties, Forties, and Fifties, Fletcher and Collins often exhumed old popular *Tracy* villains and incorporated them into new storylines when and only when the incorporation of these classic rogues did not contradict the plotting and mythologies of earlier continuities. Like Gould, Fletcher and Collins created a second generation of good and bad guys alike.

During the first week of October 1981, Rick Fletcher and Max Collins celebrated, with Chester Gould and *Tracy* readers everywhere, the fiftieth anniversary of the granddaddy of all comic strips. On April 25, 1982, Dick Tracy, Jr., and Sparkle Plenty were married. The new era of *Dick Tracy* had arrived.

On December 10, 1982, in one of the more shockingly poignant daily strips

The demise of the Iceman—*Dick Tracy*, December 11, 12, 13, 14, and 15, 1978. Reprinted by permission: Tribune Media Services.

Fifty year celebration—*Dick Tracy*, October 4, 5, and 6, 1981. Reprinted by permission: Tribune Media Services.

provided by the Fletcher/Collins team, it appeared that Pat Patton, after 51 faithful years of service in *Dick Tracy*, was making his exit. Fortunately, on the following day we found out otherwise. The sequence was moving, particularly for those readers of 1982 who first read the comic strip in newspapers and for those of us today who have a sense of the history and importance of Pat Patton to *Tracy*. Many readers knew that Pat Patton, once an integral figure of Thirties and Forties *Dick Tracy* episodes, had become increasingly unimportant to storylines as time went by. It seemed entirely possible that Patton could be killed off. When Patton became police chief in late 1948, his role in the ongoing saga was redefined, and he was relegated to the background as Chief Brandon had been before him. The artwork and writing of the daily strips of December 9–11, 1982, are impeccable, evidencing artistry within the tight constraints and parameters of comic strips in the Eighties. Fletcher's depiction of falling snow and Collins' word choice are truly masterful. Collins stated once that he wanted people to realize that, short of Dick Tracy himself, anyone was expendable in the new era of *Dick Tracy*.[56]

Rick Fletcher died in early 1983, and his artwork, done several weeks in advance of publication, concluded with work done on the story Collins would later title "The Ghost of Itchy"—a continuity which reprised some old themes and which introduced the extended families of such rogues as Itchy and B.B. Eyes. The byline of Rick Fletcher/Max Collins, now minus Gould's name, would be changed again. With the death of Rick Fletcher on March 16, 1983, Dick Locher, Pulitzer Prize–winning editorial cartoonist and Gould assistant as early as the Fifties, assumed full illustrative duties for *Dick Tracy*. Once again, the storyline and drawing remained stable as the creative torch was passed.

To their credit, Max Collins and Dick Locher were extremely faithful to Gouldian tradition in *Tracy*. Character types and family lines were continued, as was the humor of B.O. Plenty. Christmastime in the world of Dick Tracy has always been special. In 1983, Collins and Locher showcased the characters of B.O. and Gravel Gertie Plenty, Junior and Sparkle Plenty Tracy and Junior's daughter Honey Moon, and that implacable capriciousness of B.O. Plenty. They also dealt with a favorite Collins theme and important contemporary social concern—toxic waste.

One of the more noteworthy rogues to be created by early Collins/Locher collaborations was 1984's Bugsy. Locher did an excellent job augmenting Collins' creation, which paid tribute to the *Dick Tracy* rogues of the Thirties as well as the gangster movies of the same period. Bugsy's name was representative of monikers given bigger-than-life Depression-era gangsters and was a tribute to Gould's *Tracy* rogues of the early decades of the comic strip who took on names based on outrageous physiognomies or related traits. Max Allan Collins had made a very nice gesture to Chester Gould, who at the time of the Bugsy story was 84, was in rapidly failing health, and would die just a few months later.

In 1985, Dick Locher and Max Collins did an extensive sequence which centered on Dick Tracy recounting his confrontations with the rogues of the World War II years. These very successful continuities reprised grotesques like Mr. and Mrs. Pruneface and Flattop. In 1987, Dick Tracy and company continued their police work with characters like Sam Catchem, Lizz, and Tracy himself drawn and portrayed in the conservative style that marked Gould's *Tracy* prior to the Seventies. The same year also saw the emergence and murderous escapades of a classic *Tracy* villain type—Putty Puss. The tradition of Chester Gould's classic *Dick*

DICK TRACY

DICK TRACY

DICK TRACY

The shooting of Pat Patton—*Dick Tracy*, December 9, 10, and 11, 1982. Reprinted by permission: Tribune Media Services.

Tracy was back; things were both new and innovative, but were still firmly grounded in reality and old legacies. Max Collins and Dick Locher were responsible for the success achieved in this arena.

The Nineties

Today, the ongoing saga of Dick Tracy continues with no end in sight. It is thoroughly appropriate and not an overstatement to say that *Dick Tracy* is the longest running, most important single comic strip—in terms of representation of

Opposite: The marriage of Dick Tracy, Jr., and Sparkle Plenty—*Dick Tracy*, April 25, 1982. Reprinted by permission: Tribune Media Services.

Twitchy Oliver, brother of Itchy—*Dick Tracy*, April 28, 29, and 30, 1983. Reprinted by permission: Tribune Media Services.

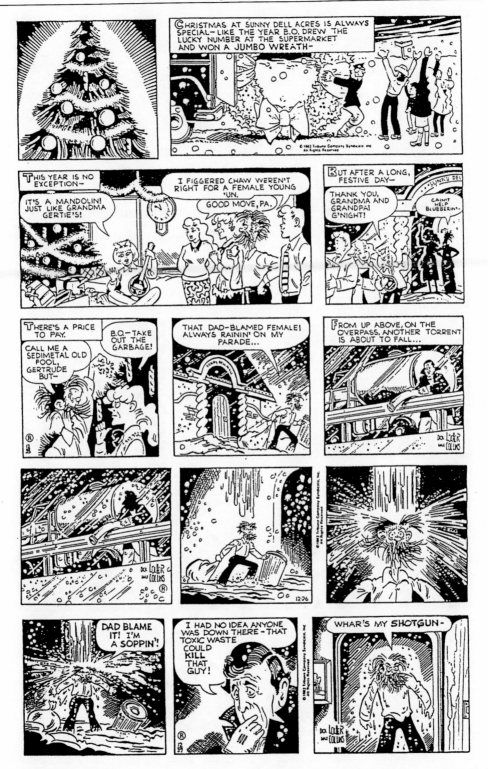

Christmastime—*Dick Tracy*, **December 25, 26, and 27, 1983. Reprinted by permission: Tribune Media Services.**

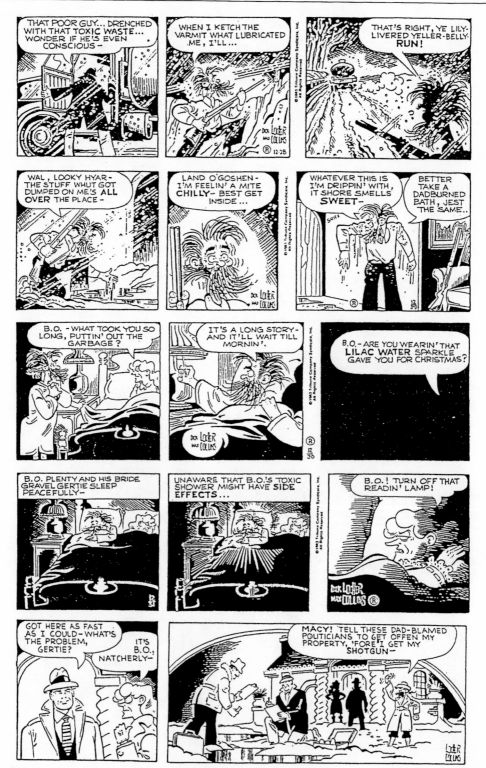

More humor with B.O. Plenty—*Dick Tracy*, December 28, 29, 30, and 31, 1983. Reprinted by permission: Tribune Media Services.

Bugsy—*Dick Tracy*, August 16, 17, and 18, 1984. Reprinted by permission: Tribune Media Services.

American culture—in the history of the medium. The continued popularity of this comic strip is attributable to the abilities of Collins, Fletcher, and Locher to retain and reprise much of Gould's original vision while at the same time moving the strip forward in the creative directions that make *Dick Tracy* their own. Collins has been the writer of the strip for more than fifteen years; Fletcher drew the strip for more than five years, and Locher has drawn it for more than ten years. The non–Gould era retains the integrity of the Gould era—both periods with many fine moments and continuities.

The 1990 Warren Beatty movie *Dick Tracy* may have brought a short-lived heightened attention to the current *Dick Tracy* comic strip, but all success attributable to the current *Tracy* is due to Collins and Locher and the vision of *Tribune* executives who work with and support this creative team. When the 1990 blockbuster movie was hyped and then eventually released, Collins and Locher paid homage to the same, though the film was not always loyal to the tradition of *Dick Tracy*. *Dick Tracy* has continued to flourish, and police detective hero Dick Tracy and his associates and extended

DICK TRACY

DICK TRACY

DICK TRACY

Tracy's wartime memories—*Dick Tracy*, August 1, 2, and 3, 1985. Reprinted by permission: Tribune Media Services.

Sam, Lizz, and Tracy—*Dick Tracy*, November 4, 1987. Reprinted by permission: Tribune Media Services.

Putty Puss—*Dick Tracy*, December 24 and 25, 1987. Reprinted by permission: Tribune Media Services.

family pursue their own manifest destiny. In 1931, Chester Gould introduced us to a grotesque rogue and gangster named Big Boy. In recent years, more than sixty years later, Max Collins and Dick Locher has given us remarkably similar characters like Crime King. Max Collins' tightly plotted stories have been the best adventures to appear in newspaper comic pages in the Seventies, Eighties, and Nineties.

In the Nineties, *Dick Tracy* maintains a careful balance of Caweltian convention and invention—fact and fantasy—which has been inherent in its nature since its beginnings in 1931. Since that time, as social sentiment has changed, so too has *Dick Tracy* changed. Shifts in actual cultural history are reflected in the inventions or fantasy element of the storyline. These inventions include the grotesque rogues and the types of crimes they perpetrate against society, as well as diverse settings and variations of established themes, plots, and motifs regarding law enforcement and the protection of socially prescribed morality. The system of myths and symbolic representations of myths utilized in *Dick Tracy* is remarkably similar to such systems in place millennia ago. The human drama, the odyssey, continues.

Notes

1. Richard Gid Powers, *G-Men: Hoover's F.B.I. in American Popular Culture* (Carbondale, Ill.: Southern Illinois University Press, 1983), pp. 29 and 31.

2. Powers, "J. Edgar Hoover and the Detective Hero," in *The Popular Culture Reader*, First Edition (Bowling Green, Ohio: Bowling Green State University Popular Press, 1977), p. 203. Edited by Jack Nachbar and John L. Wright.

3. Two valuable sources which discuss in detail J. Edgar Hoover and the public image of the F.B.I. are Richard Gid Powers' *G-Men: Hoover's F.B.I. in American Popular Culture* (Carbondale, Illinois: Southern Illinois University Press, 1983) and William W. Turner's *Hoover's F.B.I.: The Men and the Myth* (New York: Dell, 1971).

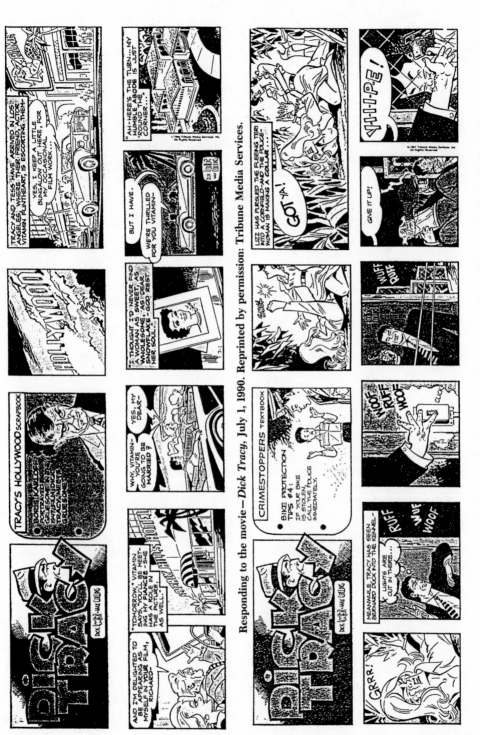

Responding to the movie—*Dick Tracy*, July 1, 1990. Reprinted by permission: Tribune Media Services.

Lizz, Tracy, and a Crimestopper—*Dick Tracy*, June 23, 1991. Reprinted by permission: Tribune Media Services.

Crime King—*Dick Tracy*, April 5, 1992. Reprinted by permission: Tribune Media Services.

4. Richard Slotkin, *Regeneration Through Violence: The Mythology of the American Frontier, 1600–1860* (Middletown, Connecticut: Wesleyan University Press, 1973), p. 4.

5. Ibid., p. 8.

6. Russel B. Nye, *The Unembarrassed Muse: The Popular Arts in America* (New York: The Dial Press, 1970), p. 236.

7. Herb Galewitz, ed., *The Celebrated Cases of Dick Tracy 1931–1951* (New York: Chelsea House, 1970), p. xi.

8. Refer to John G. Cawelti's discussion in Chapter One ("The Study of Literary Formulas") in *Adventure, Mystery and Romance* (Chicago: The University of Chicago Press, 1976).

9. Cawelti, p. 57.

10. Collins interview, October 25, 1982.

11. Charles Collins, "Happy Birthday, DICK!" *New York Sunday News*, October 14, 1956, p. 98.

12. See the origin story of Dick Tracy (not the first appearance) reprinted in *The Celebrated Cases of Dick Tracy 1931–1951*, pp. 5–12.

13. Ibid.

14. Ibid.

15. Stephen Becker, *Comic Art in America* (New York: Simon and Schuster, 1959), p. 195.

16. Ron Goulart, *The Adventurous Decade* (New Rochelle, New York: Arlington House Publishers, 1975), p. 72.

17. Ibid., p. 73.

18. Gould letter, April 13, 1979.

19. In his book *Dick Tracy: The Official Biography* (New York: Penguin, 1990), Jay Maeder provides an insightful, enthralling tale of the fact and fantasy that surrounded events in *Dick Tracy* at this time. See pages 126–129 of Maeder's book.

20. Galewitz, ed., *Dick Tracy—The Thirties: Tommy Guns and Hard Times*, p. 107.

21. Frank Redrum (note that his name is "murder" spelled backwards) wore a piece of cheesecloth over his face which had taken the brunt of a police shotgun blast. Hence, he was called "the Blank" or "Blank."

22. Richard Pietrzyk, "Dick Tracy at 50: Crime Marches On," *Collage* Vol. 3, No. 1 (Wheeling, Illinois: Collage, Inc., Jan./Feb. 1982), p. 3.

23. Most villains in *Dick Tracy* have met with permanent ends at the close of their respective escapades. Stooge Viller and later the Mole were two of the few early *Tracy* bad guys who were not immediately terminated.

24. Matt Masterson has compiled a

substantial *Dick Tracy* rogues' gallery in *Dick Tracy: The Art of Chester Gould* (Port Chester, New York: Museum of Cartoon Art, 1978). A premiere *Tracy* collector, historian, and fan, Masterson has produced in his compilation a monument and tribute to Chester Gould and *Dick Tracy* in particular, and to comic strip history in general. A one-time presentation to Gould by Masterson, this *Tracy* rogues' gallery was reprinted by Blackthorne Publishing in its *Dick Tracy* comic books of the late 1980s.

25. Cawelti, p. 60.

26. Powers, "J. Edgar Hoover and the Detective Hero," p. 209. Though Bruno Hauptmann got the electric chair for the Lindbergh baby kidnapping, considerable doubt remains today about his actual guilt. There is good reason to believe that his trial and execution was nothing less than a modern day witch hunt with the end result an attempt to appease the American public.

27. The rogue in this sequence is named Spaldoni.

28. Jackie Cooper, *Please Don't Shoot My Dog* (New York: William Morrow, 1981).

29. Powers, "The Comic Strip G-Man," *Rituals and Ceremonies in Popular Culture* (Bowling Green, Ohio: Bowling Green State University Popular Press, 1980), p. 212.

30. Ibid.

31. Goulart, ed., *The Encyclopedia of American Comics from 1897 to the Present* (New York: Facts on File, Inc., 1990), p. 378.

32. "Stepped on the gas" is Collins' terminology from the interview of November 19, 1984.

33. Galewitz, p. xii.

34. John Bainbridge, "Chester Gould: The Harrowing Adventures of His Cartoon Hero, Dick Tracy, Give Vicarious Thrills to Millions." *Life*, August 14, 1944, p. 49.

35. Al Binder and Kermit Jaediker, "Just Before the Battle, Tracy." *The New York Daily News*, May 9, 1944, p. C4.

36. *Limited Collector's Edition Presents Dick Tracy*, Vol. 4, No. C-40 (New York: National Periodical Publications, Inc., Dec./Jan. 1975/76), inside back cover.

37. Collins interview, November 19, 1984.

38. "B.O.'s Wedding Night." *Newsweek*, August 26, 1946, p. 57.

39. "Sparkle Plenty." *Life*, August 25, 1947, p. 42.

40. Maeder, p. 30.

41. Chester Gould letter interview, April 13, 1979.

42. Maeder, pp. 123-125.

43. Rick Marschall, "An Examination of the Aesthetics of Dick Tracy," *Dick Tracy: The Art of Chester Gould* (Port Chester, New York: Museum of Cartoon Art, 1978), p. 19.

44. Matt Masterson, "200 Characters from Dick Tracy 1931-1977," in *Dick Tracy: The Art of Chester Gould* (Port Chester, New York: Museum of Cartoon Art, 1978), p. 39.

45. Max Allan Collins, *The Dick Tracy Casebook: Favorite Adventures 1931-1990, Selected by Max Allan Collins and Dick Locher* (New York: St. Martin's Press), p. 55.

46. Beulah Schacht, "Straight Out of Dick Tracy: Blonde Here Gets Crewy Lou Haircut." *St. Louis Globe-Democrat*, Saturday, June 30, 1951, p. B1.

47. Collins, p. 125.

48. Maeder, p. 190.

49. Collins, p. 125.

50. "Dick Tracy in Orbit." *Newsweek*, January 14, 1963, p. 47.

51. Collins interviews, October 25, 1982, and November 28, 1984.

52. Wes Smith and Kenan Heise, "'Dick Tracy' creator Chester Gould, 84." *Chicago Tribune*, May 12, 1985, Section 2, p. 7.

53. Ibid.

54. *The Dick Tracy Casebook*, p. 125.

55. Collins interview, October 25, 1982.

56. Collins interview, November 28, 1984.

CHAPTER 5

Builders of a Legend:
The People Behind *Dick Tracy*

"The peculiarity of American institutions is, the fact that they have been compelled to adapt themselves to the changes of an expanding people—to the changes involved in crossing a continent, in winning a wilderness, and in developing at each area of this progress out of the primitive economic and political conditions of the frontier into the complexity of city life."—Frederick Jackson Turner, *The Significance of the Frontier in American History* (1893)

Cultural inheritances and personal experiences serve as primary source material for creators of the arts. It is due to the universal nature of these inheritances and experiences that selected art forms become commercially successful and culturally representative. As consumers of these forms, we relate to and embrace those forms with which we are familiar, and in which we believe. Further, the successful art form is distinguished as the one that not only reflects a collective experience and sentiment, but also legitimizes the individual consumer's experiences and places these experiences into the meaningful context of the larger society. When the men behind *Dick Tracy* presented a daily comic strip, readers embraced the work as an extension of the creative force of individuals with socially constructed realities very similar to their own. The degree of success the particular creative force and resulting art form achieve varies. Even *Dick Tracy* has had some moments

that were more successful than others; continuities from the Thirties, Forties, and Fifties are examples of the former and sequences from the Sixties and Seventies fall into the latter category.

Since the birth of *Dick Tracy* in 1931, several men have made up the creative force behind this epic comic strip. From 1931 until 1977, Chester Gould—creator and longtime champion of the work—and several assistants were that force. Since 1977, three individuals have effectively carried the famous comic strip forward, and have quite appropriately expanded and evolved Gould's established traditions—no mean feat when considering the number of famous comic strips that ended with the retirement of their creators. Indeed there is a real-life Dick Tracy; there are several of them in fact. They are the men who have recorded social history in an ongoing saga which we as a culture embrace—the saga of Dick Tracy.

Chester Gould

Chester Gould

Born on November 20, 1900, in Pawnee, Oklahoma, Chester Gould was the descendant of Cherokee Strip frontiersmen. He was one of three children. His grandfather was a preacher, and his father, Gilbert R. Gould, was a printer for the *Pawnee Courier-Dispatch* and later publisher of Stillwater, Oklahoma's *Advance-Democrat*. His mother was Alice M. Miller Gould. In numerous newspaper and magazine articles and interviews, since the rise of *Dick Tracy* in the Thirties, the comic strip master acknowledged the important influence of his father, and his father's career in journalism, on the direction he took.

As a young boy in Pawnee, Gould was impressed with several of the popular comic strips of the day. He noted:

> I bought a St. Louis paper as a boy. I would go to the newsstands, sometime on Saturday afternoons the St. Louis paper

would come in, and Sunday morning—the *Chicago Tribune*. This was before "The Gumps," before "Harold Teen" and all that. They had "Mama's Angel Child" and they had a couple of comics.... I would keep them until next week, until I got the one next week, and read them over and over.[1]

Other favorites of young Gould included Bud Fisher's *Mutt and Jeff*, George Frink's *Slim Jim*, Richard F. Outcault's *Buster Brown*, Rudolph Dirks' *The Katzenjammer Kids*, and C.W. Kahles' *Hairbreadth Harry*.[2] At age seven, Gould had further encouragement to become a cartoonist. In interviews years later, this was one of his favorite recollections:

> The Democrats in Pawnee County were having a county convention they called it, and my dad, in an effort to discourage me I guess—at seven years old, you can't argue with your father!—so Dad said, "If you want to draw, why don't you sketch some of the politicians?" Well, it sounded pretty good to me, so I did all my work on the scrap paper from the cutting machine, and I got the best pieces of it, the most recent cuttings, put them under my arm and went and made some sketches—and I can imagine how bad they must have been—but Dad would say, "Who's this?" ... And he immediately went over and put them against the window.... I remember staying after school the next day and people were still gawking at these pictures ... and I thought, "This is for me, this is my business," and that really clinched my thinking. I wanted to be a cartoonist.[3]

As a young boy, Gould had a variety of other experiences that helped convince him even further of his career goals. He was a sign painter, which he claimed was "pretty lucrative."[4] His first printed cartoon appeared in the July 1917 issue of a magazine called *The American Boy* and

" Golly! what a snap he's got!"

"Golly! what a snap he's got!" — Chester Gould's first published cartoon. This was the first prize winner of a cartoon contest sponsored by *The American Boy*. It appeared in the July 1917 issue.

won a World War I cartoon contest. The prize was five dollars.[5] Gould stated:

> What I did, I had a company of soldiers, marching down this dirt road, and there was a boy in a cornfield. It was a hot, sunny day, and he was hoeing it . . . they used to hoe corn instead of cultivate it with a team because they could get all the little weeds without harming the corn. The corn got so big they couldn't very well drive a team down the row, they'd knock it down. So they had a horrible, horrible job of hoeing the corn. Hotter than hell, no air . . . . So anyway, this kid was hoeing this, and one soldier was looking at him, they were looking right at each other and the title of it is "What a Stint He's Got." One guy doing the war and the other hoeing the corn. Each coveting the other's job."[6]

In his later teens, Gould took a correspondence course in cartooning from W.L. Evans School of Cartooning in Cleveland, Ohio, which he found both enjoyable and informative. Interestingly enough, the W.L. Evans School of Cartooning advertised regularly in *The American Boy*.

Maintaining his interest in cartooning, Gould entered Oklahoma A&M University in 1917 where he studied commerce and marketing for two years. In 1918, he joined the Lambda Chi Alpha fraternity at A&M. His father had been encouraging him to complete his college degree, and at one time was hoping that Chester would become a lawyer. "In the summer of [1921], after his second and final year at Oklahoma A&M, Chester landed a cartoon job with the *Tulsa Democrat* drawing political cartoons for $30.00 a week."[7] "For a while, he had a staff job on the *Daily Oklahoman* as a sports cartoonist."[8] In September 1921, Chester Gould moved to Chicago, and his Horatio Alger–like struggle upward hit full stride.

Gould's move to Chicago was primarily motivated by a desire to fulfill his dream of becoming a nationally syndicated

cartoonist. He also wanted to complete his degree in business at Northwestern University. Shortly after his arrival, Gould got a job on the long since defunct *Chicago Journal.* Gould stated:

> One of the guys in the art department had to go to the hospital for an appendectomy. And the second guy in command who was then in charge, looked at my art that I'd brought from Oklahoma, editorial cartoons from the *Tulsa Democrat* and sports cartoons from the *Daily Oklahoman,* and said, "Well, these aren't exactly big-city stuff, but until our man gets back from the hospital, be about a month that's all, I could put you on at $30 a week."[9]

He eventually caught on with the art department of the *Herald-Examiner* and other newspapers.

For the next ten years, the cartoonist worked at a seemingly impossible pace. In the evening he attended classes at Northwestern, and in 1923 he finished his degree. During the Twenties, Gould submitted samples of his work to virtually every major newspaper in Chicago. In an article for the September 12, 1948, edition of the *Detroit Free Press,* Fred Olmsted wrote, "By the time he [Gould] had been in Chicago 10 years, he had worked for every paper in town, except one."[10] His primary target was the *Chicago Tribune* and its co-publisher, Captain Joseph Medill Patterson. One of Gould's most noteworthy and enduring jobs at this time was with William Randolph Hearst's *Chicago American.* "His first feature, syndicated by Hearst's King Features Syndicate, was a spoof on motion pictures called *Fillum Fables.* It was followed by a strip called *Radio Cats.*"[11] *Fillum Fables* debuted in 1924, and like Ed Wheelan's *Minute Movies* (1918 to the early 1930s) was a satire of Hollywood. It ran only until 1929, and like *Radio Catts* was not a particularly strong production.

Radio was fresh and new, and getting bigger, much like the impact of television. The most common set of the day was what they call a crystal set; it had no tubes or no internal maintenance at all, but there was a little cat's whisker that you fooled around with and it touched this stone, this little hunk of stone, with a handle back here, and you hit a certain spot and you got reception. No tubes, no batteries, no nothing. That was very common and successful, so I named the strip *The Radio Cats* after the cat's whisker. They were Siamese Cats. That was my radio strip. . . . That *[Radio Catts]* was a humor strictly. *Fillum Fables* was a burlesque.[12]

Gould was particularly uninspired by the concepts of these comic strips, and they consequently lacked a vision necessary for enduring success. But he was not without triumphs during this period. Besides exerting an almost superhuman persistence at attaining his goals in cartooning, he met and married the love and inspiration of his life. Chester Gould met Edna Gauger on a blind date in Evanston, the town near Chicago that is the home of Northwestern, and in 1926 they were married. Edna and Chester were blessed with a child on August 18, 1927—a daughter named Jean. (Miss Gould became Mrs. Jean Gould O'Connell, and has been an integral part in preserving and restoring the legacies of the family and *Dick Tracy.*)

In 1928, with no ebb in determination, Chester Gould became aware of a situation which had to both please and inspire him. To many people, such an incident would have invoked jealousy and pain. But this was not the case with Gould. He had developed a tough skin and had faith in himself. The incident was this:

> In 1928, while making $100 a week, but getting nowhere, he [Gould] heard news that seemed to jeer him by showing what a cartoonist could do if good. Sidney

Opposite, top: Gabby Film—pre–*Dick Tracy* trial strip by Chester Gould. *Bottom: Jarley*—pre–*Dick Tracy* trial strip by Chester Gould.

THE RADIO CATTS   *Danny's Family Howls*

The Radio Catts, April 5, 1924.

The Radio Lanes, October 4, 1924.

Smith, who drew the tremendously popular Gumps, signed a $1,000,000 contract. Along with $100,000 a year for ten years, Smith was to get—the kingly touch—a fresh Rolls-Royce every year.[13]

Gould pushed ahead at an incredibly hard, self-disciplined pace. He had only a couple more years to wait until he hit upon the right combination to launch himself and his cartooning into the popular consciousness. Perhaps he sensed this.

Between 1921 and 1931, Chester Gould produced more than sixty marketable, semi-marketable, and sometimes unmarketable comic strips. A few met with modest success and public acceptance, but none lasted more than a couple of years. Between *Fillum Fables* and *Dick*

Tracy, Gould was offered the job of doing *Little Annie Roonie*—King Features and William Randolph Hearst's response to *Little Orphan Annie* done by Harold Gray and the Chicago Tribune Company. Gould turned down the job and, tired of *Fillum Fables,* left the *Chicago American* to pursue some more of his own ideas and creativity. He signed on with the *Chicago Daily News,* and his last major project before *Dick Tracy* was *The Girl Friends,* a comic strip which in many ways—including character types—predicted and resembled *Dick Tracy.* At this point, the aspiring artist's efforts to get Captain Patterson's attention were reaching fruition and his intense marketing of his comic art hit a new level of intensity. The *Chicago Tribune* was finally taking note of Chester Gould.[14]

Opposite, top: Peppy—pre–*Dick Tracy* trial strip by Chester Gould. *Bottom: Wordy Watkins*—pre–*Dick Tracy* trial strip by Chester Gould.

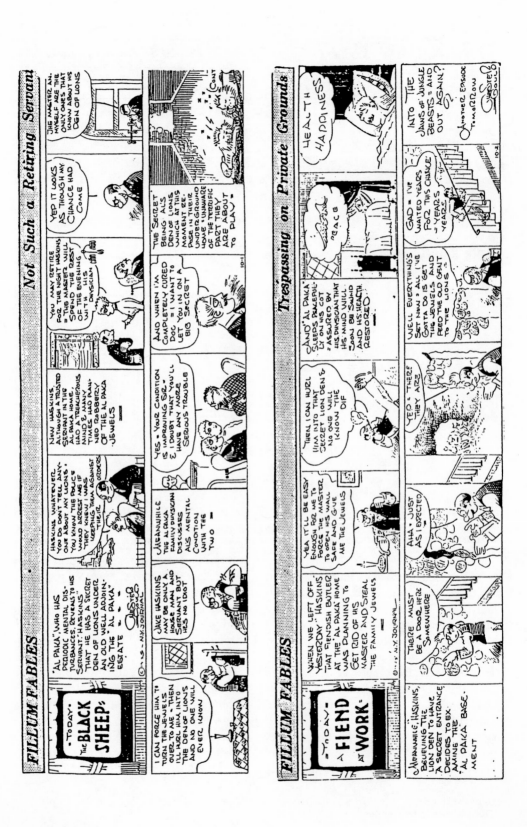

From the time he arrived in Chicago, Gould tried to capture Patterson's attention. Captain Patterson was a newspaper and comic strip mogul who had an uncanny ability to select and revise comic strips that would become immensely successful. In Twenties and Thirties America, comic strips sold newspapers. People bought newspapers sometimes for no other reason than for the comics they presented. (Today, while a handful of comics are very popular among readers, comic strips do not single-handedly sell newspapers.) Joseph Patterson knew of the power of the comic strip in the early decades of the twentieth century; so did his famous rival, William Randolph Hearst. When it came down to it, Patterson was the best and most important publisher of comic strips in the world during his times. Chester Gould knew of Patterson's abilities, but it was not easy to capture the newspaper giant's approval.

> Along with turning down everything Gould offered, Patterson moved to New York to run the *New York Daily News.* Gould kept on submitting ideas. In May of 1929 some of the rejected samples came back with a note from Patterson rather than from his secretary. Simply because Patterson had written him, Gould quit his job and traveled to New York to strike while the iron was hot. Unfortunately, the iron wasn't even warm.[15]

The rejections from Patterson continued, and any normal man would have given up long before this point. But Chester Gould was no normal man. After returning to Chicago from New York, Gould stepped up his production even further and began sending Patterson an editorial cartoon every day. "Patterson had mentioned that he needed an editorial cartoonist.... The crafty idea was to lay a cartoon on Patterson's desk at the same time every morning."[16] The famous C.S. Batchelder

Opposite: Fillum Fables, **October 1 and 2, 1925.**

was ultimately hired to fill the position.

In the late Twenties and early Thirties, gangland was running roughshod over Chicago. Events associated with gangland were major news items for citizens of the Windy City, and Chester Gould was more than a little atuned to and irate about the whole situation. He had a particular disliking for Al Capone. "Reading how this big shot spent twenty minutes in court and walked out free or got thirty days when he richly deserved the electric chair, Gould began thinking in terms of another comic strip, approximately No. 67 in a luckless series. It would have a policeman hero who would tangle with hoodlums on their own strenuous terms."[17]

Understandably a bit distraught, and with little faith in the project, Gould packaged up his first samples of *Plainclothes Tracy* and mailed them to Captain Patterson. In these first panels, the policeman hero faced a rogue named Big Boy who was quite obviously a caricature of Al Capone. "At the end of one strip, where readers would ordinarily prepare for a laugh, the hoodlums were holding an acetylene torch to Tracy's feet to make him tell who he was. Tracy wasn't telling, not if they barbecued him. It compared to all existing strips as a water-front saloon fight compares to a women's club tea."[18] Gould remembered, "I was a great follower of Sherlock Holmes on the radio for G. Washington Coffee. I said if Holmes were alive today as a young man, he wouldn't wear the two-peaked cap, and he'd have a snap-brim fedora and probably be wearing a camel's hair coat and that was the way I built Tracy."[19]

On one hot day in July 1931, Chester Gould received a telegram from Captain Joseph Patterson. Gould was shaking, probably as much from ten years of frustration as anything else, he recalled. Patterson said that the strip — *Plainclothes*

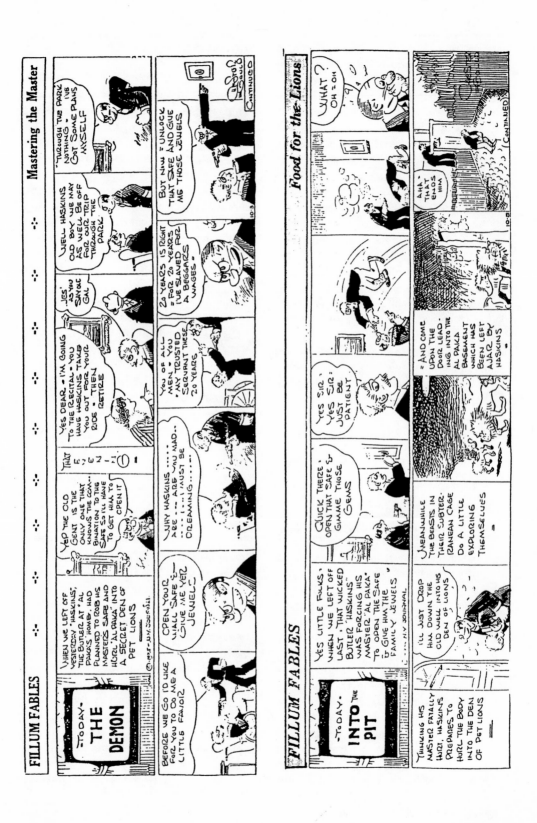

Tracy—had possibilities, and that he wanted to meet Gould in Chicago. Gould withdrew $100 of the approximately $500 he had in the bank and bought a new suit. The meeting was a landmark in comic strip history. Gould remembered:

> When I walked in his office he gave me a cordial handshake and said "Hello. I've got these strips with me here." He had no necktie on, he was in shirtsleeves, which was quite common for him, because I hardly ever saw him with a coat on, and he had on some old army shoes, just plain old army shoes. I remember this well because I had dressed up, and he said with no conversation at all, he said, "Frank Tracy, Charlie Tracy ... Dick Tracy. Let's call this guy Dick. They call cops dicks; let's call him Dick." He said, "Do you think you can have two weeks by the first of September?" Well, it was then the 15th of August. If he'd said, "Do you think you could have two weeks by eleven o'clock tonight?" I would have said "Sure thing!" So I got out two weeks. I hardly slept for those two weeks.[20]

The first strip appeared on Sunday, October 4, 1931, in the *Detroit Mirror,* and until his retirement on Christmas Day 1977, Gould never missed a deadline, something that is rare among cartoonists.

Chester Gould's intention from the beginning was to incorporate as much realism as possible into his comic strip. Thus, in the 1930s, Gould returned to Northwestern to study criminology. At the time, the crime detection laboratory of Chicago was part of Northwestern, and the policemen did not have their own facilities. (Later on, the laboratory was incorporated into the police department.) At the same time, Gould scrutinized newspaper headlines and police reports that appeared in the daily newspapers. He was particularly interested in accurately depicting real life police procedure. This was probably the closest Gould would come to

studying law and becoming a lawyer as his father had hoped. To insure realistic portrayal of police methods. the cartoonist did something else. For many years after his criminology study at Northwestern, he "employed A.A. Valanis, a retired policeman and one of the first police artists, to help keep the police procedure in *Tracy* accurate and up to the minute."[21] In some instances, Gould's study of the science of criminology enabled him to present new methods and technologies in *Dick Tracy* before they were actually employed in real life. The classic example of this, of course, was the wrist radio Dick Tracy began to use in the comic strips in the mid–Forties. There were other examples as we saw in Chapter 4.

For years Gould did the majority of his work in his second story home studio. In 1936, at the close of the Great Depression (Gould called it the "Big Depression"), Mr. and Mrs. Gould moved to their farm home near Woodstock, then a small town over an hour's drive northwest of Chicago. The suggestion to move to Woodstock came from Gould's agent and friend, Al Lowenthal, who pointed out the value of living on a farm in the event of further economic depression. The studio was in this house.[22] (Al Lowenthal was at least in part Gould's real-life model for Sam Catchem—see Chapter 4.) The farm was run as a business, and turned out corn and alfalfa plus a modest number of cattle. The farm business was more of a hobby and insurance measure for Gould than anything else. Most of Gould's time, usually six and sometimes seven days a week, was spent in perpetuating the saga of Dick Tracy. Over the years, Chester and Edna turned the once rambling, ramshackle old homestead into a beautiful, scenic country home. Gould's pioneering spirit was an all-consuming thing, and it extended beyond *Dick Tracy.*

Chester Gould enjoyed guns and

Opposite: Fillum Fables, October 3 and 5, 1925.

hunting, and he had both guns and mounted trophies in his home studio. In 1955, *Guns Magazine* related an unusual story about Gould that had to make many a reader smile. This article provided a perspective on the artist/writer's human side: a side which was often overshadowed by his famous status. The article stated in part:

> Gould occasionally gets to use a gun when he is busy at his drawing board On his 130-acre place northwest of Chicago, he finds plenty of crows to occupy his attention. "They hop over the stone fence near the front door and make a racket," says Gould. "I guess they're hunting field mice." Drafting his cartoon strips near the second story porch windows, Gould is never too busy to drop his pen and pick up his .22 Remington rifle. Cautiously opening the door, he pokes the barrel of the rifle through the crack and takes aim. The distance is about 150 feet. At last report, the crows are still alive."[23]

And so it went for some fifty years. Most assuredly, there was more drawing with the pen than drawing of the gun.

The material that appeared in *Dick Tracy* between 1931 and 1977, and to a degree from 1977 to the present, is an expression and extension of the personal life of Chester Gould, and the American society in which he lived. He commented once, "Do you know what the cartoonist is? He's a newspaper peddler. He's not a politician. He's not qualified to pass judgment on the big issues of the day. I differ greatly with people who think cartoonists should be a one-man crusaders for this and that."[24] Yet ironically, by the very nature of his medium, Gould could not help but be a politician; he could not help but pass judgment on the big issues of his day. And, there was nothing wrong with this. After all, all art is fiction, autobiography, and metaphor. After a lifetime of some eighty-four years, Chester Gould had lived the dreams of a thousand men and women. His life gave great credence to the viability of the American Dream. He died early Saturday morning, May 11, 1985, after a series of heart-related complications, his family at his side.

"He was very much the personification of Dick Tracy," said Max Allan Collins. "My last view of him — at rest, in a vintage Dick Tracy tie and a Crimestopper badge — revealed the Tracy jaw intact. Goodbye, Chet."[25]

Max Allan Collins

Born on March 3, 1948, in Muscatine, Iowa, to Max Allan and Patricia Ann Collins, Max Allan Collins, Jr., has enjoyed many different kinds of success. The famous author of detective fiction, biographer of Mickey Spillane and Jack Webb, comic strip historian, comic book scripter, and accomplished musician began writing *Dick Tracy* in 1977. As a writer of mystery novels, Collins has produced six distinct series and more than thirty novels in all,

not counting his short stories, critical studies, and edited books.

Max Collins' quest for the paper tiger in detective fiction and related fields is not, however, a recent one. In fact, this journey began for him at age six in 1954. At this time, young Al Collins was reading comics, and among his favorites were those which featured Superman and Donald Duck. (The Fifties were a high point for both characters.) By age eight, he was a

Opposite: Fillum Fables, October 6 and 7, 1925.

The Girl Friends, 1931.

Goodbye, My Friend

May 15, 1985—Dick Locher tribute. Reprinted by permission: Tribune Media Services.

hard-core comics fanatic and was reading a variety of comics—mostly books rather than comic strips—including Chester Gould's *Dick Tracy,* which was being reprinted from the newspaper page in comic book form at this time by Harvey Publishers of New York. Collins states:

> My interest in comic strips and fictional detectives harks back to the same moment: the day my mother [little did she know] put in my hot little six year old hands a tome filled with blood, thunder, villainy and detection: a *Dick Tracy* comic book. Via the covers of those first several *Dick Tracy* comics my impressionable mind was exposed to vivid color depictions of bullets flying through various bad-guy brains, much as the peculiarly grotesque and yet strangely human world of Chester Gould went crashing through my own brain, spiraling through my preadolescent sensibilities, a virtual four-color slug.[26]

It was during this period between 1954 and 1956 that Chester Gould and Dick Tracy made a profound impact on young Collins.

Collins remembers two specific events that would affect the future direction of his life. One was a particular Dick Tracy episode that he read at this time; the other was a letter he received from Chester Gould.

One of the first Dick Tracy stories young Collins read proved to be one of his all-time favorites.

It was the story about Model Jones (which is discussed in Chapter 4). Collins states:

> That was Junior Tracy's "coming of age" story—after decades of being a kid, Junior was dragged by Gould into adolescence—and nearly became a husband in the course of it. Meeting Model Jones, a pretty "older" girl, at a skating rink, Junior falls head-over-heels for her and a courtship ensues; but Model—mindful of Junior's proper upbringing—is afraid her drunken parents and juvenile delinquent brother, Larry, will taint her in her boyfriend's eyes. Junior, of course, could care less, and finally the pair prepares to elope; waiting in a diner with Junior for the honeymoon bus to arrive, Model hears a radio report saying her brother Larry was killed by a cop. Junior is unaware of this, and when Model rebuffs him ("So long, squirt!"), leaving him for his own good, he is crushed; in a singularly expressionistic panel, Gould depicts Junior alone on the highway, watching the bus disappear in the distance, as the sun goes down.
>
> The story's real impact, however, comes from the shocking death of its heroine. A sweet, innocent girl, Model is (accidentally) killed by her own brother whom she's trying to aid. Her shooting

Max Allan Collins—In Bugsy Siegel's suite at the Flamingo Hotel, Las Vegas.

was the cliffhanger of the Harvey comic book (#79), and I remember vividly waiting throughout the next month to see if Model survived—and being stunned, ruined, changed for life when she didn't. The impact of Model's death on me at age seven has shaped much of my approach to fiction writing.[27]

In 1956, Max Collins received his first letter from Chester Gould, and the moment proved to be a historical juncture in young Al's life. Collins remembered:

When I turned eight, I was still an aspiring cartoonist and dedicated fan of *Dick Tracy*. As a special gift, my mother had scooped up some of my Tracy drawings, sent them to Chester Gould, the strip's creator, and asked him to write me. And Chet, being the wonderful guy that he is, sent me a letter with a drawing of Dick Tracy saying "Hello." That birthday present was a turn-

ing point of my life. I credit that one event with really inspiring me to stick with it in the arts. It gave me confidence because right there in that very letter—which is now framed and hanging on my office wall— Chester Gould told me that I drew Dick Tracy better than any other kid my age.[28]

For the duration of grade school, and into junior high, Collins spent much of his free time writing and drawing his own comic stories. One of these homemade productions was "Ghost of the Law," which was similar to Will Eisner's *The Spirit*. The difference was that Collins had not seen Eisner's work at the time, and no one, then or since, has been able to match the legendary Eisner at his peculiarly beautiful and unique art and storytelling styles.

During his junior high days, Max Collins' emphases in the popular arts shifted and expanded. He began reading the works of three masters of hard-boiled detective fiction: Dashiell Hammett, Raymond Chandler, and Mickey Spillane. Collins notes, "The tough-and-tender works of these three men also went spiraling through my brain, like a pulpwood bullet this time, and by the ninth grade I was no longer cartooning; my artwork was limited to sketching preliminary cover art for the paperbacks I aimed to write and sell."[29] Several of his junior high teachers disapproved of Collins' literary creations, and such criticism was not new. Art teachers had disapproved of his cartoon caricatures a few years before. None of this daunted Max Collins, and in a true Chester Gould–like fashion, Collins continued to produce his art for years despite condemnation and lack of acceptance. It was a while longer before the evaluations of his work substantially improved.

During his high school years, the aspiring author wrote six novels, none of which was accepted for publication. But two events during this time provided Collins with further incentive to continue on the trail of the paper tiger. A sympathetic English teacher at West Junior High, an island in a sea of otherwise hostile, unappreciative instructors, allowed him to read his "Matt Savage" private-eye story entitled "The Girl in the River" to "a class quite astounded that their teacher was allowing them to be read such racy, violent stuff, written by one of their own, no less."[30] Collins' parents drove him to Chicago to deliver a manuscript to Tony Licata, who was the editor for Novel Books—"a notorious latterday pulp house ... they published rather traditional tough-guy novels with a little sex tossed in and foisted off on an unsuspecting public as dirty books (you'd be surprised what passed for pornography in 1964)."[31] Collins was 16 at the time, and though persistent, he was unable to sell the manuscript to Licata. "Somehow I managed not to give up, even at the University of Iowa's Writers Workshop where certain teachers and students looked

down their noses at what I was up to. This all changed when I sold the first novel in my Nolan series, *Bait Money,* just before I graduated."[32] (Collins earned an A.A. from Muscatine Community College in 1968 and a B.A. and an M.F.A. from the University of Iowa in 1970 and 1972. Between 1971 and 1977, he was an instructor of English, journalism, and creative writing at Muscatine Community College. He married Barbara Jane Mull on June 1, 1968.)

Originally entitled *First and Last Time,* that first book featured a tough-guy character named Nolan who, like true hard-boiled heroes, embraced a morality independent of socially established law enforcement and the underworld alike. To add to this tension, Nolan had broken from the ranks of the Mafia and was consequently hunted by both gang members and police. As if things were not sufficiently existential for the ironic hero, he was 50 years old and suffering from a midlife crisis. In the original version of *Bait Money* (Collins changed the title with his revision of the novel's end), Nolan's circumstances are too much for him, and "it doesn't quite work out as planned; Nolan gets shot and lies bleeding in the gutter. The tough guy dies."[33] David McDonnell and Kim Howard Johnson write:

> Despite its downbeat finale, *Bait Money* landed Collins an agent, Knox Burger (the former Dell and Gold Medal editor created with the initial paperback successes of Kurt Vonnegut, John D. MacDonald, and others), and in quick succession, several rejection slips. "With each turndown, Knox suggested I revise the book's ending and let Nolan live. It was beginning to wear on me; my original idea had been to write the last tough guy story."[34]

"A cup of coffee spilled on that manuscript by an editor at Pyramid Books is the shakey foundation on which my entire career is built," Collins laughed. "Knox told me, 'This copy's ruined. You'll have to get a new one typed up, so, for God's sake, will you please change the ending?!'"[35] Collins did just that, and his first novel sold in 1971, nine years after he had actively tried to sell his writing through the mail for the first time. Curtis Books released *Bait Money,* and its sequel, *Blood Money,* two years later in 1973.

Max Collins completed three additional books in the Nolan series for a contract which was now held by Popular Library, since Popular Library had bought out Curtis. Popular did not publish these third, fourth, and fifth Nolan stories, and Collins asked for his release from the contract. Pinnacle Books picked up the series, and Collins wrote a sixth Nolan novel. In 1981, Pinnacle Books began publishing the six books, reprinting the first two of the series initially released by Curtis Books. The series now included: *Nolan #1: Bait Money* (1981), *Nolan #2: Blood Money* (1981), *Nolan #3: Fly Paper* (1981), *Nolan #4: Hush Money* (1981), *Hard Cash (Nolan #5)* (1982), and *Scratch Fever (Nolan #6)* (1982). But the problems for the Nolan series were not over yet. Harlequin Books and its new line of Gold Eagle books took over the publishing responsibilities for Don Pendleton's "The Executioner" series in 1981 from Pinnacle Books, the new Nolan publisher.[36] Harlequin and Gold Eagle Books trumped up accusations and threatened a lawsuit. The claim was that Pendleton's Executioner, Mack Bolan, was being exploited by Collins' series and that the similarity of character names—Bolan and Nolan—was more than coincidence. The accusation was the farthest thing from the truth, as the two series and their protagonists were wholly dissimilar. Bolan was a mercenary; Nolan was a middle-aged, tough-guy detective. The audiences for the two series were dramatically different. Targeted at readers who embraced Lawrence Saunders and Robert Ludlum stories, Collins' works were far from "Executioner" status. The Nolan stories are a hybrid of traditions influenced by the work of Mickey Spillane and Donald E. Westlake. When the fifth and sixth Nolan novels came out, the Nolan name was dropped from the cover. The lawsuit never occurred, and probably would not have succeeded, but the damage was done. Sales dropped off from what was a very successful series, and Nolan numbers five and six received poor distribution to boot. Ed Abrahms did the attractive cover art for the series.

In 1987, Tor Books published a seventh Max Collins Nolan novel in hardcover. Entitled *Spree,* the book was also released in 1988 in paperback form by Tor. In 1991, Nolan numbers five and six were reprinted in one paperback volume by Carroll and Graf Books. The re-release of these Collins stories under the title *Tough Tender* was a real treat for fans of mystery fiction and of Max Allan Collins.

Between the mass market debut of Max Allan Collins and Nolan in 1973 and the temporary retirement of Nolan in 1982, Collins spawned another successful series of tough-guy novels. The Quarry series, which features a hit man with the same name, debuted in 1976 with Berkley Publishing Corporation's release of *The Broker.* Quarry is "a Vietnam Veteran who the war taught to be indifferent towards killing, and who became a hired assassin."[37] The first four books of this series initially ran from 1976 through 1977 and included *The Broker* (1976), *The Broker's Wife* (1976), *The Dealer* (1976), and *The Slasher* (1977). Countryman Press reprinted these novels in 1985 and 1986 in mass market paperback form under new titles, and added a fifth Collins Quarry novel in hardcover in 1987 entitled *Primary Target.* Collins stated about his Nolan and Quarry series, "I felt their amorality reflected the period in which they were written; I still do."[38]

Max Collins followed up his work on Nolan and Quarry with two smashing new critically acclaimed mystery series featuring hard-boiled detectives Mallory and Nathan Heller. Collins describes Mallory as "a mystery writer in a small town in Iowa (where do you get your ideas?) that took me back into private-eye territory, but only on the outskirts."[39] At this writing the Mallory series consisted of five novels: *The Baby Blue Rip-Off* (1983), *No Cure for Death* (1983), *Kill Your Darlings* (1984), *A Shroud for Aquarius* (1985), and *Nice Weekend for a Murder* (1986). Collins notes that the fourth book in the series, *A Shroud for Aquarius*, focuses on the Baby Boom generation and the hopes and dreams of that love and peace group, and how it all stacked up fifteen years later (circa 1985). He states, "The book has been described as *The Big Chill* with corpses, but I think it's different than that."[40]

When the first Mallory book was published in 1983, it was apparent that Max Collins was building upon the success of his already solid Nolan and Quarry series. The best was yet to come that same year when the first book of the author's fourth, and perhaps most famous, series to date appeared. The novel, entitled *True Detective*, featured detective Nathan Heller and was published by St. Martin's Press. Mickey Spillane called it "one of the best stories I have ever read."[41] Robert A. Baker and Michael T. Nietzel, in *Private Eyes: 101 Knights*, deemed it "probably the best historical detective novel ever written."[42] Collins himself stated, "I arrived with that book."[43] Baker and Nietzel write:

> It is the portrayal of an era—the tough-guy 1930s—with a broad sweep from the brawny shoulders of Chicago where most of the action takes place to the plastic paradise of Miami where Heller tries to prevent the murder of Chicago's mayor, Anton Cermak. This book is thoroughly researched and the many historical personages and events that are included are not mere grace notes of nostalgia; they are integral to the plot and they establish the novel's back-room, dark-alley atmosphere.[44]

In 1984, Max Collins followed *True Detective* with the second book featuring Thirties tough-guy Nate Heller, *True Crime*. The third Heller novel, *The Million-Dollar Wound*, followed in 1986. (Collins had resisted the temptation to title this third Heller novel *True War*, and then also discarded the title *Shell Shock*.) In 1984, Collins reflected on his then relatively new series:

> The Heller projects are, by my way of thinking, the major thing I do. In addition to being the second guy on *Dick Tracy*, the Heller books seem to be my best shot at some kind of posterity. They seem to be books that may last. They give my more standard crime and mystery novels a longer lease on life. Because people are interested in the Heller novels, there's a chance many of them will turn and look at the other things I've done.[45]

True Detective earned Max Collins the P.I. Writers of America Award for 1983. At this writing the series includes *True Detective* (1983), *True Crime* (1984), *The Million-Dollar Wound* (1986), *Neon Mirage: A Novel of Bugsy Siegel's Las Vegas* (1988), *Stolen Away: A Novel of the Lindbergh Kidnapping* (1991), and the short story collection *Dying in the Post-War World* (1991).

In 1986, Max Allan Collins and Countryman Press released *Midnight Haul*, a mystery novel which features the evils of corporate America and toxic waste disposal—themes that also appeared in Collins' *Dick Tracy* scripts about the same time. *Midnight Haul* was released in paperback by Knightsbridge Publishing in 1990.

In 1987, Max Allan Collins' first novel of his fifth series appeared. The well-regarded series, which like the Heller stories interweaves historical fact and fiction, features real-life hero Eliot Ness. This series of books includes the Bantam paperbacks: *The Dark City* (1987), *Butcher's Dozen* (1988), and *Bullet Proof* (1989), and the St. Martin's hardcover *Murder by the Numbers* (1993).

With the advent of the 1990 *Dick*

Tracy movie, Collins was called upon to write a novelization of the Warren Beatty production. The resulting novelization proved to be one of the finest such adaptations done in recent memory. Collins' novel was faithful to the Jim Cash and Jack Epps screenplay, and actually brought the script more into line with the legacy of Chester Gould's *Dick Tracy*. The novelization was also the first of a four-novel series featuring the exploits of Dick Tracy. The second Collins Tracy novel is entitled *Dick Tracy Goes to War* (1991); the third is entitled *Dick Tracy Meets His Match* (1992); the fourth remained to be announced at this writing. The Dick Tracy novels are complex, entertaining mystery stories which are faithful to, and expand upon, the spirit of the *Tracy* legend. They provide fast action and enthralling formula fiction. As with other Collins novels, the new Tracy books pay careful attention to issues of historical detail and context.

Beyond contributions to the mystery genre of Nolan, Quarry, Mallory, Heller, Ness, and others, Max Collins has done much to preserve the heritage of his predecessors in hard-boiled detective fiction. Among other achievements, Collins has become the definitive biographer of Mickey Spillane, his longtime hero and friend. He has written, edited, co-edited, and introduced four major Mickey Spillane studies and collections to date. These include: *Mickey Spillane's Mike Hammer: The Comic Strip, Volumes One and Two* (with Catherine Yronwode, 1982 and 1985 respectively); *One Lonely Knight: Mickey Spillane's Mike Hammer* (with James L. Traylor, 1984); and *Tomorrow I Die* (1984).

In addition, Collins has edited *Dick Tracy: The Secret Files* (with Martin H. Greenberg, 1990), a mass market paperback collection of new Tracy stories released at the time of the Beatty movie. He has edited (with Dick Locher) two volumes of *Dick Tracy* comic strip reprints: *The Dick Tracy Casebook* (1990) and *Dick Tracy's Fiendish Foes!: A 60th Anniversary*

Celebration (1991). In 1988, he edited (with John Javna) a book entitled *The Best of Crime and Detective TV*.

Collins' success as a mystery writer is largely attributable to his awareness of those who pioneered the hard-boiled detective story, and his ability to reflect and enhance that heritage. But he is not only a scholar and perpetuator of the traditions of the old masters, he is a creative force himself. Mystery writers who he acknowledges have influenced his work include Dashiell Hammett, Raymond Chandler, Mickey Spillane, Ed McBain (Evan Hunter), Donald E. Westlake, James M. Cain, Jim Thompson, Horace McCoy, and W.R. Burnett.

While mystery writing—particularly that which involves tough-guy detective fiction—has been Max Collins' primary vocation and avocation, his love of comic art has never died. Though Collins' original drawing was all but ended with the advent of high school, the young author collected and continued to voraciously read large quantities of comic art. He does so yet today. When Collins turned his attention to mystery fiction, his career in comics was far from over. About 1975, Rick Marschall, comics editor for Field Enterprises, suggested Collins create a story strip for him.[46] Marschall felt that the setting for the strip ought to be the 1930s "partially because of the new wave of nostalgia that had hit the country in recent years, partially because it would tie our new strip to the Golden Age of the comic strip continuity."[47] Collins created Nate Heller for the project, and set him in 1930s Chicago. The strip was titled *Heaven and Heller* and was an exciting prospect to the team of Collins and Marschall. But it did not work out. Collins notes:

> *Heaven and Heller* went into limbo because Rick left his position at Field, at which time all his current projects were shelved. Rick, over the next several years, tried to market the strip to other syndi-

cates; we even (at the request of King Features) had a second, beautiful batch of samples worked up by Fred DaSilva (currently the *Rex Morgan MD* artist). I went back to book-writing, figuring this brief excursion into comics was a fluke—a fun, memorable fluke, but a fluke.[48]

Yet Max Collins' big break into comics was closer than he knew at the time. In fact, it came in 1977. He states, "I was comfortably settled in a home of my own, happily married to my childhood sweetheart Barb, my writing career humming along unspectacularly, but humming along."[49] One day the phone rang. It was Don Michel, vice president and editor of the Chicago Tribune Syndicate. Michel told Collins that Chester Gould was about to retire, and he asked Collins if he would like to try out for *Dick Tracy*. Several sources indicated that Max Allan Collins would be just the kind of writer they were looking for to take over the scripting responsibilities of the famous comic strip. The syndicate was looking for a mystery writer, and Collins' work on his Nolan series and on his *Heaven and Heller* pointed to the young author's abilities and his knowledge of classic comic strips. The Nolan series continually made references to comic strips and books because Nolan's sidekick, Jon, was a comics collector and fanatic. Other things clicked also, but ironically Collins' correspondence with Gould had little if any connection with the offer to try out for the strip. Many people wrote to Gould, and Collins had only written him casually to this point. Collins remembered, "I sat down and read the last decade of *Dick Tracy* and prepared a 15-page treatment of what was right and wrong with those strips. And I followed that up with a sample story, which became my first continuity, the Angeltop story. A few weeks later, I was in Chicago, meeting the syndicate heads and negotiating a contract."[50]

Max Collins teamed up with Rick Fletcher, Gould's assistant on the comic

strip for some sixteen years, to produce *Dick Tracy* from 1977 to 1983. Collins did the writing; Fletcher did the drawing. The strip continued successfully until Fletcher's death in 1983, and it was a tribute to both writer and artist who worked together under adverse conditions. Collins lived in Muscatine, Iowa, and Fletcher lived in Woodstock, Illinois. Their collaboration was conducted largely by mail. Upon Fletcher's death in 1983, Dick Locher, an assistant to Chester Gould on *Dick Tracy* years before, assumed the responsibilities of drawing *Tracy*. More than fifteen years later, *Dick Tracy* continues to flourish. Max Collins has had a great deal to do with the continued success of Chester Gould's creation.

Collins' early work on *Dick Tracy* signaled the beginning of his break into the field of comic art. He began looking for other collaborations and other projects.

For some time I'd been keeping an eye on the developing artistic talent of a young friend of mine, Terry Beatty. He introduced himself to me at a Happy Joe's, a pizza and ice cream parlor in Muscatine, probably around 1973; he must've been about fifteen at the time. He let me know how much he liked my books, *Bait Money* and *Blood Money*. He then explained that he was the son of Ernest Beatty, my English teacher back in junior high—the very one who'd let me read my blood-and-thunder short stories to class.... Fairly early on I discovered Terry was doing very primitive, cartoony, underground-influenced art for a high school humor magazine.[51]

In 1978, Collins suggested Beatty team up with him to produce *Little Orphan Annie* samples for the Tribune syndicate. *Annie* at this time was reprinting old stories by Harold Gray, the strip's creator and single force until his death in 1968. (Between 1968 and 1978, *Annie* had been on rocky roads with Gray's first successors not making the grade. With greatly reduced cir-

The passing of the torch—Chester and Edna Gould with Max and Barbara Collins—Mr. Gould received his second Reuben award, 1978 (for 1977).

culation of *Annie,* the syndicate resorted to reprinting classic Gray stories.) With the Broadway show such a success, Collins figured that a collaboration with Beatty "had a shot at selling a revived *Annie.*"[52] Collins was commissioned by the syndicate to draft a synopsis, with the understanding that if things went well, Terry Beatty would be the artist. The syndicate offered the job of scripting to Collins, but wanted a different artist. Collins refused the deal. (Fortunately for fans of *Annie,* the Tribune syndicate landed Leonard Starr as the scripter and artist of the strip shortly thereafter. Starr has brought back much of the vitality, integrity, and original direction of Gray's famous comic strip.)

With the disappointment of *Annie* behind them, Collins decided that he and

Terry needed to launch a new project. He noted:

> Terry and I began producing a self-contained tabloid page of comics—six features of varying types, mostly humor—which we syndicated to weekly newspapers (including "shoppers") around the country; we were a moderate success, with about sixteen papers including the Chicago *Reader* (who used only our minute mystery feature, *Mike Mist*). But after a year we folded up *The Comics Page* and began working on other projects.[53]

The next stop for the Collins/Beatty team was Eclipse Enterprises, and the creation of *Ms. Tree.* Dean Mullaney of Eclipse met Max and Terry at the 1980 Chicago Comics Convention, and was an avid reader of *Dick Tracy* and *Mike Mist*. The result was that the trio put together and published a *Mike Mist* collection. Mullaney then encouraged Collins and Beatty to submit a story, maybe one about a private eye, to Eclipse. Collins developed a scenario where "the secretary marries the private eye and, on their wedding night, the private eye is killed bequeathing her the business and his unsolved murder. Mike Hammer finally marries Velda, only to be killed and she has to fill his shoes—and holster"[54] Collins named the heroine Ms. Tree, drawing on a heritage of puns provided by Dick Tracy characters. Ms. Tree has been in comic books ever since.

Today an established, award-winning mystery writer, accomplished scripter for stories of the comic arts, biographer, editor, and more, Max Collins pursues his quest for that elusive paper tiger. He might just catch the beast.

Richard E. Fletcher

Rick Fletcher at home, about 1980 (photo courtesy Beverly Fletcher).

Richard E. (Rick) Fletcher was born and raised in Burlington, Iowa, one of four children. His father was an engineer on the Burlington Route for 48 years. Fletcher always enjoyed drawing, but he also liked photography. He enjoyed tennis, and in his youth, Rick was a batboy for the local semipro team in Burlington. Beverly Fletcher, Rick's wife, recalled, "His father wanted him to be a shortstop!"[55] Mrs. Fletcher continues, "Art was his first love and he was one of the lucky people who worked and breathed all his life doing his favorite thing. He'd rather be dead than not be able to draw."[56] Joanne Springman writes:

Fletcher started his career at age 18 as the one-man art department of *Tri-City Star* in Davenport, Iowa. He had no formal art training but learned his craft by studying art books in the public library of his native Burlington, Iowa.

His career was interrupted by World War II, in which he attained the rank of captain and received the Bronze Star while serving with the U.S. Army in five European campaigns.

After the war, Fletcher joined the advertising art staff of the *Chicago Tribune* and studied comic strip technique under the Pulitzer Prize–winning cartoonist Carey Orr.

From 1953 to 1965, Fletcher drew the well-known historical strip "The Old Glory Story" for the Tribune Syndicate. Written in collaboration with Athena Robbins, the strip received several awards from national patriotic organizations. Many of the artist's original pages are in museum collections around the country.[57]

Rick Fletcher was a humanitarian, a continuously busy and industrious person who always seemed to succeed at what he did. Mrs. Fletcher stated that the awards her late husband received included "many from the VFW, DAR, and the Freedom Foundation—five medals and other awards."[58] From 1961 to 1977, Fletcher assisted Chester Gould on *Dick Tracy*, where he did the lettering and backgrounds for the strip.

Beverly Fletcher provides some important insight into Rick's role on *Tracy* during those 16 years. She writes:

> One of the things seldom mentioned is the fact that when Rick started working with Chet there were three other assistants also. Ray Gould (Chet's brother) did the lettering, Jack Ryan and Rick did backgrounds, Chet did the main characters and Al Valanis (a retired Chicago police detective) was consultant on all police details. They worked together on the story line week to week. As they left or died Rick and Chet were the only ones left and Rick did all the work except the drawing of the main characters which Chet continued to do.[59]

"'He was a nice guy,' Gould said shortly after Fletcher's death on March 16, 1983. 'We hit it off right away, and when I retired, I recommended in writing to the newspaper syndicate that they hire him to do the art. Thank goodness they liked him and did.'"[60] Chester Gould's sentiments were commonly held by others who knew Rick. Fletcher was an original talent, a team player, and a kind, gentle man. "Gould singled out Fletcher as the most versatile of all his associates, and the finest draftsman he'd ever worked with. Called the 'best gun artist' in comics, Fletcher's background work and lettering for Gould over the years has been unparalleled, and his own strip, the historical Sunday page *Old Glory Story*, had a lengthy run."[61]

With the retirement of Chester Gould from *Dick Tracy* on December 25, 1977, Rick Fletcher took over the illustrating responsibilities for the famous comic strip. At this time he collaborated with Max Allan Collins, who wrote the scripts for *Tracy*. Collins states, "Rick struck me as a very nice man. We exchanged some friendly letters and he sent me an *Old Glory* original."[62] During his stint as *Tracy's* illustrator, Fletcher, as Gould had done before him, took special care to study police techniques, procedures, and equipment. Beverly Fletcher writes:

> About the time of Art Deco [spelled "Dekko," a famous *Tracy* villain who emerged from the Fletcher/Collins collaboration] Rick became acquainted with Julio Santiago of the Hastings, Minnesota, police department who, with a partner, invented the nite-site which was used in the Art Deco story line. Rick and Julio became good friends and if anything came up Rick would consult Julio about details on how to handle a situation in a story. Rick was a stickler on detail and accuracy.[63]

Max Collins stated, "The Art Dekko/Sue Reel story was based, partially, on the famous Chicago Art Institute heist of several years before. . . . Rick's portrayal of Johnny Adonis—who was later to become a regular in the strip—was based on a real-life NYC art cop, Robert Volpe. . . ."[64] "Black policewoman Lee Ebony, introduced in that continuity was, of course, named in tribute to Will Eisner's character Ebony."[65]

Beyond being a major force behind the overall success of *Dick Tracy*, Rick Fletcher was the most important individual in the transition from the Gould years into the post–Gould years. More than anyone else, perhaps even Gould himself who stayed on for a while in the late Seventies as a consultant, Fletcher was responsible for the smooth shift from

Opposite: Old Glory Story, **January 17, 1960. Reprinted by permission: Tribune Media Services.**

Rick Fletcher's Dick Tracy

tinued, but at the same time indicate a new direction. What better way to indicate a second generation of *Tracy* than to introduce the second generation of villains: Flattop's daughter Angeltop and the Brow's son? The "Deathtrap" finale [felt by many fans to be Rick Fletcher's finest hour] takes the strip literally back to the climax of the most famous *Tracy* story of all, the replica ship in the lagoon where Flattop drowned in 1944—but such elements as Angeltop's media appearances, decrying the deaths of her father and brother as the result of police brutality, were meant to show the strip was connected to the '70s, not just the '40s.[66]

"Rick was especially proud of his 'hardware'—guns were a particular passion, and Tracy's .357 magnum always had a high-tech, chrome look that gave our strip a sheen," writes Collins, who also believes that Rick Fletcher brought a very glossy, modern, high-tech look to *Tracy* in general, and who believes that two of their finest contributions as a team to the comic were the villains Angeltop and, later, Torcher.[67] "I think Rick Fletcher outdid himself on the design of Torcher, who may be the best villain we did together," noted Collins.[68] "Rick said he enjoyed doing 'the Ghost of Itchy' story [the final Fletcher *Tracy* sequence] very much—it was one of his favorites of our stories; possibly his very favorite. He always brought great vitality to the strip, but this story has a special flair," Collins remarked.[69]

Gould's *Tracy* to the *Tracy* of those that followed. Rick Fletcher was the bridge, and *Dick Tracy* very likely might have died in 1977 when Chester Gould retired had not Fletcher been on hand to provide insight and continuity.

Rick Fletcher and Max Collins became the second generation of *Dick Tracy* storytellers when Gould retired. While Fletcher and Collins admirably succeeded in maintaining many of Gould's long-standing traditions and his integrity, they brought to the comic strip a freshness and vitality of their own. Collins remembered:

We wanted to show that the traditions of Chet Gould's classic strip would be con-

On Friday, March 11, 1983, Rick Fletcher produced his final work for *Dick Tracy*. The next day, he went into Memorial Hospital for McHenry County near his home in Woodstock, Illinois. On Wednesday, March 16, 1983, the greatest comics artist of guns, hardware and machinery in the history of the medium died. "He had drawn the first few Sunday pages of the next story [in which Junior's daughter, Honey, starts a Crime Stoppers Club] and finished up all but the last week of dailies of the 'The Ghost of Itchy' story."[70] "I'm proud of the work Rick Fletcher and

I did together, writes Collins. "His legacy is his work.... Rick Fletcher was a real pro."[71] Chester Gould said it all: "He was a nice guy."[72]

Fletcher's survivors include his wife, Beverly; his daughter, Kathryn Sue Werr-bach, and her daughters, Sara Jane and Emily Grace; his son, R. Ross Fletcher, and his daughter, Jessica Anne. His ashes are buried, at his request, at the Rock Island National Military Cemetery, Rock Island, Illinois.[73]

Dick Locher

Upon Rick Fletcher's death in March of 1983, editorial cartoonist Dick Locher assumed the responsibility of drawing *Dick Tracy*. Working on *Tracy*, however, was not a new experience for Locher. In the late Fifties and early Sixties (just before Rick Fletcher joined the Dick Tracy family), Locher was an assistant to Chester Gould. Just prior to the time Locher rejoined *Dick Tracy* in 1983, he won a Pulitzer Prize for his editorial cartooning. According to Max Collins, Locher provides "a great sense of humor" and "beautifully designed villains" for *Dick Tracy*.[74]

Dick Locher was born in Dubuque, Iowa, in 1929 and became interested in art at a young age.[75] One highlight from this early period of his artistic work that he recalls is when he won one dollar and a blue ribbon at a county fair for drawing (copying) Pappy Yokum—Li'l Abner's father. In grade school, he drew caricatures of his teachers in his textbooks. After high school, Locher studied art at the University of Iowa and the Chicago Academy of Fine Arts, where he met Rick Yager who was drawing *Buck Rogers* at the time. He also attended the Arts Center in Los Angeles. Locher remembered of Yager, "He asked me to be his assistant—I was twenty-one at the time. I worked half a year with him before I enlisted in the Air Force."[76] Locher became a captain, flying and testing new aircraft at Wright-Patterson Air Force Base (Dayton, Ohio). During this time also, Locher submitted gags to *Stars and Stripes* where, he claimed, "the money was great."[77]

In 1957, Dick Locher met Chester Gould. Locher recalls their first meeting and early collaborations:

I worked as a cartoonist in an art studio when Chet asked me to join him in 1957. We hit it off pretty good—and as far as I can find out—I was the only assistant he let ink his figures. He was strict—sometimes he didn't like what I did at all—and we'd erase and start all over. Towards the end of my stint with him [1961], he would give me the entire six dailies to take home and ink. I felt pretty proud. I put a few figures in on the Sundays—and colored the Sunday page. In 1958—I contributed to the story that was cited in his Reuben win.[78]

After leaving Gould in 1961, Locher branched into other areas of the arts. Among other things, he started his own advertising company and helped design some McDonald's characters, including Ronald McDonald in 1967. Locher remained good friends with Gould during these years and kept in touch with him. In a 1990 interview with Neil Hansen, Locher recalled:

One day he [Gould] called and said that the editorial cartoonist of the *Chicago Tribune* was going to retire, and why not go down and be their editorial cartoonist. I said, "Cripes, Chet, I've never done an editorial cartoon in my life." I went because I was a friend of Chet's, not expect-

Dick Locher (photo courtesy Sally Good).

ing to even come close, and they liked me. I had a room right next to Chet's and well, we were good friends and we used to have lunch together and the whole shooting match. And then, 1983 came by and I won the Pulitzer, I was fortunate enough to win that, and that made Chet kind of proud, I guess. He called me about five in the morning and then later that very same morning he says, "Why don't you do Dick Tracy, too?"[79]

For more than twenty years, Dick Locher has been an editorial cartoonist for the *Chicago Tribune;* for more than ten years he has drawn *Tracy.* Though very proud of his work for the comic strip, Locher notes that political cartoons are the art form he prefers.[80] Among his accomplishments and awards in this area are his Pulitzer Prize, the Overseas Press Club Award (won twice), the Sigma Delta Chi Award, the Dragonslayer Award (won five times), and the Heath Journalism Gold Award (won six times). His work has been reprinted in *Time, Newsweek, U.S. News,*

Dick Locher's Dick Tracy

and *Congressional Record*. He adds, "I like my job."[81]

In 1986, when asked what he saw as the future for *Dick Tracy*, Locher commented, "*Dick Tracy* will continue to thrive as one of the few adventure strips—because he [it] reflects today's (and tomorrow's) crimes with genuinely 'fun' characters, unusual characters—and crime solving techniques."[82] He has been exactly right in his prediction. Locher adds that the strength of the characters determines *Tracy's* future. Locher's son, John, helped draw the famous comic strip for several years.

John Locher

John Locher, born in 1961, was the son of Dick and Mary Locher. He assisted his father with the drawing of *Dick Tracy* for three years after having studied art for four years at Northern Illinois University. He also did "extensive freelance artwork for Chicago radio stations, insurance companies and thrift institutions."[83] Dick Locher noted of his son:

> John did the pencil drawing of the daily strip and I would ink it in. I would do the Sunday pencils and he would ink them in and then we would switch. That's how Chester Gould used to do it with me. He said it was a good way to get to know each other's work and style. John greatly loved Chester and admired his work. He really thought highly of his sharp black and white etchings when most of the other comics were grays.[84]

Dick Locher also stated that John "loved to focus on details such as tire marks in portraying a chase sequence or photographing a car or diesel engine to help him sketch it into the strip. He also often included his friends' names on street signs or the names of famous musicians on the sides of trucks as company logos."[85] John also "enjoyed adding to the story line and thinking up new characters to match the evil they represented. His forte, his father said, was focusing on facial expressions."[86] John Locher died at home on Sunday, May 18, 1986.

Richard Arnold "Dick" Moores

The first known assistant to Chester Gould on *Dick Tracy* was a young aspiring artist named Dick Moores. Moores was

John Locher (photo courtesy Val Mazenga).

born in Lincoln, Nebraska, on December 12, 1909, and grew up in Omaha. He graduated from high school in Fort Wayne, Indiana, and "he worked with his father in the family wholesale radio business, managed a theater, and eventually saved enough money to go to Chicago and enroll in the Academy of Fine Arts."[87] During this time in the early 1930s, Moores

was kicked out of art school, and upon the advice of his friend, Bob York (who was assisting on Carl Ed's *Harold Teen*), Moores submitted samples of his lettering to Chester Gould, who was looking for an assistant on *Dick Tracy*. Moores told Ron Goulart, "So I went to my basement room, shared with three other broke and jobless, and sat up all night lettering. I took it in the

Dick Moores

next morning, and Chester Gould hired me. Not because the lettering was good, but because there was so much of it."[88] This was April 1932.

Gould paid Moores five dollars a week, and over the next five years, Moores received raises to ten, fifteen, and eventually twenty dollars a week. Moores noted, "I did the lettering and backgrounds on the daily and Sunday and colored the Sunday prints. I never inked a figure."[89] "Chester wrote and drew both dailies and Sundays, inked all the characters and did the shading. All I did was letter them, clean up and ink the backgrounds, fill in the blacks and color two Sunday page prints. It took about three and a half days and I was free to work in a little advertising studio the rest of the week."[90] Yet Max Collins gives more credit to Moores and his early contributions to *Tracy* and notes that the distinctive style of lettering that Dick Moores provided *Tracy* in the early 1930s is the favorite lettering of most of those who have followed the

strip through the years.[91] Ron Goulart writes, "The characteristic *Tracy* style of lettering, carried on by subsequent assistants, seems to be Moores' invention."[92] *Jim Hardy* followed and Moores left Gould, though he often recounted years later that he missed Gould and *Dick Tracy*. Moores, in an entertaining and enthralling fashion, relates the birth of *Hardy* and his departure from *Tracy* to pursue his own career in *Jim Hardy: A Complete Compilation: 1936–1937*.

While an assistant of Chester Gould between virtually the beginning of *Dick Tracy* and 1935, Moores spent much of his free time working up ideas for strips of his own. None of these were accepted for publication by the syndicates until he produced *Jim Conely* for United Feature Syndicate. United asked Moores to submit further samples, and eventually asked him to come to New York. The strip's title was changed to *Jim Hardy*, and Dick Moores received a ten-year contract since "UFS felt a man who'd spent five years in close proximity to Chester Gould was just the man to do an adventure strip they could sell opposite *Dick Tracy*."[93] Ron Goulart, in his remarkable and insightful book on 1930s comic strips entitled *The Adventurous Decade*, elaborates on Moores' efforts to sell *Jim Hardy*. The art and storylines of *Jim Hardy* showed a strong influence by Chester Gould and *Dick Tracy*. Saalfield Publishing Company marketed a Big Little Book–type book about Moores' detective hero entitled *Jim Hardy: Ace Reporter* in 1940.

In October of 1942, Dick Moores and his wife were living in southern California when he left *Jim Hardy* and United Feature Syndicate for Walt Disney Studios. *Jim Hardy* had been an interesting and entertaining but not terrifically successful comic strip. (Moores' introduction to *Jim Hardy, A Complete Compilation: 1936–1937* provides the definitive history of the ill-fated strip.) Dick Moores spent 14 years with Disney Studios.[94] Anyone who follows the famous comic book *Walt Disney's Comics and Stories,* which is more than fifty years old, knows that Moores contributed much artwork and many storylines to these books. During his stint with Disney, Moores did a number of Mickey Mouse stories—his illustration of Mickey being more cartoony and rounder, and more broad-faced than previous interpretations. Moores once stated, "My first job [with Disney] was inking the *Mickey* strip for Floyd Gottfredson. I had never seen such meticulously drawn, beautiful pencil work. And here I was going to have to take my clumsy pen and go over those beautiful lines. That was about as scary a thing as I ever had to do."[95] In an interview with Tor Odemark for *The Duckburg Times* 20 (June 9, 1984), Moores recalled that he liked working with all the established Disney characters—including the "Remus" bunch, Goofy, the Peter Pan gang, Dumbo, Bongo, and Bambi—but his favorite was Goofy.[96] Moores related that his friends and favorite artists for Disney included Floyd Gottfredson (the man who made Mickey Mouse famous in the newspaper comic strips of the 1930s), Manuel Gonzales (whom he collaborated with on several occasions including in 1949 for the Simon and Schuster Golden Story Book entitled *Mystery in Disneyville*), Bill Peat, and Fred Moore.[97] In the interview with Odemark, Moores cited Chester Gould, Frank King (the creator of *Gasoline Alley*), and Carl Buettner of Whitman Publishing Company (Racine, Wisconsin) as inspirations; he added that the stories of Harold Gray *(Little Orphan Annie),* Roy Crane *(Wash Tubbs and Captain Easy),* and Milt Caniff *(Terry and the Pirates* and *Steve Canyon)* also inspired him.[98] He continued that his favorite story that he did for Disney was "Mickey Mouse and the Wonderful Whizzix" and that this story might have been "the germ of the idea" for the Disney movie *The Love Bug* (1969).[99]

"Moores' involvement in the lives of *Gasoline Alley* began in 1956 when at the age of forty-six he moved to Florida and

became Frank King's assistant and almost immediately took over the story line. Although King lived until 1969, *Gasoline Alley* has [had], in effect, been Moores' strip since 1960."[100] It was in *Gasoline Alley* that Moores made his biggest contribution to the history of the comic strip. (The Moores era of *Gasoline Alley* is aptly discussed in Nat Hentoff's introduction to his edited book entitled *Gasoline Alley.)* The National Cartoonists Society awarded Dick Moores its highest honor, the annual Reuben award as "Outstanding Cartoonist of the Year," in 1974. Moores continued *Gasoline Alley* until his death on April 22, 1986, in an Asheville, North Carolina, hospital. He had started as Chester Gould's assistant on *Dick Tracy* in the 1930s, created his own comic strips, worked for Walt Disney, and ended with great flair as the successor to Frank King on *Gasoline Alley.*

On February 10, 1986, the author sent a letter interview to Dick Moores. Moores died on April 22, but he had begun his response to his letter. The completed portion of the interview was returned to the author by his estate in June 1986. Shortly thereafter, the author began a correspondence with Dick Moores' daughter, Sara Campbell, who has been most kind and helpful. He has decided to reprint the contents of what was surely one of Dick Moores' last interviews as they were presented to him. Moores' charm and wit will not be lost in translation that way.

Can you tell me briefly about your youth? Where were you born, your early interests and experiences?

I was born in Lincoln, Neb. in Dec. 1909. My father was in the music business. My mother was a piano teacher. At the age of four she was a child prodigy. She studied in Germany and played for Kaiser Wilhelm. Later toured with Victor Herbert. I didn't pick up any of her musical talent. We lived on the main street and had to walk six blocks to the Bryant School. Kids would waylay my brother and me in a brick yard on the way to school. We always carried a few rocks in our pockets. There was a little blood spilled but nothing serious. I was glad when we moved to Omaha (I was ten) and bought a house in a better neighborhood. I entered high school at the age of eleven and wore knee high pants. It was here I first started to take a serious interest in drawing. Henry Fonda was a senior there and did some fine drawings for the yearbook. My first drawing was published in the school paper in my sophomore year. Then we moved to Fort Wayne, Ind. where I finished high school. Drew cartoons for the school paper and the yearbook. They weren't very good.

How did you get interested in comic strips? and How did you break into the field? How did you arrive at the idea for Jim Hardy? *and Why do you feel that* Gasoline Alley *has enjoyed such a popularity? What was and is it now like, to work for the syndicate?*

I attended Chi. Academy of Art for one year then in April, 1932, I went to work as Chester Gould's asst. I just did the lettering at first but soon did backgrounds and the color prints. I drew the first *Jim Hardy* page one New Year's Night when my girlfriend, Gretchen, went to a party with another guy. (I married her in May, 1937.) I sat up all night doing the page. It was about an ex-convict (who was innocent of course). United Features liked it and asked me for two weeks of strips. I sent them within a week and they hired me. I tried to draw *Jim Hardy* so he wouldn't look like *Tracy*. But for years my work looked like Chester's. The strip was a failure but I continued to do it for 6½ yrs. In 1942 we decided to axe it and I went to work for Walt Disney in the comic strip dept. *Jim Hardy* failed because I got most of my ideas watching movies, I kept changing Jim's character trying to get the right combination, but I *did* learn a lot by mistakes, improved my writing and drawing, and finally toward the end of the strip wasn't looking so much like *Tracy*.

Gasoline Alley is the only strip that has a feel of true realism. This is partly because the characters age, but mostly it is because I learned from Frank King how to put them in human interest situations and to insert a certain amount of humor. Also I have kept up with the times.

When I took over *Gasoline Alley,* thanks to the syndicate I inherited a nice list of papers, but I have found over the years the syndicate can't do much to help you retain the list. It is all up to the artist. Example—about 40 papers that now run *Gas Alley* have tried to drop the feature and had to put it back in the paper, because of reader complaints. The readers are the people you have to please, not the editors of the newspapers or the people at the syndicate.

What was your role on Dick Tracy? *What was it like working with Chester Gould? What do you most remember about working on* Tracy? *What years did you work on the strip?*

I worked for Chester from April 1932 to Jan. 1936. Chester was great to work with, he had a wonderful sense of humor, but he didn't pay too well. I put in three or four days a week and when I left in 1936 I was making $25 a week. I started at $5 a week. All the time I worked for him I never wrote a strip or inked a character. This was sacred ground to him. I *did* get a chance now and then to contribute an idea. Capt. Patterson would come to Chicago once a month and summon the cartoonists to his office (no assistants). They would have to take their current work to show him. Chester occasionally got brain-lock before these sessions. So as he paced the floor I would try to think of something. One time I suggested a thing where this street car racing down a hill would finally collide with an oil truck. He decided to go with it and it took me 17½ hours to put the bg's [probably backgrounds] in it. But Patterson liked it. We didn't have many arguments. Came close one time when a friend of mine and I had a double date at Riccardo's with Vivian Decca Chiasa, the opera singer. Gail Borden from another Chicago paper was there and reported that Vivian was there with the man who drew "Dick Tracy." I hadn't talked to Borden so it came with as much shock to me as it did to Chester.

When I came to work for Chester there was a stack of letters 2 or 3 feet high on top of his file cabinet from PTAs, etc. about violence in the strip. Patterson told him to ignore them so Chester did, I think up to his dying day. As well as being Chester's asst I was also custodian of the door. Anytime anyone would knock at the door, he would hide behind his desk and tell me to tell them he wasn't there. If it was someone he wanted to see he would jump up and call to the guy to come in. He could be ruthless at times. All the time I was with him I was drawing up Pirate pages. I always showed them to him. I had done five pages of a feature called "Bill Bones," a "humorous," I thought, group of pirates. I put them on his desk and he read them. It was very quiet. No reaction not even a chuckle. Then he leafed back through them, picked one out and said "This one is the worst." He was right!

What can you tell me about Jack Ryan, Russell Stamm, and Ray Gould, and their work on Tracy?

I went to art school with Jack Ryan. I met him on the street one day and he had just seen the first "X-Nine" drawn by Alex Raymond. He felt I would be out of a job in a month or so because "X-Nine" was so much better than "Tracy." We younger artists just out of art school had a tendency of thinking of Gould's work as crude and drawn with a screw-driver. But it didn't take long for me to realize that the man was a genius. He had the ability to get the drawing and writing off the paper and into the reader's mind. In my opinion he was the outstanding cartoonist of our time. It was a thrill and blessing to have had the honor of working with him in his formative years. I still feel at times he is looking over my shoulder.

I recommended Bart Toomey for the job when I left. He didn't work out and Chester soon hired Russell Stamm (at $55 a wk.). Russell and I were good friends. I remember being at his house one night right after he had received a $500 ck. for doing a Big Little Book on Tracy. It was the most money he had ever seen in his life. He converted it into one dollar bills and was tossing it above his head. The floor was covered with money.

One last thought, Norman Marsh who later did "Dan Dunn" helped Chester with his income tax. He was one of the guys who were allowed in the studio. He came in one day and told Chester he was thinking of drawing a strip with a mosques [sic] as the main character. He needed some information about sizes and pens. Three months later he came out with "Dan Dunn."

Russell Stamm

A Chicago native born in 1915, Russell Stamm went to work for Chester Gould drawing backgrounds for *Dick Tracy* while he was still a teenager. Ron Goulart writes that Stamm had gotten "most of his training at the Academy of Fine Arts there [Chicago]. Interested in drawing since childhood, he had also taken the Landon mailorder course. In 1934 he got a job in the art department of the *Chicago Tribune* and after assisting for short spells on *Tiny Tim* and *The Gumps* he began a five year stint helping out on *Dick Tracy*."[101] Chester Gould noted, "He couldn't draw a straight line when he came with me, and his cousin Stanley Link [Link had assisted on *The*

Gumps and later drew *Tiny Tim*] tutored him and I went along with him, and he learned to rule and letter—no figures—but he did all my lettering eventually. He was a nice boy."[102] In June of 1940, Stamm sold *Invisible Scarlet O'Neil* to Marshall Fields' Chicago Times Syndicate. The heroine was an "unconventional lady crime-fighter," and as Dick Moores had done in his post–*Tracy* work, Stamm developed and employed much more sentimental and humorous characters than Chester Gould did in his Depression-era *Dick Tracy*.[103] According to Max Collins, Stamm did the work for the two Whitman *Dick Tracy* hardcover books of the 1940s—*Dick Tracy: Ace Detective* (1943) and *Dick Tracy Meets the Night Crawler* (1945)—and some of the work for the Whitman Tracy Big Little Books.[104] Ron Goulart

notes that Stamm's accomplishments include two original Tracy Big Little Books in the early 1940s, and a non–Tracy Big Little Book entitled *Gangbusters Smash Through* (1942).[105] Goulart continues, "When he [Stamm] entered the service in 1944, the strip was ghosted for a time. He returned to *Scarlet* full time after the war and stayed with it until the end [1956] when, as he put it, 'she became completely invisible.' He then left comics for good and formed Russ Stamm Productions, creating and producing animated television commercials for a number of national clients."[106] Russell Stamm, like Dick Moores, evolved a style that years later would be original, yet reflective of the Gould art style to which he was intimately exposed in the 1930s.

Jack Ryan

In the early 1930s, Jack Ryan, along with Ed Moore, assisted Norman Marsh on *Dan Dunn*, a comic strip which debuted on September 25, 1933, and which was highly derivative of *Dick Tracy*. A few years later, "Jack Ryan drew *Steamer Kelly*, about a heroic fireman" for the *Chicago Tribune*'s answer to the comic book called *Comic Book Magazine*. This debuted in the spring of 1940, and "some of the Chicago-based cartoonists began to do original strips for *The Comic Book*."[106] John Bainbridge, in his article entitled "Chester Gould: The Harrowing Adventures of His Cartoon Hero, Dick Tracy, Give Vicarious Thrills to Millions" for the August 14, 1944, issue of *Life* magazine, related two events which occurred while Ryan assisted Gould on *Tracy* in the early 1940s. The first involved the daily routine of the two *Tracy* artists. Typically, Ryan arrived before Gould in "a cluttered room on the 14th floor of the Tribune Tower in downtown Chicago."[107]

Once here, Ryan ruled clean Bristol boards into rectangles. After drawing the other characters, Gould would hand the page back to Ryan who completed it by filling in background objects such as lampposts and buildings, and by inking in solid black spaces. The second event dealt with the naming of the famous *Dick Tracy* villain called the Brow. Bainbridge writes:

> Gould decided that he needed a shrewd, cold, intellectual scoundrel to portray the master mind of a spy ring. He accordingly drew a character who had lost both his ears in a knife fight and who possessed a deeply furrowed brow, presumably caused by thinking all the time. Gould couldn't settle on a suitable name for him, though he worried about it for a week and considered and discarded such possibilities as "The Head," "Wrinkles" and half a dozen others. Studying sketches of the villain one day, Gould's assistant, Jack Ryan, said, "Chet, what's the matter with calling this

guy 'The Brow?'" "Just exactly nothing," Gould replied happily.[108]

Prior to this time, Gould had named all his characters himself.

Coleman Anderson

Jean O'Connell writes, "In 1942, Coleman Anderson became my father's assistant until 1957. All of my father's assistants came out to his studio in Woodstock, except for Mondays when they met at the Tribune Tower."[109] The short article entitled "Dick Tracy and Me," which was written by Chester Gould for *Colliers* in 1948, acknowledges Anderson as the background artist for *Tracy* at this time.[110]

Ray Gould

Ray Gould, Chester's younger brother, was born in 1904 in Pawnee, Oklahoma, where their family lived until Chester graduated from high school. The family then moved to Stillwater, Oklahoma, to be near Oklahoma University (then Oklahoma A&M). Jean O'Connell remembers that her uncle "graduated from A&M and during those years worked for his father, Gilbert Gould, in his newspaper office learning typesetting and how to use the presses. After graduating, he continued in this field."[111]

Ray assisted his brother Chester on *Tracy* longer than anyone else. Mrs. Edna Gould writes, "Chester asked Ray and his parents to join him in Woodstock, and in 1945, they moved here [Woodstock] from Stillwater, Oklahoma. It was at this time that Ray joined Chester in doing the lettering for the strip. He continued until his death on November 12, 1974, at the age of 70."[112] Ray Gould married Mabel Wade in 1950. Chester Gould reflected on his younger brother:

He was a great guy. He was a real credit to the business. Ray was a quiet fellow and he was very capable. And I tried to coach him in art, and kind of carried on a little school for him, but he didn't take to drawing. It just wasn't in him, he didn't have the drawing desire, nor the ability to follow through. So he just did the lettering, and he colored the photostats of the Sunday pages and the daily strips, which in itself takes a lot of time. So we had a happy situation.[113]

"Ray had been a Linotype operator and that's where he learned the shaping of the letters—what they looked like and what they should look like."[114] Dick Locher writes, "I didn't know Jack Ryan or Russell Stamm—but was a close friend of Ray. He and Mabel and my wife and I socialized quite a bit. Ray was slow, deliberate—contributed to the story line—and re-cut the Sunday pages for sizing for the different newspapers. He did all the lettering. Ray had a tremendous sense of humor. I missed him when I left Gould [1961]."[115]

―――― Ray Shlemon and Susan Anderson ――――

Dick Locher writes of two recent assistants on *Dick Tracy,* "Ray Shlemon was my assistant on the strip after I lost my son John. His tour was from 1986 (June) to 1989. He retired and I hired Susan Anderson who does lettering, mailing, research, etc. Ray Shlemon was a Tribune artist from 1938 to 1986 with a tour in the Army during WWII. He is an acknowledged and renowned airbrush artist. He has paintings and art works hanging in major museums."[116]

― An Overview of the Contributors to *Tracy* ―

Chester Gould held tight control over his creation from 1931 until his retirement from *Dick Tracy* in 1977. His assistants and successors have each contributed substantially to the ongoing saga which is *Tracy.* To summarize then, Dick Moores served as Gould's first assistant from about 1931 to 1936. Moores' distinct style of lettering for the comic strip became his primary contribution to *Tracy.* Recently, however, evidence has emerged which suggests that an individual named Dick Hartly may have been another very early assistant from 1931 or 1932. (The author, during the spring of 1992, saw a copy of the very first Big Little Book — *The Adventures of Dick Tracy* [1932] — signed by Gould to Hartly whom Gould identified in the inscription as an assistant of sorts.) From about 1935 to 1940, Russell Stamm assisted Gould with ruling and lettering duties for *Dick Tracy.* Jack Ryan and Coleman Anderson began assisting Gould in the early 1940s, and both continued in this capacity for several years — Anderson until about 1957 or 1958. About 1945, Chester Gould's younger brother Ray moved to Woodstock, Illinois — Chester Gould's residence — and assisted on the comic strip until his death in 1974. About the time Coleman Anderson was finishing his stint with Gould and *Tracy,* Dick Locher joined Gould. Locher assisted Gould until 1961. In 1961, established cartoonist Rick Fletcher became an assistant for the famous comic strip. Fletcher's responsibilities on *Tracy* steadily increased as the years passed. In 1977, Fletcher assumed full illustrative duties on *Tracy* and continued in this capacity until his death in 1983. In 1977 also, critically acclaimed mystery novelist Max Allan Collins became Fletcher's collaborator and wrote the scripts for *Dick Tracy.* In 1983, political cartoonist Dick Locher, assisted by his talented son John, took over illustrative duties on the comic strip. John passed away in 1986. Max Allan Collins and Dick Locher have written and drawn *Dick Tracy* for more than ten years. Locher hired Ray Shlemon as his assistant from 1986 to 1989, and currently employs Susan Anderson to do lettering and research.

Notes

1. Max Allan Collins and Matt Masterson, "Bringing in the Reward: Detectives and Determination, Comics and Cadillacs: The Chester Gould Interview," *Nemo: The Classic Comics Library* 17 (February 1986), p. 9. (This interview is also reprinted in Max Allan Collins and Dick Locher's *Dick*

Tracy's Fiendish Foes!: A 60th Anniversary Celebration.) Through the years, there were a number of published interviews with, and magazine and newspaper articles about, Chester Gould. Though conducted in 1980, when the famous comic strip writer/artist was almost eighty years old, this particular interview reveals Gould's amazingly accurate and detailed memory and witty sense of humor. It is probably the best interview ever done with him.

2. These are some of the comic strips that Gould consistently acknowledged in interviews and articles as early influences on his work.

3. Collins and Masterson, p. 9.

4. Ibid. Gould related some interesting anecdotes about his sign painting days in Oklahoma in the interview with Collins and Masterson in *Nemo* 17.

5. Charles Green claims that the prize was five dollars in "Chester Gould: A Biographical Sketch," published in *Dick Tracy: The Art of Chester Gould* by the Museum of Cartoon Art of Port Chester, New York, in 1978. Gould remembered the award being ten dollars in his interview with Collins and Masterson published in *Nemo* 17.

6. Charles Green in "Chester Gould: A Biographical Sketch" deems the cartoon, "What a Snap He's Got." In the original cartoon, the title is "Golly! what a snap he's got!"

7. Green, p. 12.

8. Shel Dorf, *The Original Dick Tracy* 1 (September 1990), inside cover.

9. Collins and Masterson, p. 11.

10. Fred Olmsted, "Tracy Tops His Tutor, Artist Gould Is as Mild as Fearless Tracy Is Bold." *Detroit Free Press*, September 12, 1948.

11. Green, p. 12. The correct spelling is *Radio Catts.*

12. Collins and Masterson, p. 13.

13. Robert M. Yoder, "Dick Tracy's Boss." *The Saturday Evening Post*, December 17, 1949, p. 44. The Gumps were very average people and were typical of lower-middle class America. In 1935, when the comic strip appeared in hundreds of newspapers and was at its height, Smith died in an automobile accident.

14. Jay Maeder very adeptly captures the atmosphere—a rather hard, tough environment—in which young, aspiring cartoonists were enmeshed in the 1920s in his preface to his book, *Dick Tracy: The Official Biography* (New York: Penguin, 1990), p. v.

15. Yoder, p. 44.

16. Ibid.

17. Ibid.

18. Ibid.

19. Collins and Masterson, p. 15.

20. Ibid.

21. Max Allan Collins, "The World's Most Famous Detective," in *Reuben Award Winner Series: Dick Tracy, Book #4* (El Cajon, Calif.; Blackthorne Publishing, Inc., January 1986), p. 68. Series edited by Shel Dorf.

22. Gould elaborates on the story of their arrival in Woodstock in the interview with Collins and Masterson in *Nemo: The Classic Comics Library* 17, p. 21.

23. William B. Edwards, "How Dick Tracy Gets His Man." *Guns Magazine*, August 1955, p. 19.

24. William K. Stuckey, "Dick Tracy: The Inner Man." *Northwestern Review*, Winter 1967, p. 22.

25. Collins and Masterson, p. 8.

26. Max Collins and Terry Beatty, *The Files of Ms. Tree* (Canada: Aardvark-Vanaheim, Inc., 1984), p. 1.

27. Max Allan Collins, "Strip Search: Dick Tracy." *Comics Feature* 28 (March-April 1984), p. 16.

28. David McDonnell and Kim Howard Johnson, "Max Allan Collins: The Mystery Novelist Who Writes Comics." *Comics Scene* 6 (November 1982), p. 29.

29. Collins and Beatty, p. 1.

30. Ibid.

31. Ibid.

32. Ibid.

33. McDonnell and Howard Johnson, p. 30.

34. Ibid.

35. Ibid.

36. The Gold Eagle line of books from Harlequin specialized in stories of avengers, mercenaries, tough guys, and similar adventure characters.

37. Peter Sanderson, Jr., "An Interview with Max Allan Collins." *Comics Feature* 18 (August 1982), p. 16.

38. Collins and Beatty, p. 2.

39. Ibid.

40. Collins interview, November 19, 1984.

41. Max Allan Collins, *True Detective* (New York: St. Martin's, 1984), dust jacket.

42. Robert A. Baker and Michael T. Nietzel, *Private Eyes: One Hundred and One Knights* (Bowling Green, Ohio: Bowling Green State University Popular Press, 1985), p. 280.

43. Collins interview, November 19, 1984.

44. Baker and Nietzel, p. 280.

45. Collins interview, November 19, 1984.

46. Rick Marschall and Bill Blackbeard co-edited and published the complete E.C. Segar *Popeye* Sunday and daily comics in the conjunction with the San Francisco Academy of Comic Art and Fantagraphic Books. Both Marschall and Blackbeard have become recognized authorities of comic strip history.

47. Collins and Beatty, p. 2.

48. Ibid.

49. Ibid.

50. McDonnell and Howard Johnson, p. 30.

51. Collins and Beatty, p. 2.

52. Ibid.

53. Ibid.

54. Ibid., pp. 2–3.

55. Mrs. Beverly Fletcher letter interview, March 4, 1986.

56. Ibid.

57. Joanne Springman, "Rick Fletcher, 66 dies; Tracy artist for 22 years." *Daily Sentinel* (Woodstock, Illinois), p. 1.

58. Mrs. Beverly Fletcher letter interview, June 16, 1992.

59. Mrs. Beverly Fletcher letter interview, March 4, 1986.

60. "'Dick Tracy' artist Rick Fletcher; took over drawing of strip in 1977." *Chicago Tribune*, March 18, 1983.

61. Shel Dorf, ed., *Reuben Award Winner Series: Dick Tracy, Book #4* (El Cajon, Calif.: Blackthorne Publishing, Inc., January 1986), p. 68.

62. Max Allan Collins, "Strip Search—Dick Tracy: The Fletcher Years, Part One." *Comics Feature* 35 (May-June 1985), p. 48.

63. Mrs. Beverly Fletcher letter interview, March 4, 1986.

64. Max Allan Collins, "Strip Search—Dick Tracy: The Fletcher Years, Part Two." *Comics Feature* 36 (July-August 1985), p. 43.

65. Ibid., p. 44.

66. Max Allan Collins, "Strip Search—Dick Tracy: The Fletcher Years, Part One," p. 48.

67. Ibid., p. 47; Collins interview, November 19, 1984.

68. Max Allan Collins, "Strip Search—Dick Tracy: The Fletcher Years, Part Two," p. 44.

69. Ibid., p. 47.

70. Ibid.

71. Ibid.

72. "'Dick Tracy' artist Rick Fletcher; took over drawing of strip in 1977."

73. Mrs. Beverly Fletcher letter interview, March 4, 1986.

74. Collins interview, November 19, 1984.

75. Much of the information on Dick Locher comes from the Locher letter interview of February 21, 1986.

76. Locher letter interview.

77. Ibid.

78. Ibid.

79. Neil Hansen, "CVM Profile on Dick Locher," *Comics Value Monthly* 1 (South Salem, New York: Attic Books, Inc., 1990), p. 11.

80. Locher letter interview.

81. Ibid.

82. Ibid.

83. Kenan Heise, "Artist John Locher; Drew 'Dick Tracy,'" *Chicago Tribune,* May 20, 1986, Section 2/p. 6.

84. Ibid.

85. Ibid.

86. Ibid.

87. Ron Goulart, *The Adventurous Decade* (New Rochelle, New York: Arlington House Publishers, 1975), p. 93.

88. Ibid.

89. Ibid.

90. Dick Moores, "Jim Hardy and Me," *Jim Hardy: A Complete Compilation* (Westport, Conn.: Hyperion Press, Inc., 1977), p. v.

91. Collins interview, November 19, 1984.

92. Goulart, p. 93.

93. Ibid.

94. Nat Hentoff's introduction to *Gasoline Alley* by Dick Moores (New York: Avon, 1976).

95. Ron Goulart, *The Encyclopedia of American Comics from 1897 to the Present* (New York: Facts on File, 1990), p. 266.

96. Tor Odemark, "A Little Chat with Dick Moores," *The Duckburg Times* 20 (June 9, 1984), p. 26.

97. Ibid., p. 27.

98. Ibid.

99. Ibid.

100. Hentoff.

101. Ron Goulart, *The Encyclopedia of American Comics*, p. 345.

102. Collins and Masterson, p. 20.

103. See Ron Goulart's *The Adventurous Decade* for further explanation of the comic characters of Moores and Stamm.

104. Refer to Chapter Six for more information on the two Whitman hardcovers and the Dick Tracy Big Little Books.

105. Goulart, *Encyclopedia of American Comics*, p. 345.

106. Goulart, *Adventurous Decade*, p. 174.

107. John Bainbridge, "Chester Gould: The Harrowing Adventures of His Cartoon Hero, Dick Tracy, Give Vicarious Thrills to Millions." *Life*, August 14, 1944, p. 45.

108. Ibid., p. 51.

109. Mrs. Jean O'Connell letter interview, May 9, 1992.

110. Chester Gould, "Dick Tracy and Me." *Colliers,* December 11, 1948, p. 54.

111. O'Connell letter.

112. Mrs. Chester Gould letter interview, March 11, 1986.

113. Collins and Masterson.

114. Ibid.

115. Locher letter interview, February 21, 1986.

116. Locher letter interview, May 20, 1992.

CHAPTER 6

A Proliferation of Moral Storytelling: Dick Tracy in Media Other Than the Comic Strip

Willie [a thirteen-year-old boy accused of murder and sentenced to an indeterminate sentence at the state reformatory] was always a rabid comic-book reader. He "doted" on them. He spent a large part of the money he earned to buy them. Seeing all their pictures of brutality and shooting and their endless glamorous advertisements for guns and knives, his aunt had become alarmed . . . [but] Workers at a public child-guidance agency connected with the schools made her distrust her natural good sense and told her she should let Willie read all the comic books he wanted. — Fredric Wertham, M.D., *Seduction of the Innocent* (1954)

The story of Dick Tracy has traditionally been an effective form of communication in a variety of media including the comic strip because, for the most part, since its inception it has struck a responsive chord in its audience—a chord of socially prescribed *morality,* not immorality. Some media have been more successful in relating the saga than others—the comic strip being most effective since the story of Dick Tracy was created for this medium; television adaptations (both dramatic teleplays and animation aimed at children) have not worked nearly as well. Nonetheless, Chester Gould's original concept and moral storytelling—which do *not* celebrate gratuitous violence or inspire violent antisocial behavior—have been expanded in a proliferation of diverse media for more than sixty years.

Tony Schwartz, in *The Responsive Chord* (1974) and again in *Media: The Second God* (1981), provides keen insight into the role of the media as forms of communi-

cation and purveyors of social thought. To paraphrase, he claims that media create a context for education and that they reorder existing knowledge rather than provide a wealth of new information.[1] He further notes that communications media should not attempt to capture the reality of a situation, but instead should create stimuli that affect the consumer in a manner similar to that individual's own experiences in a real situation. The role of a television program or a newspaper article is to reaffirm the place of the individual, and his/her beliefs and experiences, in the larger socially constructed reality. The media work best when they hit the responsive chord—a chord that does not have to be taught, but is discovered from within oneself.

In his book *Media: The Second God,* Schwartz characterizes the media as being "all-knowing and all-powerful," a spirit that exists both outside and inside of us, and which is always with us because it is

203

everywhere.[2] The media are indeed a pervasive, mysterious lot. They profoundly affect and reflect social attitudes, political structures, and the perceptions of whole groups of people. Because of their timeliness—that is, their ability to relate news and other information almost instantaneously—the electronic media may be the most widespread and coercive of media forms today. Further, originality in communications today comes from the invention of new technologies, and extensions of existing technologies, rather than from a multiplicity of new themes, genres, and story forms produced for established media. Contemporary communications reorder past knowledge and socially constructed realities, and reintroduce them under the guise of a new technology. They rarely provide breakthroughs in message.

Chester Gould created Dick Tracy for the comic strip medium. Hence, Dick Tracy is best appreciated and is found in its purest form on the newspaper page. The story of Dick Tracy was invented for a linearly organized medium which thrives on the progression of ideas through stylized usage of seemingly simplistic and relatively crude, two-dimensional black and white illustrations. *Dick Tracy* does not present "news" as do feature articles on the front pages of daily newspapers; instead, it interprets and adds an element of fantasy to the news—it reflects real history. Employing this formula for success—carefully blending fact and fantasy—Gould and company more often than not have hit a chord to which their audiences respond.

For a moment, let us look at an opposing viewpoint. In *Learning to See: Historical Perspectives on Modern Popular/Commercial Arts*, Alan Gowans proclaims that:

Not so long ago, illustrations of violence seemed a black-and-white, wrong-and-right matter. Everybody could see through the pretensions of detective "heroes" like Dick Tracy. Only finks and stooges would believe that.... The real-life inspiration for *Dick Tracy* was the state of law and order in America, especially in the big cities.... A tidal wave of crime and corruption had all but submerged the big cities of this country.... Chester Gould, concerned citizen and artist, did something about it. And inevitably what he did reflected the hard, rough times that had America in its gangster grip. Chester Gould produced a contemporary knight in shining armour who was ready, willing and able to fight the criminal with, if necessary, the criminal's own weapons.... Dick Tracy's job was to regain the almost vanished respect for the law and to be the instrument of its enforcement. As Chester Gould once said in an interview, "I decided that if the police couldn't catch the gangsters, I'd create a fellow who would." Anybody who could pronounce the word sociology knew that "law and order" was a cover for "institutionalized violence to minority groups."[3]

Gowans, in his often perceptive and ingenious book, is dead wrong here. This is the kind of logic that makes criminals some form of protected ethnic group. The inspiration for *Dick Tracy was* the state of law and order in America, and the fertile imagination of Chester Gould and his successors. But this comic strip was never intended to be, and never has been, a wholly factual representation of reality. Its popularity and commercial prosperity are attributable to its fine balance of fact and fantasy, Caweltian convention and invention. *Dick Tracy* has worked because it hits a responsive chord, not because it is exclusively representative of real life.

The diverse media that showcased the Tracy legacy experienced varying degrees of success, yet all advanced the saga in one way or another. Beyond comic strips, Dick Tracy appeared in Big Little Books, Feature Books, comic books, radio programs, movie serials, "B" movies, a television series, and animated cartoons.

Big Little Books

Whitman Publishing Company of Racine, Wisconsin, was the originator of what it called and trademarked "Big Little Books." As a medium, Big Little Books are a detailed study in themselves, and it has not been until recent years that their significance to the evolution of popular literature, the evolution of newspaper comic strips, and the evolution of motion pictures has begun to be recognized. So popularly accepted and mass consumed were these books that more than a dozen publishing houses of the Thirties and Forties began to produce a variety of imitations — sometimes pretty close to direct rip-offs — of the Whitman product.[4] In all, more than 600 distinct titles appeared from Whitman and its followers during the Depression, World War II, and the first years of the Cold War. Most of these books were approximately 4½ inches square and 1½ inches thick — though variations existed among and even within publishing companies — and were printed on inexpensive pulpwood paper. Color pictures (often art done by illustrators contracted by publishers, or sometimes merely enhanced reprints of movie stills) adorned cardboard and paper covers. Soft covers (paper as opposed to cardboard) appeared on "premium" Big Little Books — those given away free with the purchase of grocery store items as inducements to purchase the larger items. Non-premium books sold for nine or ten cents apiece, and profit margins on the retail price were measured by the penny and half-penny. Press runs for single titles typically reached the hundreds of thousands, and for the more popular titles — like Flash Gordon, Mickey Mouse, and Dick Tracy — probably even more. The heyday for Big Little Books was between 1932 and 1938, a period deemed the Golden Age of Big Little Books by scholars of this medium. In 1938, when Whitman

Publishing realized that its trademarked "Big Little Book" had become a generic term for a variety of similar publications of other companies, it recoined "Big Little Book" as "Better Little Book" and the Silver Age for the medium was under way. This second period lasted until 1950. Several resurrections of the Big Little Book were attempted in the years that followed 1950, but by the early Eighties, the Big Little Book, no longer a profitable business venture, was extinct.[5]

Big Little Books (in the generic sense of the term) cannibalized storylines from motion pictures, classic novels, radio programs, pulp magazines, and later television programs and popular animated cartoons. But without doubt, Big Little Books relied most heavily on newspaper comic strips for their content base. Such was the case of Whitman's first Big Little Book, which appeared in 1932 and was the only one marketed that year. It was entitled *The Adventures of Dick Tracy*. Lawrence F. Lowery, author of *Lowery's The Collector's Guide to Big Little Books and Similar Books* (1981), writes: "The first Tracy BLB was not from the first comic strip. It was one in which he [Tracy] was already established as an Ace Detective. Chester Gould's art was crude and not representational of reality. Its surrealistic content often used harsh contrasts of black and white."[6] Dick Tracy Big Little Books were among the most prolific titles produced by Whitman.[7] The Wisconsin-based company alone published 27 different Tracy titles between 1932 and 1967. With rare exception, the Tracy Big Little Books were adaptations of newspaper comic strips. The usual format for these books was a page of text for each page of illustration, though there were exceptions to this rule also. Each illustration was captioned. The text consisted of comparatively large print which further ex-

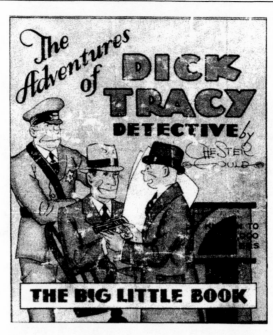

The Adventures of Dick Tracy — Whitman Publishing, 1932. The first Big Little Book and the first Dick Tracy Big Little Book. Reprinted by permission: Tribune Media Services.

plained the illustrations. Most Tracy Big Little Books exceeded 300 pages in length; many ran upwards of 400 pages. Three Dick Tracy Big Little Books were adaptations of Republic Pictures movie serials: *Detective Dick Tracy and the Spider Gang* (1937), *Dick Tracy Returns* (1939), and *Dick Tracy and His G-Men* (1941). Only *Detective Dick Tracy and the Spider Gang*, however, contained actual stills from the 15-chapter serial which starred Ralph Byrd as Gould's detective hero. The pen and ink illustrations for *Dick Tracy Returns* and *Dick Tracy and His G-Men* were specially drawn for these two books. One Big Little Book — *Dick Tracy and the Phantom Ship* (1940) — was based on a Dick Tracy radio drama.

Big Little Books and similar books enhanced the Dick Tracy mythology in two important ways. The first was that as a transitional stage between newspaper comic strips and comic books, Big Little Books were the earliest major mass medium to assemble collections of comic strips in book form.[8] What usually happened in the case of Tracy titles — and many other Big Little Books which adapted famous comic strips — was that the original panels of the comic strip were reproduced one panel per every other page. The word balloons were removed, and were replaced by pages of text opposite pages of illustrations. Because of this editing process, Big Little Books based on comic strips sometimes compromised the original stories and art. But the more important flip side was that the Tracy saga was being assimilated in book form and presented to another market. Famous newspaper comic strips had been collected and presented in book form several years prior to 1932, but Whitman was the first publisher to market such compilations on a grand scale. As Big Little Books as a whole were moving comic strips to comic books, so too were Dick Tracy Big Little Books moving Dick Tracy comic strips to Dick Tracy comic books. Early comic books, after all, relied on sequentially ordered reprints of comic strips for material.

Taking Them by Surprise

A Nice Reception

One for Good Measure

Excerpts from *The Adventures of Dick Tracy* Big Little Book. Whitman Publishing, 1932. Reprinted by permission: Tribune Media Services.

The only Dick Tracy Big Little Book with stills from the movies. *Detective Dick Tracy and the Spider Gang*—Whitman Publishing, 1937. Reprinted by permission: Tribune Media Services.

The second way in which Big Little Books enhanced the Dick Tracy phenomenon was in providing complete stories in one publication at a comparatively inexpensive price. The continuity of Chester Gould's stories was being preserved. A Dick Tracy adventure sometimes took as long as several months to unfold in newspaper comic strips when only four panels appeared each weekday. For the first time, Tracy stories were presented to the public in their entirety, and especially in the 1930s and 1940s, Gould's stories read very well when collected together. Big Little Books made these adventures more easily understood as readers could follow the uninterrupted action to its conclusion.

As noted earlier, of the over 600 titles of Big Little Books and imitations of the same that were released in the 1930s and 1940s, 27 Whitman books were Dick Tracy titles. Besides *Tracy*, only *Little Orphan Annie, Flash Gordon, Buck Rogers, Donald Duck, Mickey Mouse,* and a select few other series had more than a handful

of titles assigned to them. So successful were the Dick Tracy editions at hitting the responsive chord in their audience that Whitman—with rare exception the only publisher of Dick Tracy Big Little Books and similar books—produced several variants of its own works. In 1934, Whitman released a "Big Big Book" which was the equivalent of a Big Little Book with one important exception—it was approximately 7×10×2 inches in size. Two other Big Big Books followed, in 1936 and 1938. There were also premiums, "Penny Books," two radio drama script adaptations, and two hardcover novels—*Dick Tracy Ace Detective* (1943) and *Dick Tracy Meets the Night Crawler* (1945)—published by Whitman in an attempt to capitalize on the prosperity of the Dick Tracy Big Little Books and the original *Dick Tracy* comic strip. Dell Publishing of New York City, which in the 1940s became renowned for its line of comic books, produced five Dick Tracy titles under the rubric "Fast Action Books" which proved one of the primary competitors of the

SAMPLE COPY   Size $3\frac{3}{8} \times 4\frac{1}{2} \times 1\frac{1}{2}$ "

No.   1479   No. of Pages   432

Detective DICK TRACY vs. Crooks in Disguise BETTER LITTLE BOOK New

Price per dozen   72¢

Weight per dozen $3\frac{1}{2}$ lbs.

Terms: 2% 10 days, net 30 days. F.O.B. Racine, Wis., or Poughkeepsie, N. Y.

OCT 30 1941

Packed: 10c items—1 doz.; 25c items—¼ doz.; higher-priced items—¼ doz. (Packed assorted where there is more than one title under one number.)

WHITMAN PUBLISHING CO.

Racine, Wisconsin   Poughkeepsie, N. Y.

Wholesale information for Whitman Publishing Company's Better Little Book, *Detective Dick Tracy vs. Crooks in Disguise*, 1941. Reprinted by permission: Tribune Media Services.

Whitman products. There were others utilizing Tracy storylines.

The last Whitman Dick Tracy Big Little Book was published in 1967. Ironically, it was the first of a new revival of Big Little Books published by Whitman, just as *The Adventures of Dick Tracy* in 1932 was the first of the grand medium as a whole. Readers knew these books were not wholly realistic; in many ways they were reality-based fantasy and just plain fun. But Gould's saga of Dick Tracy had transcended the comic strip and had become an invaluable aspect of a second medium.

The Big Little Book, like the newspaper comic strip, did not attempt to provide exacting truths, but it did help legitimize the experience of the individual reader who found himself/herself trying to fit into the larger framework of society. The Dick Tracy Big Little Books hit a responsive chord.[9]

In all, Tracy appeared in the following Big Little Books and Better Little Books:* *The Adventures of Dick Tracy* (the first Big Little Book as well as the first Dick Tracy Big Little Book), 1932; *The Adventures of Dick Tracy and Dick Tracy, Jr.*, 1933; *Dick*

The citations for the Dick Tracy Big Little Books and related books came from the author's personal collection and Lowery's The Collector's Guide to Big Little Books and Similar Books *(Danville, California: Education Research and Applications Corporation, 1981). Further references were made available by Bill Blackbeard of the San Francisco Academy of Comic Art, and the Popular Culture Library of Bowling Green State University, Bowling Green, Ohio.*

Dick Tracy: Ace Detective—Whitman Publishing Company, 1943. Reprinted by permission: Tribune Media Services.

Dick Tracy Meets the Night Crawler—Whitman Publishing Company, 1945. Reprinted by permission: Tribune Media Services.

Dick Tracy: Detective and Federal Agent: Fast-Action Book #1B (identical to #1A except softcover). Dell Publishing, 1936. Reprinted by permission: Tribune Media Services.

Tracy Out West, 1933; *Dick Tracy from Colorado to Nova Scotia* (issued in both cardboard and paper covers), 1933; *Dick Tracy and the Stolen Bonds,* 1934; *Dick Tracy Solves the Penfield Mystery* (issued in both cardboard and paper covers), 1934; *Dick Tracy and the Boris Arson Gang,* 1935; *Dick Tracy on the Trail of Larceny Lu,* 1935; *Dick Tracy in Chains of Crime,* 1936; *Dick Tracy and the Racketeer Gang,* 1936; *Dick Tracy and the Hotel Murders,* 1937; *Detective Dick Tracy and the Spider Gang* (based on Republic Pictures' fifth movie serial and the first Dick Tracy serial, 1937's *Dick Tracy;* the only Dick Tracy Big Little Book which includes movie stills), 1937; *Dick Tracy and the Man with No Face* (two versions—one with "Big Little Book" logo on cover, one without), 1938; *Dick Tracy on the High Seas* (first Dick Tracy "Better Little Book"), 1939; *Dick Tracy*

Returns (based on Republic Pictures' eleventh movie serial, the second Dick Tracy movie serial—*Dick Tracy Returns* from 1938; pen and ink illustrations created for this book), 1939; *Dick Tracy the Super Detective,* 1939; *Dick Tracy and the Phantom Ship* (based on the radio script reprinted in Whitman Radio Script Play, *Dick Tracy and the Ghost Ship;* pen and ink illustrations created for this book; published in Spanish as *Dick Tracy y el Bogue Fantasma*), 1940; *Dick Tracy and His G-Men* (based on Republic Pictures' fifteenth movie serial; the third Dick Tracy movie serial, from 1939; pen and ink illustrations created for this book), 1941; *Detective Dick Tracy vs. Crooks in Disguise,* 1941; *Dick Tracy Special F.B.I. Operative,* 1943; *Dick Tracy on Voodoo Island,* 1944; *Dick Tracy and the Wreath Kidnapping Case,* 1945; *Dick Tracy and*

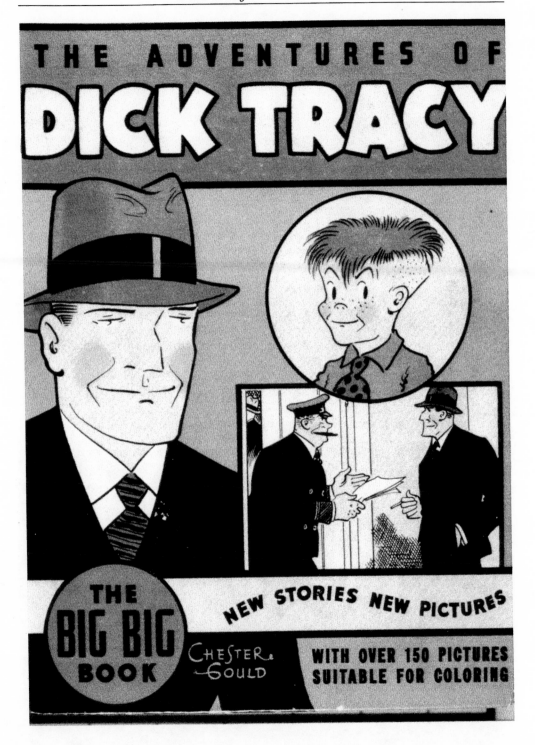

The Adventures of Dick Tracy—Big Big Book, Whitman Publishing Company, 1936. Reprinted by permission: Tribune Media Services.

Dick Tracy Gets His Man—**Whitman Publishing Company, 1938. (Penny Book.) Reprinted by permission: Tribune Media Services.**

Yogee Yamma†, 1946; *Dick Tracy and the Mad Killer†*, 1947; *Dick Tracy and the Bicycle Gang†*, 1948; *Dick Tracy and the Tiger Lilly Gang†*, 1949; *Dick Tracy Encounters Facey* (story by Paul S. Newman; three identical versions except for varying endpapers: 1. white trademarks on blue, 2. gray trademarks on white, 3. plain white), 1967.

In addition Tracy appeared in the following related books: as Whitman Karmetz premiums in *The Adventures of Dick Tracy* (1933) and *Dick Tracy and Dick Tracy, Jr.* (1933); as a Whitman Perkins premium in *Dick Tracy the Detective and Dick Tracy, Jr.* (1933); as a Whitman Tarzan ice cream premium in *Dick Tracy Meets a New Gang* (1934); as a Whitman Buddy book premium in *Dick Tracy Smashing the Famon Racket* (1938); in two Whitman Big Big Books, *The Adventures of Dick Tracy* (1934 and 1936; identical except for cover illustrations) and *Detective Dick Tracy and the Mystery of the Purple*

†*Stories adapted from Chester Gould newspaper comic strips by Helen Berke.*

Dick Tracy the Detective and Dick Tracy, Jr.—**Whitman Publishing Company, 1933. (Premium.) Reprinted by permission: Tribune Media Services.**

Cross (1938); in two Whitman Penny Books, *Dick Tracy Gets His Man* (1938) and *Dick Tracy the Detective* (1938); in two Whitman Radio Script Plays, *Dick Tracy and the Invisible Man* (1939) and *Dick Tracy and the Ghost Ship* (1939); in two Whitman hardcover novels, *Dick Tracy Ace Detective* (1943) and *Dick Tracy Meets the Night Crawler* (1945); in five Dell Fast Action Books, *Dick Tracy Detective and Federal Agent* (1936; issued in both cardboard and paper covers), *Dick Tracy and the Chain of Evidence* (1938), *Dick Tracy and the Maroon Mask Gang* (1938), *Dick Tracy and the Blackmailers* (1939), and *Dick Tracy and the Frozen Bullet Murders* (1941); and as a Quaker Oats premium in *Dick Tracy's Secret Detective Methods and Magic Tricks* (1939).

--- **Feature Books** ---

Dick Tracy expanded into a third major print medium in February 1936 when Dell Publishing Company reprinted selected *Dick Tracy* newspaper comic strips in its *Popular Comics* #1; Tracy would continue to appear as late as #27 in the series, which ended with #145, July–September 1948. Early issues of *Popular Comics* were not, however, "comic books" in the truest sense of the term; they were, like Big Little Books, more accurately a bridge between newspaper comic strips and the soon-to-evolve comic book; they were simply reprints of newspaper comics. About a year later in early 1937, David McKay Publishers began its "Feature Book" series. Like Dell's *Popular Comics* line, McKay's Feature Books were forerunners to what would eventually become recognized as a standard for comic books; other than standard physical format, this meant stories created for comic books, not reprinted from newspaper pages.

The first Dick Tracy Feature Book was not numbered or dated. It was an experimental book, and there were not many copies published as indicated by existing records and the rarity of that first title. It seems apparent that Feature Books took a good deal of their lead from Whitman Publishing's Big Little Books. The difference between the two was primarily in size and format, and the fact that Feature Books reprinted comic strips sequentially and largely unchanged and unedited. (Remember that Big Little Books were much more liberal in their editing of original comic strips and their presentation of the strips.) Feature Books were only a moderately enduring form of popular literature; they lasted until about 1948. But, like Whitman's Big Little Books and Dell's *Popular Comics* line, they helped Dick Tracy make the expansion into comic books. The aspects of these publications (i.e. Feature Books and similar publications) that most differentiated them from standard comic book formats were that they were larger in size, measuring approximately $8\frac{1}{4} \times 11\frac{1}{4} \times \frac{1}{4}$ inches, and that they only reprinted newspaper comic strips as opposed to motion picture storylines, radio scripts, and so on.[10]

Between 1937 and 1938, David McKay marketed four Dick Tracy Feature Books: *Dick Tracy* (May 1937), *Dick Tracy the Detective* (#4, August 1937), *Dick Tracy the Detective* (#6, October 1937), and *Dick Tracy and the Famon Boys* (#9, January 1938). Although McKay continued to publish Feature Books which reprinted famous newspaper strips of the day such as *Popeye, Little Orphan Annie,* and *The Phantom* until 1948, no additional Feature Books were marketed by the company after 1938. In 1939, Dell Publishing introduced the oversized "Black and White Comics" series which, except for publisher, were essentially identical to the McKay product. Six Dick Tracy Black and White Comics appeared between 1939 and 1940: *Dick Tracy Meets the Blank* (#1, 1939), *Dick Tracy Gets His Man* (#4, 1939), *Dick Tracy the Racket Buster* (#8, 1939), *Dick Tracy Foils the Mad Doc Hump* (#11, 1940), *Dick Tracy and Scottie of Scotland Yard* (#13, 1940), and *Dick Tracy and the Kidnapped Princes* (#15, 1940). Between 1941 and 1943, Dell continued the Black and White series as "Large Feature Comics," running as the third Large Feature Comic *Dick Tracy* (#3, 1941). In March 1938, Dell debuted a second line of books very similar to its *Popular Comics* series, which reprinted newspaper comic strips. The line was deemed *Super Comics* and showcased a variety of comic strip heroes. Dick Tracy appeared between #1 (May 1938) and #115 (December 1947); the series ended with #121 in February-March 1949.

The significance of *Popular Comics,* Feature Books, Black and White Comics, Large Feature Books, and *Super Comics* to the evolution of Dick Tracy in media other than the newspaper comic strip is that these publications, like Big Little Books, provided readers with complete adventures and thereby contributed to the continuity of Dick Tracy's saga. Prior to the advent of these kinds of books, even the most avid of newspaper comic strip readers had had to wait months for Tracy storylines to reach fruition, and it was very likely that in that period of several months the reader would miss some of the daily strips. The Feature Books (in a generic sense of the term) were the third major print medium for Dick Tracy, and in the 1930s and early 1940s were the medium that most faithfully reproduced the original Gould comic strips as they appeared on the newspaper page. The more standardized "Four-Color" comic books that followed were excessively liberal in editing and revising the newspaper strips. In a sense, these early Feature Books of David McKay and Dell Publishers were the equivalent of today's paperbacks that reprint contemporary comic strips like Garry Trudeau's *Doonesbury,* Jim Davis' *Garfield,* and Bill Watterson's *Calvin and Hobbes* in sequence.

Feature Books were a comparatively short-lived media phenomenon, but in their time they were vital forerunners of the emerging comic book industry. Along with Big Little Books, Feature Books were the transition between comic strips and comic books, and Dick Tracy flourished in this medium. Adventure comic strips like *Dick Tracy* became the primary content base for the McKay and Dell productions because of all newspaper comics, they provided the best ongoing stories, the best continuities. These books furthered the ability of Chester Gould's *Dick Tracy* to hit a responsive chord in its audience; they reinforced and celebrated the newspaper medium of *Tracy's* origin. People now had proof of what they had suspected all along—stories of Dick Tracy in their entireties could be just as effective as the daily installments of the same.

Comic Books

Dell Publishing Company was a prominent comic book publisher during the Forties, Fifties, and Sixties. It was publishing comic books as early as the late Thirties and as late as the early Seventies. In fact, the New York City–based company's Fast Action Books (1938–1943) were highly imitative of Whitman's Big

Dick Tracy the Detective: **Feature Book #4. David McKay Publishing, 1937. Reprinted by permission: Tribune Media Services.**

Little Book line, and its Black and White Comics and Large Feature Books (1939–1943) were highly imitative of David McKay's Feature Books.[11] But Dell is most often remembered for its wide array of ti-

tles—produced in the standard format of comic books from the late 1930s to the present. One of Dell's most famous series in this standard format was its "Four-Color Series" which included a wide variety of

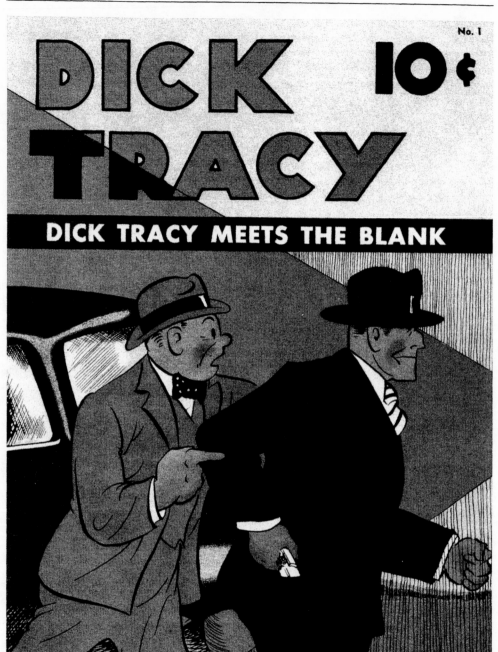

Dick Tracy Meets the Blank: **Black and White Comic #1 (aka Large Feature Comic #1, Series I). Dell Publishing, 1939. Reprinted by permission: Tribune Media Services.**

artists and fictional characters in over 1,300 titles from 1939 to 1962. Chester Gould's story of Dick Tracy expanded into a fourth print medium when in 1939 it first appeared in its own publication—an un-

numbered Dell Four-Color comic book. The Four-Color series ran until 1962; Dick Tracy made frequent appearances here between 1939 and 1948.

Dick Tracy was granted his own

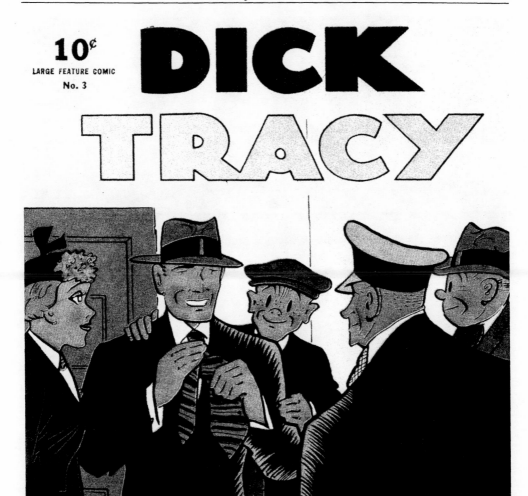

Dick Tracy: **Large Feature Comic #3, Series II. Dell Publishing, 1941. Reprinted by permission: Tribune Media Services.**

comic book series for the first time in 1947. The line, *Dick Tracy Monthly,* debuted with a January 1948 issue; *Super Comics* had last used Tracy stories in its issue #115 (December 1947). Again, Dell was the publishing company behind the project. But after just 24 issues the series was taken over by Harvey Publications (also of New York City), which revised the title for the line to read *Dick Tracy Comics*

Super Comics #105. Dell Publishing, February 1947. Reprinted by permission: Tribune Media Services.

Monthly. Harvey kept Dell's numbering system intact and presented the twenty-fifth issue with a March 1950 date. "Except for 'new' stories in [Dell] issues 19–24 of which Gould had no part, the first 18 issues reprise strips from 1934 to 1936, while the Harvey Publications go straight from Flattop in 1943 to Flattop, Jr., in 1956 with nary a break."[12] The series continued until #145 in April 1961; the final five issues were titled simply *Dick Tracy.*

However, even when the comic books were based on the newspaper comic strips, both Dell and Harvey Publishers (particularly Harvey) were guilty of intense editing and condensing of storylines. One reason for this editing was that the audience for the comic books was substantially more homogeneous—they were almost exclusively young readers—than the audience for the newspaper strips. The comic books cut back on guns and gunplay and other tools and forms of violence to make storylines and artwork tolerable to scrutinizing parents. The unfortunate thing was that much of the original intensity and flair of the Gould Dick Tracy stories was lost.

In addition to the various Feature Books, comic books, and related series already discussed which showcased Dick Tracy, there were many other comic books and similar publications that presented adventures of the ace detective. Many of these publications were designed as premiums, others were intended as one-shot books, and so on. Robert M. Overstreet's *The Overstreet Comic Book Price Guide,* issued annually, accurately and quite comprehensively catalogs these other publications. Overstreet also provides additional information on all Feature Books, comic books, and related series.

In recent years (specifically 1984 to 1989), longtime *Dick Tracy* fan Shel Dorf and Blackthorne Publishing of El Cajon, California, have produced several fine Dick Tracy comic book series. One such series, the *Dick Tracy Reuben Award Win-ner* series, consisted of 24 issues which reprinted, in black and white, classic Gould newspaper comic strips. This series ran from December 1984 to June 1989. Another Blackthorne comic book line was the *Dick Tracy Monthly* which began in May 1986 and concluded in 1989. As of #26, issues were released on a weekly basis, and the line was retitled *Dick Tracy Weekly.* *Dick Tracy Monthly/Weekly* also reprinted Gould newspaper strips. Blackthorne did three other Tracy series, though each of these was short-lived. August 1987 saw the beginning of a four-issue series which would in August 1989 be entitled *Dick Tracy: The Early Years.* September 1987 saw the beginning of another four-issue series which would end in June 1988 entitled *Dick Tracy: The Unprinted Stories.* Between January 1988 and August 1989 Blackthorne relesed three issues under the rubric *Dick Tracy Special.* All the Blackthorne Tracy comic books have black and white interiors and attractive color covers.

In conjunction with the 1990 Warren Beatty *Dick Tracy* movie, Walt Disney Productions released a series of three high-gloss, brightly colored Dick Tracy graphic novels written by John Moore and illustrated in a rather abstract, surrealist pop art style by Kyle Baker. These were entitled *Dick Tracy: Big City Blues, Dick Tracy vs. the Underworld,* and *Dick Tracy: the Movie.* The third graphic novel was based on the Beatty movie; all three were later reissued as one volume entitled *Dick Tracy: The Complete True Hearts and Tommy Guns Trilogy.*

Most recently, Gladstone Publishing of Prescott, Arizona, has produced two fine, though short-lived, Dick Tracy comic book series. This publisher marketed three oversized, high-gloss, colorful, and attractive books for its *Gladstone Comics Album* line in 1990. Between September 1990 and May 1991, Gladstone produced five standard format color comic books for its *The Original Dick Tracy* line.

Sparkle Plenty: **Four-Color #215. Dell Publishing, 1948. Reprinted by permission: Tribune Media Services.**

The significance of Dick Tracy comic books is that they provided complete (though edited) episodes to rapidly expanding audiences for Dick Tracy and the new medium. These comic books, with the exception of the *Dick Tracy* Sunday newspaper pages, were the only color presentation of Gould's detective hero done to this time. The importance of color to Dick Tracy illustrations may be

***Dick Tracy Monthly* #9. Dell Publishing, September 1948. Reprinted by permission: Tribune Media Services.**

debatable since Chester Gould's use of black and white was most effective. What is of major consequence with the Tracy comic books is that the detective hero became available to readers in a fourth print medium; America's number one police officer was becoming increasingly popular, his adventures more pervasive.

Dick Tracy Monthly #10. Dell Publishing, October 1948. Reprinted by permission: Tribune Media Services.

Radio Drama

Radio detectives were popular in the 1930s and 1940s for the same reason the Dick Tracy comic strip was popular: the storylines and themes were highly relevant to their audiences in terms of life experiences. They did not educate so much as they hit a responsive chord in the consumers. Phillips H. Lord's *Gangbusters*,

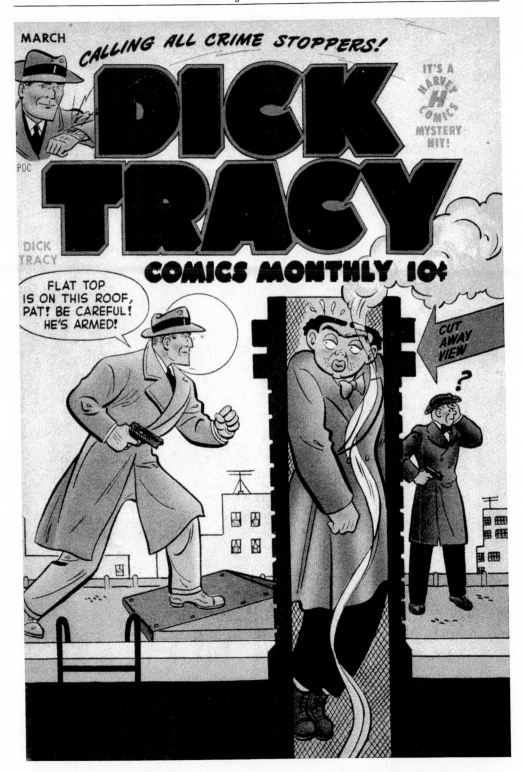

***Dick Tracy Comics Monthly* #25.** Harvey Publishing, March 1950. Reprinted by permission: Tribune Media Services.

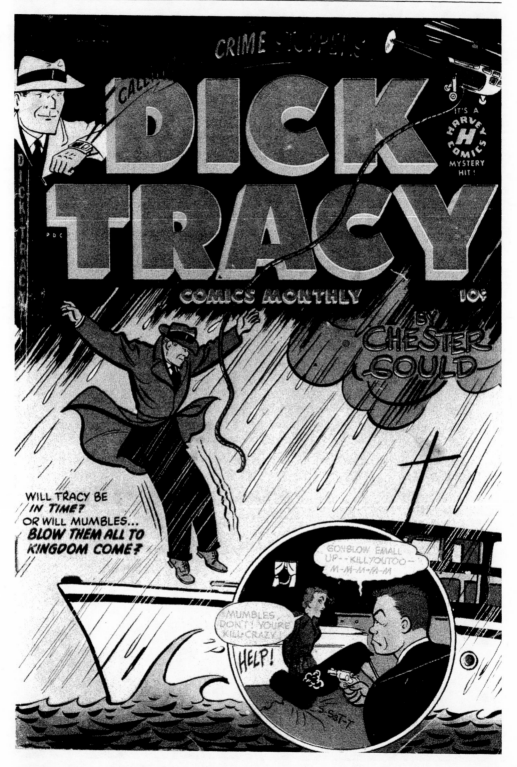

Dick Tracy Comics Monthly #49. Harvey Publishing, March 1952. Reprinted by permission: Tribune Media Services.

***Dick Tracy Comics Monthly* #131. Harvey Publishing, February 1959. Reprinted by permission: Tribune Media Services.**

based on actual documented police cases, was probably the most famous and successful of these programs. At one time it was estimated that the clues that *Gangbusters* provided the listening audience led to an astounding 92 percent effectiveness rate at capturing criminals still at large. Of course, the figure was probably greatly inflated as many of the wrongdoers would have been eventually apprehended

Motorola Presents Dick Tracy Comics by Chester Gould. Giveaway, 1953. Reprinted by permission: Tribune Media Services.

by established police procedure regardless of listener input. Nonetheless, the claim was sensational. Lord's program was one of the very few to present the monotony of established police procedure and make it interesting. The show was also one of the leading innovators for new sound effects, utilizing two or three sound effects men per show. Some of the more difficult and inventive sounds these technicians pro-

Dick Tracy. Giveaway, 1958. Reprinted by permission: Tribune Media Services.

duced included the sounds of a shot gangster falling to the floor, police chases over icy streets, the trap door falling in an execution scene, and the bubble sound as a speedboat sank. In an average half-hour episode of *Gangbusters,* there were 275 gunshots fired! Other radio dramas that stressed reality rather than fantasy usually met with dismal failure. Obviously, television's audience-participation true crime programs so popular in the early 1990s had predecessors.

As a radio drama, *Dick Tracy* was of course not a true crime program; it did not contain nearly the amount of historical fact the already highly fantastic comic strip did. At its inception in 1935, the show was entertaining, formulaic adventure fiction. At its demise in 1948, the story of Tracy on radio was nothing more than mildly interesting, campy farce. In short, as a radio hero, Tracy met with mixed success, surviving best in the afternoon serial format. The late thirties (circa 1938 and 1939) may have been Tracy's finest years on radio. At this time, the sponsor (Quaker Oats) teamed up with the network (NBC) to offer a variety of captivating premiums and related surprises available by mail. At this time too, plots were at their most intricate and inventive, as NBC had not yet gotten into wholesale reworkings of old programs. As the years passed, the stories of Dick Tracy on radio became highly conventional and reworked much old material without providing major changes in storyline.

But for the hard-core serial adventure fan, the radio saga of America's number one detective did have its appeal. One such appeal was a vast array of credible and original sound effects, including those representing screeching tires, Tommy guns, explosions, and the like. Yet Tracy was not the only radio detective to become more adventurer than the sleuth indicated by the print medium of his origin — Dashiell Hammett's Sam Spade and Arthur Conan Doyle's Sherlock Holmes experienced similar treatment. Dick Tracy was best received in the very visual, hard-edged, and stark medium of the comic strip. Chester Gould's line drawings and style could be replicated nowhere else.

Mutual Radio began serializing *Dick Tracy* on September 30, 1935, almost four years after the comic strip debuted in the *Detroit Mirror.* In 1937, the serial moved to NBC; in 1939, it went off the air. All the installments of the program at this point had been 15 minutes long. The radio series began anew in 1943 when it moved to NBC's Blue Network. (The Blue Network became ABC in 1945.) Here, Tracy's war on crime filled the airwaves until 1948. In 1946, *Tracy* also began appearing weekly as a half-hour radio program for ABC. These episodes were complete in themselves (i.e., not serial in nature), and were sponsored by Tootsie Rolls — a product which had been around since the late 1800s, according to the announcers. These Saturday evening programs were short-lived, though the daily serial continued successfully.

The half-hour Saturday performances of the middle and late 1940s were over-dramatized and sensational. For the Dick Tracy purist, this was not a good thing. Vitamin Flintheart, his wife Snowflake, and Gravel Gertie were mainstays of these evening presentations. Flintheart, always the rube and often charming, was the most obnoxious of the three, but his portrayal was not that far removed from Gould's depiction of the character in the comic strip. Tracy's creator on several occasions attempted to provide some comic relief for his often bleak, ongoing tale. Pat Patton had appeared from the beginning in 1935, and was still present at the program's retirement in 1948; Tracy's adopted son, Dick Tracy, Jr. (Junior), was a staple of the early years of Tracy radio drama (the middle and late Thirties). Tess Trueheart — Tracy's beautiful, bright, sometimes fickle girlfriend, fiancée, and eventual wife — appeared sporadically (as she did in Gould's comic strip) throughout the 14-year period.

The villains in the Dick Tracy radio drama were different from those of the comic strip since Gould did not write for the radio productions. However, as might be expected, several of the more popular themes, settings, and character types of the comic strip made their way into the programming. Villains and storyline formulas were heavily influenced by other contemporary adventure dramas. Writers and producers often worked on several shows for a given network, and in an effort to save time and money, they regularly recycled formulas. *Dick Tracy, Jack Armstrong: The All-American Boy,* and *Sky King,* which at one time had neighboring time slots on the same station, often had similarities of plots, themes, settings, and so on. Old radio programs were often reworked for new broadcasts. For example, in the case of *Dick Tracy,* a program which appeared in 1943 might be slightly altered and re-presented in 1946. This meant that the later renditions had been, in the words of the announcer, "transcribed from a earlier broadcast." Transcriptions were economical, and hence common—they were a form of the rerun.

The actors and actresses who paraded across the sound stage of *Dick Tracy* were many and varied. Radio networks had interchangeable stock players, as do television networks today. Of those who played the title role in *Dick Tracy,* Ned Wever was the most renowed. Matt Crowley and Barry Thomson also did stints as the radio detective hero. Junior Tracy was played by Andy Donnelly and Jackie Kelk. Walter Kinsella played Pat Patton, Howard Smith played Chief Brandon, and Helen Lewis played Tess Trueheart. Other characters were played by Beatrice Pons, John Griggs, Mercedes McCambridge, Craig McDonnell, Gil Mack, James Van Dyk, and Ralph Bell. Directors included Mitchell Grayson, Charles Powers, and Bob White; writers included Sidney Slon (who

was responsible for Saturday scripts), and John Wray and Everett S. Crosby, who worked on the Monday through Friday serials. There were others, too—for example, Tracy's sidekick and underling, Pat Patton, was played by several different actors. The early writers, actors, directors, and announcers are some of those most forgotten, though they ironically produced the finest Tracy radio dramas. Don Gardiner and George Gunn were the two most distinctive announcers, but Dan Seymour and Ed Herlihy also served in this capacity. Charlie Cantor, an old vaudevillian and radio bit player, sometimes played criminal parts on *Dick Tracy.*[13]

Ned Wever was not necessarily the best radio Dick Tracy, but he is most often equated with that role because he was a dashing, well-known actor in a variety of soap operas, mysteries, and related radio serial dramas. Wever's most famous role was probably that of H.C. McNeile's British detective and adventurer Bulldog Drummond for the program of the same name. (He was one of two actors who played the part of Drummond for Mutual Radio between 1942 and 1947.[14]) With its trademark foghorn, *Bulldog Drummond* was one of the premiere mystery programs of its time. Ned Wever's many roles as a radio actor included the following: Alan Bishop in *Betty and Bob* (begun on NBC Blue in 1932); Nick in *Little Italy* (begun on CBS in 1933); Jerry Miller in *Big Sister* (begun on CBS in 1936); Anthony Hale, the D.A. in *Her Honor, Nancy James* (begun on CBS in 1938); Colin Kirby in *Valiant Lady* (begun on NBC in 1938); Dr. Anthony Loring in *Young Widder Brown* (which ran on Mutual then on NBC, from 1938 to 1956); Peter Carver in *Lora Lawton* (begun on NBC in 1943); Jeff Spencer in *Two on a Clue* (begun on CBS in 1944); and Captain Scott in the later years of *Under Arrest* (1947–1954). Wever also did some speaking lines for *Showboat,* a top variety hour done by NBC; played in the serial drama *Pages of Romance* (begun on NBC

Blue in 1932); and appeared in the serial drama *True Confessions*.[15] This popular actor played Dick Tracy during the ABC run (NBC Blue prior to 1945). "He [Wever] may be seen in a frequently rerun *Perry Mason* episode, 'The Case of the Hesitant Hostess.' There he plays a gum-chewing head of a model agency, really a front for dope smuggling."[16]

Recordings of old-time radio are comparatively rare today. Several reputable companies commercially market such recordings, but even their collective inventories constitute only a terribly small fraction of the radio programming that was done during the Golden Age of the form (the Thirties and Forties). There is a horror story about numerous tapes with one-of-a-kind *Shadow* episodes being inadvertently erased. Many programs originally aired live and were never recorded. So those radio programs still existing from that period are indeed treasures. The 29 *Dick Tracy* episodes discussed here took five years to collect, and the author would be most grateful to learn of other existing episodes. As stated earlier, from all indications it appears that the years 1938 and 1939 were two of the best for Dick Tracy adventures on radio. At this time, Quaker Puffed Wheat and Puffed Rice (red and blue boxes respectively) were the products endorsed by the program. During February 1938, Dick Tracy completed "The Case of the Baron and Sub-Stratosphere Airplane Plans" (imagine the announcer repeating that case title on a daily basis!) and was beginning "The Case of the Black Pearl of Osiris." Three important codes from *Dick Tracy's Secret Code Book* (1938) were used in the episodes to relay messages.

Prisoner:

1	2	3	4	5	6	7	8	9	10
B	K	T	G	X	L	Q	R	A	U

11	12	13	14	15	16	17	18	19
H	M	D	Y	N	E	S	I	Z

20	21	22	23	24	25	26
C	O	J	V	P	W	F

Buffalo:

1	2	3	4	5	6	7	8	9	10
L	X	G	T	K	B	H	U	Q	R

11	12	13	14	15	16	17	18	19
A	E	N	C	D	M	O	Y	W

20	21	22	23	24	25	26
I	S	F	Z	J	V	P

Football:

1	2	3	4	5	6	7	8	9	10
J	V	P	W	F	O	C	Z	I	S

11	12	13	14	15	16	17	18	19
E	N	Y	D	M	H	R	U	Q

20	21	22	23	24	25	26
A	L	B	X	K	G	T

Each episode opened with a familiar summons: "Calling all adventure fans. Calling all Dick Tracy fans. Stand by. Dick Tracy is on the air!"

Following are synopses of a representative run of episodes, "The Case of the Black Pearl of Osiris," from the series' original stretch of 1935–39. Asterisks beside a few names indicate uncertain spelling.

Tuesday, February 8

Dick Tracy and Pat Patton are called upon to help Scotland Yard and to escort Egyptologist Dryden* Small to the United States via ship.[17] Strange warnings, scarabs (meant as symbols of death and destruction), and the Man with the Yellow Face all haunt Small on the voyage. However, the famed Egyptologist withholds useful information from Dick Tracy that could help our hero better protect Small. Tracy presses the man for more information; he learns little. There is a muddled attempt on Small's life, and the daily installment ends with the emergence of a mysterious message above Small's bed. We also learn that Osiris is an ancient Egyptian god. But now it is time for the

Dick Tracy Secret Service Patrol meeting, run by Junior Tracy. Junior announces that in this the nineteenth meeting, the show is saluting the twenty-eighth anniversary of the Boy Scouts of America. The day's code for patrol members is provided by Junior. It is: "Prisoner, 25, 9, 3, 20, 11, 26, 21, 8, 17, 16, 20, 8, 16, 3, 8, 18, 15, 4." Junior repeats the code, though he makes the eighth number "eighteen" instead of "eight" this time. The second reading is in error, as the code only makes sense with "eight" in the eighth place. Listeners who are not yet members of the Dick Tracy Secret Service Patrol are invited to send two box-tops from Quaker Puffed Wheat or Quaker Puffed Rice (these box-tops should be printed "3 Wrappings Guard Its Freshness") to Dick Tracy, Box L, Chicago. They would receive the secret code book, the patrol pledge, and a special badge.

Wednesday, February 9

Pat Patton draws duty guarding Dryden Small. Tracy goes below deck to speak with the ship's captain, and while there receives a message from Patton. It reads: "Prisoner, 20, 21, 12, 16, 7, 10, 18, 20, 2." On deck, Patton is mysteriously and brutally pushed overboard. Tracy arrives on deck and dives into the water after his pal. Now it is time for the Dick Tracy Secret Patrol meeting—number 20 according to Junior's records. The day's code reads: "Buffalo, 21, 12, 14, 10, 12, 4, 10, 20, 13, 3, 6, 10, 20, 13, 3, 21, 1, 8, 14, 5."

Thursday, February 10

Pat Patton, thrown overboard by the Man with the Yellow Face, is rescued by Dick Tracy in the opening moments of the show. Later, the Man with the Yellow Face threatens Patton when he (Patton) claims that he does not know where the black pearl is. During the twenty-first meeting of

the Dick Tracy Secret Service Patrol meeting, Junior relays a message from the great detective: "Football, 10, 11, 7, 17, 11, 26, 17, 9, 12, 25, 5, 17, 6, 15, 11, 25, 13, 3, 26."

Friday, February 11

Today listeners learn with Tracy that the Man with the Yellow Face is Humi Batique*, High Priest of the Cult of Osiris, and that the black pearl represents the anatomical heart of the statue of Osiris found earlier by Small. Batique shoots Tracy in the leg with Small's pearl-handled revolver and escapes. When the ship docks, Junior is there to meet Tracy and Patton. Tracy suspects Batique may be hiding in a mummy case coming ashore. During the last patrol meeting for the week, the code provided reads: "Prisoner, 20, 6, 10, 16, 3, 21, 17, 16, 20, 8, 16, 3, 8, 18, 15, 4, 12, 21, 15, 13, 9, 14."

Monday, February 14

The S.S. *Mulvania** docks. Dick Tracy's suspicions were correct, and he locates and captures Batique, who is hiding in a mummy case brought on shore. A doctor digs out the bullet from Tracy's leg (which is by now quite painful). The projectile is strange to say the least. Tracy and Junior visit Batique in jail, and the Egyptian further explains his religious motive. We have sympathy for him, and Dryden Small appears more and more the villain. Batique shows his secret compartment ring to Tracy and Junior and gives the same to Tracy so that when the great detective recovers the pearl, he will have a place to hide it. The ring also brings good luck. Dick Tracy rushes to the ballistics lab to talk to Cooper about the "bullet." There are no codes or messages during the short patrol meeting.

Promotion Record

I became a full-fledged member of the Dick Tracy Secret Service Patrol, entitled to all patrol privileges, on _____

Paste Sergeant's Insignia Here

I was promoted to the rank of Sergeant on _____

Paste Lieutenant's Insignia Here

I was promoted to the rank of Lieutenant on _____

Paste Captain's Insignia Here

I was promoted to the rank of Captain on _____

Paste Inspector-General's Insignia Here

I was promoted to the rank of Inspector-General on _____

Printed in U.S.A.

Dick Tracy Secret Service Patrol

This is to certify that:

I, _____
(SIGN NAME HERE)

am a member of the Dick Tracy Secret Service Patrol, and I hereby pledge myself to . . .

- stand for law and order
- be trustworthy, honest, honorable
- be kind, courteous and helpful to others
- be fearless, courageous in what I know is right

- be alert and healthy in thought and action
- honor and obey my parents
- keep the secrets of the Dick Tracy Secret Service Patrol strictly confidential.

Certified by: *Dick Tracy Jr.*
DICK TRACY SECRET SERVICE PATROL

Witness: _____
(PARENT OR GUARDIAN)

Tuesday, February 15

Scene One: In the ballistics lab, Cooper shows Dick Tracy that the Black Pearl of Osiris was inside the bullet. Scene Two: At a meeting of a society of unscrupulous art dealers and collectors, the High Mogul introduces Remo* from Madagascar, who is a "master of the silken cord." Remo's target is to be Tracy, as the society wants to recover the black pearl and eliminate its foe. Scene Three: From his jail cell, Batique tells Tracy that his friend will get the pearl from our hero, and that this friend will identify himself via a secret code. During the Dick Tracy Secret Service Patrol meeting, it is revealed that a special announcement is to come from the great detective himself on Friday. Excitement and speculation are high. There is no message today, but there is a call for membership, and for everyone to save box-tops from the sponsor's products — Quaker Puffed Wheat and Quaker Puffed Rice.

Wednesday, February 16

It is Tracy's night to use the car that he and Patton share. In the car, en route to picking up Tess for a date, Tracy is attacked by Remo, master of the silken cord. Remo fails. Later, an agent pretending to be sent by Batique fails to talk Tracy out of the ring and the pearl it encases. Soon after, Tracy follows the agent by cab, only to see him mysteriously killed when the agent's cab is stopped in a traffic jam. Tracy theorizes that an air rifle was employed during the traffic congestion. Later, when the detective visits Batique in prison, the latter promises a surprise for Junior. That night Tracy, Patton, and Junior go out for dinner. They are surrounded by the Mogul's agents, and escape

looks improbable at best. At the Patrol meeting, there is again mention of the surprise promised Junior and the patrol members, but there is no clue yet as to the nature of the surprise.

Thursday, February 17

When Dick Tracy, Pat Patton, and Junior leave the restaurant, the Mogul's agents attack, and a fight breaks out. During the skirmish, Tracy gets the coat off one of the foes. Later, from the dust he recovers from the garment, Tracy determines that the Mogul's society might be holed up near a mattress factory. Patton and other officers search the city's mattress factories, and at the close of today's episode, Patton calls Tracy with a coded message. It reads: "Buffalo, 14, 1, 11, 18, 21, 4."

Friday, February 18

Dick Tracy and fellow cops raid the mattress factory which Patton investigated. The High Mogul and his group are captured and taken to HQ. Humi Batique calls for Tracy and Junior to come see him in jail. Here, the Egyptian presents Junior with a Dick Tracy Secret Compartment Ring that sports the image of Tracy. (It is modeled after Batique's Osiris ring.) The detective is called to another cell where the Mogul appears to be dead. En route to the medical examiner, the Mogul escapes. The Dick Tracy Secret Service Patrol meeting centers on the very exciting news of Dick Tracy's announcement. Rings just like Junior's will be available to patrol members! More news Monday, but in the meantime, save those box-tops.

Opposite: **Dick Tracy Secret Service Patrol certificate.**

Monday, February 21

It is revealed that the High Mogul used a hypnotic trance to baffle police and escape. Humi Batique is exonerated. Later, the Mogul approaches Patton at the apartment he shares with Tracy and hypnotizes Tracy's pal so that he might get him to retrieve the black pearl from Tracy. During the patrol meeting, Dick Tracy provides more information about the secret compartment ring. A jeweler has been located who will not only produce the ring, but who will also make a new item selected by Tess Trueheart—a Dick Tracy bangle bracelet! Both are gold-plated, and can be obtained for five box-tops each.

Tuesday, February 22

Dryden Small is discovered to be a member of the High Mogul's society. A hypnotized Pat Patton talks Dick Tracy out of Batique's secret compartment ring which houses the Black Pearl of Osiris, saying no one would suspect that he (Patton) has it. Pat turns the ring over to the Mogul, and the Mogul ends the hypnotic trance, leaving Patton clueless. Dick Tracy appears, having followed Patton to the Mogul; Dryden Small appears, having followed the High Mogul. As the episode ends, Mogul and Small, with the upper hand on our heroes, plan to kill Tracy and Patton. There is further discussion of the Dick Tracy Secret Compartment Ring and Bangle Bracelet during the patrol meeting.

Wednesday, February 23

Dryden Small, as yet not a killer, does not want to add murder to his list of crimes. Small and the Mogul leave with what they believe to be the ring and pearl. Alert to the Mogul's hypnotic effects on

Patton, Tracy had switched the pearl to Junior's ring—the Mogul had only gotten the ring, which admittedly was a treasure in itself. Dick Tracy, believing that Small and the Mogul are also mixed up in international art heists, pursues them. The great detective believes that there is an even higher power behind the Mogul. Humi Batique leaves for Egypt with the pearl in tow, and it seems that "The Case of the Black Pearl of Osiris" has been completed. But when Dick Tracy and Pat Patton return home, they discover that Junior is gone. Dick Tracy takes charge of the Secret Service Patrol meeting and promotes the secret compartment ring and bangle bracelet.

Thursday, February 24

Listeners are advised to look for the Dick Tracy Headquarters sign at stores. Junior has been kidnapped by the Mogul and Dryden Small. The crooks force Junior to write Tracy a note, but the young ward is able, through some trickery, to get a coded message incorporated in the forced note. The code reads: "Prisoner, 8, 18, 23, 16, 8, 8, 13." Tracy detects the code. Meanwhile, the Mogul puts Small in charge of Junior (who is gagged and bound to a chair) when he leaves to meet with "Number One." Then a mysterious, cloaked figure shrouded in darkness comes to rescue Junior when Small exits the room. The figure identifies himself as "the Unknown." Who are Number One and the Unknown? At the Dick Tracy Secret Service Patrol meeting, the code message is repeated, and there is a reminder about the secret compartment ring and bangle bracelet.

Friday, February 25

Listeners learn little more about the Unknown except that he dons a large black hat and a large black cape and that he does good but does not want to encounter the police. While it seems certain that the Shadow would not appear on *Dick Tracy*, listeners hope this might be some superhero team-up. (It is not.) Number One turns out to be the power behind the art treasure thieves. Junior is freed by the Unknown and meets Tracy on the street after an unsuccessful attempt to get the Unknown to come with him. Tracy is already on the street because of the code message Junior sent yesterday. Tracy begins an investigation of art collectors and their sources. Number One sends a chauffeur to retrieve Small, but as Small waits for the driver, the Unknown enters and abducts him. Dick Tracy and Pat Patton are about to leave the office when the Unknown calls and tells Tracy there is a surprise waiting for him. The surprise is a bound and gagged Dryden Small, with a note pinned to him. The note reads: "With the compliments of the Unknown." At the patrol meeting, listeners are reminded about the ring and bracelet premiums.

The Dick Tracy Secret Service Patrol meetings, combined with fascinating membership offers, related premiums, and entertaining storylines, helped to make "The Case of the Black Pearl of Osiris" a high point in *Dick Tracy*'s almost 15-year run on network radio. In 1938 and 1939, this radio drama offered not only the famed secret compartment ring and bangle bracelet, but also that precious code book, a membership certificate, and patrol badges for various ranks within the patrol. The ranks included: Member, Sergeant, Lieutenant, Captain, and Inspector-General. Advancements in rank could be achieved by following directions set forth in the code book, and by sending more box-tops. Apparently, the Inspector-General badge was quite rare. In a 1983 newspaper article, Dorothy Hammond and Rachelle D. Brisk wrote, "For those with bigger appetites, forty-one box-tops

got them the rare Inspector-General's badge which now sells for up to $100."[18] But the offers of giveaways and promotions by mail were certainly not unique to *Tracy*. Writes Jim Harmon, "The barrage of premiums had started with Orphan Annie giving away a Shake-Up Mug for Ovaltine mixed beverages [malted milk]. Tom Mix then offered a wooden model of his six shooter. (The sponsor, Ralston, hoped for a thousand replies. They received three million.) Jack Armstrong then gave away a pedometer to measure how far one walked on a hike."[19]

The Dick Tracy Secret Compartment Ring and Bangle Bracelet were plated with 14-karat gold and, as noted, required five Quaker Puffed Wheat and/or Quaker Puffed Rice box-tops apiece. "The request for five box-tops was unusual. Most offers required only one box-top, sometimes two. Five would have the kids eating cereal until it came out of their ears. There was no request for 'a dime to cover the cost of handling and mailing.' Other sponsors, such as Ralston and Ovaltine, sometimes sent their merchandise without requesting cash and only asked for one proof of purchase. The reason for the premium offer was usually to test how many kids were really listening. Sometimes, such as with Quaker, it also seemed aimed at moving product off the shelves."[20]

Jim Harmon attributes some of the success of radio *Dick Tracy* to the writing skills of George Lowther.[21] Lowther wrote radio scripts for *Superman, The Tom Mix Ralston Straightshooters,* and *Dick Tracy.* Harmon claims that Lowther added "atmospheric fantasy" to the stories of Tracy on radio, and that he [Lowther] packed in twice as much action into his stories.[22] George Lowther is perhaps best known for his important contributions to the Superman story in his rare, highly collectable book *Superman* (1942).

In 1939, *Dick Tracy* went off the air. By this time the producers had discontinued the daily serial in favor of a half-hour Saturday evening presentation with self-contained stories. The switch was not popular among listeners, and soon *Dick Tracy* appeared as neither a daily serial nor as a weekly program. But in 1943 NBC's Blue Network brought *Dick Tracy* back to story radio with slightly different trappings and players. The storylines were often re-workings of earlier broadcasts; hence they were dubbed "transcribed." Case titles were not as prominent as they had been in the NBC programs of the late Thirties, and the Dick Tracy Secret Service Patrol meetings disappeared. Following is a sampling of synopses of episodes that survive. "Boys and girls, here's Dick Tracy. . . ."

Tuesday, September 14, 1943

In yesterday's story, a jewelry store robbery was perpetrated during a mysterious blackout. Today Marge and Slip, two crooks, enter a radio store and test a short-wave radio set in a booth. They are waiting for a message. Listeners learn that the mysterious blackouts that have occurred in recent days have been masterminded by Mrs. Johnson. While in the radio store sound booth, Marge and Slip await news of the next blackout. When it comes, the pair leave the radio store, enter a bank, and rob it. They knock out a clerk in the process. Later Tracy arrives and investigates the bank. An advertisement cuts in calling for listeners to increase their purchases of War Bonds. Then there is a minute of dialogue between Marge and Slip, and as the story closes there is another call to buy War Bonds.

Thursday, September 30, 1943

Listeners are reminded that this program is transcribed. Two weeks' worth of episodes have passed since the last encounter with Mrs. Johnson's gang. At this point, most of Mrs. Johnson's henchmen have been caught, but the mastermind herself is still at large. Today Dick Tracy is analyzing a perfumed handkerchief found at a robbed pawnshop while Pat Patton looks on. Tess Trueheart arrives and identifies the fragrance as "Dusk," a rare import. Tracy tries to find out where Dusk is sold. He locates such a store and learns that a man (probably confidence man Doc Benson*) purchases the exotic fragrance. The detective buys the last bottle of Dusk. Ten days later, Tess takes the perfume to Mrs. Johnson saying that it is a present from Doc Benson. Mrs. Johnson traps Tess into moving in with her as an accomplice. Don Gardiner identifies himself as the announcer, and a Tootsie Roll commercial follows.

Thursday, October 7, 1943

A variety of blackouts and related crimes have occurred over the last few weeks. Those arrested in connection with the crimes point to Mrs. Johnson as their leader. Recently, bank robber Doc Benson has been captured and released, much to the dismay of Detective Dick Tracy. Prosecutors believe Benson to be Mrs. Johnson's chief lieutenant, and they are convinced that he will lead them to her. However, after leaving HQ, Benson loses the detective tailing him and escapes. An anonymous phone call puts Tracy and Patton back on the trail of Mrs. Johnson and sends them to Apartment 3F, where Benson is tied up. (A trace of the phone call indicates that the caller was a woman.) It appears that Mrs. Johnson, the presumed phone caller, has double-crossed Doc. Tracy and Patton take Benson and head for the inventor of the blackouts, one Wayne Holt*. Ruby, a girl Tracy befriended in an earlier episode, intercepts the threesome. She has a gun and wants Doc Benson.

Friday, May 5, 1944

The circus provided many a backdrop for radio dramas and fiction as a whole during the 1930s and 1940s. Tom Mix, Jack Armstrong, the Shadow, and many others appeared in stories with this setting. Dick Tracy and associates had their share of encounters with the big top. In this episode, from the adventure "Espionage at the Circus," Tracy, Patton, and Junior continue to track Nazi spies at the circus. (One of the spies is ringmaster Spaulding.) Junior helps Stumbles (an uncoordinated circus hand) feed the animals, and also delivers the mail. While in one tent, Tracy's ward accidentally knocks over a jar of grease paint and discovers something in the paint which he rushes to Tracy. Meanwhile, Federal Agent Nicholson* visits with Dick Tracy in another part of the circus grounds. Nick is tracing a missing agent, Tracy is tracking a missing trapeze artist, and it appears that the two old friends might be able to help each other. Junior bursts into the room with his as yet undisclosed discovery. The announcer breaks in.

Tuesday, May 1, 1945

The Blue Network today presented another installment of Dick Tracy on "The Case of the Empty Safe." But a special news bulletin breaks in: "The British Broadcasting Company has just reported that Adolph Hitler died of a stroke at the Reich Chancellory in Berlin. There has been no Allied confirmation of the report." Yesterday on the show, evidence piled up that made Tracy sure that Spike Connelly* was responsible for the dynamiting of the empty safe. Sergeant Martin reported his suspicions concerning the occupants of a certain house, and Tracy and Patton went to that house. Tracy rang the front doorbell, and Patton covered the back.

Spike and his girlfriend, Gert, headed for the back door. Today Spike and Patton have a fistfight, but Gert knocks Patton out with her shoe. The crooks head for a car in the garage and make their escape. The police pursue but lose the chase. When the pair run out of gasoline, a motorist pulls up and offers assistance. Spike knocks the man cold, and the escape continues. Meanwhile, back at the house, Tracy pulls Patton to his feet, and together they head to their squad car to contact HQ by radio. Here they learn about the assaulted motorist and get a license number and auto make for the car Spike and Gert are driving. Dick and Pat take up the chase, and they learn via radio that a farmer has sighted the car moving northwest. Later Tracy and Patton stop at a house and question a man who acts very strangely, and then leave. Tracy believes that the man is being manipulated by Spike and Gert, who are watching, and he radios for a police barricade. The announcer cuts in and talks about teamwork and World War II as an advertisement for War Bonds.

Thursday, September 13, 1945†

Prior to the presentation of the next installment of "The Case of the Buried Treasure," the announcer makes reference to Phillips H. Lord's *Gangbusters* in his salute to radio sound effects men. Yesterday, Tracy, Patton, and Sheriff Blackwood were pursuing the Curry* Brothers when they stumbled upon a treasure chest containing a coded map. Meanwhile, the Currys (Jason and Oliver) went deeper into the southern swampland, taking with them the sheriff's dog, Dan. Today, Dick Tracy and Sheriff Blackwood unload the treasure chest from the back of a tractor and take it into the sheriff's kitchen. Here Patton empties the chest while Tracy and Black-

†*The NBC Blue network is now ABC.*

wood examine the map. Benefit, the sheriff's black servant, interrupts, claiming he has heard Dan baying. As a character, Benefit adheres to racial stereotypes of the times, and he is afraid Patton might find some skeleton bones in the chest. The servant recognizes the shoreline on the map as Cook's Cove, named for the dead body once found there. Tracy, Patton, and the Sheriff head for the swamp. Up ahead, the Curry brothers hear the approaching tractor, and Jason strikes Dan when he starts to bark. A thunderstorm approaches. George Gunn, the announcer, promotes *Gangbusters* by saying that the program will come to this station in just two days, and that this is ABC.

Friday, September 13, 1946

George Gunn prefaces the day's episode in "The Case of the Broken Window" by discussing forest fires. Yesterday, Dick Tracy and Pat Patton nearly caught up with the youthful jewel thieves, Spider and Mickey, but the crooks barely escaped a trap. In fact, the squad car carrying Tracy and Patton passed the pair on the street. Spider and Mickey got new clothes and haircuts and planned to lay low for a while. Today, Tracy calls Patton over to look at a broken window at the scene of the latest crime. Patton takes the blood-stained pane of glass as evidence at Tracy's request, and the two detectives make the rounds of the local pawnshops for clues. Shortly thereafter Spider and Mickey walk along the waterfront, where they see a "Help Wanted" sign at an industrial plant. The job entails loading 40-pound crates at a rate of $17.50 per week apiece. The boys do good work, and their boss rewards them with salary raises and advances. For several days, the boys continue to work hard while Tracy and Patton comb the city for them. One day, the boss asks Mickey to take money to a bank teller. Mickey completes the errand without incident, and Spider

tells Mickey to come to him next time he is given money for a bank deposit. Spider has a plan for another quick take. George Gunn announces that the final round of the U.S. Amateur Golf Tournament will be broadcast tomorrow. Tracy and Patton listen to the squad car radio which repeats the tri-state alarm for Spider and Mickey.

One Saturday Evening, 1946

In a half-hour self-contained episode sponsored by Tootsie Roll and entitled "The Case of the Firebug Murders," Vitamin Flintheart, his wife Snowflake, and Gravel Gertie all make important appearances. The overly melodramatic tale opens at a warehouse where two arsonists are setting a fire. About the same time, nearby, Gravel Gertie calls Tracy, thinking she might have an idea about the motive behind the recent rash of blazes. J.P. Doom wants to buy her house and other property in the area. Tracy goes to Doom's office, where Doom is holding a late night meeting with his henchmen Hotfoot and Gimmick. When Tracy leaves, Doom instructs Hotfoot and Gimmick to burn down Gertie's house. (An intermission and a Tootsie Roll ad follow.) Snowflake arrives at Gertie's house looking for Vitamin. Hotfoot and Gimmick arrive shortly thereafter, asking to buy more magnesium from the junk dealer Gertie. They then reveal themselves as the arsonists, and tie up Gertie and Snowflake. The fire is just about to start when Tracy and Vitamin arrive to save the ladies. But Hotfoot and Gimmick are waiting and subdue the foursome. The process starts again, whereby a burning candle is positioned in the middle of a pile of magnesium scraps. When the candle burns low enough, it will ignite the highly flammable material. Tracy rolls over to the precariously placed candle and uses it to burn through his ropes. The shack catches fire as Hotfoot, Gimmick, and Doom look on. Tracy and Vitamin jump and subdue the unsuspecting three-some, and our hero quips, "The next time these boys come in contact with anything hot, it will be a chair in the death house of the state prison." (An ad for nickel-size Tootsie Rolls follows; Ray Carter is the maestro.) Dick Tracy, at HQ, re-ceives a phone call from the owner of a trucking company. It seems one of the owner's drivers is missing, and with him some 50,000 nylons! Listeners are urged to tune in next week for "The Case of the Hot Nylons," written by Sidney Slon, and directed by Mitchell Grayson. This pro-gram was transcribed from an earlier broadcast.

One Saturday Evening, 1946

Tootsie Rolls and *The New Dick Tracy Show* present Dick Tracy on "The Case of the Dark Corridor." It is 11:30 on a cold, rainy night. Vitamin, Snowflake, and their cabbie, Alonzo, pick up a drenched, for-lorn young lady and give her a ride. The girl does not know who she is and is fright-ened about going back—where, she does not know. Vitamin and company take the girl to Dick Tracy at HQ. Meanwhile, Dr. Frantic has come to HQ looking for his missing female patient. When Vitamin, Snowflake, and Alonzo enter with the girl and meet Frantic, the girl becomes hyster-ical. The doctor takes his patient, whom he calls "Am," and leaves with Alonzo in the cabbie's rig. Tracy fears that the girl's hysteria might be well founded. At his home, Vitamin gets a phone call from Alonzo at 2:30 A.M. The driver is looking for Tracy and fears that the doctor "is not on the up and up." Alonzo picks up Vita-min and Snowflake at their house, and the threesome proceed to the sanitarium. Meanwhile, on a hunch Dick Tracy also heads to the facility. During intermission, Vitamin and the announcer advertise Tootsie Rolls. Upon returning to the story, we find Dr. Frantic speaking with his assis-tant, Phobia, at the hospital. Frantic ex-plains that he had to go to the police in his effort to locate Am. The doorbell rings, and Phobia meets Vitamin, Snowflake, and Alonzo. The assistant has the threesome wait as she goes to get Frantic. The doctor traps the group, after they explain that they are bent on retrieving Am. Frantic uses an experimental nerve gas on the trio in an attempt to coerce them, and, after ex-posing his victims to the gas for about one hour, Frantic discovers that Alonzo is not completely under his influence. He de-cides to kill all three. When Dick Tracy comes to the door with an arrest warrant for Frantic (for practicing medicine with-out a license), the phony doctor tries to hypnotize the detective. Thinking Tracy is under his influence, Frantic turns his at-tentions to the girl, Amnesia, and states, "I am going to drive her mind down the long dark corridor that leads to oblivion and death." Tracy, still in charge of his facul-ties, talks with Vitamin, Snowflake, and Alonzo while Frantic and Phobia plan to burn down the sanitarium with everyone else inside. Fortunately, the fire is never ignited. Tracy shoots Frantic as he tries to escape, and then hauls Phobia to HQ. In the final scene, Dick Tracy visits the home of Vitamin and Snowflake. The gas man comes to the door to read the meter, and Vitamin goes into hysterics. After one final advertisement for Tootsie Rolls, liste-ners learn that next week's adventure will be "The Case of the Man Who Died Twice."

Thursday, May 15, 1947

Before launching into the next install-ment of Dick Tracy on "The Case of the No-Account Swindle," the announcer dis-cusses some fielding practices for baseball players. Tracy and Patton have been called in to investigate a racket headed by Slip Sales, an embezzler who is crippling local department stores. One of Slip's girls,

Winnie the Weasel, was killed yesterday when she double-crossed the embezzler. Today, Winnie's body and purse reveal identification for five different people. Dick Tracy talks to the cabbie who hit Winnie; with her dying breath, Winnie said she was pushed in front of the man's vehicle. Back at HQ, the motive for the killing is still a mystery. It is learned that Winnie had been using credit cards extensively. In another part of town, Feather meets with Slip Sales. Feather is to pose as Mrs. Banks Daily, and to begin embezzling for Slip. Her first job takes her to a department store, where she is stopped as she is about to make a purchase while the clerk checks her credit. The announcer steps in to talk about other current ABC programs including *Sky King, Jack Armstrong,* and *Terry and the Pirates*. The store manager wants to see Mrs. Daily, as she does not have an account at his store. This serial episode was written by John Wray and Everett S. Crosby; Charles Harrell* was the producer.

Monday, July 14, 1947

Before opening the next installment of "The Case of the Crooked Fingers," the announcer, George Gunn, notes that the Bastille was stormed 158 years ago today, and tells listeners of the significance of this historical event and place as critical to the cause of freedom. Last Friday, Fingers, the sinister jewel thief, was making a desperate attempt to escape with Captain Ash* as his hostage in a speedboat, but Dick Tracy and Pat Patton were in pursuit of the villain in a faster boat. When he was about to be overtaken, Fingers threw the old barge captain overboard, knowing that Tracy and Patton would stop to save Ash. Fingers used the delay to escape and headed through the fog to Dead Man's Reef. The warning bell on the reef suddenly stopped ringing, and the boats ran blindly into danger. Today, Ash tells Tracy

to slow their boat down. With the engine cut, they hear Fingers crash—his gas tanks have broken, and burning gasoline races across the water. There is an explosion, and so ends Fingers' career as a thief. Dick Tracy takes the boat back to investigate why the buoy did not sound. The clapper on the bell had been frozen by the Terarra Tierra*, a prized jewel, which had slipped down and had frozen the clapper against the side of the bell. Captain Ash is to face charges for concealing stolen goods. Tracy and Patton thus finish "The Case of the Crooked Fingers" and head for dinner, for which Patton talks Tracy into paying. Patton treats Tracy to the circus afterwards, and a new case is under way—once more at the circus. Here a man and woman are talking about life and death. They are Medium Rare, a fortune teller, and the ringmaster. Medium claims she is legitimate and can predict the future. Then she predicts death, saying that when the ringmaster snaps his whip in the center ring tonight, Rosar*, the equestrian and daring rider, will die. George Gunn cuts in with a discussion of the hit program *So You Want to Lead a Band* which played on ABC Monday nights. Medium asks for Simi-An*, her pet monkey, whom she says will help kill the equestrian tonight. The episode features Jeff Morrell* and Carl Eastman*. George Gunn closes with a promo for *Sky King*.

Wednesday, July 23, 1947

The announcer talks baseball, and tells the story of Rube Waddell and the heroism that killed him.[23] Deeply immersed in "The Case of the Unfunny Clowns," which began at the beginning of the previous week, Dick Tracy and Pat Patton investigate villainy at the circus. Yesterday Bull Hooker, the elephant attendant, went to Medium Rare and told her that he had seen her monkey, Simi-An, start the fire that put the whole circus in an uproar. Medium agreed to pay Hooker well for his silence, but Patton had been following, and asked Bull what he had been doing in the fortune-teller's tent. Bull was furious and tried to beat up Pat, but he picked on the wrong guy. Much later, after the evening show was over, Tracy and Patton saw a beautiful girl climb to the high trapeze and perform acrobatic miracles. Today Whipper, the ringmaster, enters Medium Rare's tent. Medium tells him that if he does not follow her directions, she will inform the police that he killed her husband, Pierre, and that he (Whipper) had tried to kill the two clowns (Tracy and Patton) during the fire. The murderess explains to Whipper that Bull Hooker saw Simi-An start the diversionary fire, and that she wants him to kill the elephant attendant. She says the two clowns are next. Tracy and Patton talk to Hooker, but can get no further information from him. Then the circus owner calls for Tracy and Patton. Meanwhile Medium, Whipper, and Simi-An visit Bull Hooker. Simi-An incites Titan the elephant to kill his trainer. The announcer cuts in and promotes *The Eddie Albert Show*. Tracy and Patton run to the elephants when they hear the creatures becoming frenzied.

into the country via submarine. As they landed, the pair were questioned by a member of the Coast Guard. Today, just as the illegal aliens refuse to go with the patrolman, a car pulls up behind the guard. Belacosie warns the guard that there is a man standing behind him. The Coast Guard agent believes Belacosie is bluffing, but he is fatally incorrect when the man behind him, Rider, opens up with a Tommy gun. Ringer and Rider take the body back to the boat. When they are driving into town, Rider says that Slim Chance, famed broadcaster, announced on the radio earlier in the evening that Belacosie was coming back into the country via submarine. Belacosie thinks his girlfriend, Molee Cule*, might be the information leak and plans to threaten Slim Chance. Elsewhere, Slim Chance approaches Dick Tracy and Pat Patton, claiming that he (Chance) is going to be killed. He presents Tracy with the threatening note he received. George Gunn promotes *The Bing Crosby Show* where Barry Fitzgerald will make a guest appearance. Belacosie asks Ringer to turn on the radio so he will not miss Slim Chance's retraction, but Slim Chance will make no such statement. Charles Powers is the producer.

Wednesday, November 18, 1947

In a transcription from an earlier broadcast, today we get the first installment of "The Case of the Deadly Tip-Off." George Gunn, the announcer, talks about botany and the value of studying plants. Yesterday, Benton Malice* was electrocuted as he attempted to throw the switch on the oncoming super streamer, and his butler, Wormser Crawley*, was brought to justice for his part in the train wreck. Thus Dick Tracy and Pat Patton conclude "The Case of the Honorable Mr. Malice." But yesterday a new threat appeared—the international gangster Belacosie* and his henchman Ringer, who made illegal entry

Thursday, November 19, 1947

George Gunn commemorates the 84th anniversary of Lincoln's Gettysburg Address. Yesterday, international gangster and undesirable Belacosie smuggled four cases of contraband ashore on a desolate beach and killed a Coast Guard agent. When the gangster finds out that famed announcer Slim Chance has revealed his presence on radio, Belacosie threatens Chance and demands a retraction. This same announcer had been largely responsible for the original deportation of the crook. Two henchmen, Ringer and Rider, listen to Chance's broadcast and wait for the retraction. Dick Tracy and Pat Patton, in the client's booth at the radio station, await the broadcast also. During his broadcast, Slim Chance calls again for authorities to capture the fat gangster and throw him out of the country. When Chance leaves the studio, he is hijacked by Ringer and Rider. The pair escape with Chance via cab and lose the trailing detective. George Gunn talks about the origins of the team of Abbott and Costello, the comedy team's ABC program, and the center they established for delinquent children. Tracy worries when he gets no report from the detective he has assigned to protect Slim Chance.

Wednesday, December 31, 1947

Since this is New Year's Eve, George Gunn talks about the celebration of the holiday in New York City. To date, in "The Case of the Big Black Box," Dick Tracy and Pat Patton were on a speeding train headed for a three-week vacation when they met Oompa-Pa-Pa the Great*, who professed to have the ability to cure any illness. Tracy persuaded Patton to acquire a sudden, unknown malady so that they might further investigate the stranger's claim. Today we find our heroes locked in a California sanitarium. The invention Oompa-Pa-Pa sells, which supposedly cures any disease, is the Electronic Thermo Dynaminator and Health Dispenser. The invention is a fraud, and sales of the machine are a racket for Oompa-Pa-Pa. Rusty Blade is the fraudulent inventor's butler. Harris, who is now broke and whose wife is in the hospital with a seemingly fatal disease because of Oompa and his black box (the ETDHD), comes to the sanitarium and confronts the racketeer. Rusty Blade overpowers Harris and locks him up. Tracy and Patton hear Harris scream. After a brief interlude from announcer George Gunn, we rejoin Blade and Harris. Blade tells Harris he got excited when Harris screamed, and that is why he beat him up.

On February 15, 1945, the Armed Forces Radio Service Command Performance presented the hourlong farce *Dick Tracy in B-Flat*. More than a little bit campy, this program was played for laughs and starred, among others, Bing Crosby (as Tracy), Jimmy Durante, Judy Garland (as Tess), Bob Hope, and Frank Sinatra. The plot of the comedic operatta was sketchy at best as the major emphases were humor and singing. What storyline there was focused on Tess Trueheart's neverending attempts at getting Dick Tracy through a wedding ceremony. Of course, every time Tracy is about to say "I do," there is a delay of some sort. The first scene opens with Tess and Dick at the altar, about to complete the formalities. The wedding party sings "Happy Wedding Day" when the police chief telephones to inform Tracy of a bank robbery. The detective leaves his own wedding, but only after singing a duet with his sweetheart. Bob Hope plays the villainous Flattop, the perpetrator of the bank robbery. Flattop, like everyone else, gets his moments to sing. He then locks Tracy in the bank vault.

Back at the wedding scene, Vitamin Flintheart sings with the chorus of the wedding party. Tracy returns in his long underwear after escaping from the vault. When Tess asks him how he escaped, Tracy responds, "Through the trap door in the back." When the minister tries to begin the wedding ceremony anew, the chief calls once again. Tracy must pursue the Mole (played by Jimmy Durante) and recover the missing Snowflake Flintheart, who has disappeared. The Mole sings and tells Tracy that Snowflake is at Flattop's apartment. As Snowflake, Judy Garland sings "Somewhere Over the Barrell," after Flattop claims he has her over a barrel. Snowflake and Flattop sing a duet.

Dick Tracy knocks on Tess Trueheart's door, mistaking it for Flattop's, and says he has been going backwards because he has Serutan in his gas tank. The wedding guests have left for a Sinatra broadcast. Tracy sings, thinking Tess has deserted him. Flattop, the Mole, and the chief of police stick Tracy up.

One week later, Tracy is with Vitamin and the Summer Sisters—May, June, and July. Vitamin tells July, "You're for me, you're the hottest." The Summer Sisters sing, and the chorus joins in. The minister is once again about to pronounce Dick and Tess "man and wife" when the phone rings. It seems that Shaky has shaken loose from prison. At the drugstore Tracy confronts Shaky, and the criminal sings. The detective is about to take Shaky in when Flattop sticks him up. Shaky and Flattop sing with Tracy.

The Mole has taken Snowflake to Gravel Gertie's gravel pit. A car carrying Tracy, Shaky, and Flattop crashes with one carrying the Mole and Snowflake. Gertie serenades, recounting the first time Tracy arrested her. As Gertie, Judy Garland sings "Clang, Clang Went the Wagon." The program ends when Vitamin, Tess, and the Summer Sisters arrive on horseback. Everyone sings "Happy Wedding Day."

In 1947, Mercury Records, in conjunction with the Chicago Tribune–New York News Syndicate, released a double 78 rpm record set which featured Dick Tracy and "The Case of the Midnight Marauder." The story was adapted by Lou Schofield and Sherman Marks, and was produced by Sherman Marks. Jim Ameche, perhaps best known for his famous radio portrayals of Jack Armstrong, the All-American Boy, from 1933 until 1938, played Tracy,[24] Cliff Sobier played Vitamin Flintheart, and Richard Rober played Flattop. In a story that is even less complicated than any of the Tracy radio programs, Dick Tracy and Pat Patton run into Vitamin Flintheart in Miami. Vitamin has been disturbed by a midnight visitor whom he describes as having a flat head. Soon after, Flattop, in a wig he has taken from Vitamin's makeup box, deceives Tracy and Vitamin while in a cab. He

points a gun at the pair and takes them to his place. Once there, Flattop telephones Croaker King from the next room. Flattop asks the gangster how much money he will pay to have Tracy rubbed out. The amount is $50,000. Tracy overhears this phone conversation and jumps Flattop's henchman, Sparrow. Flattop enters, takes Vitamin hostage, and then shoots Tracy in the shoulder and leaves. Dick Tracy feigns death and calls Patton to have a newspaper extra produced which announces his (Tracy's) death. The detective follows Flattop and Vitamin to the bay, where a ship awaits. Here Tracy confronts, tricks, and shoots Flattop.

In 1939, after the Dick Tracy radio series had moved from Mutual Radio, where it began in 1935, and as NBC was completing its stint as the program's sponsor, famed children's book and Big Little Book publisher Whitman of Racine, Wisconsin, released two small books based on two NBC Dick Tracy radio plays. These two books, *Dick Tracy and the Invisible Man* and *Dick Tracy and the Ghost Ship*, were premiums given away to listeners, just like the patrol badges, secret compartment ring, code book and other items that were made available at this time. These softcover, staple-bound books were about 3¾ inches square and about ⅜ inch (64 pages) thick. In the first book, the preliminary 20 pages were occupied by a section entitled "Behind the Scenes in Radio with Dick Tracy" which contained 8 rather simplistic line drawings. (These drawings were quite faithful to the depictions in the famous comic strip, but probably were not Gould art—most likely one of Gould's assistants did the pen and ink drawings for these books.) The balance of the book provided a crude, rather detail-free dialogue which encapsulated the essence of the NBC radio play.

Contemporary history, social thought and cultural values were each reflected in radio drama *Dick Tracy*. And there was a degree of satire in these stories that eventually became the strength of their presentation. In the first years, producers relied on intricate plotting, intriguing sound effects, and alluring premiums to sell their stories of Tracy on the airwaves. As the 14-year period in which Chester Gould's flatfoot appeared on radio evolved, changes in format and content were employed to keep stories attractive to the listening audience. Plot conventions became increasingly sensational and ridiculous, and characters became outrageous and comic. When the Armed Forces Command Performance produced the hour-long farce *Dick Tracy in B-Flat* in 1945, it was obvious that the standard serial presentation had been reduced to sheer comedy. At this time, the stories became satires of themselves. Conventions and formulas had simply worn out, and transcriptions had run their course. It was only a matter of months before *Dick Tracy* radio programs disappeared into oblivion.

In 1923, the world was enthralled with the excavation of Tutankhamen's tomb.[25] Mysterious Egypt, long acknowledged as a cradle of civilization, was once again the subject of much speculation and conjecture. In a role that rivaled his portrayal of the monster in *Frankenstein* (1931) for notoriety, Boris Karloff played the title role in Universal Studios' screen classic *The Mummy* (1932). When NBC radio produced the *Dick Tracy* serial entitled "The Case of the Black Pearl of Osiris" in 1938, there was a conscious exploitation of historical precedence and social consciousness. Tales of Egypt were very common. At this time also, travel by ship was still very popular despite the fact that commercial airlines now offered another form of intercontinental transportation. Such nautical travel had unique qualities. One such quality, confinement to a limited space for a two- or three-week period with a fixed set of fellow passengers, made ships an excellent setting for mystery stories, and the frequent focus of contemporary fiction. The ship became

the locked room in the locked-room mystery.

During the "Black Pearl of Osiris" serial, too, the celebration of the 28th anniversary of the Boy Scouts of America and the appearance of a character named the Unknown are significant. Englishman Robert Baden-Powell established the world famous boys' organization in 1910, and for many decades the Scouts flourished worldwide. In the Thirties, the Boy Scouts of America were a highly visible organization with a total membership in the millions. The Secret Service Patrol so closely tied with the *Dick Tracy* radio programs of the late Thirties was a direct tribute to this great boys' organization. The Boy Scouts have traditionally been divided into troops and component patrols and have emphasized advancements in rank in a somewhat militaristic fashion. *The Dick Tracy Secret Code Book* that was offered to patrol members in 1938 was a direct, though more simplistic, imitation of *The Handbook for Boys* (later retitled *The Boy Scout Handbook*). Like the Handbook, the Code Book detailed requirements for advancement in rank and detailed specific codes. For the Boy Scouts the codes were semaphore and Morse; for Secret Service Patrol members the codes were those listed earlier in this chapter and Morse. In February 1938, the same month as the presentation of Dick Tracy on "The Case of the Black Pearl of Osiris," *The Handbook for Boys* was on its 28th printing; by November of that same year, the manual had sold some 6,100,000 copies since 1910.

When the Unknown appeared at the end of the Osiris affair, radio *Dick Tracy* afforded the listener the unique opportunity to compare the two most popular and controversial detective types in contemporary fiction. Dick Tracy, of course, represented that socially prescribed institution for the preservation of American culture, the policeman. As noted in earlier chapters, policemen were not always revered and celebrated by their entrusted public. The Unknown represented an even more popular hero of Thirties mystery fiction — the avenger. The archetypal Depression-era avenger made his debut on radio, unlike Tracy who had comic strips origins. On Thursday night, July 31, 1930, Columbia Broadcasting System (CBS) first showcased a mysterious narrator with mocking, blood-curdling voice to introduce stories of mystery and intrigue from the pages of Street and Smith's *Detective Story Magazine.* The identity of the character was for several months a mystery that served as a device to attract listeners. In 1931, the character was identified as "The Shadow," and famed newspaperman and amateur magician Walter B. Gibson (September 12, 1897–December 6, 1985) began writing the legendary pulp magazine novels about this character.[26] The first Gibson story about this now legendary avenger, published by Street and Smith in April 1931, was entitled *The Living Shadow.* When the Unknown appeared on *Dick Tracy,* comparison to CBS' famous radio avenger was unavoidable and intended.

Advertisements for War Bonds during the years 1943 through 1945 reflect civilian contributions to the war effort. Chester Gould was once asked why Dick Tracy, unlike other famous comic strip heroes of the time like Frank King's Skeezix of *Gasoline Alley,* did not travel to Europe or the Pacific to engage the enemy abroad. Gould's response was that someone had to stay home and provide necessary civil services. He saw no problem with Tracy's lack of participation in the foreign theaters of battle. Tracy was engaged in a different but nonetheless very important war of his own — the war on crime. But, always the patriot and upstanding American, it follows that Dick Tracy would support the sale of War Bonds on his own radio show.

The circus provided many a backdrop for Dick Tracy mysteries on radio (and indeed for radio dramas as a whole). In May of 1944 and again in July of 1947, Tracy and Patton found themselves pursuing criminals at the circus. In 1944, the rogues took the form of Nazi spies, so Tracy was doing his part at home to end World War II. Circuses proved to be one of America's earliest and most enduring entertainment forms. The circus itself dates back to ancient times, but the entertainment form became uniquely American with the rise of P.T. Barnum (1810–1891) and the Ringling Brothers, who opened their first circus in 1882 and later joined with Barnum and Bailey to become "The Greatest Show on Earth." The popularity of circuses diminished as new entertainment forms like motion pictures and professional sporting events rose in popularity to replace them, but virtually all of the formula print, film, and radio detectives of the 1930s and 1940s spent time investigating wrongdoings at the circus.

On May 1, 1945, when *Dick Tracy* was preempted by the special news bulletin reporting Hitler's death in Berlin, the fantasy of the *Tracy* episode that day was played against a background of vivid reality. The BBC's unconfirmed report of Hitler's fatal stroke seemed unreal for two reasons. First, while any death is in its own way tragic, the rumored demise of history's greatest monster to date had to be received by the listening audience with a degree of satisfaction. The tone of the announcer evidenced relief and the feeling that this news was too good to be true. Second, World War II had produced in more than six years enough propaganda from all sides to last the duration of the century. Certainly the validity of the bulletin had to be questioned at the time. Listening to this *Tracy* episode in the 1990s, we can see the fallacy and propaganda of the announcement, yet we still do not know for sure how the Nazi leader eventually died.

The year 1945 also saw the introduction of the racially stereotyped Benefit in the *Tracy* episode "The Case of the Buried

Treasure." One of the many values in studying Chester Gould's creation is the insight Gould provided into racial stereotypes of those times. The image of the Black servant (in this case, Benefit) was not unique to the *Dick Tracy* radio stories. Gould had portrayed Asians, Blacks, Native Americans, and other non-white racial groups in his comic strip almost from the start. But in Gould's *Dick Tracy* and in the radio programs about his creation, racial diversity, unlike grotesqueness, was not equated with evil. This attitude differed, of course, from Milton Caniff's portrayal of Asians in *Terry and the Pirates*. Caniff capitalized on and reinforced the negative "Yellow Peril" stereotype so popular in this country between the era of the Transcontinental Railroad and the close of World War II. In the *Dick Tracy* radio presentation, as in the comic strip, Benefit was simply a faithful servant who spoke in a slow manner and who was afraid of death and all its trappings—like skeleton bones. Eddie "Rochester" Anderson made this stereotype popular in many film appearances and in his collaborations with Jack Benny.

Forest fires, golf tournaments, and anniversaries of the storming of the Bastille and the Gettysburg Address all were important news items of the 1940s. Today, forest fires and golf tournaments are still with us, but the French Revolution is rarely remembered. Perhaps the heightened awareness of the cause of freedom represented in the Bastille and Lincoln's famous address was partially due to a heightening of patriotism caused by the war. Perhaps in the Forties Americans were simply more conscious of such history because the events were not quite as distant in time as they are today. And perhaps too the patriotic, altruistic values reflected and prescribed in stories about Dick Tracy lent themselves to these kinds of news items. An entire framework of morality, and the importance of the individual within that construct, was pre-

sented in the news items that were an integral part of the radio adventures of Dick Tracy. The Boy Scouts of America, the heroism of Hall of Fame baseball pitcher Rube Waddell, and more examples reinforced the morality play in Dick Tracy radio drama.

The stereotypical mad scientist hellbent on world domination at any cost was a staple of popular fiction long before Chester Gould introduced Americans to Dick Tracy. The dime novels of the era just following the Civil War exploited this conventional story character. Nick Carter, who debuted in a Street and Smith weekly entitled *The Old Detective's Pupil; or The Mysterious Crime of Madison Square* on September 18, 1886, battled the evil Dr. Quartz. (Street and Smith of New York published dime novels long before they began publishing pulp magazines in which Walter Gibson's Shadow later appeared.) Sir Arthur Conan Doyle introduced the world to master sleuth Sherlock Holmes in 1887 in *A Study in Scarlet*. Soon Holmes began matching wits with the sinister Dr. Morarity. In 1913, Sax Rohmer introduced the most famous of all mystery series revolving around the villain—the Dr. Fu Manchu stories. The archetypal Yellow Peril of fiction first appeared in *The Insidious Dr. Fu Manchu*. So when Dick Tracy faced the likes of Dr. Frantic and J.P. Doom in his radio adventures, this criminal type was already a well-established convention. However, Dr. Frantic in particular reveals something about 1940s public visions of psychologists and other doctors of the mind. The father of psychoanalytic theory, Dr. Sigmund Freud (1856–1939), had been dead for only a few years at this point, and the Menninger Clinic of Kansas was in its infancy. In short, the field of psychoanalytic study was very new and experimental, and was greatly distrusted by people of those times. Public skepticism and paranoia generated about psychologists and their practices led to some outrageous stock players whose portrayals were only partly founded in fact. Exaggeration in portrayals of these doctors was the order of the day, just as it was in the depictions of Asians as "Yellow Perils." In *Dick Tracy* then, Dr. Frantic takes on added significance as one of the most vile criminal types of the period's fiction.

Stories of Dick Tracy on radio were generally different from the tales Chester Gould provided in his comic strip. Radio *Dick Tracy* was highly formulaic from the start, using plots, themes, settings, and character types very similar to those of other contemporary radio adventures like *Sky King* and *Jack Armstrong*. The *Dick Tracy* comic strip was much more consciously patterned after real history, and it reflected documented police procedure which Gould himself had acquired from Chicago area police forces. While both media presented the story of Dick Tracy as a morality play, the comic strip emphasized this aspect much more than the radio drama did. While the radio adventures of Tracy were highly formulaic, Chester Gould's comic strip tales were created from day to day. (In an earlier chapter, Max Collins is quoted as saying that Gould "flew by the seat of his pants.") Both radio and comic strip renditions of *Dick Tracy* emphasized both realistic and outrageously fantastic characters. In his comic strip, Gould made his criminals grotesque because he wanted crime and its perpetrators depicted as ugly. However, Tracy's creator also provided the sharp contrast of very straight, moralistic characters in the likes of Dick Tracy and his police and nuclear families. In the radio programs, criminals remained outrageous and grotesque, and often—particularly in the middle and late Forties—the good guys also deviated from established conventions. In short, at one time or another, all the radio characters were played for laughs.

Chester Gould named his comic strip rogues (e.g. Big Boy and Flattop) based on their physiognomies as a reflection of the monikers attributed to real villains like Pretty Boy Floyd and Baby Face Nelson. The names given the radio criminals in *Dick Tracy* did reflect Gould's naming techniques in the comic strip. In the radio programs, characters like J.P. Doom (a mastermind behind apocalyptic arson fires), Dr. Frantic (a mad inventor and pseudo-psychologist), Medium Rare (a half-baked fortune-teller), Fingers (a jewel thief), and Rusty Blade (a murderous butler) and more appeared. And, like its comic strip cousin, *Dick Tracy* on radio also provided non-criminals with names based on their physiognomies. There were Benefit (a Black servant), Bull Hooker (an elephant attendant), Stumbles (an uncoordinated circus hand) and others.

In the radio program, Dick Tracy was an adventure hero rather than a police detective hero. Unlike the comic strip, the *Dick Tracy* radio stories employed little if any established police procedure. During the "Black Pearl of Osiris" sequence, Cooper of ballistics did discover that the pearl was encased in the bullet shot into Tracy, and Tracy did determine from dust fibers that the High Mogul was hiding out in a mattress factory, but these were isolated uses of scientific police procedure. Historical fact could be found in the storylines of the comic strip; it only really appeared in the news items which preceded the radio shows. The audience for the comic was diverse—children, men, and women all read the newspaper strip. The radio adventures of Dick Tracy were almost exclusively consumed by children and adolescents, as suggested by the fact that the only format in which the drama succeeded was the afternoon serial. Chester Gould's comic strip has remained commercially marketable and reflective of public sentiment since 1931 because it has changed with cultural values and social thinking. When the formulas of the Tracy radio serials became increasingly conventional and worn out, the program survived for only a few months more as characters and themes became outrageous and the program became a parody of itself.

The adventures of Dick Tracy have taken a variety of forms and have been strongly influenced by the media in which they appear. Comic strips, Big Little Books, movie serials, "B" movies, television and other media have showcased the ongoing story of America's number one detective in unique fashions. The radio programs about Tracy did not have the advantage of the stark black and white line drawings of Chester Gould, but these programs did perhaps play on the metaphoric stage of the greatest theater of all, a theater that not even Gould's comic strip could equal on some levels. This was the theater of the mind, the forum where listener interaction and imagination were every-

thing. Fortunately and unfortunately, imagination can be both enduring and fleeting. So in a sense, one cannot fully comprehend the relationship between the radio players and their listening audiences some fifty and sixty years ago. But, from the few *Dick Tracy* radio programs that have been preserved on audio tape, one gets a sense of the grandeur and romance of those earlier but still trouble-fraught times. Don Gardiner, George Gunn, Ned Wever and all the other radio players for *Dick Tracy* brought happiness, entertainment, and romance to their audiences. The live radio broadcast is assuredly more ephemeral than the printed word or drawing, but its consequences, at least at the time of its presentation, could in its own way be unequalled.

Movie Serials

In 1937, Chester Gould's detective hero debuted in the first of four Dick Tracy movie serials created by Republic Pictures. By the time the fourth Dick Tracy serial was released in 1941, it was quite apparent that these fast-moving, visually stimulating, cliffhanging productions would stand not only as more than worthy contributions to the Tracy legacy, but also as landmark contributions to the medium of the motion picture serial. Ralph Byrd (April 22, 1909–August 18, 1952) played the title character in each of the four 15-chapter serials and was quite successful in that role; because of Byrd's performances, a good deal of the integrity and charm of the Chester Gould comic strip remained intact in these celluloid interpretations of the Tracy legend. Alan G. Barbour writes, but perhaps overstates a bit, that the relationship between Byrd and his motion picture interpretation of Dick Tracy was "one of those rare cases where the actor and the

role are [were] completely unified: Ralph Byrd was Dick Tracy."[27] By the time Byrd appeared in that first Republic Dick Tracy serial (Republic's fifth serial at that time), he had appeared in Columbia Pictures' movie *Hellship Morgan* (1936) and Puritan Pictures' *Border Caballero* (1936).[28] The movie serial, a very sensual medium in terms of sight and sound, expanded the horizons of Gould's newspaper strip hero. The four Dick Tracy movie serials produced by Republic Pictures Corporation were *Dick Tracy* (1937), *Dick Tracy Returns* (1938), *Dick Tracy's G-Men* (1939), and *Dick Tracy vs. Crime, Inc.* (1941).[29]

Dick Tracy (1937) is entertaining even by today's standards, though Ralph Byrd's Dick Tracy has more super-hero characteristics than does his comic strip counterpart. This 15-chapter serial was broken down into six or seven discernible adventures that fit together with more than a minimal continuity. The Gouldian grotesque villain was center stage here as in the newspaper stories. In this first Tracy serial, the grotesque is a mysterious figure of the shadows called "the Spider" and also "the Lame One." However, there were liberties taken with Chester Gould's traditions. Instead of Tess Trueheart, the weekly installments featured Kay Hughes as Gwen. The chemistry between Tracy and his female foil was lost. Interestingly enough, in this serial Republic gave Dick Tracy a brother named Gordon who falls victim to the evil undertakings of the Lame One and Moloch—the Mad scientist assistant of the Lame One who has operated on Gordon's brain to inspire him to do dastardly things like murder. All in all, this 1937 Republic work was, and remains, quite enthralling for adventure fans and those impassioned by the cliffhangers of the silver screen so popular in the 1930s and 1940s.

The second Dick Tracy motion picture serial, *Dick Tracy Returns,* appeared in 1938. Republic's eleventh serial to date; this too was 15 chapters in length. It was even better than the highly effective and satisfying *Dick Tracy* of the year before. Ralph Byrd was again masterful in his portrayal of the title hero, and again the grotesque rogue took center stage. In *Dick Tracy Returns,* that villain is Pa Stark, tyrannical father of a crime family. Charles Middleton, best remembered for his wonderful portrayals of Ming the Merciless, archenemy of the title hero (played by Buster Crabbe) in the Flash Gordon movie serials done by Universal Pictures (*Flash Gordon* [1936], 13 chapters; *Flash Gordon's Trip to Mars* [1938], 15 chapters; and *Flash Gordon Conquers the Universe* [1940], 12 chapters), stars as Pa Stark. Alan G. Barbour captures the essence of the opening episode of *Dick Tracy Returns:*

> Young David Sharpe, playing a new police recruit graduate [named Ron Merton], is brutally gunned down by one of Pa's sons. Sharpe, not quite dead but paralyzed, is placed in an iron lung. Pa Stark sneaks into the hospital and sadistically unplugs the iron lung, dooming young Sharpe. That was pretty vicious stuff to feed an audience composed primarily of young kids.[30]

Yet what Barbour describes from the early stages of *Dick Tracy Returns* is precisely in line with Gould's intentions in the *Tracy* comic strip; crime is indeed a very dark, vile, evil occupation which must be dealt with in harsh but appropriate fashions. Grotesques performed insidiously conceived devilry throughout the newspaper presentation of the Tracy saga. While the violent act was less frequent in *Dick Tracy* of the newspaper page than people tend to remember, it did help illustrate the truly undesirable, antisocial nature and behavior of the bad guys. The effective Dick Tracy stories, regardless of the medium in which they appeared, were those that focused on the diametrically opposed black and white—"evil" and "good." The morality play, which resolves the conflict at least temporarily, has been a hallmark of the Dick Tracy story and has helped Gould and associates strike the responsive chord in their audience. In the fifteenth and concluding installment of *Dick Tracy Returns,* Pa Stark receives the demise he has so justly earned since the first episode. Here, a struggle between Tracy and Stark in an airborne plane ends as Tracy bails out, and Stark crashes with the plane to his death.

In 1939, *Dick Tracy's G-Men,* the third Republic serial which featured Dick Tracy in 15 chapters (Republic's fifteenth serial to date), again featured Ralph Byrd as Dick Tracy. The first chapter of this production, as in the cases of most movie serials, was a little longer than ensuing chapters (approximately 30 minutes as opposed to 20 minutes) and featured a scene which was only alluded to in Gould's work—public, legally sanctioned execution. International spy Nicholas Zarnoff (played by

Ralph Byrd as Tracy.

talented veteran actor Irving Pichel) dies in the gas chamber as Dick Tracy looks on. (Rough stuff indeed that, depending upon your viewpoint, is as intense as the opening sequences of *Dick Tracy Returns* in which Pa Stark coldly dispenses of police recruit Ron Merton.) Zarnoff's body is quickly hijacked by members of his gang, and he is later brought back to life via some powerful drugs. The game is once again afoot. *Dick Tracy's G-Men*, like most movie serials, featured many chapters which ended with elaborate cliffhangers like seemingly inescapable death traps for the detective hero. It is important to remember, however, that Chester Gould had devised many such perilous conditions for Dick Tracy ever since 1931 when the comic strip began. At the close of *Dick Tracy's G-Men*, Zarnoff reaps the harvest he has sown. Trapped on a desert with Tracy, Zarnoff subdues the hero. But he

drinks from a spring, unaware that the water is laden with arsenic.

Each new Dick Tracy movie serial became increasingly complex, polished, fast-moving, and enthralling. The fourth and final Republic serial about Tracy appeared in 1941 and, in its own way, may have been the best of the four released. Republic Pictures' twenty-fourth serial was the 15-chapter *Dick Tracy vs. Crime, Inc.* of 1941. The grotesque rogue of the picture is a character called "the Ghost"—an individual who has mastered a technique to become invisible to the naked eye. In order to capture the Ghost, Dick Tracy (Ralph Byrd) has to lure the Ghost into a room which has an infrared lightbulb. It was all very exciting. The Dick Tracy motion pictures done by Republic and Ralph Byrd were over, and they had ended on a high note. Byrd and Tracy left the silver screen, but they would be back....[31]

Dick Tracy
Republic Pictures, 1937

Chapters: 1. The Spider Strikes. 2. The Bridge of Terror. 3. The Fur Pirates. 4. Death Rides the Sky. 5. Brother Against Brother. 6. Dangerous Waters. 7. The Ghost Town Mystery. 8. Battle in the Clouds. 9. The Stratosphere Adventure. 10. The Gold Ship. 11. Harbor Pursuit. 12. The Trail of the Spider. 13. The Fire Trap. 14. The Devil in White. 15. Brothers United.

Cast: *Dick Tracy* Ralph Byrd, *Gwen* Kay Hughes, *Mike McGurk* Smiley Burnette, *Junior* Lee Van Atta, *Moloch* John Picorri*, *Gordon Tracy (#1-good)* Richard Beach, *Gordon Tracy (#2-evil, then good)* Carleton Young, *G-man Steve Lockwood* Fred Hamilton, *G-man Clive Anderson* Francis X. Bushman, *Brewster* John Dilson, *Clayton* Wedgewood Nowell, *Paterno* Theodore Lorch, *Odette* Edwin Stanley, *Cloggerstein* Harrison Greene, *Martino* Herbert Weber, *Burke* Buddy Roosevelt, *Flynn* George De Normand, *Korvitch* Byron K. Foulger, *Henchman* Roy Barcroft, *Oscar and Elmer* actor unknown, *The Spider (aka The Lame One)* actor unknown.

Crew: *Producer* Nat Levine, *Associate Producer* J. Laurence Wickland, *Co-Directors* Ray Taylor, Alan James, *Original Story* Morgan Cox, George Morgan, *Screenplay* Barry Shipman, Winston Miller, *Supervising Editor* Murray Seldeen, *Film Editors* Helene Turner, Edward Todd, Bill Witney, *Camera* William Nobles, Edgar Lyons, *Sound Engineer* Terry Kellum, *Music* Harry Grey, *Special Effects* Howard Lydecker.

Black and white, first chapter approx. 30 minutes, subsequent chapters approx. 20 minutes each.

Dick Tracy Returns
Republic Pictures, 1938

Chapters: 1. The Sky Wreckers. 2. The Runway of Death. 3. Handcuffed to Doom. 4. Four Seconds to Live. 5. Death in the Air. 6. Stolen Secrets. 7. Tower of Death. 8. Cargo of Destruction. 9. The Clock of Doom. 10. High Voltage. 11. The Kidnapped Witness. 12. The Runaway Torpedo. 13. Passengers to Doom. 14. In the Hands of the Enemy. 15. G-Men's Dragnet.

Cast: *Dick Tracy* Ralph Byrd, *Gwen Andrews* Lynn Roberts, *Pa Stark* Charles Mid-

dleton, *Mike McGurk* Lee Ford, *Steve Lockwood* Michael Kent, *Junior* Jerry Tucker, *Ron Merton* David Sharpe, *Champ* John Merton, *Trigger* Raphael Bennett, *Dude* Jack Roberts, *The Kid* Ned Glass, *Joe Hanner* Edward Foster, *Snub* Alan Gregg, *Rance* Reed Howes, *Reynolds* Robert Terry, *Hunt* Tom Seidel, *Slasher* Jack Ingram, *Carson* Gordon Hart.

Crew: *Associate Producer* Robert Beche, *Co-Directors* William Witney, John English, *Screenplay* Barry Shipman, Franklyn Adreon, Ronald Davidson, Rex Taylor, Sol Shor, *Production Manager* Al Wilson, *Unit Manager* Mack D'Agostino, *Film Editors* Helene Turner, Edward Todd, *Camera* William Nobles, *Music* Alberto Columbo.

Black and white, first chapter approx. 30 minutes, subsequent chapters approx. 20 minutes each.

Dick Tracy's G-Men
Republic Pictures, 1939

Chapters: 1. The Master Spy. 2. Captured. 3. The False Signal. 4. The Enemy Strikes. 5. Crack Up! 6. Sunken Peril. 7. Tracking the Enemy. 8. Chamber of Doom. 9. Flames of Jeopardy. 10. Crackling Fury. 11. Caverns of Peril. 12. Fight in the Sky. 13. The Fatal Ride. 14. Getaway. 15. The Last Stand.

Cast: *Dick Tracy* Ralph Byrd, *Gwen* Phyllis Isley (Jennifer Jones), *Nicholas Zarnoff* Irving Pichel, *Steve Lockwood* Ted Pearson, *Robal* Walter Miller, *Sandoval* George Douglas, *Clive Anderson* Kenneth Harlan, *Scott* Robert Carson, *Foster* Julian Madison, *First G-Man (Bruce)* Ted Mapes, *Second G-Man (Murchison)* William Stahl, *Third G-Man (Wilbur)* Robert Wayne, *Tommy* Joe McGuinn, *Ed* Kenneth Terrell, *Warden Stover* Harry Humphrey, *Baron* Harrison Greene, *Dr. Shang* Stanley Price.

Crew: *Associate Producer* Robert Beche, *Co-Directors* William Witney, John English, *Screenplay* Barry Shipman, Franklyn Adreon, Rex Taylor, Ronald Davidson, Sol Shor, *Production Manager* Al Wilson, *Unit Manager* Mack D'Agostino, *Film Editors* Edward Todd, William Thompson, Bernard Loftus, *Camera* William Nobles, *Music* William Lava.

Black and white, first chapter approx. 30 minutes, subsequent chapters approx, 20 minutes each.

*Misspelled in the serial's credits as "Piccori."

Dick Tracy vs. Crime, Inc.
Republic Pictures, 1941*

Chapters: 1. The Fatal Hour. 2. The Prisoner Vanishes. 3. Doom Patrol. 4. Dead Man's Trap. 5. Murder at Sea. 6. Besieged. 7. Sea Racketeers. 8. Train of Doom. 9. Beheaded. 10. Flaming Peril. 11. Seconds to Live. 12. Trial by Fire. 13. The Challenge. 14. Invisible Terror. 15. Retribution.

Cast: *Dick Tracy* Ralph Byrd, *Billy Carr* Michael Owen, *June Chandler* Jan Wiley, *Lucifer* John Davidson, *Morton* Ralph Morgan, *Lieutenant Cosgrove* Kenneth Harlan, *Henry Weldon* John Dilson, *Stephen Chandler* Howard Hickman, *Daniel Brewster* Robert Frazer, *Walter Cabot* Robert Fiske, *Wilson* Jack Mulhall, *Arthur Trent* Hooper Atchley, *John Corey* Anthony Warde, *Trask* Chuck Morrison, *Dr. Jonathan Martin* C. Montague Shaw, *Brent* John Merton, *Drake* Terry Frost, *Other Players* Forrest Taylor, David Sharpe, *The Ghost* actor unknown.

Crew: *Associate Producer* William J. O'Sullivan, *Co-Directors* William Witney, John English, *Screenplay* Ronald Davidson, Norman S. Hall, William Lively, Joseph O'Donnell, Joseph Poland, *Production Manager* Al Wilson, *Unit Manager* Mack D'Agostino, *Film Editors* Tony Martinelli, Edward Todd, *Camera* Reggie Lanning, *Music* Cy Feuer, *Special Effects* Howard Lydecker.

Black and white, first chapter approx. 30 minutes, subsequent chapters approx. 20 minutes each.

"B" Movies

In 1945, RKO Pictures produced the first of four feature length movies about the exploits of the now world famous Dick Tracy. These were *Dick Tracy* (1945 — later referred to as *Dick Tracy, Detective*), *Dick Tracy vs. Cueball* (1946), *Dick Tracy's Dilemma* (1947), and *Dick Tracy Meets Gruesome* (1947); each ran about an hour in length. Morgan Conway played the title character in the first two movies; Ralph Byrd returned to the silver screen in the title role for the third and fourth productions. Both actors were successful — Byrd, because of the serials, was identified with the role; Conway, because of his sharp physical features and subdued, dark demeanor, may have been, in his own way, celluloid's best Dick Tracy ever.

Dick Tracy Meets Gruesome, the fourth of the set, is the most revered, though each of the others has its own distinct merits. Boris Karloff played the grotesque, murderous Gruesome, Ralph Byrd played Tracy, and the storyline was the most colorful of the four — but not the darkest, and in that sense not as satisfying as, for example, *Dick Tracy* (1945).

Morgan Conway was superb in *Dick Tracy* (1945). Conway may have possessed the most fitting physical appearance of all movie players who have donned the trenchcoat and snap-brimmed fedora of Dick Tracy. His features are sharper than Byrd's, and his physical countenance and personality are appropriately less humorous and less comedic. His build is slender, almost gaunt, and his voice is deep, cold, and hard. He reflects Chester Gould's vision of Tracy.

The violence in the first Dick Tracy movie is found in suspense — particularly the suspense of the opening tracking and murder of schoolteacher Dorothy Stafford (played by Mary Currier) and near the end of the movie when maniacal slasher Splitface (Mike Mazurki) repeatedly stabs Professor Starling (Trevor Bardette). While the film is dark in tone, atmosphere (the story takes place primarily at night), and message, violence is relatively moderate in frequency and depiction. Tracy tracks

---

*Re-released in the 1940s as Dick Tracy vs. The Phantom Empire.

Splitface throughout the course of the movie, and ultimately captures him and leads him off to prison. The formulaic plot (Splitface's motive is revenge on the twelve jurors and two alternates who found him guilty years earlier and sent him to prison) is not complex, but it is entertaining. Splitface is indeed ugly in every sense of the term.

Likewise, Dick Wessel plays a vicious, hot-tempered tough guy as Cueball, the nemesis of Tracy in RKO's 1946 *Dick Tracy vs. Cueball*. Morgan Conway reprises his role as the hero. The bald Cueball specializes in strangling people and serves as Tracy's quarry throughout the film. Violence is even more moderate in frequency and depiction than it was in the movie from the previous year—Cueball strangles people off camera. The rogue, initially in cahoots with Little (Byron K. Foulger), steals some diamonds and then has a hard time fencing them. Ultimately, Tracy chases Cueball to a train stockyard where the villain gets caught in a track and is killed by a speeding train. This movie features a somewhat more complex storyline than its predecessor and showcases a variety of colorful characters like Vitamin Flintheart, Priceless, Filthy Flora, and Jules Sparkle—all of whom are tributes to, and reflections of, Gouldian tradition. Much of the action takes place near and around a place called the Dripping Dagger—a sort of safehouse/hideout for crooks that is run by Flora. This setting of the hideout with a name indicative of death and destruction would appear also in the third and fourth RKO Tracy movies. In *Dick Tracy's Dilemma* and *Dick Tracy Meets Gruesome*, the respective settings include the Blinking Skull and the Hangman's Knot.

In *Dick Tracy's Dilemma* Ralph Byrd returned to the film role he pioneered in the four Republic serials. The physically and socially deformed Claw (Jack Lambert) limps and lurches his way through the story with the artificial appendage

(which replaces his missing hand) for which he has been rechristened. The Claw is a volatile, scowling maniac just like Splitface and Cueball. His special brand of violence involves bludgeoning people with his metal hook. The Claw initially steals a valuable cache of furs and murders a night watchman, and the chase is on. Eventually, Dick Tracy pursues the Claw into a junkyard where the villain electrocutes himself on a live wire. The movie features Vitamin Flintheart, Longshot Lillie (quite similar to Filthy Flora of the Cueball escapade), Sightless (a not-so-blind street-corner pencil seller and informant for Tracy), and others. Humor and comic relief remain staples of *Dick Tracy* on film.

Dick Tracy Meets Gruesome, though perhaps a little lighter in tone and atmosphere, brings together all the successes and strengths of the first three RKO Dick Tracy movies and adds the screen legend Boris Karloff. The plot is really no more complex than those of its predecessors—in fact, *Dick Tracy vs. Cueball* may have been the best plotted of the four—yet the film is wonderful. Themes of poison gas and atomic science in the film are representative of war and postwar concerns at this time. It would be a shame to spoil the plot here, so no elaborate summary will be provided. Tracy fans should see the movie; it is indeed a treasure for film fans and scholars, and for followers of Dick Tracy.

On a related note, David Wilt recently published a book entitled *Hardboiled in Hollywood: Five Black Mask Writers and Their Movies* (1991). Herein, Wilt provides an insightful and entertaining discussion of five mystery fiction authors who wrote for the prestigious pulp magazine entitled *(The) Black Mask*. Eric Taylor, one of these authors, wrote the screenplays for *Dick Tracy* (1945) and *Dick Tracy Meets Gruesome* (1947). *Hardboiled in Hollywood* is a good source for further information on Taylor.[32] Two other very famous detective fiction authors for

Morgan Conway, as Tracy, with Anne Jeffreys in a poster for *Dick Tracy vs. Cueball*.

the pulps proved mainstays for the Dick Tracy television series that followed just a few years later. They were Robert Leslie Bellem and W.T. (Todhunter) Ballard.

Dick Tracy
An RKO Radio Picture, 1945*

Cast: *Dick Tracy* Morgan Conway, *Tess Trueheart* Anne Jeffreys, *Splitface* Mike Mazurki, *Judith Owens* Jane Greer, *Pat Patton* Lyle Latell, *Chief Brandon* Joseph Crehan, *Junior* Mickey Kuhn, *Professor Starling* Trevor Bardette, *Steven Owens* Morgan Wallace, *Deathridge* Milton Parsons, *Mayor* William Halligan, *Mrs. Caraway* Edythe Elliot, *Dorothy Stafford* Mary Currier, *Manning* Ralph Dunn, *Radio Announcer* Edmund Glover, *Sergeant* Bruce Edwards, *Miss Stanley* Tanis Chandler, *Pedestrians* Jimmy Jordan, Carl Hanson, *Bystander at Murder* Franklin Farnum, *Cops* Jack Gargan, Sam Ash, Carl Faulkner, Franklin

Meredith, Bob Reeves, *Johnny Moko* Tom Noonan, *Detectives* Harry Strang, George Magrill, *Busboy* Robert Douglass, *Jules the Waiter* Alphonse Martell, *Woman* Gertrude Astor, *Head Waiter* Jack Chefe, *Girl* Florence Pepper, *Motorists* Wilbur Mack, Jason Robards, Sr.

Crew: *Executive Producer* Sid Rogell, *Producer* Herman Schlom, *Director* William Berke, *Assistant Director* Clem Beauchamp, *Screenplay* Eric Taylor, *Camera* Frank Redman, A.S.C., *Music* Roy Webb, *Musical Director* Constantin Bakaleinikoff, *Editor* Ernie Leadlay, *Art Directors* Albert S. D'Agostino, Ralph Berger, *Set Design* Darrell Silvera, *Sound* Jean L. Speak, Terry Kellum.

Black and white, 61 minutes.

Dick Tracy vs. Cueball
An RKO Radio Picture, 1946

Cast: *Dick Tracy* Morgan Conway, *Tess Trueheart* Anne Jeffreys, *Pat Patton* Lyle Latell,

Though 1945 is the date most often associated with this film, the copyright date in the opening credits is 1946. This movie was later retitled Dick Tracy, Detective, *presumably to differentiate it from the 1937 Republic serial entitled* Dick Tracy.

Mona Clyde Rita Corday, *Vitamin Flintheart* Ian Keith, *Cueball* Dick Wessel, *Priceless* Douglas Walton, *Filthy Flora* Esther Howard, *Chief Brandon* Joseph Crehan, *Little* Byron K. Foulger, *Junior* Jimmy Crane, *Higby* Milton Parsons, *Rudolph* Skelton Knaggs, *Cop* Ralph Dunn, *Jules Sparkle* Harry Chesire, *Lester Abbott* Trevor Bardette.

Crew: *Executive Producer* Sid Rogell, *Producer* Herman Schlom, *Director* Gordon M. Douglas, *Original Story* Luci Ward, *Screenplay* Dane Lussier, Robert E. Kent, *Camera* George E. Diskant, *Music* Phil Ohman, *Musical Director* Constantin Bakaleinikoff, *Editor* Philip Martin, Jr., *Art Directors* Albert D'Agostino, Lucius O. Croxton, *Set Design* Darrell Silvera, Shelby Willis, *Sound* Robert H. Guhl, Roy Granville, *Special Effects* Russell A. Cully, A.S.C., *Dialogue Director* Leslie Urbach.

Black and white, 62 minutes.

Dick Tracy's Dilemma
An RKO Radio Picture, 1947

Cast: *Dick Tracy* Ralph Byrd, *Tess Trueheart* Kay Christopher, *Pat Patton* Lyle Latell, *The Claw* Jack Lambert, *Vitamin Flintheart* Ian Keith, *Longshot Lillie* Bernadene Hayes, *Sightless* Jimmy Conlin, *Peter Premium* William B. Davidson, *Sam* Tony Barrett, *Pred* Richard Powers, *Night Watchman* Harry Strang, *Cop in Squad Car* Tom London, *Watchman* Jason Robards, Sr., *Donovan the Cop* Harry Harvey, *Cop* Sean McClory, *Police Detective* Al Bridge, *Police Technician* William Gould.

Crew: *Producer* Herman Schlom, *Director* John Rawlins, *Screenplay* Robert Stephen Brode, *Camera* Frank Redman, A.S.C., *Music* Paul Sawtell, *Musical Director* Constantin Bakaleinikoff, *Editor* Marvin Coll, *Art Directors* Albert S. D'Agostino, Lucius O. Croxton, *Set Design* Darrell Silvera, *Sound* Jean L. Speak, Terry Kellum, *Special Effects* Russell A. Cully, A.S.C., *Makeup* Gordon Bau.

Black and white, 60 minutes.

Dick Tracy Meets Gruesome
An RKO Radio Picture, 1947

Cast: *Dick Tracy* Ralph Byrd, *Tess Trueheart* Anne Gwynne, *Gruesome* Boris Karloff, *L.E. Thal* Edward Ashley, *Professor I.M. Learned* June Clayworth, *Pat Patton* Lyle Latell, *Melody* Tony Barrett, *X-Ray* Skelton Knaggs, *Dan Sterne* Jim Nolan, *Chief Brandon* Joseph Crehan, *Dr. A. Tomic* Milton Parsons, *Other Players* Lex Barker, Lee Phelps, Sean McClory, Harry Harvey, Harry Strang.

Crew: *Producer* Herman Schlom, *Director* John Rawlins, *Original Story* William H. Graffis, Robert E. Kent, *Screenplay* Robertson White, Eric Taylor, *Camera* Frank Redman, A.S.C., *Music* Paul Sawtell, *Musical Director* Constantin Bakaleinikoff, *Editor* Elmo Williams, *Art Directors* Albert S. D'Agostino, Walter E. Keller, *Set Design* Darrell Silvera, James Altweis, *Sound* Jean L. Speak, Terry Kellum, *Special Effects* Russell A. Cully, A.S.C., *Makeup* Gordon Bau.

Black and white, 65 minutes.

Television Drama

Ralph Byrd and Dick Tracy came to television on September 13, 1950.[33] American Broadcasting Company, one of the companies which produced and aired *Dick Tracy* radio programs, was the network sponsor. Tim Brooks and Earle Marsh write, "Chester Gould's famous comic-strip hero appeared briefly on network television in 1950–1951 in this very violent series. With him were the famous supporting characters, including his sidekick Sam Catchem, Chief Murphy, and an array of incredible villains...."[34] Sam Catchem was played by Joe Devlin, and Police Chief Murphy was played by Dick Elliott, who in the 1960s would become better known as the mayor on *The Andy Griffith Show*. Murphy was unique to the Tracy television dramas; Chief Brandon and then Chief Pat Patton had been Tracy's immediate superiors in Gould's comic strip.

At least three of the writers for the short-lived *Dick Tracy* television program were seasoned mystery authors. These were Dwight Babcock (1909–   ), author and screenplay writer of hundreds of works; W.T. (Todhunter) Ballard (1903–1980), famed author of several popular genres, including mysteries and westerns, who had appeared regularly in *(The) Black Mask*, where he published his stories of tough-guy detective Bill Lennox, and in *Dime Detective;* and Robert Leslie Bellem (1902–1968), famed author of pulp magazine stories and writer of the tremendously popular Dan Turner, Hollywood Detective, stories. Bellem in particular wrote and advised extensively for the *Dick Tracy* television program. His name appears frequently in the few lists of episode credits that exist today. John Wooley edited and introduced a nice selection of facsimile reprints of Bellem's Dan Turner stories entitled *Robert Leslie Bellem's Dan Turner, Hollywood Detective* (1983).[35] Likewise, renowned scholar of detective fiction James L. Traylor edited a fine selection of W.T. Ballard's Bill Lennox stories entitled *Hollywood Troubleshooter: W.T. Ballard's Bill Lennox Stories* (1985).

Traylor credits W.T. Ballard as the writer of four teleplays for this television series.[36] Buddy Barnett credits Ballard with co-writing four teleplays with Robert Leslie Bellem.[37] Traylor's list includes "Dick Tracy and the Sapphire Mystery," "Dick Tracy and the Smugglers," "Dick Tracy Is Missing," and "Last Man Murders"; Barnett's list includes "Episode #10: Junior and the Sapphire Mystery," "Episode #16: Tess and the Smugglers," "Episode #17: Tracy Is Missing!" and "Episode #26: The Case of the Dangerous Dollars."

The *Dick Tracy* television series lasted only a couple of years on ABC. Vincent Terrace writes, "On August 18, 1952, Ralph Byrd's death ended the legend of a live Dick Tracy."[38]

Several unanswered questions regarding this television series remain. If, as evidenced in the credits for the series assembled largely by Buddy Barnett and in the entry by Tim Brooks and Earle Marsh in *The Complete Directory to Prime Time*

Network TV Shows, 1946–Present (third edition), *Dick Tracy* appeared on television for 26 episodes between 1950 and 1951 on the ABC network (September to October 1950, Wednesday 8:30–9:00; October to December 1950, Monday 8:30–9:00; and January to February 1951, Tuesday 8:00–8:30), then why were new episodes not created between February 1951 and August 1952 when Byrd's death supposedly made continuation impractical? Was the period between 1951 and 1952 only a period of reruns from 1950 and 1951?[39]

There is another confusing piece of evidence. It appears likely that there existed a pilot episode or episodes separate from the 26 episodes identified by Barnett. With the release of the 1990 Warren Beatty *Dick Tracy* movie and the ensuing hype, Simitar Entertainment, Inc., of Plymouth, Minnesota, released a set of two VHS videotapes that contained two uncredited half-hour installments from the television series. The first, entitled "Dick Tracy and Flattop," includes a byline for P.K. Palmer (a pioneer of the very first episodes for the series) and is seemingly contradictorily copyrighted 1952 in its closing credits. (Was this copyright added in 1952 when the program may have aired as a rerun?) The second, simply entitled "Dick Tracy," again includes a P.K. Palmer byline, but is also obviously the immediate sequel to the episode entitled "Dick Tracy and Flattop," since the opening moments of the second episode include scenes from the first, and since Sam Catchem (Joe Devlin) and Chief Murphy (Dick Elliott) spend several minutes reviewing the specifics of the case of "Dick Tracy and Flattop." In "Dick Tracy and Flattop," Flattop holds Tracy captive and plans to kill him as soon as he gets paid for the job by Namgib (Bigman spelled backwards); in the episode entitled "Dick Tracy," the storyline revolves around a group of car thieves.

There is still more to the story of the Ralph Byrd *Dick Tracy* television dramas.

Simitar was not the only VHS videocassette producer to market selected 1950s *Tracy* television dramas featuring Byrd in 1990. Wavelength Video of Burbank, California, released a set of four hourlong videotapes collectively entitled *Dick Tracy: The Lost Episodes*. Each of the first three tapes contained two half-hour *Tracy* television programs. The fourth contained one half-hour show and a short video overview of Dick Tracy on film and on television. (This overview states that many of these episodes are indeed lost for the moment but expresses optimism that they may someday be unearthed.) Four of the dramas matched up with the list of episodes that follows, but three do not in any apparent way. These three, titled either in the early 1950s or by Wavelength at the time of release on video, are "Dick Tracy Meets (vs.) the Foreign Agents," "Hi-Jack," and "The Mole." Unfortunately, the Wavelength videotapes contain virtually no original credits for the programs. "Dick Tracy Meets (vs.) the Foreign Agents" comprises two half-hour installments. Famed *Tracy* rogue Influence makes a cameo appearance in the first half hour and stars in the second half hour. Ultimately, one has to wonder if there were more than 26 episodes. It appears possible.

Upon a viewing of the few episodes available on videotape, one final observation becomes possible and important. The *Dick Tracy* television dramas featuring Ralph Byrd in the title role were entertaining, and did evolve and get better each week. These are indeed treasures, and the author would be most appreciative to hear more about these programs. The following are the 26 episodes known to have aired.

1. Dick Tracy and the Brain (Parts 1–5)
Cast: Ralph Byrd, Joe Devlin, Thurston Hall, Lyle Talbot, Christine Larson, John O'Malley, Tony Rocke, Jane Easton, John Demler, George Magrill, Dick Alexander, Howard Chamberlan, Frank Jenks, Pat Coleman, Dick Eliott, John Henry, Chuck Hamilton, John Harmon.
Crew: *Story* P.K. Palmer, *Producer* P.K. Palmer, *Director* William Sheldon, *Additional Dialogue* Robert Leslie Bellem.

6. Dick Tracy and B.B. Eyes (Parts 1–2)
Cast: Ralph Byrd, Joe Devlin, Richard Kean, Wyott Ordung, Isabel Randolph, Paul Fierro, Ned Roberts, William Woodson.
Crew: *Story* Robert Leslie Bellem, *Director* Charles Haas.

8. B.O. Plenty's Folly
Cast: Ralph Byrd, Joe Devlin, Cy Jenks, Almira Sessions, Norman Rice, Skelton Knaggs, Leander DeCordova, Carl Davis.
Crew: *Story:* Edmond E. Kelso, *Director* Nate Watt.

9. Dick Tracy and the Brow
Cast: Ralph Byrd, Joe Devlin, Margia Dean, Norman Rice, William Bakewell, Isabel Randolph, William Woodson.
Crew: *Story* Robert Leslie Bellem, William Livey, *Director* Nate Watt.

10. Junior and the Sapphire Mystery
Cast: Ralph Byrd, Joe Devlin, Angela Greene, Martin Dean, George Pembroke, Percy Helton, Don Brodie.
Crew: *Story* W.T. (Todhunter) Ballard, Robert Leslie Bellem, *Director* Nate Watt.

11. Dick Tracy and Pruneface (Parts 1–2)
Cast: Ralph Byrd, Margia Dean, Alan Keyes, Gene Roth, George Pembroke, Martin Dean, Hans Schumm, John Sebastian, Noel Cravat, Bruce Edwards, William Woodson.
Crew: *Story* William Livey, Robert Leslie Bellem, *Director* Thomas Carr.

13. Dick Tracy: Pruneface Returns (Parts 1–2)
Cast: Ralph Byrd, Joe Devlin, Margia Dean, Alan Keyes, Gene Roth, George Pembroke, Martin Dean, Bruce Edwards, James Fairfax, William Woodson.
Crew: *Story* William Livey, Dwight Babcock, Robert Leslie Bellem, *Director* Thomas Carr.

15. Heels Beals
Cast: Ralph Byrd, Joe Devlin, Isabel Randolph, Billy Benedict, Karl Davis.
Crew: *Story* Don Brinkley, *Director* Thomas Carr.

16. Tess and the Smugglers
Cast: Ralph Byrd, Joe Devlin, Angela Greene, Martin Dean, Don Harvey, Don Brodie, George Pembroke, John Halloran.
Crew: *Story* W.T. (Todhunter) Ballard, Robert Leslie Bellem, *Director* Nate Watt.

17. Tracy Is Missing!
Cast: Ralph Byrd, Joe Devlin, Don Harvey, Pierre Watkin, Frank Jacquet, Marc Krah.
Crew: *Story* W.T. (Todhunter) Ballard, Robert Leslie Bellem, *Director* Thomas Carr.

18. The Brow Returns
Cast: Ralph Byrd, Joe Devlin, Margia Dean, Norman Rice, Frank Nordstrom, Hugh Snaders, Don Brodie, Tennessee Jim.
Crew: *Story* William Livey, *Director* Nate Watt.

19. Shaky's Secret Treasure
Cast: Ralph Byrd, Joe Devlin, Dabs Greer, Lois Hall, Richard Reeves, Stephen Carr.
Crew: *Story* Roy Hamilton, *Director* Thomas Carr.

20. The Mosquito Murders
Cast: Ralph Byrd, Joe Devlin, Lyle Talbot, Percy Helton, Patricia Wright, Paul Purcell.
Crew: *Story* Dwight Babcock, Robert Leslie Bellem, *Director* Thomas Carr.

21. The Egyptian Mummy Case
Cast: Ralph Byrd, Joe Devlin, Charles Evans, Lorin Baker, Noel Cravat.
Crew: *Story* Fritz Blocki, Robert Leslie Bellem, *Director* Duke Goldstone.

22. Dick Tracy and Influence
Cast: Ralph Byrd, Joe Devlin, Frank Gerstle, Richard Reeves, Leslie O'Pace, Henry Rowland.
Crew: *Story* William Livey, Robert Leslie Bellem, *Director* Thomas Carr.

23. Dick Tracy Meets the Shark
Cast: Ralph Byrd, Joe Devlin, Dabbs Greer, Monica Keating, Stan Blystone, Paul Hoffman.
Crew: *Story* Robert Leslie Bellem, *Director* Duke Goldstone.

24. The Ghost of Gravel Gertie
Cast: Ralph Byrd, Joe Devlin, Almira Sessions, Sy Jenks, Paul Maxey, Jessie Adams, Frank de Kova, Skelton Knaggs.

Crew: *Story* Edmond E. Kelso, Robert Leslie Bellem.

25. Dick Tracy and Big Frost
Cast: Ralph Byrd, Joe Devlin, Lyle Talbot, Phillip Van Zandt, Paul Wexler, Harry Arnie.
Crew: *Story* Milton M. Raison, Robert Leslie Bellem, *Director* Thomas Carr.

26. The Case of the Dangerous Dollars
Cast: Ralph Byrd, Joe Devlin, George Eldredge, Leonard Penn, Luther Crockett, Stephen Carr, John Doucette.
Crew: *Story* W.T. (Todhunter) Ballard, Robert Leslie Bellem, *Director* Duke Goldstone.

Credits for "Dick Tracy and Flattop" and its sequel, "Dick Tracy," are as follows:

"Dick Tracy and Flattop"

Cast: *Dick Tracy* Ralph Byrd, *Sam Catchem* Joe Devlin, *Flattop* John Cliff, *Namgib* George Pembroke, *Chief Murphy* Dick Elliott, *Tess* Angela Greene, *Mole* Pedro Regas, *Chief Patton* Pierre Watkin, *Jenk* Frank Stanlow, *Dixon* Richard Reeves, *Timmy* Danny Welton.
Crew: *Executive Producer* Herbert Moulton, *Associate Producer* Robert M. Snader, *Director* B. Reaves Eason, *Camera* Harold Stine, Ira Morgan, A.S.C., *Production Managers* Jesse Corallo, Willard Sheldon, *Story Editor* Robert Leslie Bellem, *Edited by* Harvey Manger, A.C.E., George McGuire, A.C.E., *Art Director* Rudi Feld, *Recorded by* John Kean, Buddy Myers, *Assistant Director* Richard Dixon, *Dialogue Directors* Stephen Carr, Gloria Welsch, *Makeup* Armand Delmar, Curly Batson, *Script Supervisor* M.E.M. Gibsone
Copyright 1952.

"Dick Tracy"
(Sequel to "Dick Tracy and Flattop")

Cast: *Dick Tracy* Ralph Byrd, *Sam Catchem* Joe Devlin, *Chief Murphy* Dick Elliott, *Hijack* Michael Ragan, *Doke* Ward Blackburn, *Ruff* Riley Hill, *Mr. Rones* Bob Rose.
Crew: *Cinematography* Ira Morgan, A.S.C., *Production Manager* Harry O. Jones, *Film Editor* George McGuire, *Sound Engineer* Buddy Myers, *Makeup* Curly Batson, *Dialogue Director* Gloria Welsch, *Written and Produced by* P.K. Palmer, *Directed by* Willard H. Sheldon.

Animated Cartoons

Dick Tracy animation had both strengths and weaknesses. While some of the Dick Tracy comic books suffered from liberal editing that reinterpreted Chester Gould's original newspaper comic strips, the animated cartoons were even less loyal to Gould's stories. These cartoons contained comparatively little plotting and much less development of the same than the strips; they were targeted strictly at children.

Between 1960 and 1962, UPA (United Productions of America) released *The Dick Tracy Show*, a syndicated series of 130 five-minute shorts which, upon presentation, were interspersed with some interesting, but not always practical, crimestopper tips. Utterly fantastic assistants and exaggerated stereotypes of the period joined a very cardboard, desk-bound Dick Tracy. The good guys—the ones who did Tracy's legwork in the series—included a dog named Hemlock Holmes who talked like Cary Grant and his Keystone Cop–like Retouchables, a highly stereotyped Asian (presumably Japanese) named Jo Jitsu, a likewise highly stereotyped Hispanic (presumably Mexican) named Go Go Gomez, and a very lazy, overweight Irish cop named Heap O'Callory and his hip generation tip-off man, Nick. Villains in the series included Flattop, B.B. Eyes, Sketch Paree, Mole, Brow, Oodles, Pruneface, and Itchy. On occasion there were others. The series was produced by Henry G. Saperstein and Peter DeMet. Everett Sloane was the voice of Dick Tracy; additional voices were provided by Mel Blanc, June Foray, Benny Rubin, Paul Frees, and Joan Gardiner.[40]

Episodes of *The Dick Tracy Show* were as follows:

"Air Freight Fright"
  (Jo Jitsu, Pruneface, Itchy)
  Story: Dick Shaw. *Director:* John Walker.

"(The) Alligator Baggers"
  (Hemlock Holmes and the Retouchables, Brow, Oodles)
  Story: Homer Brightman. *Director:* Brad Case.

"Baggage Car Bandits"
  (Hemlock Holmes and the Retouchables, B.B. Eyes, Flattop)
  Story: Al Bentino/Dick Kinney. *Director:* John Walker.

"(The) Banana Peel Deal"
  (Hemlock Holmes and the Retouchables, Brow, Oodles)
  Story: Kin Platt. *Director:* Paul Fennell.

"(The) Bank Prank"
  (Jo Jitsu, B.B. Eyes, Flattop)
  Story: Cal Howard. *Director:* John Walker.

"(The) Bearskin Game"
  (Hemlock Holmes and the Retouchables, Stooge Viller, Mumbles)
  Story: Ralph Wright. *Director:* Clyde Geronimi.

"Bettor Come Clean"
  (Hemlock Holmes and the Retouchables, B.B. Eyes, Flattop)
  Story: Dave Detiege. *Director:* Paul Fennell.

"Big Bank Bungle"
  (Heap O'Callory, Pruneface, Itchy)
  Story: Al Bentino/Dick Kinney. *Director:* Steve Clark.

"(The) Big Blowup"
  (Go Go Gomez, B.B. Eyes, Flattop)
  Story: Al Bentino/Dick Kinney. *Director:* Jerry Hathcock.

"(The) Big Punch"
  (Go Go Gomez, Sketch Paree, Mole)
  Story: Dave Detiege. *Director:* John Walker.

"(The) Big Seal Steal"
  (Hemlock Holmes, B.B. Eyes, Flattop)
  Story: Homer Brightman. *Director:* Clyde Geronimi.

"(The) Big Wig"
  (Go Go Gomez, Stooge Viller, Mumbles)
  Story: Al Bentino/Dick Kinney. *Director:* Steve Clark.

"(The) Bird Brain Pickers"
  (Hemlock Holmes and the Retouchables, Pruneface, Itchy)
  Story: Homer Brightman. *Director:* Clyde Geronimi.

"Bomb's Away"
  (Hemlock Holmes, Stooge Viller, Mumbles)
  Story: Al Bentino/Dick Kinney. *Director:* John Walker.

"(A) Boodle of Loot"
(Hemlock Holmes and the Retouchables, Stooge Viller, Mumbles)
Story: Al Bentino/Dick Kinney. *Director:* Grant Simmons.

"(The) Boomerang Ring"
(Jo Jitsu, Pruneface, Itchy)
Story: Homer Brightman. *Director:* Brad Case.

"Bowling Ball Bandits"
(Hemlock Holmes and the Retouchables, B.B. Eyes, Flattop)
Story: Homer Brightman. *Director:* Clyde Geronimi.

"Brain Game"
(Jo Jitsu, Brow, Oodles)
Story: George Atkins. *Director:* Clyde Geronimi.

"(The) Camera Caper"
(Go Go Gomez, Stooge Viller, Mumbles)
Story: Bob Ogle. *Director:* Steve Clark.

"(The) Casbah Express"
(Jo Jitsu, Sketch Paree, Mole)
Story: Tedd Pierce. *Director:* Paul Fennell.

"(A) Case for Alarm"
(Go Go Gomez, B.B. Eyes, Flattop)
Story: Al Bentino/Dick Kinney. *Director:* Grant Simmons.

"(The) Castle Caper"
(Go Go Gomez, Pruneface, Itchy)
Story: Cecil Beard/Bob Ogle. *Director:* Clyde Geronimi.

"(The) Catnap Caper"
(Hemlock Holmes and the Retouchables, Stooge Viller, Mumbles)
Story: Bob Ogle. *Director:* Ray Patterson.

"Champ Chumps"
(Jo Jitsu, Stooge Viller, Mumbles)
Story: Homer Brightman. *Director:* John Walker.

"Cheater Gunsmoke"
(Heap O'Callory, Cheater Gunsmoke)
Story: Brad Case. *Director:* Dave Detiege.

"(The) Chinese Cookie Caper"
(Hemlock Holmes, Stooge Viller, Mumbles)
Story: Bob Ogle. *Director:* Grant Simmons.

"Choo Choo Boo Boo"
(Hemlock Holmes and the Retouchables, B.B. Eyes, Flattop)
Story: Al Bentino/Dick Kinney. *Director:* John Walker.

"(The) Cold Cash Caper"
(Hemlock Holmes, Stooge Viller, Mumbles)
Story: Bob Ogle. *Director:* Paul Fennell.

"Cooked Crooks"
(Jo Jitsu, Stooge Viller, Mumbles)
Story: George Atkins. *Director:* Paul Fennell.

"(The) Cop and Saucer"
(Jo Jitsu, Brow, Oodles)
Story: Kin Platt. *Director:* Jerry Hathcock.

"(The) Copped Copper Caper"
(Go Go Gomez, Flattop, B.B. Eyes)
Story: Bob Ogle. *Director:* John Walker.

"(The) Copy Cat Caper"
(Go Go Gomez, Sketch Paree, Mole)
Story: Bob Ogle. *Director:* John Walker.

"Court Jester"
(Go Go Gomez, Stooge Viller, Mumbles)
Story: Al Bentino/Dick Kinney. *Director:* Steve Clark.

"Crime Flies"
(Jo Jitsu, Stooge Viller, Mumbles)
Story: Bob Ogle. *Director:* Ray Patterson.

"Crookster's Last Stand"
(Go Go Gomez, Stooge Viller, Mumbles)
Story: Al Bentino/Dick Kinney. *Director:* John Walker.

"Down the Drain"
(Jo Jitsu, Sketch Paree, Mole)
Story: Kin Platt/Dave Detiege. *Director:* Steve Clark.

"(The) Elephant Caper"
(Jo Jitsu, Sketch Paree, Mole)
Story: Al Bentino/Dick Kinney. *Director:* Grant Simmons.

"(The) Elevator Lift"
(Jo Jitsu, B.B. Eyes, Flattop)
Story: Dick Shaw. *Director:* Jerry Hathcock.

"Escape from Sing Song"
(Hemlock Holmes and the Retouchables, Brow, Oodles)
Story: Dave Detiege. *Director:* Brad Case.

"Evil Eye Guy"
(Hemlock Holmes, Sketch Paree)
Story: Homer Brightman. *Director:* John Walker.

"Feathered Frenzy"
(Go Go Gomez, Stooge Viller, Mumbles)
Story: Al Bentino/Dick Kinney. *Director:* Ray Patterson.

"(The) Film Can Caper"
(Go Go Gomez, Stooge Viller, Mumbles)
Story: Bob Ogle. *Director:* Grant Simmons.

"(The) Fish Filchers"
(Hemlock Holmes and the Retouchables, Brow, Oodles)
Story: Bob Ogle. *Director:* Grant Simmons.

"(The) Fixed Stare Case"
(Go Go Gomez, Sketch Paree, Mole)
Story: Ralph Wright. *Director:* Steve Clark.

"Flea Ring Circus"
(Hemlock Holmes and the Retouchables, B.B. Eyes, Flattop)
Story: Bob Ogle. *Director:* Steve Clark.

"(The) Flower Plot"
(Jo Jitsu, Sketch Paree, Mole)

Story: George Atkins/Vic Haboush. *Director:* Brad Case.

"Football Brawl"
(Jo Jitsu, Pruneface, Itchy)
Story: Dick Shaw. *Director:* John Walker.

"Fowl Play"
(Go Go Gomez, Sketch Paree)
Story: Homer Brightman. *Director:* Clyde Geronimi.

"Funny Money"
(Hemlock Holmes and the Retouchables, Stooge Viller, Mumbles)
Story: Homer Brightman. *Director:* Clyde Geronimi.

"Gang Town"
(Go Go Gomez, B.B. Eyes, Flattop)
Story: Dave Detiege. *Director:* John Walker.

"Ghostward Ho!"
(Hemlock Holmes, Stooge Viller, Mumbles, The Lone Stranger and Quicksilver)
Story: Bob Ogle. *Director:* Ray Patterson.

"(The) Gold Grabbers"
(Go Go Gomez, Pruneface, Itchy)
Story: Dick Shaw. *Director:* Clyde Geronimi.

"Grandma Jitsu"
(Jo Jitsu, Sketch Paree, Mole)
Story: Bob Ogle. *Director:* John Walker.

"(The) Great Whodunit"
(Go Go Gomez, B.B. Eyes, Flattop)
Story: Tom Hicks/Bob Ogle. *Director:* Steve Clark.

"Gruesome Twosome"
(Heap O'Callory, Pruneface, Itchy)
Story: Homer Brightman. *Director:* Ray Patterson.

"Gym Jam"
(Jo Jitsu, Flattop)
Story: George Atkins. *Director:* Clyde Geronimi.

"Ham on the Lam"
(Hemlock Holmes, Brow, Oodles)
Story: Homer Brightman. *Director:* Steve Clark.

"Hawaiian Guy"
(Jo Jitsu, Stooge Viller, Mumbles)
Story: Bob Ogle. *Director:* Steve Clark.

"Hooked Crooks"
(Hemlock Holmes and the Retouchables, Pruneface, Itchy)
Story: Dave Detiege. *Director:* Paul Fennell.

"Horse Race Chase"
(Go Go Gomez, Brow, Oodles)
Story: Homer Brightman. *Director:* Ray Patterson.

"(The) Hot Ice Bag"
(Hemlock Holmes and the Retouchables, Stooge Viller, Mumbles)
Story: Homer Brightman. *Director:* Ray Patterson.

"Hot on the Trail"
(Go Go Gomez, Pruneface, Itchy)
Story: Al Bentino/Dick Kinney. *Director:* Paul Fennell.

"Hotel Havoc"
(Go Go Gomez, Stooge Viller, Mumbles)
Story: Bob Ogle. *Director:* Steve Clark.

"Island Racket"
(Go Go Gomez, Pruneface, Itchy)
Story: Dick Shaw. *Director:* Clyde Geronimi.

"(The) Ivory Rustlers"
(Go Go Gomez, Stooge Viller, Mumbles)
Story: Al Bentino/Dick Kinney. *Director:* Jerry Hathcock.

"Jewel Fool"
(Jo Jitsu, Flattop)
Story: George Atkins. *Director:* Brad Case.

"Kidnap Trap"
(Hemlock Holmes and the Retouchables, Brow, Oodles)
Story: Homer Brightman. *Director:* Brad Case.

"Lab Grab"
(Jo Jitsu, Brow, Oodles)
Story: George Atkins. *Director:* John Walker.

"(The) Last Blast"
(Hemlock Holmes, Stooge Viller, Mumbles)
Story: Ralph Wright. *Director:* Clyde Geronimi.

"(The) Lie Detector"
(Hemlock Holmes, Stooge Viller, Mumbles)
Story: Homer Brightman. *Director:* Clyde Geronimi.

"Lighthouse Creepers"
(Go Go Gomez, Brow, Oodles)
Story: Bob Ogle. *Director:* Grant Simmons.

"(The) Loch Mess Monster"
(Go Go Gomez, Brow, Oodles)
Story: Homer Brightman. *Director:* Clyde Geronimi.

"(The) Log Book Case"
(Jo Jitsu, Mole)
Story: Ralph Wright. *Director:* Paul Fennell.

"Lumber Scamps"
(Hemlock Holmes and the Retouchables, Brow, Oodles)
Story: Homer Brightman. *Director:* John Walker.

"(The) Manor Monster"
(Go Go Gomez, Pruneface, Leon the Mechanical Monster)
Story: Bob Ogle. *Director:* Jerry Hathcock.

"Mardi Gras Grab"
(Jo Jitsu, Pruneface, Itchy)
Story: Al Bentino/Dick Kinney. *Director:* Ray Patterson.

"(The) Medicine Show Case"
(Go Go Gomez, Sketch Paree, Mole)

Story: Ralph Wright. *Director:* Jerry Hathcock.

"Mole in the Hole"
(Hemlock Holmes, Mole)
Story: Homer Brightman. *Director:* Jerry Hathcock.

"(The) Monkey Tale"
(Hemlock Holmes, Sketch Paree, Mole)
Story: Al Bentino/Dick Kinney. *Director:* Steve Clark.

"Mummy's the Word"
(Jo Jitsu, Pruneface, Itchy)
Story: Bob Ogle. *Director:* John Walker.

"(The) Newspaper Caper"
(Jo Jitsu, Pruneface, Itchy)
Story: Dick Shaw. *Director:* Steve Clark.

"(The) Nickel Nabbers"
(Hemlock Holmes and the Retouchables, Pruneface, Itchy)
Story: Dave Detiege. *Director:* Paul Fennell.

"Oil's Well"
(Go Go Gomez, Sketch Paree, Mole, A La Mode Jones)
Story: Al Bentino/Dick Kinney. *Director:* Grant Simmons.

"(The) Old Mummy Case"
(Go Go Gomez, Brow, Oodles)
Story: Ralph Wright. *Director:* Clyde Geronimi.

"(The) Old Suit Case"
(Go Go Gomez, B.B. Eyes)
Story: Ralph Wright. *Director:* Clyde Geronimi.

"(The) Onion Ring"
(Hemlock Holmes and the Retouchables, Stooge Viller, Mumbles)
Story: Bob Ogle. *Director:* Clyde Geronimi.

"(The) Oyster Caper"
(Jo Jitsu, Pruneface, Itchy)
Story: Ed Nofziger. *Director:* Clyde Geronimi.

"(The) Parrot Caper"
(Jo Jitsu, B.B. Eyes, Flattop)
Story: Al Bentino/Dick Kinney. *Director:* Clyde Geronimi.

"Pearl Thief Grief"
(Jo Jitsu, Sketch Paree, Mole)
Story: Homer Brightman. *Director:* Grant Simmons.

"Penny Ante Caper"
(Heap O'Callory, Pruneface, Itchy)
Story: Dave Detiege. *Director:* Steve Clark.

"Phony Pharmers"
(Hemlock Holmes and the Retouchables, B.B. Eyes, Flattop)
Story: Ed Nofziger/Bob Ogle. *Director:* Ray Patterson.

"(The) Pigeon Coup"
(Jo Jitsu, Stooge Viller, Mumbles)

Story: Cal Howard. *Director:* Clyde Geronimi.

"(The) Platterpuss Plot"
(Hemlock Holmes and the Retouchables, Pruneface, Itchy)
Story: Al Bentino/Dick Kinney; *Director:* Clyde Geronimi.

"(The) Purple Boy"
(Hemlock Holmes and the Retouchables, Pruneface, Itchy)
Story: Ed Nofziger. *Director:* Brad Case.

"Quick Cure Quacks"
(Jo Jitsu, Pruneface, Itchy)
Story: Dick Shaw. *Director:* John Walker.

"Racer Chaser"
(Jo Jitsu, Stooge Viller, Mumbles)
Story: Bob Ogle. *Director:* Grant Simmons.

"Red Hot Riding Hoods"
(Hemlock Holmes and the Retouchables, Flattop, Mumbles)
Story: Homer Brightman. *Director:* Ray Patterson.

"(The) Retouchables"
(Hemlock Holmes and the Retouchables, Stooge Viller, Mumbles)
Story: Al Bentino/Dick Kinney. *Director:* Clyde Geronimi.

"Rock-a-Bye Guys"
(Hemlock Holmes and the Retouchables, Stooge Viller, Mumbles)
Story: Homer Brightman. *Director:* John Walker.

"Rocket 'n' Roll"
(Jo Jitsu, Hemlock Holmes and the Retouchables, Stooge Viller, Mumbles)
Story: Al Bentino/Dick Kinney. *Director:* Clyde Geronimi.

"Rocket Racket"
(Hemlock Holmes and the Retouchables, Sketch Paree, Mole)
Story: Bob Ogle. *Director:* Grant Simmons.

"Rogues Gallery"
(Heap O'Callory, Mole, Sketch Paree)
Story: Al Bentino/Dick Kinney. *Director:* John Walker.

"(The) Ruby of Hamistan"
(Jo Jitsu, Sketch Paree, Mole)
Story: Al Bentino/Dick Kinney. *Director:* John Walker.

"Scrambled Yeggs"
(Heap O'Callory, Brow, Oodles)
Story: Homer Brightman. *Director:* Ray Patterson.

"(The) Skyscraper Caper"
(Go Go Gomez, B.B. Eyes, Flattop)
Story: Kin Platt. *Director:* Clyde Geronimi.

"Small Time Crooks"
(Jo Jitsu, Brow, Oodles)
Story: Bob Ogle. *Director:* Steve Clark.

"Smashing the Ring Ring"
  (Jo Jitsu, Pruneface, Itchy)
  Story: Chris Hayward/Lloyd Turner. *Director:* Jerry Hathcock.
"Snow Job"
  (Go Go Gomez, Pruneface, Itchy)
  Story: Al Bentino/Dick Kinney. *Director:* Paul Fennell.
"(The) Snow Monster"
  (Jo Jitsu, Flattop)
  Story: George Atkins. *Director:* Brad Case.
"Stamp Scamp"
  (Hemlock Holmes and the Retouchables, B.B. Eyes)
  Story: Dave Detiege. *Director:* Clyde Geronimi.
"Steamboat Steal"
  (Go Go Gomez, Sketch Paree, Mole)
  Story: Al Bentino/Dick Kinney. *Director:* Grant Simmons.
"Stockyard Caper"
  (Hemlock Holmes and the Retouchables, Brow, Oodles)
  Story: Al Bentino/Dick Kinney. *Director:* Brad Case.
"(The) Stuffed Pillow Case"
  (Go Go Gomez, Stooge Viller, Mumbles)
  Story: Bob Ogle. *Director:* Steve Clark.
"Surprised Package"
  (Heap O'Callory, Brow, Oodles)
  Story: Homer Brightman. *Director:* Steve Clark.
"(The) Sweepstakes Caper"
  (Jo Jitsu, Stooge Viller, Mumbles)
  Story: Cal Howard. *Director:* John Walker.
"Tacos Tangle"
  (Go Go Gomez, Jo Jitsu, B.B. Eyes)
  Story: Bob Ogle. *Director:* Ray Patterson.
"Tanks a Heap"
  (Heap O'Callory, Stooge Viller, Mumbles)
  Story: Dave Detiege. *Director:* Steve Clark.
"Tick Tock Shock"
  (Heap O'Callory, Brow, Oodles)
  Story: Homer Brightman. *Director:* John Walker.
"Tobacco Load"
  (Hemlock Holmes and the Retouchables, Cheater Gunsmoke)
  Story: Dave Detiege. *Director:* Brad Case.
"(The) Tower of Pizza"
  (Hemlock Holmes, Brow, Oodles)
  Story: Homer Brightman. *Director:* Steve Clark.
"Trick or Treat"
  (Jo Jitsu, Sketch Paree, Mole)
  Story: Al Bentino/Dick Kinney. *Director:* Clyde Geronimi.
"Trickery at Sea"
  (Jo Jitsu, Stooge Viller, Mumbles)

Story: Dick Shaw. *Director:* Grant Simmons.
"Two Goons in the Fountain"
  (Jo Jitsu, Pruneface, Itchy, Antonio)
  Story: Al Bentino/Dick Kinney. *Director:* Ray Patterson.
"Two Heels on Wheels"
  (Hemlock Holmes and the Retouchables, Stooge Viller, Mumbles)
  Story: Homer Brightman. *Director:* Grant Simmons.
"(The) Two Way Stretch"
  (Jo Jitsu, Brow, Oodles)
  Story: Nick Bennion. *Director:* Ray Patterson.
"(The) Van Vandals"
  (Jo Jitsu, Brow, Oodles)
  Story: Ralph Wright. *Director:* Jerry Hathcock.
"(The) Venetian Blind"
  (Jo Jitsu, Sketch Paree, Mole)
  Story: Al Bentino/Dick Kinney. *Director:* Grant Simmons.
"(The) Vile in Case"
  (Jo Jitsu, Brow, Oodles)
  Story: Ralph Wright. *Director:* Steve Clark.
"Wheeling and Stealing"
  (Hemlock Holmes and the Retouchables, Sketch Paree, Mole)
  Story: Al Bentino/Dick Kinney. *Director:* Paul Fennell.
"(The) Windmill Caper"
  (Go Go Gomez, Brow, Oodles)
  Story: Bob Ogle. *Director:* John Walker.

On September 11, 1971, *Dick Tracy* became a regular feature of the Saturday morning animated children's program *Archie's TV Funnies* on CBS. *Archie's TV Funnies* lasted two seasons, ending on September 1, 1973. In this particular Archie series (there were several of them on Saturday morning television in the 1960s and 1970s), Archie and his gang (Reggie, Jughead, Betty, Veronica, Moose, and Hotdog) run a television station. This allows the gang to showcase a variety of "funnies," including stories of Nancy and Sluggo, Moon Mullins, Emmy Lou, Smokey Stover, Broomhilda, the Captain and the Kids, the Dropouts, and, of course, Dick Tracy. Rogues that confronted Tracy on the Archie program included Mole, Flattop, Pruneface, Mumbles, Brow, and Pear Shape. The individual funnies that made up *Archie's TV Funnies* were untitled.

In comparison to the UPA Dick Tracy animation of ten years earlier, the Tracy funnies were a bit more complex and a little better plotted. One particular episode which featured Pruneface has the villain training attack dogs for evil purposes. In fact, Pruneface has masterminded an international dognapping ring which converts canines of all sorts into anti-police dogs. Pruneface uses the naïve and innocent Miss Canine's mansion as the headquarters for his nefarious operations. Tracy uses a mechanically controlled artificial dog (Rookie the Robot Dog) to track Pruneface. After Rookie is nabbed by the villain's henchmen, Tracy and Sam Catchem follow the thugs in their magnetic flying buckets. (This Tracy episode does indeed remain loyal to Chester Gould's science fiction themes found in *Dick Tracy* of the newspaper comics page at the time.) Meanwhile, Tess Trueheart approaches Miss Canine's mansion on her own, unaware that she is about to be captured by Pruneface. Tracy, circling the mansion in the air above in his flying bucket, decides not to approach Pruneface with Tess in the way. The criminal binds and gags Tess and Miss Canine. Tess accidentally kicks open a water pipe, and she and Miss Canine are in danger of drowning in the cellar of the mansion. Needless to say, Tracy ultimately rescues the pair, subdues Pruneface, and returns to headquarters—only to hear a television announcement which states that Flattop has escaped from prison. The whole episode is roughly seven or eight minutes long, by far the longest of the TV funnies to be showcased by Archie and the gang. *Archie's TV Funnies* was directed by Hal Sutherland and was produced by Lou Scheimer and Norm Prescott.

Television Pilot

In 1966, Twentieth Century–Fox, William Dozier, and James Fonda began work on a half-hour pilot for a proposed *Dick Tracy* television series. Dozier had been quite successful producing the *Batman* series for ABC. Ultimately, however, the *Tracy* pilot did not sell and was never aired on network television.

The pilot starred Ray MacDonnell in the title role, and Victor Buono (King Tut in the *Batman* series) as Mr. Memory. Other players included Ken Mayer as Chief Patton, Allen Jaffe as Mr. Memory's assistant, Hook (who was highly reminiscent of a variety of characters from folklore and literature and, more specifically to the Dick Tracy heritage of Jack Lambert as the Claw in the 1947 RKO movie *Dick Tracy's Dilemma*), and Eve Plumb (later Jan in *The Brady Bunch*) as Bonny Braids. The pilot was written by Hal Fimberg and directed by Larry Peerce. In a statement for *Comics Scene* (#16, 1990), William Dozier said, "We made the pilot and the network didn't pick it up. Nobody bought it. I don't think it was quite far out enough. I don't know."[41] Robert Borowski provides a nice discussion of the pilot and proposed series in an article entitled "Dick Tracy: The Series That Never Was" for *Model and Toy Collector* (Summer Special #2, 1990).[42]

The pilot is entitled "The Plot to Kill NATO" and begins with the kidnapping of three ambassadors who are about to leave for "a secret and vital NATO conference." After this brief prologue, the pilot turns to a rather uninspired, campy, though strangely catchy theme song which relies heavily on the chorus, "D-i-c-k T-r-a-c-y . . .

He's a Good Cop!" During this theme, the major players of the episode are introduced in a series of visual credits. Though Tess Trueheart Tracy and Bonnie Braids are introduced in these credits, they appear nowhere else in the pilot. Tracy does, however, refer to them more than once during the episode, claiming that they are out of town.

In short, this pilot episode is quite entertaining and satisfying. It is played neither totally campy—as were Dozier's *Batman* television programs starring Adam West and Burt Ward—nor totally straight. Probably since there were already Dozier's *Batman* and the *Green Hornet* series on television, network executives felt there was no room for another similar production. This was unfortunate; the *Tracy* pilot offered much of merit.

While somewhat imitative of Dozier's *Batman* in terms of music and editing (and the fact that Dick Tracy's secret laboratory in the basement of his house is accessed by a device strangely similar to the Batpole in *Batman*), Dozier's *Dick Tracy* owes much to the Tracy conventions established in Chester Gould's comic strip. In fact, Gould himself and Henry G. Saperstein (responsible for much of the success of the UPA *Dick Tracy* animation) are acknowledged in the closing credits with providing an idea and characters for the pilot. The program does consciously attempt to showcase specific detection of crime and scientific advances in that detection—Dick Tracy utilizes a laboratory invention or two, rather ingeniously fingerprints Dr. Alexander (Mr. Memory's accomplice, who is later eliminated by Memory), and disguises himself as a chauffeur to gain access to Memory's hideout. And there is substantial action and adventure in the program. Characters in the story—both morally good and bad—are also quite faithful to Gouldian tradition. Mr. Memory, while not as physically deformed and violent as, for example, Pruneface of the newspaper *Dick Tracy*, is indeed a worthy

contribution to the *Dick Tracy* rogues' gallery. The pilot also features the Gouldian conventions of a death trap for the hero—in this case a poison gas–filled room—and a secret passageway or two. The pilot seems to have offered great potential (particularly by 1960s standards), featuring an array of characters, inventions, and situations for further exploration and development. The storyline is even reflective of social concerns of the day as it suggests that Mr. Memory is an enemy in the Cold War—he is, after all, attempting to thwart NATO and world peace.

In the end, Mr. Memory attempts to force the hands of a subdued Dick Tracy into his piranha tank—the same tank which claimed Hook's missing appendage. As one might suspect, Tracy breaks free; he turns up the volume on Mr. Memory's computer/radio device, immobilizing the villain. Memory is committed to a mental institute. After the closing credits, viewers learn that "Next week, in 'A Plot to Destroy a Metropolis,' Dick Tracy encounters Global Enemy Number One." Most likely, a second episode was never made.

Credits for the pilot were as follows:

Cast: *Dick Tracy* Ray MacDonnell, *Mr. Memory* Victor Buono, *Tess Trueheart Tracy* Davey Davison, *Lizz* Jan Shutan, *Chief Patton* Ken Mayer, *Sam Catchem* Monroe Arnold, *Junior* Jay Blood, *Bonnie Braids* Eve Plumb, *Hook* Allen Jaffe, *Ben* Tom Reese, *Higgins* Richard St. John, *Markov* Gregory Gay, *Dr. Alexander* Vinton Hatworth.

Crew: *Executive Producer* William Dozier, *Producer* James Fonda, *Production Supervisor* Jack Sonntag, *Assistant to Executive Producer* Charles B. Fitzsimons, *Unit Production Manager* Maxwell O. Henry, *Post Production Supervisor* James Blakeley, A.C.E., *Post Production Coordinator* Robert Mintz, *Director* Larry Peerce, *Assistant Director* Max Stein, *Screenplay* Hall Fimberg, *Director of Photography* Frederick Gately, A.S.C., *Film Editor* Bob Mosher, A.C.E., *Music* Billy May, *Music Supervision* Lionel Newman, *Supervising Music Editor* Leonard A. Engel, *Music Editor* Ken Spears, *Supervising Sound Effects Editor* Ralph B. Hickey, *Sound Effects Editor* Harold Wooley, *Art Directors* Jack Martin Smith, Serge

Ray MacDonnell as Tracy in the unaired television pilot of 1966.

Krizman, *Makeup Supervision* Ben Nye, *Set Decorators* Walter M. Scott, James Payne, *Hair Styling Supervision* Margaret Donovan. Color by De Luxe. Theme composed and performed by The Ventures. William Self in charge of production for Twentieth Century–Fox Television, Inc. A Greenlawn Production in association with Twentieth Television Personalities, Inc. and Twentieth Century–Fox Television. Copyright 1967. Based on an idea and characters created by Chester Gould and Henry G. Saperstein.

In 1993, *Dick Tracy* appears almost exclusively in comic strips, where it remains a strong statement about, and reflection of, American values and attitudes. The 1990 Warren Beatty movie *Dick Tracy* did inspire a variety of new book publications — primarily containing classic *Tracy* newspaper comic strips — and a variety of premiums and toys and related paraphernalia. In 1970, Tempo Books released a paperback novel simply entitled *Dick Tracy* under what could be a pseudonymous byline — William Johnston. Between 1975 and 1976, Fawcett Publishers published three paperback books which reprinted classic *Tracy* adventures from the Forties *(Dick Tracy — His Greatest Cases No. 1: Pruneface; Dick Tracy — His Greatest Cases No. 2: Snowflake and Shaky Plus the Black Pearl;* and *Dick Tracy — His Greatest Cases No. 3: Mrs. Pruneface)*. Between 1979 and 1980, Tempo Books published two paperback books of Max Collins and Rick Fletcher *Tracy* reprints *(Dick Tracy Meets Angeltop* and *Dick Tracy Meets the Punks)*. The William Johnston novel and the two Collins/Fletcher paperbacks were reissued in 1990 in conjunction with the Warren Beatty movie.

Chester Gould's 1931 creation of *Dick Tracy* for the newspaper comic strips has expanded into a variety of media over the years. This expansion not only points to the success of the original art form in terms of public acceptance, but testifies to the enduring cultural values of a story — an ongoing novel — more than sixty years old.

Chester Gould's brainchild, still celebrated each summer in Woodstock, Illinois, during "Dick Tracy Days" by the Chester Gould–Dick Tracy Museum, and by Andy Feighery's *Dick Tracy Fan Club* of Manitou Springs, Colorado, continues to hit a responsive chord.

Notes

1. Tony Schwartz, *The Responsive Chord* (Garden City, N.Y.: Anchor Books/Doubleday, 1974).
2. Tony Schwartz, *Media: The Second God* (Garden City, N.Y.: Anchor Books/Doubleday, 1981).
3. Alan Gowans, *Learning to See: Historical Perspectives on Modern Commercial Arts* (Bowling Green, Ohio: Bowling Green State University Popular Press, 1981), p. 223.
4. Among the imitators of Whitman Publishing were Saalfield Publishing of Akron, Ohio, who produced the "Little Big Book," and Dell Publishing of New York who marketed the "Fast Action Book." "Big Little Book" is a protected trademark of Whitman Publishing Company, Racine, Wisconsin.
5. The definitive study to date on Big Little Books is Lawrence F. Lowery's *The Collector's Guide to Big Little Books and Similar Books* (Danville, California: Educational Research and Applications Corporation, 1981). While more remains to be done on the study of the Big Little Books from a socio-historic perspective, Lowery's book provides an admirable general history of this once popular medium.
6. Lowery, p. 26.
7. Only Mickey Mouse had more Whitman Big Little Book and Better Little Book titles—29 in all. The early Mickey Mouse Big Little Books were reworkings of classic Floyd Gottfredson newspaper comic strips.
8. The first comic book was *New Fun Comics* of February 1935, according to Robert M. Overstreet in *The Overstreet Comic Book Price Guide* (Cleveland, Tennessee: Overstreet Publications, Inc., 1992). This book was the first to possess original stories and the standard format that was and is characteristic of comic books. Precisely what is held to constitute a comic book varies from authority to authority, so other claimants exist for the title of first comic book.
9. Lawrence F. Lowery's Volume IV, Number 6 (November 1985) and Volume V, Number 1 (January/February 1986) of *The Big Little Times* (Danville, California) provide even further information regarding the Dick Tracy Big Little Books. In these two volumes, Lowery discusses, with precision and accuracy, the content base for each book, where that base came from, publishing history, and more. Lowery's material is detailed and insightful.
10. Overstreet discusses some of the history behind, and qualities of, the Feature Book. "Feature Book" was a trademark of David McKay Publishing Company.
11. See Lowery's *The Collector's Guide to Big Little Books and Similar Books* for more additional explanation of Dell's Fast Action Books.
12. *Comics Scene* 3, p. 24. It should be noted that although Dick Tracy first appeared in standard comic books in the Dell Four-Color series in 1939, there was not a comic book title solely dedicated to Dick Tracy comics until 1948.
13. John Dunning, *Tune in Yesterday: The Ultimate Encyclopedia of Old-Time Radio 1925–1976* (Englewood Cliffs, N.J.: Prentice-Hall, 1976), p. 72.
14. Ibid., p. 102. The other actor was Santos Ortega.
15. Frank Buxton and Bill Owen, *The Big Broadcast: 1920–1950—A New, Revised, and Greatly Expanded Edition of Radio's Golden Age* (New York: Viking, 1972).
16. Jim Harmon, "Dick Tracy's Radio Patrol" in James Van Hise's *Calling Tracy!—Six Decades of Dick Tracy* (Las Vegas: Pioneer Books, Inc., 1983), p. 62.
17. As noted, the spellings provided in these plot synopses are based on the audio radio program, not printed scripts. Words followed by an * are spelled based on the author's best guess. Just prior to publication, the author acquired four additional Dick Tracy radio programs. These are: "The Case of the Low Hijack," Monday, August 16, 1947; "The Case of the Poisonous Timber," Tuesday, December 16, 1947; "The Case of the Poisonous Timber," Friday, December 19, 1947; and "The Case of the Big Black Box," Thursday, January 9, 1948.
18. Dorothy Hammond and Rachelle D. Brisk, "Dick Tracy badge was a cereal box-top reward, worth varies." *Green Bay Press Gazette*, January 9, 1983, Scene 5.
19. Harmon, p. 58.

270 Dick Tracy and American Culture

20. Ibid., p. 59.

21. Ibid.

22. Ibid.

23. In 1946, George Edward "Rube" Waddell (October 13, 1876–April 1, 1914), a famous pitcher for Louisville, Pittsburgh, Philadelphia, and St. Louis respectively from 1897 to 1910, was enshrined in the Baseball Hall of Fame. Waddell had died of complications of a cold incurred two years earlier while standing shoulder-deep in the icy water of a Kentucky river piling sand bags to thwart the river from flooding a small town. Among his baseball feats was the record of 343 strikeouts in 377 innings in 1904 (a record which stood until Bob Feller broke it in 1946), and 16 strikeouts in one game in 1908 (Feller eventually topped this record too). According to the announcer during the opening minutes of the July 23, 1947, episode of "The Case of the Unfunny Clowns," the program had also discussed Waddell on a previous day.

24. Jim Ameche (1915–February 4, 1983) went on to do dramatic performances for the Woodbury Hollywood Playhouse and the Lux Theater after his stint as Jack Armstrong. Ameche eventually became a successful disc jockey, and his voice was heard on several commercials.

25. The Egyptian king's name is also spelled "Tutankhamon" and "Tutankhamun." The stairway leading to his tomb was discovered in 1922.

26. For more information on the origins of the Shadow on radio, refer to Anthony Tollin's article "The Invisible Shadow" in Walter B. Gibson's *The Shadow Scrapbook* (New York: Harcourt, Brace, Jovanovich, 1979) and Will Murray's book *The Duende History of the Shadow* (Greenwood, Mass.: Odyssey Publications, 1980).

27. Alan G. Barbour, *Cliffhanger: A Pictorial History of the Motion Picture Serial* (New York: A&W Publishers, Inc., 1977), p. 38.

28. Buddy Barnett provides a brief biography and filmography for Ralph Byrd in "Dick Tracy on T.V." *Videosonic Arts* 2 (North Hollywood, California: Videosonic Arts, Summer 1990), p. 9.

29. Barbour's *Cliffhanger* provides additional information about the Republic movie serials featuring Dick Tracy.

30. Ibid.

31. Suggested further readings on the Dick Tracy serials include: Barbour's *Days of Thrills and Adventure*, Roy Kinnard's *Fifty Years of Serial Thrills*, Jim Harmon and Donald F. Glut's *The Great Movie Serials: Their Sound and Fury*, Jon Tuska's *The Detective in Hollywood*, William C. Cline's *In the Nick of Time: Motion Picture Sound Serials*, and Charles Lee Jackson's "A Complete History of Dick Tracy—The Films, Serials, TV and Cartoons . . ." for *Filmfax* 21 and 22 (July and September, 1990). (See Bibliography for complete citations.) Jackson's work does provide a technical history for the four Republic Tracy serials and includes some nice photos and stills.

32. David Wilt, *Hardboiled in Hollywood: Five Black Mask Writers and the Movies* (Bowling Green, Ohio: Bowling Green State University Popular Press, 1991).

33. Tim Brooks and Earle Marsh in *The Complete Directory to Prime Time Network TV Shows: 1946–Present,* third edition (New York: Ballantine, 1985) cite the debut date as September 11, 1950. Alex McNeil in *Total Television: A Comprehensive Guide to Programming from 1948 to the Present,* third edition (New York: Penguin, 1991) cites the debut date as September 13, 1950. Since the program probably debuted on a Wednesday, as did the rest of the first few episodes, the September 13, 1950, date appears more credible. Both sources agree that the program terminated with the February 12, 1951, episode.

34. Brooks and Marsh, p. 217.

35. John Wooley, ed., *Robert Leslie Bellem's Dan Turner, Hollywood Detective* (Bowling Green, Ohio: Bowling Green State University Popular Press, 1983).

36. James L. Traylor, ed., *Hollywood Troubleshooter: W.T. Ballard's Bill Lennox Stories* (Bowling Green, Ohio: Bowling Green State University Popular Press, 1985), p. 155.

37. Barnett, pp. 7–8.

38. Vincent Terrace, *The Complete Encyclopedia of Television Programs 1947–1976* (Cranbury, N.J.: A.S. Barnes, 1976), p. 207.

39. Barnett, pp. 7–8; Brooks and Marsh, p. 217.

40. These voice credits for the Dick Tracy animated cartoons are found in Jeff Lenburg's *The Encyclopedia of Animated Cartoon Series* (New York: Plenum House Pub. Corp., 1981), p. 112.

41. Duane S. Arnott, "Dick Tracy: The Lost Casebook," *Comics Scene* 16 (December 1990), pp. 57–60.

42. Robert Borowski, "Dick Tracy: The Series That Never Was," *Model and Toy Collector* (Summer Special, #2—Dick Tracy Special) (Seville, Ohio: Cap'n Penny Productions, Inc., 1990).

CHAPTER 7

Premiums, Paraphernalia, and Material Culture: The Dick Tracy Toys

"Please, sir, I want some more." — Oliver Twist in Charles Dickens' *Oliver Twist* (1837)

In the early Thirties, as Dick Tracy moved quickly into a variety of media other than the comic strip, he likewise moved quickly into a proliferation of toys, games, and peripheral premiums. Dick Tracy enjoyed a resurgence in such items in 1990 which coincided with the release of the Warren Beatty movie, but for all practical purposes, Dick Tracy toys, games, and related products have been around since the beginnings of Chester Gould's famous comic strip. There have been literally hundreds of these things.

When *Dick Tracy* was in its infancy in the waning months of 1931 and the early months of 1932, there were already promotional items intended to advertise and enhance the debut of the newspaper comic strip. There was an early Dick Tracy button that had a cardboard backing which announced that *Dick Tracy* appeared in the *Detroit Mirror* (where *Tracy* first appeared), and there has been a multitude of buttons and badges since that time. There have been Dick Tracy board games, card games, and even a Crimestopper game from the Ideal Toy Corporation which came out on the heels of the animated cartoon series. There were Dick Tracy rings (some with secret decoders and secret compartments), decoders, police sirens, whistles, and watches. Among the more

unusual Tracy toys and premiums were a Dick Tracy tie clip, a Dick Tracy glider plane, and a Dick Tracy bubble bath container. There were also Dick Tracy's handcuffs for Junior, Dick Tracy police cars, and several different Dick Tracy toy pistols. The Marx Company marketed two target games, and appropriately enough, considering the profession of the comic strip hero, there were a Dick Tracy fingerprint set, an electronic wrist radio, a pen light, and a model police station. There was also a viewer which featured Tracy's exploits from the movies.

Since Dick Tracy appeared in a variety of media, many of the toys and games were intended to reinforce the stories presented in these diverse media. The Dick Tracy radio dramas, motion picture serials, B movies, and television animation were the inspiration for many of these items. There were even toys and games and related items based on the Tracy Big Little Books and comic books, and the television pilot which never aired. Republic Pictures and Quaker Oats (a major Tracy radio sponsor) were behind several of these products. Richard Gid Powers writes:

> There was Quaker Puffed Rice's Dick Tracy Secret Service Patrol that gave kids

the chance to "be a master detective like Dick Tracy." For a dime and four box-tops, kids got a Dick Tracy Secret Code Book, the Patrol Pledge, a Badge, the Secret Detecto-Kit, and a chance to "amaze your friends." The "Genuine, Official Detecto-Kit" contained photographic negatives of Dick Tracy, Tess Trueheart, Pat Patton, and Dick Tracy, Jr., a photo developer (Secret Dick Tracy Formula Q-11), a stylus for secret writing and an official Dick Tracy Secret Instruction Book.[1]

Coca-Cola also produced a couple of Tracy collectibles including a long-play record that contained the Dick Tracy radio program "The Case of the Firebug Murders."[2]

Sometimes the media themselves became Dick Tracy toys, premiums, and collectibles. For example, as discussed in Chapter 6, there were Dick Tracy comic books, some of which were issued as premiums for gas stations and the like. In the most general sense, all Tracy feature books, comic books, Big Little Books, and related books could be deemed Tracy toys and paraphernalia.

Some Big Little Books were given away as premiums for products like Cocomalt, a malted milk powder. There were other such books which were reprints of radio scripts, detective guides, and at least one book which contained magic tricks. The magic book, *Dick Tracy's Secret Detective Methods and Magic Tricks,* was produced in 1939 by the Quaker Oats Company of Chicago. The best source of information on comic books, feature books, and related premiums is Robert M. Overstreet's *The Comic Book Price Guide* (updated annually); the best source on Big Little Books and related books is Lawrence F. Lowery's *The Collector's Guide to Big Little Books and Similar Books* (1981).

There were several different Dick Tracy coloring books published through the years; Saalfield Publishing Company of Akron, Ohio, did some of these. Whether by the publishers' intent or not, the Big Little Books featuring line drawings instead of film stills often served as coloring books for children. Retailing for 29¢, the 1962 Little Golden Book entitled *Dick Tracy,* written by Carl Memling and illustrated by Hawley Pratt and Al White, was another famous Tracy item. This book featured Hemlock Holmes, Go Go Gomez, and Jo Jitsu—stars of the popular Dick Tracy animation series.

In 1947, shortly after Sparkle Plenty was born to B.O. Plenty and Gravel Gertie, *Life* magazine (August 25, 1947) carried a full-page article with photos of the new Sparkle Plenty doll marketed by the Ideal Toy Company. One of the photos showed people crowded into a Gimbel's Department Store waiting to purchase the doll. The article stated that former All-American football player William M. McDuffee, now manager of the toy department at Gimbel's (one of the largest department stores in the U.S. in 1947), had read *Tracy* and decided that, because of the popularity of the comic strip, little advertising and promotion would be needed to market a Baby Sparkle Plenty doll.[3] The article read, in part:

> McDuffee took his idea to the Ideal Toy and Novelty Co. Forty-eight days later, the production of Baby Sparkle Plenty dolls began. On July 28 they went on sale. At a stiff $5.98 apiece, 10,000 sold in the first five days. Sales in the next two weeks zoomed to 22,000. At this rate more Baby Sparkle Plenty's will be sold in the last five months of this year than all other types of dolls put together. McDuffee, who knows a good thing when he has it, is getting ready to bring out a Baby Sparkle Plenty cradle and a Gravel Gertie banjo.[4]

Ideal's Baby Sparkle Plenty doll, if not the single most popular, was one of the most popular and famous Dick Tracy toys ever produced.

With the birth of Bonny Braids to the Tracys in 1951, the Ideal Toy Corporation produced a Bonny Braids doll. But the idea for a doll of Dick and Tess' firstborn predated Bonny's birth. An article from the July 7, 1951, issue of *The New Yorker* related the following:

> Benjamin Franklin Michtom, chairman of the board of Ideal Toy, perceived at once that a Tracy marriage could mean a Tracy baby, which could mean a Tracy doll, which could mean a gold mine for Ideal. He got Gould on the telephone and announced flatly, "When the baby's born, it's mine." Gould thought it over, then said that was all right with him. "Why not?" Miss [Charlotte] Klein [a publicity representative for Ideal] asked us. "He gets a percentage on every Bonny Braids that comes out of the factory, and the Sparkle Plenty doll we did from his strip grossed five million dollars."[5]

At $5.98 per doll, that is over 800,000 Sparkle Plenty dolls sold.

The story of the Bonny Braids doll continues. Miss Klein noted that the doll, which retailed for $6.98, was being produced at the time at a rate of more than 7,000 a day. In *Dick Tracy*, Bonny Braids was born in a police car; in real life, Klein hoped that local police could be persuaded to rush the first Bonny Braids doll from the Ideal factory to Gimbel's via patrol car. "Commissioner Murphy wouldn't hear of it. 'Something about the money,' Miss Klein said."[6] The Los Angeles cops did help with Ideal's publicity stunt. In New York, on the Sunday before the Bonny Braids doll went on sale, Klein donned a nursemaid costume and wheeled a sample doll in a baby buggy up Fifth Avenue from Forty-Fifth Street to the Central Park Zoo. Klein stated, "I had a banner around the carriage reading, 'Nobody But Nobody But Gimbel's Has Bonny Braids.' Drew quite a crowd."[7] Shortly after Honey Moon Tracy was born to Junior and Moon Maid in 1965, Ideal Toys released a Honey Moon doll.

There have been a vast number of different Dick Tracy toys and premiums produced over the years, but as of yet, there is no single publication which is entirely comprehensive and definitive in listing and discussing these toys and premiums. There are, however, several fine books, magazines, and articles which go a long way to enhancing our understanding of the depth and breadth of these products. Robert M. Yoder, in his article "Dick Tracy's Boss" for *The Saturday Evening Post* (December 17, 1949) suggested that, at that time, there were 63 Dick Tracy games, toys, premiums, and so on. Yoder's list included:

> wrist radios, burglar alarm kits, masks, wallets, detective sets, Tommy guns, masquerade costumes, flashlights, suspenders, belts, sweat coats, sweat shirts, cameras, fountain pens, field glasses, puzzles, comic books, three kinds of watches, Gravel Gertie's banjo, Sparkle Plenty dolls, clothes and other girls toys, Sparkle Plenty Christmas Tree lights . . . even a Sparkle Plenty glass cleaner, and a B.O. Plenty soap. . . .[8]

The dolls to which Yoder refers may include Sparkle Plenty paper cut-out dolls as well as the famous Ideal doll. There were also Bonny Braids paper dolls.

A variety of Dick Tracy games—board games, card games, and more—have also been marketed through the years. These are hard to find and quite desirable among collectors. They are difficult to find with all pieces intact and even more rarely found in mint or near mint condition.

In addition, there were at least four distinct series of Dick Tracy collectible cards. One set dates from the 1930s and was part of a product called Dick Tracy Caramels. A package of these caramels and cards originally sold for a penny apiece; there were 144 cards in a complete set. The series was issued by the Walter H. Johnson Candy Company of Chicago. One side of each card had a titled color illustration; the other side provided a brief synopsis of the ongoing story retold in the cards. That story dealt with Junior, Steve the

Tramp, Hank Steele, and others, and had originally appeared in newspapers in 1933. Christopher Benjamin and Dennis W. Eckes' *The Short Americana Price Guide to Non-Sports Cards* (1983) lists the titles for each of the 144 cards in this set.

Another set of Tracy cards included 32 individual pieces. This set was one of seven sets which made up the larger Big Little Book cards set. This set contained 32 cards for each of 7 characters including Flash Gordon, Popeye, Tom Mix, G-Man, Buck Jones, Dan Dunn, and Dick Tracy. Benjamin and Eckes date these cards circa 1939-40, and claim that "each has rouletted edges, suggesting that they were issued in strips or were attached to a tab in the books."[9] Like the Walter H. Johnson Candy Company set, these cards had an illustration on one side and text on the other.

Yet another Dick Tracy card set reprinted "Exciting Adventures of Dick Tracy" and was released in 1953. This set contained 48 separate cards, each of which had an illustration or illustrations on one side and text on the other. Benjamin and Eckes note that the cards of this set were cut directly from the candy boxes distributed by the Novel Package Corporation, and that the text was printed in blue ink on a gray-colored back.[10]

In 1990, Topps Company issued a set of 88 glossy movie cards and 11 stickers in conjunction with the Warren Beatty movie. These cards showcased color stills from the motion picture bordered in yellow—the color of Tracy's slicker in both Sunday comic pages and the movie—and a brief synopsis on the reverse side.

Many of the most ephemeral, and consequently rare and most desirable, Dick Tracy toys were premiums and paper items. Such premiums were generated by several companies, but in the case of Dick Tracy premiums, they more often than not came from Quaker Oats, the breakfast cereal company which sponsored Tracy on radio. Quaker Oats was able to advertise its products—primarily Quaker Puffed Wheat and Quaker Puffed Rice—on the airwaves and then lure children of all ages to buy its breakfast food simply to acquire the necessary box-tops to be sent in so that the prizes (or premiums) could be procured. It was ingenious marketing all the way around. Code books, patrol badges, rings, bangle bracelets, and other items became available through the marriage of radio drama and cereal manufacturer.

There are other Dick Tracy collectibles or items that at one time or another since 1931 symbolized or reinforced the Tracy mythology. Some were more specialized than others; for example, movie posters from the movie serials and "B" movie were relatively limited in number since they were originally intended just as theater advertisements. Chester Gould and his assistants and successors have been exceptionally good at responding to correspondence so letters from Gould and others associated with *Tracy* are unique collectibles. A market exists for original art (e.g. daily comic strips) by Gould, Fletcher, and Locher. Original comic strips, however, are one of a kind, and in a very real sense can be compared to an original Picasso—they are museum pieces which can often be the stuff of auctions. The more desirable the original art (depending on factors like age, characters portrayed, and so on), the harder to find and more expensive the piece is to obtain. Vintage pieces of Gould *Dick Tracy* art currently command prices of several thousand dollars apiece. Much original art was discarded or given away by Gould. Thankfully, however, there are institutions like the Museum of Cartoon Art in Port Chester, N.Y., that have assembled some rather impressive collections.

The 1990 *Dick Tracy* movie generated many related toys and Tracy products. There were mugs, shirts, special edition cards and comic books, model figures, cereal premiums (like those found in Cap'n Crunch), sticker books, coloring books, various novelizations, and picture books. Probably the most interesting toy related to the 1990 movie was the action figure of the Blank. When Gould first introduced the Blank to *Dick Tracy* in post–Depression America, readers learned that Blank was also known as Frank Redrum. One of the many liberties taken by writers of the 1990 Beatty film was making the alter ego of Blank be Breathless Mahoney (Shaky's daughter, who was introduced in *Tracy* in 1945 long after Frank Redrum was disposed of), played by Madonna. Movie producers feared that the Blank's "surprise" identity—revealed at the end of the film to the small percentage of the moviegoers who had not already guessed it—would be spoiled by the release of this figure, which had been announced but held back. The figure had a mask attached to a hat which, when removed, revealed Breathless' countenance. In 1991, *Tomart's Action Figure Digest* revealed the hoax:

> The Blank sold exclusively in Canada. . . . By the time the figure was cleared, Dick Tracy merchandise had died and no one was reordering. Except there was a major back order situation in Canada which had to be filled by Christmas '90. The Blank was finally delivered around December 15 and figures have been slowly filtering into the U.S. Canadian dealers are estimated to own between 2,000 to 8,000 Blank figures.[11]

Should there be another *Dick Tracy* movie, which is indeed possible, more movie related collectibles will appear.

Today, authorities are able to list several hundred Dick Tracy items. The most comprehensive lists of such toys and related items are based on two things: personal collections and antique dealer inventory and related sales records. In order to be as comprehensive as possible when investigating the material culture arising from *Dick Tracy*, one needs to consult about a half dozen specialized books. Lowery's and Overstreet's guides on Big Little

Books and comic books respectively are tops. Likewise, Benjamin and Eckes' guide, which has a section on Tracy cards, is also exemplary. There are a few other guides that should be noted as quite useful. The first such book is based on the Tracy collection of Lawrence Doucet. Doucet and William Crouch collaborated to produce what to date is the best volume on Dick Tracy toys, premiums, and paraphernalia, *The Authorized Guide to Dick Tracy Collectibles* (1990). Though not thoroughly comprehensive (no one has been able to collect one of every Tracy item ever produced), the book is highly accurate. Photographic illustrations are a highlight of this work.

Tom Tumbusch's *Tomart's Price Guide to Radio Premium and Cereal Box Collectibles* (1991) is a stunning and wonderfully insightful book chock-full of information and illustrations regarding Tracy material culture. *Model and Toy Collector*, Dick Tracy Special (Summer Special #2) contains many illustrations and much information regarding Dick Tracy toys and premiums. It is the finest magazine issue ever devoted to the topic. Likewise, *The Antique Trader*, Volume 30, Issue 19 (May 7, 1986) contains much useful information on the topic. Specialty magazines like *Collectible Toy Values Monthly* #7 and #8 (1992) are also important resources when investigating Tracy paraphernalia, as are David Longest's book *Toys: Antique and Collectible* (1990) and the magazine *Comic Values Monthly Special* Volume 1, Number 1(1990).

Telescopes, telephones, paint books, postcards, and an enormous range of other items have sported Dick Tracy insignia and logos through the years. There have been hundreds of such diverse items produced and marketed since 1931. This material is fascinating to the fan and the cultural archaeologist alike; it serves as cultural iconography, as symbols of mythology, and as emblems of morality. It brings us a little closer to, and intimately ties us in with, our hero's world.

Notes

1. Richard Gid Powers, *G-Men: Hoover's F.B.I. in American Popular Culture* (Carbondale, Ill.: Southern Illinois University Press, 1983), pp. 191–192.

2. Deborah Goldstein Hill's *Price Guide to Coca-Cola Collectibles* (West Des Moines, Iowa: Wallace-Homestead Book Company, 1984) features a brief discussion and two illustrations of Coca-Cola Dick Tracy collectibles.

3. "Sparkle Plenty." *Life,* August 25, 1947, p. 42.

4. Ibid.

5. "Bonny Braids." *The New Yorker* 27, July 7, 1951, p. 15.

6. Ibid.

7. Ibid.

8. Christopher Benjamin and Dennis W. Eckes. *The Sport Americana Price Guide to Non-Sports Cards* (Laurel, Md.: Den's Collectors Den, and Lakewood, Ohio: Edgewater Book Company, Inc., 1983), p. 99.

9. Ibid.

10. Ibid.

11. *Tomart's Action Figure Digest,* Vol. 1, No. 1 (Dayton, Ohio: Tomart Publishers, 1991), inside cover.

CHAPTER 8

The 1990 Blockbuster Movie

"Imitation is the sincerest of flattery."—C.C. Colton, *Lacon: Reflections,* Vol. 1, No. 217 (1820)

On Friday, June 15, 1990, Touchstone Pictures premiered its new motion picture *Dick Tracy* to the public, starring Warren Beatty in the title role. The movie had been years in the making. Coupled with the latest Roger Rabbit cartoon, "Rollercoaster Rabbit," it was intended to be the Disney company's response to the 1989 summer smash hit *Batman,* which starred Michael Keaton as the winged avenger. Though not the equal of *Batman* in box office ticket sales and in other generated revenues, *Dick Tracy* was indeed wildly successful in 1990. Chester Gould's famous comic strip was finally getting its deserved big-screen treatment—due largely to the efforts of Warren Beatty.

The movie was not without its failures and weaknesses, but its tremendous successes far overshadowed any shortcomings. Some of the Gould *Tracy* diehards were apprehensive, many were optimistic, but most everyone seemed to be willing to give Warren Beatty and associates a chance at working with the sacred legend. Imitation—even bad imitation—is in its own way the sincerest of compliments. In the case of this 1990 filmic adaptation of the comic strip *Dick Tracy,* the imitation was more often good than bad.

The movie was set in 1930s America, a period defined by the Great Depression, urban corruption, and gangland; this was the same setting for Chester Gould's ex-periences and observations, and their transposition onto the newspaper comics page in *Dick Tracy.* In the movie, the lifestyle of gangland—characterized by "the rubout" and "the bath"—was juxtaposed against a sort of Dickensian world where people were down on their luck and where a small Oliver Twist–like waif who called himself "Kid" lived under the thumb of a mean, nasty, selfish, and exploitative individual named Steve the Tramp. Several concurrent plots were woven together to produce the larger story.

These plots include the saga of the Kid, the romance between police detective Dick Tracy and his sweetheart Tess Trueheart, the rise and downfall of gang lord Big Boy Caprice, the tragedy of Breathless Mahoney and her relationship with Tracy, and smaller but nonetheless significant plots like those surrounding gangster Lips Manlis; Tracy's assistants Pat Patton, Sam Catchem, and Bug Bailey; the crooked D.A. Fletcher; love-blinded 88 Keys (spelled Keyes in Gould's *Tracy* of the newspaper pages of 1943), and so on. The result is formulaic melodrama—somewhat loyal to the tradition of *Dick Tracy* of the comics page—of a satisfactory variety.

Chester Gould's comic strip detective was now immortalized on the silver screen. This is not to say, however, that the movie serials and B movies starring Ralph

Warren Beatty as Dick Tracy. (Photo courtesy Ted Okuda.)

Byrd and Morgan Conway in the 1930s and 1940s did not serve useful purposes and succeed on at least modest levels. But never before had this sort of big-scale Hollywood production been undertaken on Dick Tracy's behalf; never before had Dick Tracy appeared in Technicolor. Warren Beatty produced and directed the film and helped finance it in several ways. Con-

sidering the years of preproduction and related complications, it is amazing that the movie was completed and released at all, much less at what has to be considered a high level of success.

There are admittedly some weaknesses in the movie. The first deals with Beatty's portrayal of Tracy. While no one can deny that Beatty was the champion behind the movie and the most important individual working on the project, he brought with him some baggage which did cause some problems. It is no secret that, correctly or incorrectly, Warren Beatty has been typecast based on both his legendary personal life and screen performances. Newspapers, magazines, and other media forms, quick to exploit the announcement of the upcoming film and later the highly publicized release of the movie, were also quick to enumerate Beatty's past relationships with a variety of famous and beautiful women offscreen. Earlier onscreen performances in movies like *Shampoo* (1975) also came back to haunt the actor. Reminders of these past incidents were unfortunate for Beatty and his latest film. Dick Tracy of the comic strips was, particularly in the 1930s and 1940s, a model of puritanical moral fiber—especially in the arena of intimate relationships with females. This sharply defined, unwavering trait helped characterize Gould's fictional hero. The exploitation and perhaps misrepresentation of Beatty's personal prowess and selected previous movie appearances directly compromised the title character of *Dick Tracy*. This largely media-created image was further worsened by the insistence of magazines like *People* and *Newsweek* that Beatty and Madonna were carrying on a torrid romance offscreen.

Thomas Godfrey, in an article for the Winter 1991 issue of *The Armchair Detective* entitled "What Have Hollywood, Warren Beatty, and Madonna Done to 'Plain Clothes' Tracy?" was emphatic in his viewpoint:

> Beatty's Dick Tracy is a major casting mistake. He never comes near to being a square-jawed, two-fisted crimefighter. For years, he has been trying to put across the standard Warren Beatty screen persona, the boyish, aw-shucks heartthrob of fraternity row, the appealing hunk of untested sexuality who will somehow prove himself in the end. At age 53, this routine

is starting to look a little overripe for all its years on the vine. This is not Dick Tracy. This figure has no bravado and no cutting edge. He's all fluff and cuddly, like a frothy *Shampoo*—Rodeo Drive where Michigan Avenue is clearly wanted.[1]

Godfrey's position is well taken and largely representative of public sentiment, if somewhat heavy-handedly stated. In an idyllic world of Hollywood filmmaking, an unknown, sharper-featured, perhaps even physically darker-haired individual of about thirty-five years of age would have been cast. Yet one must remember that without Beatty's persistent efforts and undying devotion to the project, there very likely would never have been a big-scale Dick Tracy movie at all.

Conversely, however, Madonna's documented sexual escapades—both on and off celluloid—did not detract from her portrayal of *Tracy* villainess, Breathless Mahoney. In Chester Gould's famous comic strip, Breathless did not appear until May 10, 1945—she was not part of Thirties *Dick Tracy* as suggested by the 1990 movie. Like Madonna, Chester Gould's Breathless flaunted what could best be described as a "naughty" side; in fact, Gould's Breathless was a ruthless killer. Madonna's established image played well into the character of Breathless Mahoney; her singing was one of several highlights of the motion picture production.

And the band played on. Stephen Sondheim's original songs (many of which Madonna sings) coupled with Danny Elfman's score make *Dick Tracy* one of the most successful musicals of all time. Songs like "Sooner or Later (I Always Get My Man)," "More," and "What Can You Lose," became classics of the movie and Madonna's repertoire. As a period torch singer, Madonna is unsurpassed. Her vitality, expressionism, passion, and sensuality perfectly augment her wonderful singing voice. Sondheim's "What Can You Lose," performed as a duet by Breathless (Madonna) and 88 Keys (Mandy Patinkin), is especially poignant as the two singers' voices blend in beautiful harmonies. Danny Elfman, grandmaster of dark, gothic, Wagnerian strains for blockbuster movie scores like *Beetlejuice* (1987), *Batman* (1989), and *Batman Returns* (1992), provides a hauntingly moving atmosphere for the movie.

Writing, casting, and acting for the movie are, for the most part, quite effective. The writing and resulting screenplay provide a predictable, formulaic musical—but there is indeed a craft and an aesthetic associated with this type of screenplay. There is nothing profound in the area of scripting except the showcasing of the various interesting characters, the visually stimulating and carefully designed backgrounds, and the music and singing of the film. The storyline, while generally faithful to Gouldian tradition, liberally deviates from that tradition at times. Max Collins and Dick Locher, the greatest living *Tracy* authorities, should have been much more intimately involved with the scripting of the film, if only in consultant roles.

While Madonna is very effective as the torch-singing Breathless Mahoney (this may have been her best film role yet), and the grotesque rogues are likewise effective, the two stars of *Dick Tracy* are probably Glenne Headly as Tess Trueheart and Charlie Korsmo as the Kid (later Dick Tracy, Jr., or simply Junior). Glenne Headly has undertaken a variety of distinct roles on both stage and screen in recent years, and has been most effective in all cases. She was quite visible and renowned immediately before *Dick Tracy* in the 1988 motion picture *Dirty Rotten Scoundrels* (with Michael Caine and Steve Martin) and the 1989 television miniseries *Lonesome Dove*. Though Tess Trueheart was blonde in Chester Gould's *Dick Tracy*, she is red-headed in Beatty's film—probably to ensure a contrast in appearance to the blonde Breathless in this very visual medium. Hers is the most complex and best acted role in the film. In an article for the *Chicago Tribune* (Sunday, July 1, 1990), Hugh Boulware wrote:

> After reading the Tracy screenplay, Headly agreed to the role. Once committed, she managed to invest her relatively thankless role—as the "good" girlfriend who remains loyal to Tracy despite his attraction to Madonna's Breathless Mahoney—with an integrity and texture that lend an emotional core to the brilliant visual design of the film.[2]

Without Headly's performance, Beatty's and Madonna's performances would have been substantially compromised. She set the stage for these two typecast, media-created superstars.

Likewise, Charlie Korsmo's portrayal of the Kid proved pivotal to the ultimate success of the movie. The 11-year-old actor's sincerity and honesty in real life, chronicled in newspaper and magazine articles which hyped the movie, helped define his character as the Kid in the 1990 movie. The story of Dick Tracy, Jr., may have been Chester Gould's most powerful ongoing saga in *Dick Tracy* during the Thirties. Jim Cash and Jack Epps, Jr., two of the screenplay writers of *Tracy*, are to be credited with the insightful use of the Junior storyline in the script for the movie. Charlie Korsmo is effective in the sharply drawn, straightforward, Dickensian little boy who is harnessed with poverty but endowed with great emotional and physical strength. His honesty, on and off screen, was most endearing. A Minneapolis native, "Korsmo said before he got the role as the street-smart orphan he had never read Dick Tracy. 'They gave me some comic books to read on the set and I thought it was good.' But Korsmo said he and his older brother prefer superhero comic books."[3] He continued that acting was not his "supreme goal." "In fact, Korsmo said the main reason he started acting was, 'I wanted to make enough money to buy a Nintendo.'"[4]

The grotesque *Dick Tracy* rogues, always a strength of the famous comic strip, are also a highlight of the 1990 Warren Beatty film. Al Pacino as Big Boy Caprice with his witless witticisms is as perversely charismatic, though in a much different fashion, as he was as Michael Corleone in *The Godfather* (1972) and its two sequels. The makeup for the rogues is excellent, though in one of the biggest mistakes or shortcomings of the movie many of the classic *Tracy* rogues, introduced at the beginning of the movie, are summarily executed in a St. Valentine's Day–like massacre. These include Shoulders, Stooge Viller, Rodent (spelled Rhodent in Gould's *Tracy* of the newspaper pages of 1957), Brow, and Little Face.

For the *Dick Tracy* purist, the 1990 blockbuster movie did contain some striking inaccuracies, both intended and unintended, and some perhaps unimportant. Breathless Mahoney, 88 Keyes, and Sam Catchem did not appear in *Dick Tracy* at all in 1930s newspaper pages, and the movie is set entirely in the Thirties. (They debuted in 1945, 1943, and 1948 respectively.) There exist several other similar cases of 1940s and 1950s characters appearing in the 1930s setting of the movie. Some of the rogues, like Big Boy and Itchy, were given last names that were inconsistent with Gould's names for his characters. Some of this divergence from Gould's comic strips may not be important. At times it actually seemed that too much of the Dick Tracy legacy was incorporated— more correctly jammed—into the movie, thus leaving many complex characters and important themes undeveloped.

One of the great strengths of what is in itself a very fine movie and achievement for Warren Beatty and company was Max Allan Collins' novelization for the film. In his adaptation of the screenplay, Collins produced one of the finest novelizations ever done for a motion picture. Collins, as a talented writer and scholar of the Tracy mythos, was able to smooth out and explain away some of the inconsistencies inherent in the Beatty production. The movie also benefited greatly from the talents of Jim Cash and his partner Jack Epps, Jr., the highly successful screenwriting team for *Top Gun* (1986), *Legal Eagles* (1986), and *The Secret of My Success* (1987) that initially adapted Gould's comic strip saga for a contemporary film medium. But Collins' novel must be noted as one of the great uncredited keepers of the faith, maintainers of Gould tradition, and rectifiers of inconsistencies and errors for the movie.

As might be expected, the deluge of reporting devoted to the movie contained its share of errors also—errors which were much more extreme and numerous than those in the film. There were errors in reporting concerning virtually all aspects of the movie, and many errors regarding the Tracy legacy. A number of self-proclaimed "authorities" emerged in a variety of newspaper and magazine articles, as well as on television. Ironically, one such authority appeared in the *New York Times,* a publication which has never published comic strips, and is hence unqualified to comment on the medium and its many manifestations. One article from the *Times* stated that Chester Gould's Dick Tracy "had no feelings, no nerves, no dreams, no inner life, no outer life."[5] Apparently, the author was not reading about the same newspaper strip hero millions of others had read about for sixty years. This kind of uninformed analysis was, however, not unique to just one or two publications.

When all is said and done, Warren Beatty's *Dick Tracy* was a very important, highly successful movie. The cartoonish appearance of settings and backdrops which relied on three primary colors— red, blue, and yellow—and the secondary color green was magnificent. The cinematography was legendary and in some ways yet unequalled. And, perhaps most important, without Warren Beatty it is doubtful that any Dick Tracy movie would have been made in contemporary times. Though somewhat exploitive of Chester Gould's creation, the movie is more importantly celebrative of the famous newspaper police detective and his legacy.

Imitation is indeed the greatest form of flattery, and when all the criticisms have passed, this is one thing that should be remembered about this movie. *Mad* magazine spoofed the Beatty movie in its 300th issue (January 1991), thus paying tribute to a tribute to Gould's *Dick Tracy*. John Moore and Kyle Baker produced a three-volume graphic novel which, like Andy Warhol's 1960 painting of Dick Tracy and Sam Catchem entitled "Dick Tracy," was a somewhat unsettling, somewhat disappointing pop art interpretation which compromised but nonetheless paid tribute to *Dick Tracy*.[6] Chester Gould's original newspaper comic strip was so good, so popularly appealing through the years, that many people have felt obligated to wrestle with it, to interpret it, and to assimilate it into their own world views and creative endeavors. Whether one likes or dislikes the 1990 movie *Dick Tracy* — clearly, most people justifiably like the production — it is important to remember the original source to which it pays tribute. The film is best appreciated as a compliment to, and imitation and celebration of, Chester Gould's creative masterpiece.

Credits

Cast, in order of appearance: *Dick Tracy* Warren Beatty, *Kid* Charlie Korsmo, *McGillicuddy* Michael Donovan O'Donnell, *Stooge* Jim Wilkey, *Shoulders* Stig Eldred, *The Rodent* Neil Summers, *The Brow* Chuck Hicks, *Little Face* Lawrence Steven Meyers, *Flattop* William Forsythe, *Itchy* Ed O'Ross, *Tess Trueheart* Glenne Headly, *Soprano* Marvelee Cariaga, *Baritone* Michael Gallup, *Sam Catchem* Seymour Cassel, *Pat Patton* James Keane, *Chief Brandon* Charles Durning, *Reporters* Allen Garfield, John Schuck, Charles Fleischer, *Breathless Mahoney* Madonna, *88 Keys* Mandy Patinkin, *Lips Manlis* Paul Sorvino, *Lips' Bodyguard* Robert Costanzo, *Customer at Raid* Jack Kehoe, *Lips' Cop* Marshall Bell, *Doorman* Michael G. Hagerty, *Lefty Moriarty* Lew Horn, *Diner Patron* Arthur Malet, *Mike* Tom Signorelli, *Steve the Tramp* Tony Epper, *Big Boy Caprice* Al Pacino, *Numbers* James Tolkan, *Pruneface* R.G. Armstrong, *Mumbles* Dustin Hoffman, *Mrs. Green* Kathy Bates, *Lab Technicians* Jack Goode, Jr., Ray Stoddard, *D.A. Fletcher* Dick Van Dyke, *Store Clerk* Hamilton Camp, *Cops at Tess'* Ed McCready, Colm Meaney, *Texie Garcia* Catherine O'Hara, *Influence* Henry Silva, *Ribs Mocca* Robert Beecher, *Spaldoni* James Caan, *Bartender* Bert Remsen, *Judge Harper* Frank Campanella, *Club Ritz Patrons* Sharmagne Leland-St. John, Bing Russell, *Bug Bailey* Michael J. Pollard, *Uniform Cop at Ritz* Tom Finnegan, *Newspaper Vendor* Billy Clevenger, *Radio Announcers* Ned Claflin, John Moschitta, Jr., Neil Ross, Walker Edmiston, *Mrs. Trueheart* Estelle Parsons, *Forger* Ian Wolfe, *Welfare Person* Mary Woronov, *Night Clerk* Henry Jones, *Old Man at Hotel* Mike Mazurki, *Dancers* Rita Bland, Lada Boder, Dee Hengstler, Liz Imperio, Michelle Johnston, Karyne Ortega, Karen Russell, *Stunt Coordinator* Billy Burton, *Stunts* Gary Baxley, William H. Burton, Steve Chambers, Gilbert B. Combs, Louie Elias, Randy Hall, Bear Hudkins, Duane Katz, Larry Nicholas, Dennis Scott.

Technical Credits: *Produced and Directed by* Warren Beatty, *Written by* Jim Cash & Jack Epps, Jr. Based on characters created by Chester Gould for the Dick Tracy® comic strip distributed by Tribune Media Services, Inc. *Executive Producers* Barrie M. Osborne, Art Linson & Floyd Mutrux, *Cinematography by* Vittorio Storaro AIC-A.S.C., *Production Designer* Richard Sylbert, *Editor* Richard Marks, *Co-Producer* John Landau, *Costume Designer* Milena Canonero, *Casting by* Jackie Burch, *Original Songs by* Stephen Sondheim, *Music by* Danny Elfman, *Visual Effects Produced by* Michael Lloyd, Harrison Ellenshaw, *Unit Production Manager* Jon Landau, *First Assistant Director* Jim Van Wyck, *Second Assistant Director* Princess McLean, *Special Character Make-up by* John Caglione, Jr., Doug Drexler, *Musical*

Numbers Staged by Jeffrey Hornaday, *Associate Producer* Jim Van Wyck, *Production Supervisor* Rodney M. Liber, *Art Director* Harold Michelson, *Set Decorator* Rick Simpson, *Supervising Sound Editor* Dennis Drummond, *Music Editor* Bob Badami, *Special Consultant* Bo Goldman, *Associate Costume Designer* Judianna Makovsky, *Make-up Consultant* Richard Dean, *Head Costume Supervisor* Robert Chase, *Men's Costume Supervisor* Bruce R. Hogard, *Women's Costume Supervisor* Elisabetta Beraldo, *Costumers* John M. Young, Alice Daniels, Bernadene Morgan, Diah Wymont, Vicki Graef, *Make-up Artist* Cheri Minns, *Assistant Make-up* Hallie D'Amore, *Hairstylist* Lynda Gurasich, *Assistant Hairstylist* Virginia Hadfield, *Key Character Make-up Artist* Kevin Haney, *Special Character Makeup Artists* Ve Neill, Craig Reardon, *Lab Manager* Anthony Fredrickson, *Lab Crew* Gregory Smith, Bruce Fuller, Gil Mosko, *Lab Coordinator* Dawn Severdia, *Camera Operators* Enrico Umetelli, James M. Anderson, *1st Assistant Camera* Giuseppe Alberti, Billy Clevenger, *2nd Assistant Camera* Deborah Morgan, Jeffrey Thorin, *Additional 2nd Assistant Camera* Lorna Wiley, *Script Supervisor* Ana Maria Quintana, *Sound Mixer* Thomas Causey, *Boom Operator* Joseph Brennan, *Second Boom* Richard Kite, *Video Assist* Bradford Ralston, *Production Associates* George Bamber, Carol Kim, *Chief Lighting Technician* Gary Tandrow, *Assistant Chief Lighting Technician* Steve McGee, *Rigging Gaffer* Kevin J. Lang, *Dimmer Operator* Fabio Cafolla, *Electricians* Michael J. Bailey, George Dunagan, Brad Emmons, James Keys, John Brumshagen, Art Monzo, Charles Spillar, Montey Menapace, *Key Grip* Decker, *Best Boy Grip* Hank Sheppherd, *Dolly Grip* Bernie Schwartz, *Grips* John Phillip Morris III, Matthew Nelson, Gregg Guellow, *Property Master* C.J. Maguire, *Assistant Property Master* Frank L. Brown, *Special Effects Coordinator* Larry Cavanaugh, *Special Effects Supervisor* Bruce Steinheimer, *Special Effects* Casey Cavanaugh, Dave Kelsey, Joe Montenegro, John Stirber, Ron MacInnes, Ed Felix, *1st Assistant Editor* David Moritz, *2nd Assistant Editors* Karen Rasch, Stephanie Ng, *Apprentice Editors* Maria Lee Silver, Stephen L. Meek, Margaret Guinee, *Supervising Sound Effects Editor* Patrick Drummond, *Sound Effects Editors* Jacqueline Cristianini, John S. Wilkinson, Jr., Joan Giammarco, *Supervising Dialogue Editor* George H. Anderson, *Dialogue Editors* Lucy Coldsnow, David Giammarco, *Supervising ADR Editor* Nicholas Vincent Korda, *ADR Editors* Beth Bergeron, Mary Andrews, Karen I. Stern, Jeff Watts, *Foley Editors* Joe R. Dorn, Michael Dressel, *1st Assistant Sound Editor* Kevin Barlia, *Assistant Dialogue Editor* Margaret Guinee, *Assistant Foley Editors* Renee Tondelli, Valeria Davidson, *Assistant ADR Editors* Michele Perrone, Jonathan Klein, *Assistant Music Editor* Andrew Silver, *Assistant Sound Editors* Carol A. Fleming, Karen L. Minahan, Brenda Sowa, Anne Grodzicki Haschka, Lisa Dorney, *Additional Assistant Editors* Karen Wanderman, John Ganem, *Apprentice Sound Editors* Richmond Riedel, Roy Seeger, *Production Coordinator* Jacqueline George, *Assistant Production Coordinator* Rachel Jaffe, *Production Secretary* Penny Segal, *Location Manager* Judson Schwartz, *Accountant* Paul "Numbers" Steinke, *Assistant Accountant* Barbara Gutman, *Payroll Accountant* Connie Dolph, *2nd Assistant Director* Brian Fong, *DGA Trainees* Mark Catone, Cynthia A. Potthast, *Producer Associate* Maggie Kusik, *Post-Production Associate* Jane Payne, *Administrative Assistant* Michael Davison, *Assistant to Richard Sylbert* Sharmagne Leland-St. John, *Lead Set Designers* James J. Murakami, Henry Alberti, *Set Designer* Eric Orbom, *Leadman* Mike Higelmire, *Set Dressers* John Scott III, William Wright, Richard Bisutti, *Sculptor* Thomas Prosser, *Storyboard Illustrator* Maurice Zuberano, *Matte Layout Illustrator* Leon R. Harris, *Set Illustrator* William Major, *Art Department Assistant* Pamela Glintenkamp, *Construction Coordinator* Roger Irvin, *Construction Foremen* William Iiams, Bennett Sperber, Thomas Lawson, *Paint Foreman* David Goldstein, *Production Assistants* G. Spence Bove, Scott Fort, Michael Fitzpatrick, Alisa Statman, Victor Bazaz, Aaron Osborne, Michael Gurasich, Brent Lon Hershman, *Post-Production Assistants* Marc Story, Letitia J. Rogers, *Studio Teacher* Laura Gary, *Unit Publicists* Pat Newcomb, Dick Guttman, *Still Photographer* Peter Sorel, *Casting Assistant* Ferne Cassel, *Extras Casting* Carissa Blix/Cenex Casting, *ADR Voice Casting* Barbara Harris, *Sound Re-Recorded at* Todd A-O/Glen Glenn Studios, *Re-Recording Mixers* Chris Jenkins, David E. Campbell, C.A.S., D.M. Hemphill, Steve Pederson, Paul Sharpe, *Sound Engineer* Jack Snyder, *Sound Re-Recordist* Scott Austin, *P.D.L.* Pete Gregory, J.D. Ward, *Special Sound Processing* Craig Harris, *Foley by* Taj Soundworks, *Foley Artists* John Roesch, Ellen Heuer, *Foley Recorded by* Greg Orloff, *Visual Effects* Buena Vista Visual Effects Group, *Visual Effects Producer* Brooke Berton, *Visual Effects Production Supervisor* Lynda Lemon, *Supervising Visual Effects Coordinator* Carolyn Soper, *Optical Supervisor* Kevin Koneval, *Effects Camera Supervisor* Peter Montgomery,

284 Dick Tracy and American Culture

Line-up Supervisor Bernie Gagliano, *Matte Artists* Michele Moen, Paul Lasaine, Tom Gilleon, David Mattingly, *Assistant Matte Artist* Lucy Tanashian, *Effects Camera Operators* Glenn Campbell, Stephen Brooks, David R. Hardberger, Dick Kendall, Brandy Hill, Philip Huff, *Effects Animators* Allen Gonzales, S.O.C., Samuel Recinos, *Effects Editors* Rob Yamamoto, Kelly Tartan, *Optical Cameramen* Douglas R. Ulm, James Mann, S.O.C., James L. Clay, Steve Rundell, *Visual Effects Coordinator* Melissa Taylor, *Optical Libraian* Brian Raymond, *Post-Production Controller* Kim Costalupes, *Graphics Artist* Linda Folden, *Auditors* Gayle Fraser-Baigelman, Sharon Simon.

    Miniature Shoot: *Director of Photography* Bill Neil, *Production Associate* Thomas D. Adelman, *Camera Operator* Peter Montgomery, *Gaffer* Mark Cane, *Electrician* Mark Hadland, *Key Grip* Fred Albrecht, *Grip* Essil Massinburg, *Additional Miniature Photography* The Chandler Group, *Miniatures Provided by* Stetson Visual Services, Inc., *Miniature Supervisor* Mark Stetson, *Chief Mechanical Design* Robert Spurlock, *Chief Modelmaker* Tom Valentine, *Modelmakers* Dennis Schultz, Ian Hunter, *Modelshop Coordinator* Laurel Schneider, *Transportation Coordinator* Joel Marrow, *Transportation Captain* Dusty Saunders, *Mechanic* Robert Johnson, *Drivers* Randy Cantor, John Marendi, John Pratt, Lucianne Renfro, Dennis Yank, Jim Vargas, *Craft Service* John Moy.

    Second Unit: *Directors* Billy Burton, Richard Marks, Barrie M. Osborne, *Director of Photography* James M. Anderson, *Camera Operator* George Mooradian, *1st Assistant Director* Paul C. Moen, *Video Assist* Dwight Dalzell, *Sound Mixer* James E. Webb, *Boom Operator* Randy Johnson, *Costumes* Thomas Johnson, Colin Booth, *Make-up* John Norin, *Hairstylist* Carol Meikle, *Property Masters* Rudy Reachi, Joseph R. Olsen, *Script Supervisor* Wayne Damore, *Title Design* Wayne Fitzgerald, *Opticals* Cinema Research Corporation, Clayton R. Marsh. *Color Timer* Carlo Labella, *Negative Cutter* Donah Bassett, *Post-Production Accounting* Prep/Shoot/Post, *Orchestrations* Steve Bartek, *Additional Orchestrations* Shirley Walker, *Supervising Copyist* Joel Franklin, *Contractor* Patti Fidelibus, *Score Conducted by* Shirley Walker, *Score Recorded by* Dennis Sands at Columbia Studios, *Score Mixed by* Shawn Murphy at CBS Television City, *Songs Performed by Madonna Recorded by* Bill Bottrell at Ocean Way Recording, *Mixed by* Brian Maulouf at CBS Television City, *Dick Tracy Album Executive Producer* Seymour Stein, *Producer* Andy Paley.

    Songs: "Sooner or Later (I Always Get My Man)," written by Stephen Sondheim, performed by Madonna, arranged by Jeremy Lubbock, strings arranged by Shirley Walker, courtesy of Sire Records; "More," written by Stephen Sondheim, performed by Madonna, arranged by Jeremy Lubbock, courtesy of Sire Records; "What Can You Lose," written by Stephen Sondheim, performed by Madonna and Mandy Patinkin, arranged by Shirley Walker, courtesy of Sire Records; "Live Alone and Like It," written by Stephen Sondheim, performed by Mel Torme; "Back in Business," written by Stephen Sondheim, performed by Janis Siegel, Cheryl Bentyne and Lorraine Feather, arranged by Jeremy Lubbock, vocal arrangement by Janis Siegel; "Die Schlumpf" (opera sequence), composed and conducted by Thomas Pasatieri, performed by Marvelee Cariaga and Michael Gallup; "Pep, Vim and Verve," written by Bill Elliott, Ned Claflin and Andy Paley, performed by Jeff Vincent and Andy Paley; "You're in the Doghouse Now," written by Andy Paley, Jeff Lass, Mike Kernan and Ned Claflin, performed by Brenda Lee, courtesy of Warner Bros. Records; "Some Lucky Day," written by Mike Kernan and Andy Paley, performed by Andy Paley; "Now I'm Following You," written by Andy Paley, Jeff Lass, Ned Claflin and Jonathan Paley, performed by Andy Paley; "Rompin' & Stompin'," written by Jeff Vincent and Ned Claflin, performed by Al Jarreau, courtesy of Reprise Records; "Ridin' the Rails," written by Ned Claflin and Andy Paley, performed by k.d. lang and Take 6, k.d. lang courtesy of Sire Records, Take 6 courtesy of Reprise Records; "Blue Nights," written by Andy Paley, Jeff Lass and Jonathan Paley, performed by Tommy Page, courtesy of Sire Records; "It Was the Whiskey Talkin' (Not Me)," written by Andy Paley, Ned Claflin, Jonathan Paley and Mike Kernan, performed by Jerry Lee Lewis; "Looking Glass Sea," written by Vince Clarke and Andy Bell, performed by Vince Clarke and Andy Bell of Erasure, Vince Clarke and Andy Bell courtesy of Mute Records.

    The following albums available on Sire Records: Madonna's "I'm Breathless," "Dick Tracy," "Dick Tracy" the Original Score, composed by Danny Elfman.

    Costumes made by Western Costume. Dick Tracy rain coats made by Burburry's. Furs by Somper Furs of Beverly Hills.

    Special thanks: Craig Baxley; Dr. Leroy Perry, Chiropractor and The International Sportsmedicine Institute. Color Processing and E.N.R. Prints by Technicolor®. MPAA #30562. Dolby Stereo®. Dick Tracy® is a registered trademark of Tribune Media Services, Inc. This motion picture was created by Touchstone Pictures. ©MCMXC Touchstone Pictures. All Rights Reserved. Distributed by Buena Vista Pictures Distribution, Inc. This film is rated PG.

Notes

1. Thomas Godfrey, "What Have Hollywood, Warren Beatty, and Madonna Done to 'Plain Clothes' Tracy?" *The Armchair Detective* Vol. 24, No. 1 (Winter 1991), pp. 16–18. The 1990 *Dick Tracy* movie aired on Valentine's Day (Sunday, February 14), 1993, beginning at 9:00 p.m. E.S.T. on ABC television.

2. Hugh Boulware, "Headly's Headway: From Steppenwolf to 'Dick Tracy' and Back (Briefly)." *Chicago Tribune*, Sunday, July 1, 1990, Section 13, pp. 6–7.

3. Donna Faulk, "Dick Tracy's 'Kid.'" *Wausau Daily Herald*, 1990.

4. Ibid.

5. John Russell, "How a 30's Stiff Became a Charmer for the 90's." *The New York Times*, Sunday, June 10, 1990, Section 2, pp. 1, 36.

6. Warhol apparently did more than one tribute to Dick Tracy. The painting referenced here features profiles of Dick Tracy and Sam Catchem, and was done on canvas. In 1960 also, Warhol did a crayon rendering of Chester Gould's famous comic strip detective.

CHAPTER 9

The Second Most Famous Detective

"You know that there is another man, then?"—Dr. John Watson in *The Hound of the Baskervilles* (*The Strand Magazine,* January, 1902) by Arthur Conan Doyle

The Great Depression was the birthplace of numerous significant, enduring socio-historic events and advancements in American culture. Among these was the emergence a variety of popular media like Big Little Books, Feature Books, and comic books; other existing media like motion pictures, pulp magazines, and comic strips evolved and flourished. In 1931, a comic strip was born which documented American social history by chronicling a major event of the day—the "war on crime." It took depictions of violence to new graphic heights on the newspaper comics page. Storylines and rogues were intentional exaggerations of actual historic events and people. It was Chester Gould's *Dick Tracy*.

Tracy was born out of the ashes of the Depression, just as the mythic phoenix was born out of death. The success of this newspaper comic strip, in terms of reflecting cultural history in a meaningful fashion and in terms of commerciality, should be attributed to Chester Gould's ability (and the abilities of his assistants and successors on *Tracy*) to tap into social consciousness, to carefully blend convention and invention, reality and fantasy, and present the result in a fashion palatable to readers. With the close of the Depression and the onset of World War II, *Dick Tracy* could have easily fallen into obscurity. Instead, Gould turned the war years into some of

Tracy's finest hours. *Dick Tracy* grew with changing cultural history and social sentiment, and Chester Gould, himself a product and producer of American culture, remained a dedicated student of newspaper headlines and police procedures. His cultural inheritances and personal experiences and observations shaped his mindset into one highly congruent with established public sentiment. In recent years, Max Allan Collins and Dick Locher have carried on this tradition.

In terms of reality, fantasy, and an integration of the two, the *Dick Tracy* story is a beautifully crafted epic of modern times, and a chronicle of American socio-political history. If Arthur Conan Doyle's Sherlock Holmes is the most famous fictional detective of all time, Dick Tracy is assuredly the second most famous. The passage of time will provide new perspectives, new appreciation, and new credibility for Chester Gould, *Dick Tracy*, and all those who have been a part of the house of Dick Tracy. In recent years, Max Collins and Dick Locher have taken *Tracy* to new levels of success and vitality, making it in the Nineties the number one adventure continuity of modern comic art. It remains the most highly culturally representative newspaper comic strip of all time.

Dick Tracy at its best has always been a system of language, a system of symbols; it has frequently been Art with a capital

Newspapers, Circulations, Readerships

Date	Estimated Newspapers Buying Dick Tracy*	Estimated Readership†	Source of Information
end of 1932	22 newspapers		Ellen Mills Ewing, *Oregonian* (5/15/44)
end of 1933	44 newspapers		Ellen Mills Ewing, *Oregonian* (5/14/44)
May 1944	180 newspapers		Ellen Mills Ewing, *Oregonian* (5/14/44)
August 1947		26,000,000	*Life* (8/25/47)
May 1953	more than 400 newspapers	90,000,000	*TV Guide* (5/1/53)
December 1955	409 newspapers (U.S. and Canada)	24,000,000 (43 countries§)	*New York Sunday News Magazine*
October 1956	more than 500 newspapers worldwide		George Brandenburg, *Editor and Publisher* (10/6/56)
October 14, 1956	more than 450 newspapers	60,000,000 to 70,000,000	Charles Collins *New York Sunday News* (10/14/56)
late 1950s	550 newspapers		Lloyd Sachs, *Memories Magazine* (June/July 1990)
October 1961	569 newspapers (U.S. and Canada)		*Newsweek* (10/16/61)
April 1962	507 newspapers	80,000,000 daily 110,000,000 Sundays	Dennis Orphan, *The Quill* (4/62)
Winter 1967	675 newspapers		William K. Stuckey, *Northwestern Review* (Winter 1967)
June 1970	over 500 newspapers		William Johnston's novel *Dick Tracy* (1970)
March 1974	375 newspapers	38,000,000	Mark Starr, *Wall Street Journal* (3/12/74)
Summer 1990	close to 300 or 320 newspapers		Dick Locher, *Comic Values Monthly Special #1* (Summer 1990)
Summer 1990	about 250 newspapers		Lloyd Sachs, *Memories Magazine* (June/July 1990)

*Unless otherwise noted, these figures could be estimates for U.S. newspapers only, for U.S. and Canada newspapers only, or for worldwide newspapers.

†Unless otherwise noted, these figures could refer to readerships or circulations, which, depending on definitions of each, very likely mean quite different things. Also, unless otherwise noted, these figures could refer to daily, Sunday, and or an average of daily/Sunday readerships/circulations.

§It is unclear whether this figure includes the U.S. and Canada.

"A." It has been a beautiful configuration of black ink line drawings and a first-rate morality play that represents the "best that has been known and thought." *Dick Tracy* is a comic strip epic which blends real social history and police procedure with exaggerated grotesque rogues who epitomize the repulsiveness inherent in evil and its perpetrators.

The numbers of newspapers which have featured *Dick Tracy* through the years, and these newspapers' respective circulations and readerships, serve as one sort of barometer of the public acceptance and pervasiveness of this particular comic strip. While the figures compiled and listed here may be somewhat general, they do indicate two important things. First, almost since its inception in 1931, *Dick Tracy* has reached literally millions of people. Second, *Tracy's* popularity peaked in the very late 1950s and very early 1960s — not the early and middle 1940s, the period acknowledged by most *Tracy* fans and scholars as the best era for the famous comic strip.

Another barometer of popularity is imitation and satire of the original work. We have seen in chapters 2 and 3 and again in Dick Moores' biography in Chapter 5, as well as other places, that Chester Gould's *Dick Tracy* served as an inspiration for other storytellers, comic strip artists, and even politicians like J. Edgar Hoover. The original cultural product, the initial creator's conception, is truly significant as a cultural barometer if it is deemed worthy of imitation by so many talented individuals. Andy Warhol's renditions of Dick Tracy prove this. It was indeed heartening to see several very famous comic strips like *Gasoline Alley, Pogo,* and *Frank and Ernest* pay tribute to *Dick Tracy* during the summer of 1990 when the blockbuster movie was released. The tribute in *Pogo* was perhaps the most elaborate as the writer-artist team of Larry Doyle and Neal Sternecky (successors to the famous Walt Kelly) presented a comic strip within a comic strip called *Dog Gravy* which featured Beauregard Bugleboy as Detective Dog Gravy.

The greatest tribute paid to Chester Gould and *Dick Tracy* by another famous comic strip artist and storyteller and his creation was, of course, Al Capp's *Fearless Fosdick* in his *Li'l Abner* strip. This parody of Gould's famous work appeared sporadically in Capp's *Li'l Abner* between 1942 and 1977. (*Li'l Abner* itself ran from 1934 until 1977.) Written by an *Abner* character named Lester Gooch (himself an exaggeration of Chester Gould), the *Fearless Fosdick* comic strip poked fun at all of *Dick Tracy's* major characteristics and eccentricities — Fosdick's square jaw was even more pronounced than Tracy's, violence

was used much more gratuitously in *Fosdick* than in *Tracy* (and rarely with any meaning), grotesques were even more outrageous. In short, *Fearless Fosdick* was a great deal of fun but must be taken seriously as a loving tribute to Chester Gould and *Dick Tracy*. Kitchen Sink Press of Princeton, Wisconsin, has begun a series of *Fearless Fosdick* reprint collections. The first volume is introduced most adeptly by Max Allan Collins. All the stories are entertaining.[1]

There have been other tributes to Chester Gould and *Dick Tracy* through the years. In its October/November 1954 edition, *Panic* comic book featured a story called "Tick Dracy" by "Justfer Gold" Elder which parodied Chester Gould's famous newspaper strip.[2] In its January 1991 issue, *Mad Magazine* published its parody of the 1990 Warren Beatty film entitled "Schtick Tracy."[3] In addition, numerous companies have both legally and illegally used Dick Tracy as a marketing device for their products. Five companies which did so legally include the American Newspaper Publishers Association Foundation, A.B. Dick, ITT, Koh-I-Noor, and Autolite.

In the 1990s one more person and one more organization deserve special acknowledgment for their tributes to *Dick Tracy* and all the people — fans and scholars alike — who have been a part of the house of Dick Tracy. Andrew Feighery and the Dick Tracy Fan Club provide club members with a lengthy, beautiful magazine which features both fan interests and a large array of intelligent, insightful works of scholarship. *The Dick Tracy Fan Club* (the name of the magazine as well as the club itself) is fascinating, even-handed, and beautifully produced. Feighery's tremendous efforts are obvious in the publication. Chester Gould would have approved.[4]

With some luck, but more importantly the guidance of Max Allan Collins and Dick Locher and the *Chicago Tribune*

Fearless Fosdick in Al Capp's *Li'l Abner*.

and Tribune Media Services, Chester Gould's 1931 brainchild will thrive for years to come. The Dick Tracy legacy continues with no end in sight. And, this is how Gould would have wanted it. There is room for much more academic and intellectual inquiry in regard to *Dick Tracy*, and individuals like Andy Feighery, Bill Blackbeard, Shel Dorf, Matt Masterson, and others too numerous to mention have made this abundantly clear. One can see Gould's genius each day in the guise of that pillar of justice, morality, and hope, that man in the trenchcoat and snap-brim fedora whose exploits unfold daily in the pages of the newspaper — Dick Tracy.

Notes

1. Al Capp, *Fearless Fosdick* (Princeton, Wisconsin: Kitchen Sink Press, Inc., 1990). Foreword by Max Allan Collins. See also: Al Capp, *Fearless Fosdick: The Hole Story* (Princeton, Wisconsin: Kitchen Sink Press, Inc., 1992); Max Allan Collins, "Strip Search: Fearless Fosdick: The 'Ideel' Comic Strip Detective." *Comics Feature* 33 (January-February, 1985), pp. 14–15, 38–40.

2. "Tick Dracy." *Panic* Vol. 1, No. 5 (New York: Tiny Tot Comics, Inc., October/November 1954).

3. Dick Debartolo and Angelo Torres, "Schtick Tracy." *Mad* 300 (January 1991), pp. 15–19.

4. To subscribe and become a member write: *Dick Tracy Fan Club*, Andrew Feighery, Publisher, P.O. Box 632, Manitou Springs, CO 80829.

Bibliography

The citations listed in this bibliography represent only a fraction of the sources available on *Dick Tracy* and related topics. However, in the judgment of the author, these citations include some of the very best work done on the topic. Of the sources not included herein, many have been purposely omitted as some are superficial and redundant, some are inaccurate in a variety of degrees, and some are biased to the point of being useless. The real authority on *Tracy* passed away in May of 1985. The most credible of those authorities who remain are family members of, and assistants to, Mr. Gould. Of these, Max Allan Collins, Jean Gould O'Connell, and Dick Locher are primary keepers and defenders of the legend.

A.B. Dick advertisements. (Dick Tracy appeared in several advertisements in newspapers for this copying machine circa 1987.)

Abel, Robert H., and White, David Manning, eds. *The Funnies: An American Idiom.* London: Collier-Macmillan Ltd., 1963.

The Animated Adventures of Dick Tracy. U.P.A. Productions of America. Henry G. Saperstein, Executive Director; Abe Levitow, Director. 13-volume set of VHS videocassettes which contains the entire run issued in 1990-91 by Paramount studios.

Ansen, David, and Abramson, Pamela. "Tracymania: Disney and Beatty Gamble on a Square-Jawed Comic-strip Cop—and Scramble to Cover Their Bet." *Newsweek,* June 25, 1990, pp. 44–48.

Archie's T.V. Funnies with Dick Tracy, Vol. 1. (VHS tape). South Plainfield, N.J.: New Age Video, Inc. Program copyright 1968.

"Are Comics Bad for Children?" *Rotarian* 56 (March 1940), pp. 18–19; *Reply* 56 (May 1940), p. 2.

Arnott, Duane S. "Dick Tracy: The Lost Casebook." *Comics Scene* 16. New York. (December 1990), pp. 57–60.

Associated Press. "Dick Tracy Strips Stolen in N.Y." October 1989.

Astor, David. "Upcoming *Dick Tracy* Film Aiding Comic." *Editor and Publisher,* Vol. 123, No. 21 (May 26, 1990), p. 58.

_____. "*Dick Tracy* and *Gasoline Alley* Pullings." *Editor and Publisher,* Vol. 124, No. 45 (November 9, 1991), pp. 36–37.

Autolite advertisements. (Dick Tracy appeared in several comic strips which promoted these spark plugs circa 1966.)

Bainbridge, John. "Chester Gould: The Harrowing Adventures of His Cartoon Hero, Dick Tracy, Give Vicarious Thrills to Millions." *Life,* August 14, 1944, pp. 43–53.

Baker, Robert A., and Nietzel, Michael T. *Private Eyes: One Hundred and One Knights.* Bowling Green, Ohio: Bowling Green State University Popular Press, 1985.

Ballard, Todhunter. *Home to Texas.* New York: Dell, 1974.

Ballard, W.T. *The Seven Sisters.* New York: Pocket Books, October 1962.

"Banking on 'Dick Tracy.'" *Lansing State Journal,* May 31, 1990. (Wire service story.)

Barbour, Alan G. *Cliffhanger: A Pictorial History of the Motion Picture Serial.* New York: A&W Publishers, Inc., 1977.

_____. *Days of Thrills and Adventure.* New York: Macmillan, 1970.

_____. *A Thousand and One Delights.* New York: Collier Books, 1971.

Barnett, Buddy. "Dick Tracy on T.V." *Videosonic Arts* 2 (Summer 1990). North Hollywood, California: Videosonic Arts.

Becker, Stephen. *Comic Art in America*. New York: Simon and Schuster, 1959.

Benjamin, Christopher, and Eckes, Dennis W. *The Sport Americana Price Guide to Non-Sports Cards*. Laurel, Md.: Den's Collectors Den, and Lakewood, Ohio: Edgewater Book Company, Inc., 1983.

Benvenuti, Stefano, and Rizzoni, Gianni. *The Whodunit: An Informal History of Detective Fiction*. New York: Macmillan, 1980.

Benton, Mike. *The Illustrated History of Crime Comics: The Taylor History of Comics #5*. Dallas: Taylor Publishing Co., 1993.

Berger, Arthur Asa. *The Comic-Stripped American*. Baltimore: Penguin, 1973.

Best of The Chicago Tribune #2. Toronto: Dragon Lady Press, 1985 (special Dick Tracy issue).

Binder, Al, and Jaediker, Kermit. "Just Before the Battle, Tracy." *New York Daily News*, May 9, 1944.

Biskind, Peter. "Warren and Me." *Premiere*, vol. 3, no. 11 (July 1990), pp. 52–55.

"Black and White: Ken Tucker Rates the Daily Comic Strips." *Entertainment Weekly*, No. 34 (October 5, 1990), pp. 34–47.

Blackbeard, Bill, and Williams, Martin, eds. *The Smithsonian Collection of Newspaper Comics*. Washington, D.C.: Smithsonian Institution Press, and New York: Harry N. Abrams, 1977.

Blackthorne 3-D Series 8. "Dick Tracy in 3-D." El Cajon, Calif.: Blackthorne Publishing Co., July 1986.

Bonifer, Mike. *Dick Tracy: The Making of the Movie*. New York: Bantam, 1990.

"Bonny Braids." *The New Yorker* 27 (July 7, 1951), pp. 14–15.

"B.O.'s Wedding Night." *Newsweek*, August 26, 1946, p. 57.

Boulware, Hugh. "Headly's Headway: From Steppenwolf to 'Dick Tracy' and Back (Briefly)." *Chicago Tribune*, Sunday, July 1, 1990, Section 13, pp. 6–7.

Boyar, Jay. "The Changing Profile of Dick Tracy." *The Orlando Sentinel*, Sunday, May 20, 1990, pp. F1, F2.

Bradbury, Ray, and Carter, Graydon. "The Making of *Dick Tracy*." *Vogue*, vol. 180, no. 6 (June 1990), pp. 242–244.

Brandenburg, George A. "Gould-Tracy, Partners in Crime for 25 Years." *Editor and Publisher*, October 6, 1956, pp. 14, 90.

Broes, Arthur T. "*Dick Tracy*: The Early Years." *Journal of Popular Culture* 25:4 (Spring 1992). Bowling Green, Ohio: Bowling Green State University Popular Press, pp. 97–122.

Brooks, Tim, and Marsh, Earle. *The Complete Directory to Prime Time Network T.V. Shows: 1946–Present*, Third Edition. New York: Ballantine, 1985.

Bulkley, Nat. "Generosity of Guests Gives Dick Tracy Museum a Boost." *Northwest Herald* (Crystal Lake, Ill.), Monday, November 16, 1992, Community section.

Burden, Angela. "Chester Gould's Daughter Recalls Life with Father." *Northwest Herald* (Crystal Lake, Ill.), Wednesday, June 13, 1990, Community section.

Buxton, Frank, and Owen, Bill. *The Big Broadcast: 1920–1950 — A New, Revised, and Greatly Expanded Edition of* Radio's Golden Age. New York: The Viking Press, 1972.

Cagle, Jess. "Tracy's Case History." *Entertainment Weekly*, No. 86. (Friday, October 4, 1991).

Campbell, Joseph. *The Power of Myth*. New York: Doubleday, 1988.

Campbell, Sara Moores. Letter, June 20, 1992. Santa Barbara, Calif.

Canby, Thomas Y. "Satellites That Serve Us." *National Geographic*, September 1983, pp. 281–291.

Caniff, Milton. *The Complete Color Terry and the Pirates (Sunday and Dailies)*. Princeton, Wis.: Kitchen Sink Press, Inc., and Abington, Pa.: Remco Worldservice Books. 16-volume series, begins 1991.

Capp, Al. *The Best of Li'l Abner*. New York: Avon, 1976.

————. *Fearless Fosdick*. Princeton, Wis.: Kitchen Sink Press, Inc., 1990. Foreword by Max Allan Collins.

————. *Fearless Fosdick: The Hole Story*. Princeton, Wis.: Kitchen Sink Press, Inc., 1992.

————. "'It's Hideously True' — Creator of Li'l Abner Tells Why His Hero Is (Sob!) Wed." *Life*, March 31, 1952, pp. 100–108.

————. *Li'l Abner*. (Daily reprints). Princeton, Wis.: Kitchen Sink Press, Inc. Multi-volume series, begins 1988.

————. *My Well Balanced Life on a Wooden Leg*. Santa Barbara: John Daniel and Company, Publishers, 1991.

————. *The World of Li'l Abner*. New York: Ballantine, 1953.

"Cash Beats the Odds, Fifth Flick on the Way." *The State News*, Friday, October 20, 1989. East Lansing, Mich.: Michigan State University, p. 12.

Caunitz, William J. *Black Sand*. New York: Crown Publishers, Inc., 1989.

_____. *One Police Plaza.* New York: Crown Publishers, Inc., 1984.

_____. *Suspects.* New York: Crown Publishers, Inc., 1986.

Cawelti, John G. *Adventure, Mystery and Romance: Formula Stories as Art and Popular Culture.* Chicago: The University of Chicago Press, 1976.

_____. *The Six-Gun Mystique.* Bowling Green, Ohio: Bowling Green State University Popular Press, 1984.

"Chester Gould: Creator of Dick Tracy." Associated Press, May 1985.

"Chester Gould, Creator of Dick Tracy." *The Cross and Crescent.* Vol. LXXVII, No. 3. Indianapolis. Fall 1990. Publication of the Lambda Chi Alpha Fraternity.

"The Chester Gould Society." Announcement via flyer, Continuing Education Division of Northwestern University.

"Chester Gould's Golden Mouldies: Forty Years of Friends and Fiends." *Esquire,* December 1975, pp. 156–157.

Chicago Tribune. Chester Gould obituary, May 13, 1985.

Cinefantastique, vol. 21, no. 2 (July 1990).

Cinefax . . . the Journal of Cinematic Illusions 44 (November 1990). Special issue on the 1990 Dick Tracy movie. Riverside, Calif.: Valley Printers.

Clark, Kenneth R. "TV Technology Finally Catches Up with Dick Tracy." *Chicago Tribune,* Monday, June 6, 1983, Section 1, p. 14.

Cline, William C. *In the Nick of Time: Motion Picture Sound Serials.* Jefferson, N.C.: McFarland, 1984.

Colborn, Marge. "Dick Tracy Could Correct That Profile." Gannett News Service story appearing in *The Lansing State Journal,* June 28, 1990.

_____. "Keep Your Chin Up, Tracy: Doctors Can Help." *Detroit News,* June 20, 1990.

Collins, Charles. "Happy Birthday, Dick!" *New York Sunday News,* October 14, 1956.

"Collins, Max (Allan), Jr. 1948–," *Contemporary Authors* Vol. 103, p. 95.

Collins, Max Allan. *The Baby Blue Rip-Off.* New York: Walker Publishing, 1983.

_____. *The Baby Blue Rip-Off.* New York: Tom Doherty Associates, Inc., November 1987.

_____. *Bait Money.* New York: Curtis Books, 1973.

_____. *Blood Money.* New York: Curtis Books, 1973.

_____. *The Broker.* New York: Berkley, 1976.

_____. *The Broker's Wife.* New York: Berkley, 1976.

_____. *Bullet Proof.* New York: Bantam, April 1989.

_____. *Butcher's Dozen.* New York: Bantam, 1988.

_____. *The Dark City.* New York: Bantam, June 1987.

_____. *The Dealer.* New York: Berkley, 1976.

_____. *Dick Tracy.* New York: Bantam, June 1990. Novelization of 1990 Warren Beatty movie.

_____. *Dick Tracy Goes to War.* New York: Bantam, 1991.

_____. *Dying in the Post-War World.* Woodstock, Vt.: The Countryman Press, Inc., 1991.

_____. Interview, October 25, 1982, Muscatine, Iowa.

_____. Interview, November 19, 1984, Muscatine, Iowa.

_____. *Kill Your Darlings.* New York: Walker Publishing, 1984.

_____. *Kill Your Darlings.* New York: Tom Doherty Associates, Inc., February 1988.

_____. Letters, January 28, 1982; July 19, 1983; January 21, 1984; June 30, 1984; July 13, 1985. Muscatine, Iowa.

_____. *Midnight Haul.* Woodstock, Vt.: The Countryman Press, 1986.

_____. *Midnight Haul.* New York: Knightsbridge Publishing Company, 1990.

_____. *The Million-Dollar Wound.* New York: St. Martin's Press, 1986.

_____. *The Million-Dollar Wound.* New York: Tom Doherty Associates, Inc., July 1987.

_____. *Murder by the Numbers.* New York: St. Martin's Press, March 1993.

_____. *Neon Mirage.* New York: St. Martin's Press, 1988.

_____. *Neon Mirage: A Novel of Bugsy Siegel's Las Vegas.* New York: Bantam, 1991.

_____. *Nice Weekend for a Murder.* New York: Walker Publishing, September 1986.

_____. *No Cure for Death.* New York: Walker Publishing, 1983.

_____. *No Cure for Death.* New York: Tom Doherty Associates, Inc., April 1987.

_____. *Nolan #1: Bait Money.* New York: Pinnacle Books, Inc., 1981.

_____. *Nolan #2: Blood Money.* New York: Pinnacle Books, Inc., 1981.

_____. *Nolan #3: Fly Paper.* New York: Pinnacle Books, Inc., 1981.

_____. *Nolan #4: Hush Money.* New York: Pinnacle Books, Inc., 1981.

_____. *Nolan #5: Hard Cash.* New York: Pinnacle Books, Inc., 1982.

————. *Nolan #6: Scratch Fever*. New York: Pinnacle Books, Inc., 1982.

————. *Primary Target*. Woodstock, Vt.: Countryman Press, October 1987.

————. *Primary Target*. New York: PaperJacks Ltd., October, 1988.

————. "Private Consultation," in Randisi, Robert J., *Justice for Hire*. New York: The Mysterious Press, 1990.

————. *Quarry*. Woodstock, Vt.: The Countryman Press, 1985. (Formerly *The Broker*.)

————. *Quarry's Cut*. Woodstock, Vt.: The Countryman Press, 1986. (Formerly *The Slasher*.)

————. *Quarry's Deal*. Woodstock, Vt.: The Countryman Press, 1986. (Formerly *The Dealer*.)

————. *Quarry's List*. Woodstock, Vt.: The Countryman Press, 1985. (Formerly *The Broker's Wife*).

————. "Robber's Roost" in *The Further Adventures of Batman, Volume 2: Featuring the Penguin*, edited by Martin H. Greenberg. New York: Bantam Books, Inc., 1992.

————. *A Shroud for Aquarius*. New York: Walker Publishing, 1985.

————. *A Shroud for Aquarius*. New York: Tom Doherty Associates, Inc., June 1988.

————. *The Slasher*. New York: Berkley, 1977.

————. "The Sound of One Hand Clapping," in Greenberg, Martin H., ed., *The Further Adventures of Batman*. New York: Bantam, July 1989.

————. *Spree*. New York: Tom Doherty Associates, Inc., October 1987.

————. *Spree*. New York: Tom Doherty Associates, Inc., July 1988.

————. *Stolen Away* (hardcover). New York: Bantam, June 1991.

————. *Stolen Away* (mass market paperback). New York: Bantam, May 1992.

————. *Stolen Away* (trade paperback). New York: Bantam Books, June 1991.

————. "The Strawberry Teardrop" in Robert Randisi's *The Eyes Have It*. New York: The Mysterious Press, 1984, pp. 26–44.

————. "Strip Search: Dick Tracy," *Comics Feature* 28 (March-April 1984), pp. 14–18.

————. "Strip Search: Dick Tracy: The Fletcher Years, Part One," *Comics Feature* 35 (May-June 1985), pp. 47–50, 61.

————. "Strip Search: Dick Tracy: The Fletcher Years, Part Two," *Comics Feature* 36 (July-August 1985), pp. 43–47.

————. "Strip Search: Fearless Fosdick: The 'Ideel' Comic Strip Detective," *Comics Feature* 33 (January-February 1985), pp. 14–15, 38–40.

————. *Tough Tender*. New York: Carroll and Graf Publishers, Inc., 1991. (Reprints Nolan #5 and #6).

————. *True Crime*. New York: St. Martin's Press, 1984.

————. *True Crime*. New York: Tom Doherty Associates, Inc. December 1986.

————. *True Detective*. New York: St. Martin's Press, 1983.

————, and Beatty, Terry. *The Files of Ms. Tree*, Volume One. Canada: Aardvark-Vanaheim, Inc., 1984.

————, and ————. *Mike Mist Minute Mist-eries* 1. Eclipse Comics, April 1981.

————, and ————. *Ms. Tree*. New York: PaperJacks. July 1988.

————, and ————. *Ms. Tree Quarterly*. New York: DC Comics. Series begins Summer 1990.

————, and ————. *Ms. Tree Summer Special* 1. Long Beach, Calif.: Renegade Press, August 1986.

————, and ————. *Ms. Tree's Thrilling Detective Adventures*. U.S.A.: Eclipse Comics 2/83–7/84; Canada: Aardvark-Vanaheim 8/84–5/85; Long Beach, Calif.: Renegade Press 6/85–6/89.

————, and Fletcher, Rick. *The Complete Max Collins/Rick Fletcher Dick Tracy, No. 1: 50th Anniversary Dick Tracy*. Toronto: Dragon Lady Press, 1986.

————, and ————. *The Complete Max Collins/Rick Fletcher Dick Tracy, No. 2: Who Shot Pat Patton?* Toronto: Dragon Lady Press, 1987.

————, and Greenberg, Martin H., eds. *Dick Tracy: The Secret Files*. New York: Tom Doherty Associates, Inc., 1990.

————, and Javna, John. *The Best of Crime and Detective TV: Perry Mason to Hill Street Blues, The Rockford Files to Murder, She Wrote*. New York: Crown Publishers, Inc., 1988.

————, and Locher, Dick. *Dick Tracy and the Nightmare Machine*. New York: Tom Doherty Associates, Inc., January 1991.

————, and ————, eds. *The Dick Tracy Casebook: Favorite Adventures 1931–1990, Selected by Max Allan Collins and Dick Locher*. New York: St. Martin's Press, 1990.

————, and ————, eds. *Dick Tracy's Fiendish Foes!: A 60th Anniversary Celebration*. New York: St. Martin's Press, October 1991.

_____, and _____. *Thrilling Adventure Strips: Dick Tracy Meets Big Brother* 6. Toronto: Dragon Lady Press, 1986.

_____, and _____. *Thrilling Adventure Strips: Dick Tracy—The Russian Exchange* 10. Toronto: Dragon Lady Press, 1987.

_____, and _____. *U.S. Classics Series: Tracy's Wartime Memories.* Park Forest, Ill.: Ken Pierce, Inc., 1986.

_____, _____, and Fletcher, Rick. *The Complete Max Collins/Rick Fletcher Dick Tracy, No. 3: The Ghost of Itchy.* Toronto: Dragon Lady Press, 1987.

_____, and Traylor, James L. *One Lonely Knight: Mickey Spillane's Mike Hammer.* Bowling Green, Ohio: Bowling Green State University Popular Press, 1984.

_____, and Yronwode, Catherine, eds. *Mickey Spillane's Mike Hammer: The Comic Strip*, Vol. 2. Park Forest, Ill.: Ken Pierce, Inc., 1985.

Color Collector's Guide 1 (Winter 1990); 2 (Winter 1993). Allen Park, Mich.: Archival Photography.

Comics Buyer's Guide 866 (June 22, 1990). Special Dick Tracy issue.

Comics Values Monthly 1. South Salem, N.Y.: Attic Books, Inc., 1990.

Conan Doyle, Sir Arthur. *The Annotated Sherlock Holmes.* New York: Clarkson N. Potter, Inc., 1967. (Annotated in two volumes by William S. Baring-Gould.)

Cooper, Jackie, and Kleiner, Dick. *Please Don't Shoot My Dog: The Autobiography of Jackie Cooper.* New York: William Morrow, 1981.

Corliss, Richard. "Extra! Tracy Is Tops; Warren Beatty Creates the Best Comic-strip Movie Yet." *Time,* vol. 135, no. 25, (June 18, 1990), pp. 74–76.

Counts, Kyle. "Dick Tracy: Gun Blazing, the Comic Strip Detective Blasts the Bad Guys at a Bijou Near You." *Comics Scene* 14 (August 1990), pp. 33–39.

Couperie, Pierre, and Horn, Maurice. *A History of the Comic Strip.* New York: Crown Publishers, Inc., 1967.

Coutros, Pete. "This Cop's the Prize, America's Ace Detective Is Dick Tracy . . . But a Guy Named Chester Gould Is the Real Brains." *New York Sunday News Magazine*, December 18, 1955.

Crane, Roy. *The Complete Wash Tubbs and Captain Easy*, Vols. 1–18. (Daily and Sunday reprints.) New York: Nantier-Beall-Minoustchine Publishing Co., 1987–92.

Crouch, Bill, Jr., ed. *Dick Tracy: America's Most Famous Detective, The Life and Times of Chester Gould's Immortal Sleuth.* Secaucus, N.J.: Citadel, 1987.

_____, and Doucet, Lawrence. *The Authorized Guide to Dick Tracy Collectibles.* Radnor, Pa.: Wallace-Homestead Book Company, 1990.

Culhane, John. "Dick Tracy: The First Law and Order Man." *Argosy*, Vol. 379, No. 6 (June 1974), cover, pp. 20–21, 44–47+.

Cuneen, Joseph, "DT a Frothy Fantasy for 10-Year-Olds of All Ages." *National Catholic Reporter*, Vol. 26, No. 34 (June 28, 1990), 1B or 18.

Daley, Robert. *Year of the Dragon.* New York: New American Library, 1982.

"A Day in the Life of Dick Tracy." *Chicago Sunday Tribune*, January 20, 1946.

Debartolo, Dick, and Torres, Angelo. "Schtick Tracy." *Mad* No. 300 (January 1991).

Dellios, Hugh."Woodstock Brings Home 'Dick Tracy.'" *Chicago Tribune*, Sunday, April 22, 1990, Section 1, p. 17.

_____. "Woodstock Welcomes Home Dick Tracy." *Chicago Tribune*, Thursday, June 14, 1990.

Demaris, Ovid. *Dillinger.* New York: Belmont Tower Books, 1973.

Diaz, Victoria, and the Associated Press. "50 Years of Crime-busting for Tracy." *Detroit Free Press*, October 4, 1981, pp. 1C, 4C.

Dick Tracy. Republic Movie Serial. 15 episodes. 1937.

Dick Tracy (radio series). Mutual Radio, 1935–1937; NBC, 1937–1939; NBC Blue, 1943–1945; ABC, 1945–1948.

"The Case of the Black Pearl of Osiris." Tuesday, February 8 through Friday, February 25, 1938.

Untitled episode. Tuesday, September 14, 1943.

Untitled episode. Thursday, September 30, 1943.

Untitled episode. Thursday, October 7, 1943.

"Espionage at the Circus." Friday, May 5, 1944.

"The Case of the Empty Safe." Tuesday, May 1, 1945.

"The Case of the Buried Treasure." Thursday, September 13, 1945.

"The Case of the Broken Window." Friday, September 13, 1946.

"The Case of the Firebug Murders." One Saturday, 1946.

"The Case of the Dark Corridor." One Saturday, 1946.

"The Case of the No-Account Swindle." Thursday, May 15, 1947.
"The Case of the Crooked Fingers." Monday, July 14, 1947.
"The Case of the Unfunny Clowns." Wednesday, July 23, 1947.
"The Case of the Low Hijack." Monday, August 16, 1947.
"The Case of the Deadly Tip-Off." Wednesday, November 18, 1947.
"The Case of the Deadly Tip-Off." Thursday, November 19, 1947.
"The Case of the Poisonous Timber." Tuesday, December 16, 1947.
"The Case of the Poisonous Timber." Friday, December 19, 1947.
"The Case of the Big Black Box." Wednesday, December 31, 1947.
"The Case of the Big Black Box." Thursday, January 8, 1948.
Dick Tracy (television series). American Broadcasting Company Television, September 13, 1950–
   February 12, 1951.
Dick Tracy: Dailies and Sundays from 3-12-40 to 7-13-40. Long Beach, Calif.: Tony Raiola Publisher,
   Copyright 1983 Chicago Tribune and New York News Syndicate.
Dick Tracy: Dailies and Sundays from 7-13-40 to 10-20-40. Long Beach, Calif.: Tony Raiola
   Publisher, Copyright 1983 Chicago Tribune and New York News Syndicate.
"Dick Tracy: 50 Years of Chasing Colorful Comic Strip Characters." *Milwaukee Journal*, Octo-
   ber 2, 1981.
Dick Tracy Adventures 1. Prescott, Ariz.: Gladstone Publishing, Ltd., May 1991.
Dick Tracy and Flattop/Dick Tracy. Two half-hour *Dick Tracy* television drama episodes copy-
   righted 1952. Marketed on VHS videotape by the Simitar Company of Plymouth, Minnesota.
"Dick Tracy and Other People You May Have Met." *Chicago Sunday Tribune*, April 23, 1944,
   Graphics section, p. 1.
Dick Tracy and the Woo Woo Sisters. New York: Dell Publishers, Inc., 1947.
"'Dick Tracy' Artist Rick Fletcher; Took Over Drawing of Strip in 1977." *Chicago Tribune*,
   March 18, 1983.
"Dick Tracy Authors, Chicago Tribune Sued for Libel by Record Store Owners." AP Wire Service
   article appearing in the *Journal Star* (Peoria, Ill.), Sunday, October 18, 1897.
Dick Tracy Better Little Books. Racine, Wis.: Whitman Publishing Company. (Continued from *Dick
   Tracy Big Little Books*.)
   Second 1400 Series (1938–1940): "Dick Tracy on the High Seas" #1454 (1939), "Dick Tracy
      Returns" #1495 (1939).
   Third 1400 Series (1939–1941): "Dick Tracy the Super Detective" #1488 (1939), "Dick Tracy and
      the Phantom Ship" #1434 (1940), "Dick Tracy and His G-Men" #1439 (1941).
   Fourth 1400 Series (1941–1943): "Dick Tracy vs. Crooks in Disguise" #1479 (1941), "Dick Tracy
      Special F.B.I. Operative" #1449 (1943).
   Fifth 1400 Series (1943–1946): "Dick Tracy on Voodoo Island" #1478 (1944), "Dick Tracy and the
      Wreath Kidnapping Case" #1482 (1945).
   Sixth 1400 Series (1946–1949): "Dick Tracy and Yogee Yamma" #1412 (1946), "Dick Tracy and the
      Mad Killer" #1436 (1947), "Dick Tracy and the Bicycle Gang" #1445 (1948), "Dick Tracy and
      the Tiger Lily Gang" #1460 (1949).
Dick Tracy Big Big Books. Racine, Wis.: Whitman Publishing Company.
   The Adventures of Dick Tracy Detective #4055 (1934).
   The Adventures of Dick Tracy Detective #4055 (1936; identical to 1934 edition with the exception
      of cover illustration).
   Dick Tracy and the Mystery of the Purple Cross #4071 (1938).
Dick Tracy Big Little Books. Racine, Wis.: Whitman Publishing Company.
   700 Series (1932–1936): "The Adventures of Dick Tracy" #707 (1932), "Dick Tracy and Dick Tracy
      Junior" #710 (1933), "Dick Tracy Out West" #723 (1933), "Dick Tracy from Colorado to Nova
      Scotia" #749 (1933), "Dick Tracy from Colorado to Nova Scotia" #749 softcover (1933).
   First 1100 Series (1934–1936): "Dick Tracy and the Stolen Bonds" #1105 (1934); "Dick Tracy Solves
      the Penfield Mystery" #1137 (1934), "Dick Tracy Solves the Penfield Mystery" no number, soft-
      cover (1934), "Dick Tracy and the Boris Arson Gang" #1163 (1935), "Dick Tracy on the Trail
      of Larceny Lu" #1170 (1935), "Dick Tracy in Chains of Crime" #1185 (1936).
   Second 1100 Series (1936–1937): "Dick Tracy and the Racketeer Gang" #1112 (1936).
   First 1400 Series (1937–1938): "Dick Tracy and the Hotel Murders" #1420 (1937), "Dick Tracy and
      the Spider Gang" #1446 (1937), "Dick Tracy and the Man with No Face" #1491 (1938), (Con-
      tinued as *Dick Tracy Better Little Books*)
   2000 Series (1967–1969): "Dick Tracy Encounters Facey" #2001 (1967).

Dick Tracy Coloring Book. Akron, Ohio: Saalfield Publishing Company, 1946.
Dick Tracy Comics Monthly 25–145. New York: Harvey Publications, Inc., March 1950–April 1961.
"Dick Tracy Creator," United Press International, May 1985.
"'Dick Tracy' Creator Cited." *Chicago Tribune,* Tuesday, July 18, 1978.
"'Dick Tracy' Creator Dies." *Chicago Tribune,* Sunday, May 12, 1985, Section 1, p. 7.
Dick Tracy, Detective. Motion Picture, 1945.
Dick Tracy Famous Comic Strip Story Books Series #1100A (Penny Books). Racine, Wis.: Whitman
    Publishing Company, 1938–1939.
  "Dick Tracy Gets His Man"
  "Dick Tracy the Detective"
Dick Tracy Fan Club. Manitou Springs, Colo.: Andrew Feighery, Publisher, 1992–present.
Dick Tracy Fast-Action Story Books. New York: Dell.
  "Dick Tracy Detective and Federal Agent" (1936) (2 versions: varnished hardcover; unvarnished
    softcover).
  "Dick Tracy and the Chain of Evidence" (1938).
  "Dick Tracy and the Maroon Mask Gang" (1938).
  "Dick Tracy and the Blackmailers" (1939).
  "Dick Tracy and the Frozen Bullet Murders" (1941).
Dick Tracy in B-Flat (radio program). Armed Forces Radio Service Command Performance,
    February 15, 1945.
"Dick Tracy in Orbit." *Newsweek,* January 14, 1963, p. 47.
"'Dick Tracy' Is Selling Like Gangbusters." *Lansing State Journal,* July 14, 1990 (wire service story).
"Dick Tracy Looks at Television." *TV Guide,* May 1, 1953, pp. 20–21.
Dick Tracy Meets Gruesome. Motion Picture. 1947.
"Dick Tracy Meets Koh-I-Noor." (Advertisement for Koh-I-Noor/Rapidograph art supplies com-
    pany circa 1988.)
Dick Tracy Monthly 1–24. New York: Dell, January 1948–December 1949.
Dick Tracy Movie Novelization. Racine, Wis.: Western Publishing Company, Inc., 1990.
The Dick Tracy *Official Souvenir Magazine.* Brooklyn: The Topps Company, Inc., 1990.
Dick Tracy premium books.
  The Adventures of Dick Tracy. Racine, Wis.: Whitman Publishing Company, 1933. Karmetz
    Premium adapted from *The Adventures of Dick Tracy* #707.
  Dick Tracy and Dick Tracy, Jr. Racine, Wis.: Whitman Publishing Company, 1933. Karmetz
    Premium adapted from *Dick Tracy and Dick Tracy, Jr.* #710.
  Dick Tracy Meets a New Gang. Racine, Wis.: Whitman Publishing Company with Lily-Tulip Cor-
    poration, 1934. Tarzan Ice Cream Premium.
  Dick Tracy Smashing the Famon Racket. Racine, Wis.: Whitman Publishing Company, 1938.
    Buddy Book Premium.
  Dick Tracy the Detective and Dick Tracy, Jr. Racine, Wis.: Whitman Publishing Company, 1933.
    Perkins Premium adapted from *Dick Tracy and Dick Tracy Jr.* #710.
  Dick Tracy's Secret Detective Methods and Magic Tricks. 1939. Quaker Oats Premium.
Dick Tracy Radio Script Plays. Racine, Wis.: Whitman Publishing Company, 1939. Vol. 1: "Dick
    Tracy and the Invisible Man"; Vol. 2: "Dick Tracy and the Ghost Ship."
Dick Tracy Returns. Republic Movie Serial. 15 episodes. 1938.
Dick Tracy Secret Service Patrol Secret Code Book. Chicago: Quaker Puffed Wheat and Quaker
    Puffed Rice, 1938 and 1939.
Dick Tracy Sheds Light on the Mole. Western Printing Company. 1949. Ray-O-Vac Flashlights
    Giveaway.
Dick Tracy Tabloid (The). Mount Carmel, Calif. Begins with Issue #1, September 1983.
Dick Tracy—The Lost TV Episodes, Vols. 1–4. (VHS tapes). Burbank, Calif.: Wavelength Video,
    1990. Vol. 1: "Dick Tracy Meets Flattop," "Dick Tracy Versus Heels Beels." Vol. 2; "Hijack,"
    "The Mole." Vol. 3: "Dick Tracy Versus the Foreign Agents" (2 part episode). Vol. 4: "Shaky's
    Secret Treasure," "A Dick Tracy Sampler."
Dick Tracy Versus Cueball. Motion Picture, 1946.
Dick Tracy vs. Crime Inc. Republic Movie Serial. 15 episodes. 1941.
Dick Tracy's Dilemma. Motion Picture. 1947.
Dick Tracy's G-Men. Republic Movie Serial. 15 episodes. 1939.
Dickens, Charles. *Bleak House.* Oxford: Oxford University Press. From the Oxford Illustrated
    Dickens Series. Original copyright 1853.

_____. *The Mystery of Edwin Drood*. Oxford: Oxford University Press. From the Oxford Illustrated Dickens Series. Original copyright 1870.

_____. *Oliver Twist*. Oxford: Oxford University Press. From the Oxford Illustrated Dickens Series. Original copyright 1838.

_____. *Sketches by Boz*. Oxford: Oxford University Press. From the Oxford Illustrated Dickens Series. Original copyright 1836.

"Disney Beats Drums for 'Tracy.'" *The Milwaukee Journal*, Monday, January 29, 1990, p. 10A.

"Dog Gravy," in *Walt Kelly's Pogo*, June 24, 1990–July 22, 1990. Distributed by the Los Angeles Times Syndicate.

"Doonesbury." *Life*, October 1984, pp. 55–62.

Dorf, Shel, ed. *Reuben Award Winner Series: Dick Tracy* (Nos. 1–24). El Cajon, Calif.: Blackthorne Publishing, Inc., December 1984–1989. Shel Dorf, Series Editor.

Dove, George N. *The Boys from Grover Avenue: Ed McBain's 87th Precinct Novels*. Bowling Green, Ohio: Bowling Green State University Popular Press, 1985.

"Dress Like Dick Tracy." *Lansing State Journal*, February 1, 1990.

Dunning, John. *Tune in Yesterday: The Ultimate Encyclopedia of Old-Time Radio 1925–1976*. Englewood Cliffs, N.J.: Prentice-Hall, 1976.

Edwards, William B. "How Dick Tracy Gets His Man." *Guns Magazine*, August 1955, pp. 16–19, 54.

Elfman, Danny (composer). *Dick Tracy: Original Score*. New York: Sire Records Co., 1990.

Ewing, Ellen Mills. "Dick Tracy: When Chester Gould Introduced Gunplay into Comics, America Got a Hawk-Nosed Hero Who Out-Sherlocked Mr. Holmes." *Oregonian* (Portland, Ore.), May 14, 1944, p. 6.

Faulk, Donna. "Dick Tracy's 'Kid.'" Pennywhistle Press, *Wausau Daily Herald* (Wausau, Wis.), Saturday, June 16, 1990, p5B.

Fitzgerald, Kate. "*Tracy* Nabs Recall; Movie's Ads Arrest Viewer Attention." *Advertising Age* vol. 61, no. 31 (July 30, 1990), p. 39.

Fletcher, Beverly. Letters, March 4, 1986; June 16, 1992. Woodstock, Ill.

Fletcher, Rick, and Collins, Max. *Dick Tracy Meets Angeltop, Flattop's Little Girl*. New York: Grosset and Dunlap, 1979, and New York: Berkley, August 1990.

_____, and _____. *Dick Tracy (#2) Meets the Punks*. New York: Grosset and Dunlap, 1980, and New York: Berkley, August 1990.

Galewitz, Herb, ed. *The Celebrated Cases of Dick Tracy 1931–1951*. New York: Chelsea House Publishers, 1970. Reprinted 1990; Secaucus, New Jersey: The Wellfleet Press.

_____, ed. *Dick Tracy—The Thirties: Tommy Guns and Hard Times*. New York: Chelsea House Publishers, 1978, and Secaucus, N.J.: The Wellfleet Press.

_____, ed. *Great Comics Syndicated by the Daily News*–Chicago Tribune. New York: Crown Publishers, Inc., 1972.

Gangbusters (radio program). "The Case of the Chicago Tunnel Gang," "The Golf Course Murders," and "The Safe Cracking Combine."

Garner, Jack. "'Dick Tracy Hits It Big.'" Gannett News Service, in the *Lansing State Journal*, June 14, 1990, What's On, p. 6.

Gehr, Richard. "Dick Tracy: The Lineup." *Mirabella* 13 (June 1990), p. 57.

Get These Valuable Gifts Free with These Box Tops (P.G.-1-39); *Get Valuable Gifts Free with Box Tops from Quaker Puffed Wheat and Quaker Puffed Rice* (P.G.-2-39). (Two retail store banners advertising Quaker Puffed Wheat and Puffed Rice Cereals, and related Dick Tracy premiums, 1939.)

Gibson, Walter B. *The Shadow Scrapbook*. New York: Harcourt, Brace, Jovanovich, 1979.

Gilbert, Elliot L. *The World of Mystery Fiction*. Bowling Green, Ohio: Bowling Green State University Popular Press, 1983.

Gleiberman, Owen. "Dick Tracy—Movie Review." *Entertainment Weekly*, June 15, 1990, pp. 16–17.

Godfrey, Thomas. "What Have Hollywood, Warren Beatty, and Madonna Done to 'Plainclothes' Tracy?" *The Armchair Detective*. Vol. 24, No. 1 (Winter 1991).

Gold, Mike. "Max Allan Collins Interview." *The Comics Journal* 77 (November 1982), pp. 68–69.

Goldberg, Lee. *Unsold Television Pilots 1955–1988*. Jefferson, North Carolina: McFarland, 1990.

Goulart, Ron. *The Adventurous Decade*. New Rochelle, New York: Arlington House Publishers, 1975.

_____. *Cheap Thrills*. New Rochelle, New York: Arlington House Publishers, 1972.

_____. *The Dime Detectives*. New York: The Mysterious Press, 1988.

_____. *The Encyclopedia of American Comics from 1897 to the Present*. New York: Facts on File, 1990.

_____. "The Funny Paper Detectives of the Thirties." *Alfred Hitchcock's Mystery Magazine*, Vol. 29, No. 3. New York: Davis Publications, Inc., March 1984, pp. 58–63.

_____, ed. *The Great British Detective*. New York: Signet Books, 1982.

Gould, Chester. Buster Brown Shoes Giveaway. Reprint of material from 1938 and 1939.

_____. *Dick Tracy* (Four Color Comic no. 1). New York: Dell, 1939.

_____. *Dick Tracy* (Four Color Comic no. 6). New York: Dell, 1940.

_____. *Dick Tracy* (Four Color Comic no. 8). New York: Dell, 1940.

_____. *Dick Tracy* (Four Color Comic no. 21). New York: Dell, 1941.

_____. *Dick Tracy* (Four Color Comic no. 34). New York: Dell, 1943.

_____. *Dick Tracy* (Four Color Comic no. 56). New York: Dell, 1944.

_____. *Dick Tracy* (Four Color Comic no. 96). New York: Dell, 1946.

_____. *Dick Tracy* (Four Color Comic no. 133). New York: Dell, 1947.

_____. *Dick Tracy* (Four Color Comic no. 163). New York: Dell, 1947.

_____. *Dick Tracy* (Large Feature Comic no. 3). New York: Dell, 1941.

_____. *Dick Tracy: Ace Detective*. Racine, Wis.: Whitman Publishing Co., 1943.

_____. *Dick Tracy: The Early Years* 1–4. El Cajon, Calif.: Blackthorne Publishing Company, August 1987–August 1988. Shel Dorf, Series Editor.

_____. *Dick Tracy: The "Unprinted" Stories* 1–4. El Cajon, Calif.: Blackthorne Publishing Company, September 1987–June 1988. Shel Dorf, Series Editor.

_____. *Dick Tracy and Dick Tracy, Jr. and How They Captured "Stooge" Viller*. New York: Cupples and Leon Publishers, 1933. (Reprints strips from 1933.)

_____. "Dick Tracy and Me." *Colliers*, December 11, 1948, p. 54.

_____. *Dick Tracy and Scottie of Scotland Yard* (Black and White Comic no. 13). New York: Dell, 1940.

_____. *Dick Tracy and the Famon Boys* (Feature Book no. 9). New York: David McKay Publishers, January 1938.

_____. *Dick Tracy and the Kidnapped Princes* (Black and White Comic no. 15). New York: Dell, 1940.

_____. *Dick Tracy Foils the Mad Doc Hump* (Black and White Comic no. 11). New York: Dell, 1940.

_____. *Dick Tracy Gets His Man* (Black and White Comic no. 4). New York: Dell, 1939.

_____. *Dick Tracy—His Greatest Cases #1: Pruneface*. Greenwich, Conn.: Fawcett Publications, 1975. Edited by Herb Galewitz.

_____. *Dick Tracy—His Greatest Cases #2: Snowflake and Shaky and the Black Pearl*. Greenwich, Conn.: Fawcett Publications, 1975. Edited by Herb Galewitz.

_____. *Dick Tracy—His Greatest Cases #3: Mrs. Pruneface—also Crime, Inc*. Greenwich, Conn.: Fawcett Publications, 1976. Edited by Herb Galewitz.

_____. *Dick Tracy Meets the Blank* (Black and White Comic no. 1). New York: Dell, 1939.

_____. *Dick Tracy Meets the Night Crawler*. Racine, Wis.: Whitman Publishing Co., 1945.

_____. *Dick Tracy Monthly* 1–25. El Cajon, Calif.: Blackthorne Publishing Company, May 1986–December 1987. Becomes *Dick Tracy Weekly* with #26 (January 1988). Shel Dorf, Series Editor.

_____. *Dick Tracy Special* 1–3. El Cajon, Calif.: Blackthorne Publishing Company. January 1988 to August 1989. Shel Dorf, Series Editor.

_____. *Dick Tracy the Detective* (Feature Book no. 4). New York: David McKay Publishers, August 1937.

_____. *Dick Tracy the Detective* (Feature Book no. 6). New York: David McKay Publishers, October 1937.

_____. *Dick Tracy the Racket Buster* (Black and White Comic no. 8). New York: Dell, 1939.

_____. *Dick Tracy Weekly* 26–99. El Cajon, Calif.: Blackthorne Publishing Company, January 1988–September 1989. Continuation of *Dick Tracy Monthly*. Shel Dorf, Series Editor.

_____. *Exploits of Dick Tracy*. Rosdon Books, Inc., 1946. (Reprints the story of "The Brow.")

_____. *How Dick Tracy and Dick Tracy, Jr., Caught the Racketeers*. New York: Cupples and Leon Publishers, 1933. (Hardcover that reprints strips from August 3, 1933, through November 8, 1933. There was a shorter paperback version of this book which reprinted strips from September 18, 1933, through November 8, 1933.)

_____. Letters, October 7, 1973; March 26, 1979; April 13, 1979. Woodstock, Illinois.

_____. Motorola Giveaway, 1953. (Tracy comic book.)

_____. *The Original Dick Tracy*, 1–5. September 1990 to May 1991. Gladstone Publishing Ltd.

_____. *The Original Dick Tracy Comic Album*, Vols. 1–3. Prescott, Arizona: Gladstone Publishing

Limited, 1990. (1: "Dick Tracy Fights the Mumbles Quartette"; 2: "Origin of the 2-Way Wrist Radio"; 3: "The Lair of the Mole.")

————. Service Station Giveaway. 1958.

————. Shoe Store Giveaway. 1939.

————. *Sparkle Plenty* (Four Color Comic no. 215). New York: Dell Publishing Co., 1948.

————. "The World Is Your Beat," *Chicago Tribune*. (May 12, 1963). Advertisement for American Newspaper Publishers Association Foundation.

Gould, Mrs. Chester [Edna]. Letter, March 11, 1986. Woodstock, Ill.

Gowans, Alan. *Learning to See: Historical Perspectives on Modern Popular/Commercial Arts*. Bowling Green, Ohio: Bowling Green State University Popular Press, 1981.

Gray, Harold. *Arf! The Life and Hard Times of Little Orphan Annie 1935–1945*. New Rochelle, N.Y.: Arlington House Publishers, 1970.

————. *Little Orphan Annie in Cosmic City*. New York: Dover Publications, Inc. No copyright date; original material reprinted from 1933.

Gray, Kevin. "The Case of the Cartoon Caper!" *The Daily Item—The Gannett Westchester Newspapers*, Sunday, March 11, 1990, pp. 1, 8.

"The Great Piggy Bank Robbery." Warner Bros. Looney Tunes Cartoon, July 27, 1946. (Stars Daffy Duck as Duck Twacy.)

Green, Tom. "Star Turns Comic Cop for 'Tracy.'" *USA Today*, June 12, 1990, Life section.

Hale, Norman F. *All Natural Pogo*. New York: Thinker's Books, 1991.

Hamlin, V.T. *Alley Oop: Mystery of the Sphinx*. Princeton, Wis.: Kitchen Sink Press, Inc., 1991.

————. *Alley Oop: The Adventures of Time-Traveling Caveman*. Princeton, Wis.: Kitchen Sink Press, Inc., 1990.

Hammett, Dashiell. *The Continental Op*. New York: Random House, 1974.

————. *Red Harvest*. New York: Alfred A. Knopf, 1929.

————, and Raymond, Alex. *Dashiell Hammett's Secret Agent X-9*. New York: International Polygonics, Ltd., 1983. Edited by Tony Sparafucile.

————, and ————. *Secret Agent X-9*. Princeton, Wis.: Kitchen Sink Press, Inc., 1990.

Hammond, Dorothy, and Brisk, Rachelle D. "Dick Tracy Badge Was a Cereal Box-top Reward, Worth Varies." *Green Bay Press Gazette*, January 9, 1983, Scene p. 5.

Harmond, Jim. *The Great Radio Heroes*. New York: Ace Books, Inc., 1967.

————, and Glut, Donald F. *The Great Movie Serials: Their Sound and Fury*. Garden City, N.Y.: Doubleday, 1972.

Harvey Comics Library: Sparkle Plenty (Dick Tracy in Blackmail). New York: Harvey Publications, 1952.

Hawkins, Robert J. "Tracy Hoopla: It's Enough to Make a Guy Squint." *San Diego Tribune*, Thursday, June 14, 1990, pp. E1, E4.

"He Can Still Leave 'Em Breathless." *People*, July 2, 1990, pp. 78–82.

Hencey, Robert. "Dick Tracy: King of the Detectives," *The Antique Trader Weekly*. Dubuque, Iowa, May 7, 1986.

Herriman, George. *George Herriman's Krazy & Ignatz: The Komplete Kat Komics*. Forestville, Calif.: Eclipse Books. Multi-volume series, begins 1988.

————. *The Komplete Kolor Krazy Kat*. Princeton, Wis.: Kitchen Sink Press, Inc., and Abington, Pa.: Remco Worldservice Books. 7-volume series, begins 1990.

Higby, Mary Jane. *Tune in Tomorrow*. New York: Ace Publishing Corporation, 1966.

Hill, Deborah Goldstein. *Price Guide to Coca-Cola Collectibles*. West Des Moines, Iowa: Wallace-Homestead Book Company, 1984.

Hinds, Julie. "Who's That Guy?" *The Detroit News*, Monday, June 11, 1990, Section C, pp. 1–3.

Hollatz, Tom. *Gangster Holidays: The Lore and Legends of the Bad Guys*. St. Cloud, Minn.: North Star Press of St. Cloud, Inc., 1989.

Holt, Kermit. "Mrs. G. Gertie Becomes Bride of B.O. Plenty." *Chicago Tribune*, August 18, 1946, Section 1, p. 19.

"Holy Dick Tracy! 2-Way Wristwatch Radio on Way." *Dallas Morning News* story appearing in the *Chicago Tribune*, June 12, 1989.

Hoppenstand, Gary. "Murder and Other Hazardous Occupations: Taboo and Detective Fiction," in Browne, Ray B., ed., *Forbidden Fruits: Taboos and Tabooism in Culture*. Bowling Green, Ohio: Bowling Green State University Popular Press, 1984.

Horn, Maurice, ed. *The World Encyclopedia of Comics*. New York: Chelsea House Publishers, 1976.

"How an Idea in Yesterday's Funny Papers Can Become Tomorrow's Front Page Headlines." 1984 advertisement, with reference to 2-Way Wrist Radio, for ITT Corporation.

Hughes, Mike. "'Top Gun' to Top Cop: Jim Cash Returns to the Spotlight with 'Dick Tracy.'" *Lansing State Journal,* June 15, 1990, pp. 1C, 4C.

Hutchens, John K. "Tracy, Superman, et al. Go to War." *New York Times Magazine,* November 21, 1943.

Illenberger, Theodora, and Keller, Avonne Eyre, eds. *The Cartoonist Cookbook.* New York: Hobbs, Dorman and Company, Inc., 1966.

"Inept Heroes, Winners at Last." *Life,* March 17, 1967, pp. 74–80.

Inge, M. Thomas. *Comics as Culture.* Jackson, Mississippi: University Press of Mississippi, 1990.

Jackson, Charles Lee, II. "A Complete History of Dick Tracy—The Films, Serials, TV and Cartoons: A Definitive Look at One of America's Most Enduring Multi-Media Heroes: Part One 'A Good Cop': The Saga of a Square-jawed Dick Who Went Gunning for America's Underworld." *Filmfax: The Magazine of Unusual Film and Television,* No. 21. July 1990, pp. 44–53.

_____. "A Complete History of Dick Tracy—Part Two: The Serials and Beyond." *Filmfax: The Magazine of Unusual Film and Television,* No. 22. August/September 1990, pp. 50–54, 98.

Johnson, Crockett. *Barnaby.* Garden City, N.Y.: Blue Ribbon Books, 1943.

_____. *Barnaby,* Volumes 1–6. New York: Random House, 1985 and 1986.

_____. *Barnaby and Mr. O'Malley.* New York: Henry Holt and Company, 1944.

Johnson, Kim Howard. "Crimestopper's Casebooks: In the Biggest Dick Tracy Year of All, Max Allan Collins Still Chronicles the Detective's Adventures," *Comics Scene* 14. August 1990, pp. 40–44, 52.

Johnston, William. *Dick Tracy.* New York: Grosset and Dunlap, June 1970, and New York: Berkley, June 1990.

Kanner, Bernice. "Will Crime Pay for *Dick Tracy?*" *New York* Vol. 23, No. 25 (June 25, 1990), pp. 20–21.

Kaye, Lenny. "Dick Tracy: The First 50 Years." *Comics Scene* 3 (May 1982), pp. 20–24.

Kelly, Walt. *Ten Ever-Lovin' Blue-Eyed Years with Pogo.* New York: Simon and Schuster. Original copyrights 1948 through 1959.

Kilday, Gregg. "Making Up Is Hard to Do: Bringing *Dick Tracy's* Comic-Strip Villains to Life." *Entertainment Weekly,* July 6, 1990, pp. 32–41.

_____. "Strip Show: The Comic-Book Look of Dick Tracy." *Entertainment Weekly,* June 15, 1990, pp. 34–43.

King, Robert. "Chester Gould's Dick Tracy." *Fanfare,* No. 5 (Summer 1983), 19+.

Kinnard, Roy. *The Comics Come Alive: A Guide to Comic-Strip Characters in Live-Action Productions.* Metuchen, N.J.: Scarecrow, 1991.

_____. *Fifty Years of Serial Thrills.* Metuchen, N.J.: Scarecrow, 1983.

Kittredge, William, and Krauzer, Steven M., eds. *The Great American Detective.* New York: Signet Books, 1978.

Knarr, Jack. "They're Revving Up for Dick Tracy's Comeback." *Burlington County Times* (N.J.), Thursday, February 8, 1990, pp. A1, A5.

Kobler, John. *Capone: The Life and World of Al Capone.* Greenwich, Conn.: Fawcett Publications, 1971.

Krulik, Nancy E. *The Dick Tracy Fun Book of Puzzles, Games and Jokes.* New York: Scholastic Inc., 1990.

Lehman, David. "Thrillers." *Newsweek,* April 22, 1985, pp. 58–61.

Lenburg, Jeff. *The Encyclopedia of Animated Cartoon Series.* New York: Plenum House Publishing Corporation, 1981.

"Lifeline." *USA Today,* January 18, 1984, Life section.

Limited Collector's Edition Presents Dick Tracy Vol. 4, No. C-40 (December-January 1975-1976). New York: National Periodical Publications, Inc.

Locher, Dick. "Goodbye, My Friend." *Chicago Tribune,* May 15, 1985, Section 1, p. 15.

_____. Letters, February 21, 1986; March 10, 1986; May 20, 1992. Chicago, Illinois.

_____. *Vote for Me and It Serves You Right or Left.* Chicago: Bonus Books, 1988.

_____, and Kilan, Michael. *Flying Can Be Fun.* Gretna, LA: Pelican Publishing Co., 1985.

Longest, David. *Toys: Antique and Collectible.* Paducah, Ky.: Schroeder Publishing Co., Inc., circa 1990.

Los Angeles Times. Chester Gould obituary, May 12, 1985.

Lowery, Lawrence F. *The Collector's Guide to Big Little Books and Similar Books.* Danville, Calif.: Education Research and Applications Corporation, 1981.

Lowther, George. *Superman.* New York: Random House, 1942.

Luciano, Dale. "A G-Man and a Drag Queen," *The Comics Journal* 94 (October 1984), pp. 41–43.

Lynes, Russell. "Dick Tracy Has Been Framed!" *The New York Times,* May 8, 1969 (late edition), p. 48.

McBain, Ed. *Cophater.* New York: The New American Library, 1973. (Originally appeared in 1956.)

McCay, Winsor. *The Complete Little Nemo in Slumberland.* Westlake Village, Calif.: Remco World-service Books and Fantagraphics. 8-volume series, begins 1988.

McCutchan, Ann. "'Dick Tracy' Items May Be Collectibles." Gannett News Service story appearing in the *Green Bay Press-Gazette,* Sunday, October 14, 1990, p. G-3.

MacDonald, J. Fred. *Don't Touch That Dial!: Radio Programming in American Life, 1920–1960.* Chicago: Nelson-Hall, Inc., 1979.

McDonnell, David, and Hutchison, David. "Dick Tracy Talks—Warren Beatty Provides the New Profile for Chester Gould's Crimestopper." *Comics Scene* 15 (overall series 25), October 1990, pp. 61–64, 66.

————, and Johnson, Kim Howard. "Max Allan Collins: The Mystery Novelist Who Writes Comics," *Comics Scene* 6. (November 1982), pp. 29–32, 40.

McGauley, John, and the Associated Press. "Artist Creator of Dick Tracy Dies." *Lansing State Journal,* May 12, 1985, p. 1A.

MacLachlan, Claudia. "Copped Comics: Authorities Retrieve Vintage Strips." *St. Louis Post-Dispatch,* Saturday, October 21, 1989, pp. 1, 5.

McNamara, Joseph. *The First Directive.* New York: Ballantine, 1986.

McNeil, Alex. *Total Television: A Comprehensive Guide to Programming from 1948 to Present* (Second Edition). New York: Ballantine Books, 1985.

————. *Total Television (Including Cable): A Comprehensive Guide to Programming from 1948 to the Present* (Third Edition). New York: Penguin, 1991.

"Mad for the Makeup." *Detroit Free Press,* June 22, 1990.

Madonna. *I'm Breathless: Music from and Inspired by the Film* Dick Tracy. New York: Sire Records Co., 1990.

"Madonna, in Part." *Newsweek,* March 19, 1990.

Maeder, Jay. *Dick Tracy: The Official Biography.* New York: Penguin, June 1990.

————. "Why Was Moon-Maid Killed?" *Miami Herald.* (August 24, 1978), p. 6E.

Magiera, Marcy. "*Dick Tracy* Nabs Tie-in Interest; Licensed Goods Precede Disney Film." *Advertising Age,* Feb. 5, 1990, (Vol. 61), p. 20.

Malloy, Alex G., and Wells, Stuart. *Collectible Toy Values Monthly,* Vol. 1, No. 8 (April 1992).

Maltin, Leonard. *Of Mice and Magic: A History of American Animated Cartoons.* New York: New American Library, Inc., 1984.

————. *T.V. Movies and Video Guide, 1990 Edition.* New York: New American Library, Inc., 1989.

Mammoth Comics 1. Racine, Wis.: Whitman Publishing Co. 1938. (Dick Tracy story among others.)

Margolick, David. "At the Bar: In Dick Tracy's Latest Caper, 'The Case of the Purloined Panels,' a Law Firm Is Embarrassed." *The New York Times,* October 20, 1989.

Marschall, Richard. *America's Great Comic Strip Artists.* New York: Abbeville Press, 1989.

Martin, John. "Look Your Best, Slug—The Lineup's Going TV," *The New York News,* January 29, 1954.

"Max Collins and Terry Beatty," *Comics Interview* 24. New York: Fictioneer Books Ltd., 1985. David Anthony Kraft, editor/publisher.

Maxwell, Philip. "Chet Gould's Colorful Career; Dick Tracy," *The Morning Herald: Evening Standard* (Uniontown, Pa.), May 12, 1942, Section B, p. 12.

Memling, Carl. *Dick Tracy* (Little Golden Book #497). New York: Western Publishing Co., 1962. Illustrated by Hawley Pratt and Al White. 24 pages.

Mercury Records Presents Dick Tracy in "The Case of the Midnight Marauder" with Flattop and Vitamin Flintheart an Adventure Story for Children with a Moral. Radio program on 78 RPM, 1947.

Merry Christmas from Sears Toyland. No number, 1939. Sears Roebuck Giveaway.

Miazga, Vicki. "Local Writer Captures Gangsters' Heyday," *Lakeland Times* (Minocqua, Wis.), October 13, 1989, p. 14.

"Miniature Wrist Radio." *Life,* October 6, 1947, pp. 63–64.

Model and Toy Collector. Summer Special #2; Dick Tracy Special. Seville, Ohio: Cap'n Penny Productions, Inc., 1990.

Mooney, Linda A., and Fewell, Carla-Marie. "Crime in One Long-Lived Comic Strip: An Evaluation of Chester Gould's *Dick Tracy.*" *The American Journal of Economics and Sociology* vol. 48, no. 1 (January 1989), pp. 89–100.

Moore, John, and Baker, Kyle. *Dick Tracy, Book One: Big City Blues*. Burbank, Calif.: W.D. Publications, Inc., 1990.

_____, and _____. *Dick Tracy, Book Three: The Movie*. Burbank, Calif.: W.D. Publications, 1990.

_____, and _____. *Dick Tracy, Book Two: Dick Tracy vs. the Underworld*. Burbank, Calif.: W.D. Publications, Inc., 1990.

_____, and _____. *Dick Tracy: The Complete True Hearts and Tommy Guns Trilogy*. Burbank, Calif.: W.D. Publications, Inc., 1990. (The three Moore/Baker graphic novels in one volume.)

Moores, Dick. *Gasoline Alley*. New York: Avon, 1976.

_____. *Gasoline Alley*, July 6–August 16, 1986. Reprinted in *Comics Revue* 35. New York: Fictioneer Books, Ltd., 1989.

_____. *Jim Hardy*, Vol. 1. Houston, Texas: Classic Comic Strips, Inc., 1989.

_____. *Jim Hardy: A Complete Compilation 1936–37*. Westport, Conn.: Hyperion Press, 1977.

_____. *Jim Hardy: Ace Reporter*. Akron, Ohio: The Saalfield Publishing Company, 1940. (Big Little Book.)

_____. Various contributions (script, art, and more) to Walt Disney comic books including "Mickey Mouse and Goofy's Mechanical Wizard" (*Walt Disney's Comics and Stories* 550, 551 and 552 — August, September, and October 1990); "Mickey Mouse: The Wonderful Whizzix" (*Walt Disney's Comics and Stories* 553, 554 and 555 — November, December, and January 1990 and 1991); "Mickey Mouse: Secret of the Whirlpool" (*Walt Disney's Comics and Stories* 564, 565, and 566 — October, November and December 1991).

Motorola Presents Dick Tracy Comics: The Case of the Sparkle Plenty T.V. Mystery. Motorola Giveaway, 1953.

"Move Over Dick Tracy: Tiny TV's Here Even for the Wrist," *Chicago Tribune*, October 18, 1985, p. 70.

Mullinax, Gary. "'Dick Tracy' Draws a Bead on Madonna, and Fires Blanks." Gannett News Service Story appearing in *The Lansing State Journal*, June 13, 1990.

Murray, Will. *The Duende History of the Shadow*. Greenwood, Mass.: Odyssey Publications, 1980.

Museum of Cartoon Art. *Dick Tracy: The Art of Chester Gould*. Port Chester, New York: Museum of Cartoon Art, 1978. Major contributions from Max Allan Collins and Matt Masterson.

Musial, Joe, ed. *The Katzenjammer Kids*. New York: Pocket Books, 1970.

Nemo: The Classic Comics Library 8 (August 1984). Little Orphan Annie Issue.

Nemo: The Classic Comics Library 17 (February 1986). "Special Issue! — Chester Gould and Dick Tracy: A Comprehensive Look at a Comics Strip Master."

Nemo: The Classic Comics Library 26 (September 1987). "T.S. Sullivant's Unforgettable Zoo."

Nemo: The Classic Comics Library 28 (December 1987). "A Special Focus! Ethnic Images in the Comics."

Neuberger, Richard L. "Hooverism in the Funnies." *The New Republic*, July 11, 1934, pp. 234–235.

The New York Times. Chester Gould obituary, May 12, 1985.

Newsweek. Chester Gould obituary, May 20, 1985.

Nicodemus, Charles. "Creator of Dick Tracy Dies." *Chicago Sun Times*, May 12, 1985.

Niderost, Eric. "Crewcut for a Flattop," *Starlog* 157. August 1990, pp. 17–19, 58.

_____. "Starting from Scratch: Blasting Away at Dick Tracy, Ed O'Ross Owns an Itchy Trigger Finger." *Starlog Spectacular* 1 (series 2, overall issue 3). Summer 1990, pp. 27–30.

Nolan, William F. Letter, June 3, 1985. Agoura, California.

_____, ed. *The Black Mask Boys*. New York: William Morrow, 1985.

Non-Sport Update Vol. 1, No. 1 (October 1990). Harrisburg, Pa.: Roxanne Tosser, Publisher, 1990.

Nye, Russel B. *The Unembarrassed Muse: The Popular Arts in America*. New York: The Dial Press, 1970.

Oaks, Richard. "Chester Gould: Sanguinary Squire from Pawnee." *The World of Comic Art* 1 (Winter 1966-67), pp. 28–31.

O'Brien, Richard. *Collecting Toys*. Florence, Ala.: Books Americana, 1980.

O'Connell, Jean Gould. Letter. *Comics Buyer's Guide* 850, March 2, 1990.

_____. Letters, May 9, 1992; June 11, 1992; June 19, 1992. Geneva, Illinois.

Official Dick Tracy Giant Sticker-Poster Set. Buena Vista Pictures Distribution, Inc., 1990.

Olmsted, Fred. "Tracy Tops His Tutor, Artist Gould Is as Mild as Fearless Tracy Is Bold." *Detroit Free Press*, September 12, 1948.

Orphan, Dennis. "Dick Tracy: For 30 Years Flint-Jawed Crime Fighter." *The Quill*, April 1962, pp. 14–15.

O'Sullivan, Judith. *The Art of the Comic Strip*. Mount Vernon, N.Y.: Press of A. Colish, 1971. Published in conjunction with the University of Maryland Department of Art.

————. *The Great American Comic Strip: One Hundred Years of Cartoon Art.* Boston: Little, Brown and Company, 1990.

Overstreet, Robert M. *The Comic Book Price Guide.* (22nd edition). Cleveland, Tenn.: Overstreet Publications, Inc., May 1992.

Pace, Eric. "Dick Tracy and Mugs, a Rogues' Gallery of Art." *The New York Times,* Friday, September 17, 1982.

Paley, Andy (producer). *Dick Tracy: Music for the Movie.* New York: Sire Records Co., 1990.

Pells, Richard H. *Radical Visions and American Dreams: Cultural and Social Thought in the Depression Years.* New York: Harper and Row, 1973.

Penzler, Otto, ed. *The Great Detectives.* Boston: Little, Brown and Company, 1978.

————, and Steinbrunner, Chris, et al. *Detectionary.* New York: Random House, 1971.

Peters, Jennifer. "Comic Relief: 5 Videos for the Cartoon-Crazed Summer." *USA Weekend,* August 3–5, 1990, p. 8.

P.G. and E. Progress (Pacific Gas and Electric Company), March 1984, pp. 2–7.

Pietryzk, Richard. "Dick Tracy at 50: Crime Marches On." *Collage* Vol. 3, No. 1 (January-February 1982), pp. 3–4.

The P.I.'s: Michael Mauser and Ms. Tree. 1–3. Evanston, Ill.: First Comics, Inc., January 1985; March 1985; May 1985.

Polskin, Howard. "TV's Love Affair with the Movies." *TV Guide* Vol. 38, No. 21 (Issue #1939), May 26–June 1, 1990.

Popular Comics 1–145. New York: Dell, February 1936–July/August 1948). Dick Tracy did not appear in all of these issues. Even Overstreet does not provide exact issue numbers for the Tracy appearances.

Powers, Richard Gid. "The Comic Strip G-Man." *Rituals and Ceremonies in Popular Culture.* Bowling Green, Ohio: Bowling Green State University Popular Press, 1980.

————. *G-Men: Hoover's F.B.I. in American Popular Culture.* Carbondale, Ill.: Southern Illinois University Press, 1983.

————. "J. Edgar Hoover and the Detective Hero," in *The Popular Culture Reader.* Bowling Green, Ohio: Bowling Green State University Popular Press, 1977.

Pre-publicity book for *Dick Tracy, The Movie.* Touchstone Pictures, 1990.

Pre-Tracy trial comic strips, provided by Max Allan Collins and by Bill Blackbeard of the San Francisco Academy of Comic Art.

Raymond, Alex. *Flash Gordon.* (Color Sunday reprints). Princeton, Wis.: Kitchen Sink Press, Inc. Multi-volume series, begins 1990.

Rea, Steven. "The New 'Dick Tracy': Hit or Bust?" Knight-Ridder Newspapers. Appeared Saturday, May 26, 1990, in the *Green Bay Press-Gazette.*

Reitberger, Reinhold, and Fuchs, Wolfgang. *Comics: Anatomy of a Mass Medium.* Boston: Little, Brown and Company, 1971.

Roberts, Garyn G., ed. *A Cent a Story!: The Best from* Ten Detective Aces. Bowling Green, Ohio: Bowling Green State University Popular Press, 1986.

————, and Hoppenstand, Gary, eds. *The Night Nemesis: The Complete Stories of the Moon Man, Volume One.* Bowling Green, Ohio: The Purple Prose Press, 1985.

————, ————, and Browne, Ray B., eds. Old Sleuth's *Freaky Female Detectives (From the Dime Novels).* Bowling Green, Ohio: Bowling Green State University Popular Press, 1990.

Robinson, Jerry. *The Comics: An Illustrated History of the Comic Strip.* New York: Putnam, 1974.

Roeburt, John. *Al Capone.* New York: Pyramid Books, 1959.

Rosemont, Franklin. "Surrealism in the Comics II," in Buhle, Paul, ed., *Popular Culture in America.* Minneapolis: University of Minnesota Press, 1987.

Ruhm, Herbert, ed. *The Hard-Boiled Detective: Stories from* Black Mask Magazine 1920–1951. New York: Random House, 1977.

Russell, John. "Gallery Season, in All Its Variety, Opens Uptown and Downtown." *The New York Times,* Friday, October 1, 1982, Weekend section.

————. "How a 30's Stiff Became a Charmer for the 90's." *The New York Times,* Sunday, June 10, 1990, Section 2, pp. 1, 36.

Sachs, Lloyd. "Tracing Tracy." *Memories: The Magazine of Then and Now,* Vol. III, No. 3 (June-July 1990), pp. 23–24.

Sagendorf, Bud. *Popeye: The First Fifty Years.* New York: Workman, 1979.

Sampson, Robert. *Yesterday's Faces,* Vols. 1–6. Bowling Green, Ohio: Bowling Green State University Popular Press, 1983–1993.

Sanderson, Peter, Jr. "An Interview with Max Allan Collins." *Comics Feature* 18 (August 1982), pp. 16–30.

Schact, Beulah. "Straight Out of Dick Tracy: Blonde Here Gets Crewy Lou Haircut." *St. Louis Globe-Democrat*, Saturday, June 30, 1951, p. B1.

Schmich, Mary T. "Dick Tracy Still Lives in Illinois Home of His Creator." *Austin American-Statesman*, Saturday, July 19, 1986, p. E2.

Schwartz, Tony. *Media: The Second God*. New York: Random House, 1981.

_____. *The Responsive Chord*. Garden City, N.Y.: Anchor Press/Doubleday, 1973.

Segar, E.C. *The Complete E.C. Segar Popeye*, Vols. 1–11. Thousand Oaks, Calif.: Fantagraphics Books 1984–91. (Vols. 1–4 reprint Sundays; Vols. 5–11 reprint Dailies.)

Serbell, John. "Fifty Golden Years." *Media Digest*, 1981, pp. 40–54.

Sharrett, Christopher. "Comic Book Cinema." *USA Today*, Vol. 119, no. 2544 (September 1990), p. 55.

Sheridan, Martin. *Comics and Their Creators*. New York: Luna Press, 1942. Reprinted 1971 and 1989.

Simmons, Walter. "The Country's Favorite Detective." *Chicago Tribune*, April 23, 1944.

"Sleuths Use Dick Tracy Ploy." Associated Press, circa 1985.

Slotkin, Richard. *Regeneration Through Violence: The Mythology of the American Frontier 1600–1860*. Middletown, Conn.: Wesleyan University Press, 1973.

Smith, Liz. "Disney, Beatty Can Relax: 'Dick Tracy' Is a Dazzling Film." *Detroit Free Press*, June 20, 1990.

Smith, Wes, and Heise, Kenan. "'Dick Tracy' Creator Chester Gould, 84." *Chicago Tribune*, May 12, 1985, Section 2, p. 7.

Snead, Elizabeth. "Jump into Lively Detective Duds." Gannett News Service story appearing in *The Lansing State Journal*, June 13, 1990, Style section.

"Sparkle Plenty." *Life*, August 25, 1947, p. 42.

Spillane, Mickey. *Tomorrow I Die*. New York: Mysterious Press, 1984. Edited and introduced by Max Allan Collins.

Spillman, Susan. "Big Gamble for Beatty and Disney." *USA Today*, May 11–13, 1990, pp. 1–2.

Springman, Joanne. "Rick Fletcher, 66, Dies; Tracy Artist for 22 Years." *Daily Sentinel* (Woodstock, Ill.), March 16, 1983.

Starr, Mark. "Durable Cop: After Four Decades Dick Tracy Remains Top Comic-Strip Hero." *Wall Street Journal*, March 12, 1974, pp. 1, 16.

Stedman, Raymond William. *The Serials: Suspense and Drama by Installment*. Norman, Oklahoma: University of Oklahoma Press, 1971.

Steinbrunner, Chris, and Penzler, Otto, eds. *Encyclopedia of Mystery and Detection*. New York: McGraw-Hill, 1976.

Steranko, James. *History of Comics*, Vols. 1 and 2. Reading, Penn.: Supergraphics Publishing, 1970 and 1972.

Sterrett, Cliff. *Polly and Her Pals*. Eternity Comics. Beings with Issue #1 on October 1990.

_____. *Polly and Her Pals*. Princeton, Wis.: Kitchen Sink Press. 4-volume series, beings December 1990.

Stone, Robert. "Sunday Mornings with Flyface." *Times Literary Supplement* 4554 (July 13, 1990), pp. 752–753.

Stryker, Hal. *NYPD 2025*. New York: Pinnacle Books, Inc., 1985.

Stuckey, William K. "Dick Tracy: The Inner Man." *Northwestern Review*, Winter 1967.

Super-Book of Comics. New York: Western Publishing Co. Omar Bread and Hancock Oil Company giveaways. (Hancock issues are reprints of the earlier Omar issues.) #1 "Dick Tracy" (Omar, 1944); #1 "Dick Tracy" (Hancock, 1947); #13 "Dick Tracy" (Omar, 1945); #13 "Dick Tracy" (Hancock, 1947); #25 "Dick Tracy" (Omar, 1946); no number "Dick Tracy" (Hancock, 1948).

Super Comics 1–115. New York: Dell, May 1938–December 1947. The series went to #121 (February/March 1949), but Dick Tracy moved to his own title (Dell *Dick Tracy Monthly*) in January 1948. Tracy appeared in selected issues of *Super Comics*.

Tangorra, Joanne, and Zinsser, John, eds. "Bantam Audio Taps New Markets with Dick Tracy Tape." *Publishers Weekly*, Vol. 237, No. 22 (June 1, 1990), pp. 25–30.

Tastee-Freez Comics 6. "Dick Tracy." New York: Harvey Publications, 1957.

Terrace, Vincent. *The Complete Encyclopedia of Television Programs, 1947–1976*. Cranbury, N.J.: A.S. Barnes, 1976.

Thomas, Bob. "Can Comics' Flatfoot Be Film Megastar?" Associated Press story appearing in the *Green Bay Press-Gazette*, Sunday, June 3, 1990.

Thomas, James Stuart. *The Big Little Book Price Guide*. Des Moines, Iowa: Wallace-Homestead Book Company, 1983.

Thompson, Maggie. "'Dick Tracy' Victim of Auto Burglary." *Comic Buyer's Guide* 730 (January 15, 1988).

————. "Gladstone to Publish Chester Gould's 'Dick Tracy.'" *Comics Buyer's Guide* 853 (March 23, 1990), pp. 1–3.

Thurman, Steve. *"Baby Face" Nelson*. Derby, Conn.: Monarch Books, Inc., 1961.

"Tick Dracy," *Panic*, Vol. 1, No. 5. New York: Tiny Tot Comics, Inc., October-November 1954. (An E.C. comic book.)

Time. Chester Gould obituary, May 20, 1985.

Tomart's Action Figure Digest Vol. 1, No. 1. Dayton, Ohio: Tomart Publications, Summer 1991.

"Too Harsh in Putting Down Evil: Violence in the Dick Tracy Strip." *Time*, June 28, 1968, p. 42.

"Top Cop." *Newsweek*, October 16, 1961, pp. 102, 105–106.

"Tracking Tracy." *The Paducah Sun* (Paducah, Ky.), January 8, 1990.

"Tracy Cartoon Series Under Fire in L.A." Associated Press article appearing in the *Wausau Daily Herald*, July 6, 1990.

"Tracy Jumps from Screens to Stores." Gannett News Service story appearing in *The Lansing State Journal*, June 13, 1990, Style section.

"'Tracy' on the Way." *The Milwaukee Journal*, Monday, December 11, 1989.

"Tracy Ring May Bring $100." *USA Today*, June 4, 1990, Money section, p. B3.

"Tracy's Influence." *Batman: The Sunday Classics 1943–46*. Princeton, Wis.: Kitchen Sink Press, 1991, p. 208.

Traylor, James, ed. *Hollywood Troubleshooter: W.T. Ballard's Bill Lennox Stories*. Bowling Green, Ohio: Bowling Green State University Popular Press, 1985.

Trivette, Don. "Disney Offers Print Kits and a Line of Inexpensive Early Learning Software." *PC Magazine*, Vol. 10, No. 16 (September 24, 1991), pp. 496–497.

Tumbusch, Tom. *Tomart's Price Guide to Radio Premium and Cereal Box Collectibles*. Dayton, Ohio: Tomart Publications, 1991.

Turner, William W. *Hoover's F.B.I.: The Men and the Myth*. New York: Dell, 1971.

Tuska, Jon. *The Detective in Hollywood*. Garden City, N.Y.: Doubleday, 1978.

20/20. American Broadcasting Company Television, Friday, June 8, 1990.

Umphlett, Wiley Lee. *Mythmakers of the American Dream: The Nostalgic Vision in Popular Culture*. Cranbury, N.J.: Associated University Presses, Inc., 1983.

Unabridged Edgar Allan Poe. Philadelphia: Running Press Book Publishers, 1983.

The Uncensored Mouse, No. 1. Newbury, Calif.: Eternity Comics, April 1989.

Van Hise, James. *Calling Tracy!: Six Decades of Dick Tracy*. Las Vegas: Pioneer Books, Inc., 1990.

————. *Serial Adventures*. Las Vegas: Pioneer Press, Inc., 1990.

Walt Disney's Mystery in Disneyville. New York: Simon and Schuster, 1949. Pictures by the Walt Disney Studio. Adapted by Richard Moores and Manuel Gonzales.

Wambaugh, Joseph. *The Blue Knight*. Boston: Little, Brown, 1972.

————. *The New Centurions*. Boston: Little, Brown, 1970.

————. *The Onion Field*. Boston: Little, Brown, Inc., 1973.

Warren, Bill. "Exerting Influence—Again a Bad Guy, Henry Silva Puts on the Plastic of Recognized Villainy." *Starlog* 158 (September 1990), pp. 53–58.

————. "Once in Love with Pruneface—According to R.G. Armstrong, Female Fans Are Already Falling for the Man with the Rubber Mug." *Starlog* 158 (September 1990), pp. 59–62, 64.

Waugh, Coulton. *The Comics*. New York: Macmillan, 1947.

Wertham, Fredric, M.D. *Seduction of the Innocent*. New York: Rinehart and Company, 1954.

Weaver, Tom. "Crimestopper's Heritage: For Decades, Dick Tracy Has Battled the Bad Guys in Serials, Movies, TV Shows and Cartoons." *Comics Scene* 14 (August 1990), pp. 29–32, 52.

Werner, Laurie. "Comic-Book Heroes Take Over Hollywood." *USA Weekend*, March 10–12, 1989, p. 6.

Westlake, Donald E. *Cops and Robbers*. New York: The New American Library, Inc., 1973.

————. *Levine*. New York: The Mysterious Press, 1984.

Wheelan, Ed. *Minutes Movies*. Comic strip reprints in *Murder City* comic book. Newbury Park, Calif.: Malibu Graphics, 1990.

White, Clinton, and Lowery, Larry. "The Dick Tracy Big Little Books: Part 1." *The Big Little Times*, Vol. IV, No. 6. Danville, Calif.: The Big Little Book Collectors Club of America, November-December 1985.

_____, and _____. "The Dick Tracy Big Little Books: Part 2." *The Big Little Times*, Vol. V, No. 1. Danville, Calif.: The Big Little Book Collectors Club of America, January-February 1986.

Who's Who 34 (1966-67), p. 809.

Wilt, David. *Hardboiled in Hollywood: Five Black Mask Writers and the Movies.* Bowling Green, Ohio: Bowling Green State University Popular Press, 1991.

"Without a Tracy." *U.S.A. Today*, January 18, 1984, Life section.

Wooley, John, ed. *Robert Leslie Bellem's Dan Turner Hollywood Detective.* Bowling Green, Ohio: Bowling Green State University Popular Press, 1983.

"Writer and Artist: Max Collins and Terry Beatty." *Comics Interview* 24, pp. 7–23, New York: Fictioneer Books Ltd.

Yoder, Robert M. "Dick Tracy's Boss." *The Saturday Evening Post*, December 17, 1949, pp. 22–23, 44–46.

Young, Dean, and Marschall, Rick. *Blondie and Dagwood's America.* New York: Harper and Row, 1981.

Yronwode, Catherine, and Collins, Max Allan, eds. *Mickey Spillane's Mike Hammer: The Comic Strip, Volume Two.* Park Forest, Ill.: Ken Pierce, Inc., 1982.

Zehme, Bill. "Warren Beatty." *Rolling Stone*, Issue 579 (May 31, 1990), pp. 42–48, 68, 70–71.

Index

Bold indicates illustration; "n" indicates footnote.

311